HIGH★HONOR

Smithsonian Institution Press·Washington and London

Recollections by Men and Women of World War II Aviation

STUART LEUTHNER AND OLIVER JENSEN

HIGH★HONOR

Editor: Michelle Smith
Designer: Alan Carter
Production Editor: Duke Johns
Copy Editor: Therese Boyd

Cover: Fighter pilot Edward Rector and his crew chief
stand in front of an SB2U dive bomber in 1941

Library of Congress Cataloging-in-Publication Data

Leuthner, Stuart.
High honor.
1. World War, 1939–1945—Aerial operations, American.
2. World War, 1939–1945—Personal narratives, American.
I. Jensen, Oliver Ormerod, 1914–   II. Title.
D790.L48 1989   940.54'4973   89-4062
ISBN 0-87474-650-7 (alk. paper)

British Library Cataloging-in-Publication Data available

Manufactured in the United States of America

9   8   7   6   5   4   3   2   1

97 96 95 94 93 92 91 90 89

∞ The paper used in this publication meets the minimum
requirements of the American National Standard for
Permanence of Paper for Printed Library Materials
Z39.48-1984.

Publisher's note: This is a book of memories, often dealing
with otherwise undocumented personal incidents
occurring more than four decades ago. It may therefore
include some inaccuracies, though we have made every
effort to verify details with the individuals profiled by the
authors.

To those who never came back, C.J., and A.J.

"And for the support of this Declaration,
with a firm Reliance on the Protection of Divine Providence,
we mutually pledge to each other our Lives, our Fortunes,
and our sacred Honor."

—Final sentence, Declaration of Independence

CONTENTS

"TRUCK DRIVERS"

ODD MAN OUT

APPENDIX

FOREWORD

As a World War II aviator, I have special reason to be interested in the stories of other individuals who flew for the United States in that war. But interest in these stories by the men and women who fought in the war is surely not limited to those who were there.

Everyone enjoys a good war story. If all you know about the Second World War is what you've learned from the history textbooks, the stories of these individuals will make it come alive in a way the schoolbooks never could. The tragedies and triumphs, the bravery and buffoonery, the heartbreak and, yes, the humor of such well-told war tales rival those to be found anywhere in literature.

The only thing better than hearing a good war story, in fact, is telling one yourself.

I was a major and commanding officer of the 717th Squadron of the 449th Bomb Group in 1944. We were stationed in Grottaglie, Italy, which is very near Taranto and very far from the area around McAllen, Texas, where I grew up.

I was only twenty-three, but they called me "the old man."

One bombing run we made over Austria that year will live forever in my memory. Our target had been a railroad marshaling yard in Vienna. There was a great deal of flak on this run. We were being fired on by 88mm antiaircraft guns.

The flight from Grottaglie to Vienna would have normally taken about 11 hours, round trip. But after we dropped our bombs we lost two engines. Flames were shooting out of one of them.

By the time I got the plane under control, I had lost several thousand feet and had given up the lead of the mission. We were not able to keep up with the formation, even though we threw overboard everything that could be dumped in order to try to lighten our aircraft.

Before long, it became obvious that we had lost so much altitude—and were continuing to lose it—that we would not be able to get back across the Adriatic Sea. I asked the navigator to find a place where we could go down, in hopes that we would not have to bail out. He advised that there was an island that was available in case of emergency; the island, which was named Vis, had changed hands in the past, but he understood it was at present in Allied hands. I told him I hoped that was the case, but knew we would have to try to land there, regardless. There was no way we could make it to the coast of Italy.

It was February and, had we gone down in the Adriatic, we probably would not have lasted more than five minutes. The water was freezing cold.

We crossed the Yugoslav coast and were able to locate the island, but by that time we were at a very low altitude and it was only at the last moment that we found the emergency strip. After spotting the runway I had to make a very sharp turn in direction to line up with it, since there were hills all around. As a result, I made a poor landing and washed out the nose gear.

At that point I still wasn't certain we were on friendly soil and, when the plane slid to a stop, I saw some women coming toward us wearing grenade belts. I climbed out of the plane and walked toward them, hoping they were friendly, only to have a man about my age emerge from the group and come toward me.

I said, "Don't I know you?"

He looked at me and said, "Sure, you're Bentsen. I used to sack groceries for your mother when she went to the store in McAllen."

I can't recall when I have ever been happier to see a fellow from home.

Twenty-eight years later I returned to Yugoslavia as a United States senator for a visit with President Tito. It was his partisans who had successfully fought off the Germans to control that emergency airstrip on the island of Vis where my B-24 set down. It was his partisans who cared for my crew until a British bomber came in and flew us to safety.

It was a real pleasure to have the opportunity to thank President Tito during that 1972 visit. And to tell him my story.

I think it will be a pleasure for you to read the adventures of these fliers in *High Honor*, as told in their own words.

LLOYD BENTSEN

U. S. Senator, Texas

ACKNOWLEDGMENTS

We would like to thank those people who helped us navigate this book through publishing's flak-filled skies. The late Donna Whiteman transcribed the vast majority of tapes with patience and accuracy. But, more than that, she brought her special understanding of history and a good word when spirits were flagging. Our greatest regret is that she could not have lived to read this book.

Felix Lowe of the Smithsonian Press believed in a book about World War II that doesn't end in 1945. Michelle Smith did an excellent job of editing a very large manuscript and never lost her sense of humor. Going beyond the usual duties expected of an agent, Robert Parke not only shared his combat experiences, but helped us stay in formation and finish the mission. Finally, thanks to each and every man and woman who talked to us about their role during the war. It was, for many, a bittersweet remembrance.

We are also indebted to a number of people who, each in their own way, helped make the final project that much better. We are grateful for their help and apologize to any we may have inadvertently overlooked. They are: Susan Attaway, Julian Bach, Mardy Bosch, Nick Bottari, Dick Calderhead, Vicki Christensen, William Dunn, Bill Flower (Sikorsky Aviation), Mary Hess, David Fritts, Col. Thomas Hanlin II (Air Force public relations), Edward Jablonski, Alison Jensen, Carolyn Jensen, Michael and Eric Jensen, Wilbur Johnson, Ed Jurist, Janet Lanphier, Richard Laska, Jon Lopez, Pat Lupke, Sam Meredith, Henry Neger, Frank Nehin, Maynard Park, Mick Pateman, Andrea Phin, Ken Ramer, Janet Roelofs, Connie Roosevelt, Art Rothenberg, John Sanduski, Frank Sloat, Richard Snow, Randy Steele, Ken Vose, Henry Walther (P-47 Alumni Association), Stephen Wilkinson, and Robert Wood.

INTRODUCTION

May it not be that the cause of civilization itself will
be defended by the skill and devotion of a few thousand airmen?

> Winston Churchill, to Parliament
> at the start of the Battle of Britain

Most people think Americans love luxury and that their culture
is shallow and meaningless. It is a mistake. . . . I can tell you
that Americans are full of the spirit of justice, fight and adventure.

> Admiral Isoroku Yamamoto,
> in warning his countrymen

The flyer, whether the single man in a fighter or the small crew of a
larger plane, has been the last "loner" of war in our apocalyptic
century. When he made his appearance in the First World War, he
was a figure of romance, "a knight of the air." If the comparison with
the medieval warrior with his horse and his lance seems trite today—
and would make the subjects of this book grimace or laugh aloud—it
is sound and true. The passage of centuries and the rise of intricate
technologies have transformed the mount and the long lance, but the
airman's skill and devotion, of which Mr. Churchill spoke, remained
throughout the second world conflict as reliable and steadfast as ever.
Whether fighting other airmen, scouting the enemy, bombing
through intense antiaircraft fire, delivering goods and men through
all hazards, or simply finding his way home over hostile lands and

empty, daunting seas (if the gas lasted), he was still as alone as the knight of ancient times.

The achievements of American airmen in World War II fill many volumes; the purpose of this book has been to examine not the war itself but the memories of a handful of flyers who survived. While two have died since we saw them, the others are (as we write) in their sixties or seventies, mostly retired, in whole or in part, and grown thoughtful. Here, in their own words, they look back in maturity upon the greatest adventures of their lives and try to fit them into the framework of their whole existence.

The interviews that appear here are often the product of many sessions, which Mr. Leuthner began conducting in 1978. As the project wore on, a few years later, Mr. Jensen joined him. Together we have edited a great bulk of material into publishable order, in each case with the approval of the subjects, to whom we are deeply indebted for their time and effort. Sometimes the subjects were at first reluctant to speak, and if they have erred, it is generally on the side of modesty. They have, on the other hand, strong opinions, especially on some of the tragic blunders and follies encountered in a war. They come from various services and fought in most of the main theaters of the war—indeed, several men were in British or other air forces before Pearl Harbor. The men who flew the missions naturally predominate in these pages, but we have also included a few of the nonflying men and women who backed them up or, in the phrase of that era, "kept them flying."

Our subjects came from many walks of American life, from classrooms, farms, factories, offices. After the war a few stayed on in aviation and even fought in Korea and Vietnam, but the majority dispersed into new careers as varied as before, in some cases finding fame. To our minds, however, they are all extraordinary people whose stories ought to be listened to and preserved, not just as tales of Homeric adventure and danger, but as annals of the human spirit.

STUART LEUTHNER

OLIVER JENSEN

FIRST BLOOD

Most people of a certain age, which is getting on to the mid-sixties or more as this book is published, and includes all those who speak to us in it, can remember where they were and what they were doing when Pearl Harbor was attacked without warning on Sunday morning, December 7, 1941. It was at first hard to believe, and the Navy, flashing the news to its many ships and stations, felt it necessary to add the words, "This is not a drill." A whole generation understood that this was one of those electric moments in the otherwise slow progress of history that change everything, like the Battle of Waterloo ("A damned near thing," said the victorious Duke of Wellington), or the Kaiser's grim host invading Belgium ("The lights are going out all over Europe," mourned Sir Edward Grey, England's foreign minister).

Those we have interviewed here were mostly in college, or in beginning jobs, or in one kind of military training or another. Two were flying with the Canadians, one of whom candidly admitted he had never previously heard of Pearl Harbor. One of the editors of this volume was a young editor on *Life* magazine, which had gone to press on the day before, Saturday, and was driving happily out to the country when he heard the bulletins on his car radio. Racing back to the office in New York in the sure knowledge that the issue would have to be changed, he encountered his boss, the late John Shaw Billings, who was handing out rewrite assignments. With a grim smile he said, "Now you can just call them 'Japs.'"

Far to the East, however, Japan's desperate stroke was a much nearer thing—to Edward Rector in Burma with the Flying Tigers and to Charles F. Willis, Jr., at Kaneohe Naval Air Station in Hawaii. For Willis, in fact, history was screaming past his barracks.

Wreckage at Naval Air Station, Pearl Harbor, December 7, 1941. The burning U.S.S. *Arizona* fills the sky with smoke and flames. National Archives.

WHISKEY

*Charles F. Willis, Jr., was a patrol plane pilot at Kaneohe seaplane base,
where the Japanese scored heavily against the rows of PBYs neatly lined up
ashore. Out of the thirty-six planes in Patrol Wing 2, their dive bombers
destroyed twenty-seven and damaged six. Only three, which had been on
patrol, escaped, and Willis himself, as he explains, was hit. By the time we
first met him, two years later, he had inflicted his revenge on the Japanese
and was half a world away, living in a Quonset hut at a muddy British
air field at Dunkeswell in southwest England. He was flying long patrol
missions over the Bay of Biscay, hunting German submarines coming in
and out of their pens in Nazi-held French ports. He was a hard but
amusing and even romantic figure who had picked up the nickname of
"Whiskey" from the name of his dog; Whiskey the dog sometimes
accompanied his master, probably against some regulation, in the big
PB4Y—a naval adaptation of the B-24 bomber—which was lettered "The
Fabulous Character." Behind him were two years of daring exploits in the
early days of the war in the Pacific, and three Distinguished Flying Crosses.*

*Over forty years after that, we were sitting with him again, on the
deck of his vintage Chris Craft at a Washington, D.C., marina. He is still
fit, if somewhat battered, a man of medium height and build, and he talks
easily and without formality about his career of wild ups and downs in
war, politics, and business.*

Charles F. Willis, Jr., as a young patrol plane pilot, at the start of an adventurous career in aviation, politics, and business.

A bunch of us had been out most of the night in Honolulu. We'd been in the sack about four or five hours when we were woken up by this terrible racket. On the way to Pearl Harbor the Japanese came across Kaneohe Naval Air Base, and in the process they shot up the quarters where we were sleeping. I looked out the window and saw a fighter go over with red circles on its wings. We figured out what was going on, pulled on our clothes, went running down the stairs, and jumped in my car. We were heading for our airplanes, which was rather stupid, because it takes about an hour to launch a PBY from the ramp into the water. I was racing to the base as fast as I could drive when a bomb hit my car. It turned upside down and caught fire. We all spilled out, and I started running for the hangar. A fighter hit me with machine-gun fire and splattered my leg, arm, and head. I managed to roll into the bushes and was out like a light for 24 hours. It was utter chaos, and the Japs wiped out most of our airplanes. Thank God they never found out how much damage they really did.

A few weeks before the attack, the Navy had been extending the runway at Kaneohe, and the bulldozers had gone right through the top of an ancient burial mound. A couple of us were wandering on the beach one day, and here was a full skeleton, clean as a whistle. I collected the whole thing, put it in a canvas bag, and threw it in the back of my car. When the Navy came around for the body count the day after the attack, there was my car, upside down and burned, with a bunch of bones in it. They said, "Poor old Whiskey really got it." Then they sent my mother and father a telegram. When they finally found me in the bushes they took me to the infirmary and asked who I was. I said, "Charlie Willis." They said, "You can't be Charlie Willis, he's dead." They told me about the bones and I said I wanted those bones, they were mine. They said, "We know, that's what we told your mother." I got to a telephone as fast as I could. My parents were having a ceremony for me when I called. Eight months later I got shot down again, and my parents got another telegram that said I was missing in action. They got another one when I had to ditch a B-24* in England and didn't get back for a couple of days. My mother said, "Would you please stop this, Charlie?"

I got the bones back, and I've hung the skull over the fireplace in every place I've lived since the war. I have five kids, and they used to ask me, "Daddy, who's that?" I'd say, "That's Uncle George. I loved him so much I've always kept him around." They would introduce Uncle George to all their friends, and it became a family joke that Daddy had Uncle George over the fireplace. I carried Uncle George

---

*See the appendix for a fuller discussion of the B-24, PBY, and other airplanes mentioned in this book.

on some combat missions because that old guy had been identified as me, and I felt I should take care of him.

I was in the infirmary for about a week, and the Navy wanted to put me in the hospital and take all the shrapnel and bullets out of me. I said, "You can't do that. The war will be over, and I'll miss it." That's how silly we were. My squadron was re-forming, and they were getting new airplanes. I was all wrapped up in bandages and I told them, "Let me out of here, I want to get back in an airplane." If I had known even one-third of what we were up against and what we would be doing for the next few years, I might have gone to the hospital for a nice long stay. While I was in the hospital, I'd been reading headlines in the *Honolulu Advertiser* that we had suffered minor casualties, and when I went over to Pearl Harbor there was the whole goddamn Navy, upside down.

★

A group of us who were flying in the Pacific during that first year after Pearl Harbor have been talking about taking an old PBY and retracing our steps across the Pacific. I've got the plane and the guys lined up. We all lived together in Hawaii, and we were as close as six guys could get. The PBY belongs to the "Confederate Air Force" down in Texas. They said we could use it if they sent one of their guys with it. The only problem would probably be the guys who would be going on this trip. I'm going to have to establish who's the boss right away, because we are all commanders or captains. The first thing my old pal, George Poulos, said to me was, "Who is going to be in command?" I said, "Each of us will take turns so you can yell at me for a while and I can yell at you for a while." You don't have much to look forward to after you get to age sixty, and this would be one last fling in a PBY for some old "Black Cats." I've even got my uniforms and my 1940 flight jacket. The jacket still fits—well, maybe a little tight here and there. We were called the "Black Cats" because we painted the airplanes all black so the Japs couldn't see us against the dark water. Most of the time we did our flying at night because we felt safer.

Our modern "Black Cat" would start out in San Diego. We would fly from there to Hawaii and then on to Johnston Island. When we got down there in 1942 it was just a little dot in the ocean with a few Marines. We landed in the water, beached the airplane, and operated out of there for about a week. From there we would go to Canton Island. We were just like scouts in the Old West, looking and probing to find out how much the Navy and its limited force could expect to run into.

A lot of things we did in those early days we did without realizing the danger we were facing. We did them because it was exciting, and we thought we could get away with it. We also felt that the Japs were terrible, terrible people. We'd seen so much damage that had been done at Pearl Harbor, and remember, over 2,400 people were killed. Half of our squadron had arms and legs blown off. It was a very vivid impression for us, and I think it affected us more than those who came later and hadn't seen their own people hit so hard. To go so suddenly from a Hawaiian vacation into combat was a real shock.

I never thought we would lose the war, and I don't think anybody I flew with did. We were the cockiest bunch of bastards that you've ever seen in your life. We didn't know what we were up against, and the powers-that-be didn't tell us anything. They said, "Just do what we tell you." The PBY only flew 100 miles an hour, and it had two .50-caliber machine guns in the waist and one .30-caliber in the bow, but it was all we had, and we could show you things that airplane could do, things that modern aviators wouldn't believe. For instance, circular takeoffs. We would go around in circles in those little lagoons until we got up enough speed to get the damn thing in the air. It was real tricky because you had the wing tilted and if you dipped a float in the water, you could turn over. I used that takeoff when we picked up some wounded Marines on Tulagi.

We landed with no lights, no nothing, and I reported to Gen. Alexander Vandergrift. He said, "I want you to take the wounded out of here because they're going to die if you don't." Vandergrift was living in a cave because he didn't think they were going to make it off the beach. I will never forget that picture. He had an ammunition box with a candle on it for a desk. I went back to the plane and found out they had loaded thirty-seven wounded Marines in there. Those men had been lying on the beach for two days. I thought there was too much weight to get the airplane off the water because I had forty-eight people in that little plane. The Marines, plus my own eleven crew members. Everybody was squashed up. I had five people in the cockpit with me. We opened all the hatches because the stink was absolutely unbearable. Gangrene, blood, and the moaning and groaning. I told this sergeant to explain to the general that I'd have to drop my bombs on takeoff. There were two 500-pound bombs, one under each wing, and they had contact fuses on them. I thought they might give me a kick in the ass—or blow our tail off.

We made a circular takeoff, and I dropped the bombs. It felt like somebody had pushed us up in the air. We cleared the trees, and when I got to Noumea I called the hospital ship. I told them what the problem was and they said, "How many people do you have?" I said, "Thirty-seven." They said, "Say again?" Two of the Marines died on

8

the way, but we got the rest of them back, and I feel better about that mission than anything in the war. We were doing something for people who otherwise would have been dead the next day.

Our next stop on our trip into the past would be at Suva, where we were based for a month. We went ashore and talked with the natives and tried to find out which Jap groups had been there and which islands actually had Japs on them. Then we'd report back to the fleet. We had five PBYs and they'd say, "Go to this island, go to that island. See what's going on." We didn't know what to expect. Either we'd find Japs or we wouldn't find Japs. We'd go in and meet with the natives and find out what they knew. I never found any of the natives down there who wanted to help the Japs. They had been mistreated for a couple of years, and they would do anything to help the Americans.

Tonga-Tabu would be another island. That's where the queen was a six-foot, six-inch woman. She served our crew a dinner of rancid fish. From Tonga-Tabu we would fly to Ndeni, which was right off Guadalcanal. It's a tiny little island, and we didn't know what we were going to find there, either. That night we went ashore and met the chief. The natives were very friendly, and they invited us to eat with them. A Jap sub came up and shelled us while we were there. The Japs knew what we were up to, and we were bothering the shit out of them. It's a good thing they didn't know there were so few of us.

The Navy sent us out to find the enemy, and we sure found them. Once we ran into a task force of about eighteen or nineteen Jap warships heading for Guadalcanal. A battleship, cruisers, destroyers, everything. Without being dramatic, you really get a feeling when you're in a situation like that. Here you are in an airplane with three machine guns flying over this enemy fleet, and I'm talking to the commander-in-chief of the Pacific Fleet. I was a lieutenant, the lowest of the low, and here I was telling Admiral Halsey, "We have a battleship, we have this, we have that." While I'm doing that, we were circling them and they were shooting at us. We had Zeros chasing us, and we kept dodging in and out of the clouds for a few hours until the Navy told us to come home. We were up there looking at the big picture, and it's hard to explain to somebody now, to tell how it really felt to be the only Americans out there, and that this whole thing was coming right at us.

★

During that war I always had two things on my mind. The first was, how was I going to get back? The second was, how could I inflict the most damage? You've got all this experience that you are trying to save for the Navy, and you also have the desire to stay alive. But you also want to really give them hell. I think that is the proper way to go about things in the military. I used to talk with people in the squadron about their philosophy, how they felt about the war, and I would eliminate about 10 percent of the people I was supposed to take into the squadron. I felt they were dangerous, to themselves and to others. It was never personal, it was just a feeling that mentally they didn't have it.

I had a problem with a guy when we were down in the water about 600 miles off Guadalcanal. We got in a fight with a Japanese seaplane. It was a Kawanishi 97, which had four engines and carried a lot more firepower than we did. We shot each other up real good, and one of my men, Frankovitch, was killed. Both of our engines quit and we ended up in the ocean. We had to take pencils from the navigator's table and break them off to plug the holes that the Jap had put in us. The sea was so rough that the plane started to come apart, so we got into two rubber boats.

The second night we were down, we had no water or food, we're way the hell out in the ocean, surrounded by sharks, a couple of guys bleeding and one dead, and my copilot started blubbering and crying. I told him to shut up. I said, "If you don't shut up, I'm going to dump you over the side." He kept crying, and it was hard on the rest of the crew. We had seven guys in those boats, and it was bad enough without somebody carrying on like that. The next morning he was still blubbering. "Oh, my God, I'll never get back. God will never take care of us." That really got me mad. God is not going to help me if I get shot down by the Japs. Every time before a strike we would have the Holy Joes. People used to say to me, "Why don't you go to services?" I said, "Why? I know what I'm going to do. Going in there and carrying on isn't going to help me do my job." If religion means anything to me, it means this. You are given what you've got, you use it the best way you can.

I took out my pistol and pistol-whipped him. He was out for two or three hours. We were finally spotted by another PBY from our squadron on the third day, and they picked us up. When I got back I surveyed him. That's Navy for an examination. I told the admiral, "This guy needs to be taken out of combat. He is no good for the other men with him." They took him out of the squadron and a year or so later, when I was with my Liberator group over in England, who comes walking in? The same guy, and now he's in command of a four-engine Liberator squadron! You can't figure the Navy out. On the first flight he went out on, he got jumped by some Me 109s, turned tail, and ran. He never flew again. When you know someone is no good, why put him in the situation? I wasn't worried about him, it was the other people he was going to take with him.

After we were rescued off Guadalcanal, they gave me a new PBY and we kept at it. Our group was very potent considering what we were working with. On one mission we took three PBYs and made a round-trip of 1,700 miles and hit a Jap cruiser and destroyer. I was out in the Pacific for almost two years and did over one hundred combat missions. We were relieved by another squadron because we lost so many people and airplanes. I think most of us had been out there long enough. They took us back to Pearl Harbor and said that we were all going to become instructors. I told them that I didn't want to be an instructor. I wanted to go back into combat because I thought I was pretty good at it.

★

I went to Washington and told the Navy Department that I wanted combat. They told me that they had a special group going over to work with the RAF, and we would be assigned to the Coastal Command. I wasn't the only one who didn't want to be an instructor. There were ten of us that went over to England. We were flying a PB4Y, which was the Navy version of the Liberator, and I got a thrill out of every mission. We would fly by ourselves, and a patrol might be 1,600 or 1,700 miles. All alone out there looking for submarines and watching for fighters or anything that might come along. We were the whole mission, one airplane and eleven guys. It was up to me to get the job done. We did the majority of our flying in the Bay of Biscay, and most of the time the weather was terrible. It seemed like it was always raining and cloudy.

We flew our thirty missions, and then they brought us into the briefing room and asked us if we would volunteer for five special missions. One of the pilots in the group was Joe Kennedy. I don't believe what I read about him now. How he went to London and was playing around with princesses and nurses, stuff like that. When he was in the squadron, he was quiet, read a lot, and didn't drink like some of the other people did. He was a nice guy and would fly just like everybody else.

We all said we'd fly, and each mission was going to be different. The Allies had not been able to hurt the German submarine pens. They were huge things with about one hundred feet of concrete on top of them. Some of them are still there. The submarines would go in to get repaired, and we couldn't do anything about it. The biggest bombs we had didn't even dent those things. We had a planning group that was thinking up really crazy stuff like going in 50 feet off the water with torpedoes. Just before the plane would get to the opening of the submarine pen, you'd drop your torpedoes and hope that they would run into the entrance and explode inside. That was crazy because, first of all, the Germans had all of these huge anti-aircraft guns on the banks of these places. As you came in you would see this wall of fire coming at you. The Germans also had flak ships sitting out in the water as a screen before you even got close. After the second mission like that, I told those planners that if they thought up more ideas like that, they could come with me.

They decided to load Kennedy's airplane with torpex. There was a very rudimentary electronic control system between his Liberator and a patrol plane, a PV-1. It was really a very primitive guided missile, but they had to have somebody take it off. The idea was that Kennedy and his copilot would take off and go up to 10,000 feet. Then they would point it at the French coast and bail out. The PV-1 plane would direct the Liberator down, and the whole thing would go smack into the submarine pen and blow it up. They took off, and as he was climbing to 10,000 feet there was either violent "clear-air turbulence" or, they think now, some errant radio signal triggered off all that torpex. The patrol plane pilot came back and said it was just one big explosion. Looking backward, it was about the dumbest idea I ever heard of. It probably would have exploded just at the mouth of the tunnel and not hurt anything inside, anyway.

That was how I got to know the Kennedys. I went to Boston and told his father how he died. All the Navy told the family was that he died in action. Since then, of course, the story has come out. I met Joe Kennedy in the Ritz Carlton Hotel in Boston. He was having lunch and I went over to his table. I said, "I'm Charlie Willis. I was with your son in England." He said, "I know." I said, "I'd like to tell you how he died. I'm sure you realize what a great guy he was." After I told him what had happened, he said, "You know that he could have been the next president of the United States." That's a quote. Then he said, "Why did he go and stick his neck out and volunteer for that mission?" I think young Joe wanted to prove something because Jack had just come back from PT-109.

I came back from that tour about a week before D-day, June of 1944. They wanted me to go to a Liberator training school in San Diego. I wanted a fighter squadron because I had always wanted to be a fighter pilot. They said, "You can't be a fighter pilot, you've never flown fighters." I said, "That doesn't mean I can't fly them." I got kind of mad. I managed to get into fighters because they couldn't get volunteers for a night fighter program they were starting. Day fighter pilots would say, "You mean we are going to land on a carrier at night with no lights? Forget it." They were going to use the Grumman F7F, the Tigercat. They were airplanes with a pair of huge engines and a tiny fuselage. The Tigercat was very fast, very new, and they were going to be equipped with radar. I flew one and said, "I like that." This officer said to me, "Goddamn it, we can't get anyone who wants to do this. We are looking for volunteers." I said, "Well, you've got one."

I went down to Vero Beach, Florida, where I was supposed to start a squadron. The pilots were there, but the airplanes weren't. They hadn't gotten any of the Tigercats off the production line, so we started to train in Hellcats, the standard day fighter, on the new carriers. I had never been in a Hellcat, and the only way you can check out in a plane like that is to get in and take off. That was pretty exciting. I was twenty-seven years old then, and I had all these young fighter pilots, twenty-one or twenty-two, who had just gotten back from one combat tour. I heard them talking about "the old fart." I realized that was me. "This old, goddamn, multi-engine fart that we got as a skipper." It really pissed me off.

The squadron went to Barber's Point, where we did some further training, and then we went aboard the *Ticonderoga*. You should have seen my first approach to land on that carrier. I'm leading the squadron and I've never made a carrier landing before, and that's not easy to do, much less at night. The Navy thought either you have a squadron and you're the commanding officer and make the landing, or you will be back teaching Liberator pilots. I managed to get down in one piece. The landing signal officer had fluorescent strips on his arms and straight down his front. He was lit up with black light, and all you would see would be a cross and that cross would move. We never did get the Tigercats, and we only chased one plane on a night mission. I don't even know if it was a Jap, because Japanese airpower had disappeared by the early part of 1945. We spent most of our time harassing the Japs on the mainland, and that was fun. We were strafing beaches, roads, bombing anything that had lights. We were pretty jolly when we came back from those missions, because we had that feeling that we were getting the Japs for all the terrible things they had done.

Everybody, I think, remembers what they were doing when Jack Kennedy was killed, and a lot of people remember what they were doing when they heard the atomic bomb had been dropped. I was on the *Ticonderoga* getting ready to take off. The strike was cancelled, and we were called into a ready room and told that a huge bomb had been dropped on Hiroshima and wiped out the whole city. We didn't know what the hell they were talking about and thought we were being spoofed. In the first place, we always laughed when the Air Force dropped anything. We were surprised if they hit the earth, never mind the target. In a few days they cancelled all operations, the fleet was ordered to Guam, and the war was over.

★

After the war I went to Patuxent, Maryland, as a test pilot. The Navy test program, at that time, was the most exciting thing a pilot could get involved with. We had every type of airplane that existed, and since I was in charge of this particular group, I could fly a different airplane every day. Four-engine, single-engine, the Messerschmitt 262 jet, a Zero, we had everything. Willy Messerschmitt himself came to give us a series of lectures. His English was better than mine. Very arrogant. He talked down to us, but everybody was taking it even though we'd say things about him when we got out. We were taking it because he was talking about things none of us knew about. When we got to fly the 262 you could see where it was going to be in the future. It was obvious to me, and still is, that if Hitler had had some decent people around him, he would have won the Battle of Britain and won the war. The biggest stupe he had was Göring. They had flown an experimental jet in 1939, and Göring said it was no good. Messerschmitt's whole story was, the Germans didn't lose the war and the United States didn't win it, that the production capability of the U.S. won the war, it wasn't the fighting ability of the soldiers. My feeling is that the German pilots were as good as anybody could have been, and the Japanese pilots were as good as anybody could expect them to be. Messerschmitt said, "You took automobile factories and one month later you were turning out tanks and airplane engines."

After a year of test work I met E. F. Hutton. I had breakfast with him one morning and he said, "Charlie, you are wasting your life in the peacetime Navy. Get out." I said, "I've got no money." I had something like $2,000 saved in war bonds. "The only thing I know how to do is push airplanes around the sky." He said, "I'll loan you $5,000. What do you want to do?" I said, "I'll start a freight airline." I thought there was a tremendous future for an airline like that because no airline was flying only freight. He said, "That's a hell of an idea. Transportation is the backbone of this country." He handed me his personal check for five big ones.

I contacted some of my old squadron mates. I said, "How would you like to come out of the Navy with me? I'm going to resign and start an airline." George Enloe resigned immediately, and we got three other Navy commanders. I called it Willis Air Service, the Commander Airline. We went down and bought two war-surplus C-47s in Georgia, where the government had stacked them up. They cost us $2,000 apiece. The ones the government didn't sell, they destroyed. There were acres and acres of them, and we couldn't even go in and take the instruments out of them. They went in there with bulldozers.

This was 1947, and we were located at Teterboro, New Jersey. There was a 3,000-foot-long grass strip, and we had the biggest airplanes there. We flew basically to Miami, Puerto Rico, and Colombia, South America. Air freight was all new, and we were flying everything. After two months we bought two C-54s because we were doing so well. Air freight prospered in those three or four years because there had been no commerce between the places we were going during the war. Everybody needed everything, and we were taking refrigerators, machinery, lots of things that would normally go by ship, but would have taken months to get there. We would haul fruits and vegetables on the way back.

I was doing all the sales work. One day a guy called up and said, "I've got the rose market cornered in Texas. I've got fifty thousand–dozen roses down here. Can you send a plane down?" Red roses were selling for $12 a dozen. I said, "Well, we aren't in the rose business, but will you pay $800 for the air freight?" He said, "I'll tell you what, we'll split the profit because I can sell all of these roses over the phone. You can make $10,000 by being my partner." I flew the airplane down to Fort Worth and picked up these great big boxes. They were exactly what he'd said, red roses, buds. I flew back to Teterboro that night, and the next morning a fleet of trucks came over from New York. The first guy takes the lids off a few boxes and says, "They're deadheads." I said, "What's a deadhead?" He said, "They were picked before they should have been, and they will never open. We don't buy that stuff." There must have been a frost scare in Texas, and they picked all the roses and dumped them on me.

I got a big truck and loaded it with those boxes. I had heard that Macy's could sell anything in those days, and we drove right up in front of the store in Manhattan. I went in and said, "Who is the chief buyer?" A guy came out. "I've got fifty thousand–dozen roses outside. Do you want to have a rose sale?" He went outside, looked at them, and said, "Rose sale." He cleaned out part of the street floor and put the roses out at twenty-five cents a dozen. You should have seen all those secretaries fighting over those flowers. He said he knew what the deal was and we laughed like hell. I got my eight hundred bucks back, and the guy in Texas wanted to know what I did with them. I told him, "None of your goddamn business. You thought you were palming them off on me."

I financed the airline by advertising for pilots, crew members, and mechanics. When people came to apply I would say, "There are two things you have to know. First, you don't get paid a salary. Second, you have to invest $2,000 in stock in the company." They'd ask, "How do we make any money?" I told them they would get paid by the trip. If the trip earns so much money, part of the profit is for the plane, part for the pilot, and so much for the copilot. By God, we had all the people we could handle, and they all ended up getting fair money.

Among the people who applied was a woman. She was English and had been a ferry pilot during the war. I told her the same thing. "You go get $2,000, and I will make you a copilot." All the guys laughed like hell until the next day when she came back with a check for $2,000 and I made her a copilot. All the pilots had funny stories about flying with her. "We'd be coming into Newark on an instrument approach, and the goddamn rain and sleet is coming down. The windshield wipers are going back and forth, and I'd scream for flaps and I'd look over—and Eleanor is powdering her nose. Then I'd scream for wheels, and she is over there putting her lipstick on." I don't know how many of those stories were true, but they all said she could fly. To make a long story short, she married one of the pilots and they went off as a team to fly an oil company's executive plane.

★

One day Eddie Rickenbacker called me up and asked me to have lunch with him at Rockefeller Center. He was the president of Eastern Airlines at that time. I went in to New York and he said, "We are going to run you out of business, but when we do I want to hire all your people. Any objections?" I said, "No, I can't keep all of those people, but why don't you look to the future? You're a visionary man." Eastern and the rest of the scheduled airlines went to the Civil Aeronautics Board and said, "We can do what they are doing, and we can do it better." They had more lawyers and more money, and the CAB was a political animal. Now the CAB is out of business, the airlines are deregulated, and you can charge anything you want and go anywhere you want.

I anticipated losing the airline, so I started a flying school in my headquarters and got the concession from the Port Authority to sell all the fuel and oil at Idlewild Airport. I lucked into that one. One day I went over there in my plane, and here was this huge airport that they had dug out of the river. The Port Authority had taken it over because the airlines were saying they wouldn't use it. They said the charges were too high, and they were going to stay at LaGuardia. I looked at it from the air, and I knew somebody was going to use that son-of-a-bitch sooner or later. It was fantastic, with 12,000-foot runways. They put out the bid for the fuel concession, and I was the only bidder. We would get a cent and three-quarters for every gallon we put in, and that may not sound like much, but you're talking about millions of gallons a day.

For six months I sat there and didn't sell one drop of gasoline because no airplanes were coming in. However, I made hay during that time and got distributor agreements with Shell, Esso, and Cities Service. I put in a Quonset hut and rented uniforms for my men. When the planes did start coming in, they'd say, "We want Shell gasoline." We'd put on the Shell uniforms and go out and fuel the airplane. The next guy would say, "I want Cities Service." We'd go in and put on our Cities Service uniforms. The fuel was all coming out of the same tank. Fuel is all made to the same specifications. The public doesn't know that. When you go into a Shell station you're getting gasoline with the same specs that you get in a Gulf station. The gasoline companies have these additives which are so much bullshit. It's all sales crust on the pie.

National and Eastern were the first to start coming into Idlewild, and sales were going like mad. At that time a lot of the airlines were flying Constellations and I loved those Connies. They ate a lot of fuel. One by one, the oil companies came out and looked at my facilities. Esso was the first one to wake up. They came to me and said, "You're commingling." I said, "Yeah, that's right." They said, "We want our own tank." I told them that if they wanted their own tank, they could build it. They were screaming at the Port Authority, and there was an emergency meeting. "Willis is commingling. Our fuel is an Esso product and we have to have it identified." I said, "It is identified. We go out with Esso uniforms on when we sell Esso." That was the beginning of commingling in this country. It's all commingled today.

We had a real booming business. I was selling all this fuel, doing maintenance for all the foreign airlines at Idlewild, and my school was filled with students under the G.I. Bill. That's when I lost my first wife. She said, "You love airplanes and flying more than me." I was out there every Sunday because Sunday was a big day for the airlines. One day who taps me on the shoulder but Captain Rickenbacker. After what he had done to Willis Air Service, I really didn't look too kindly at the man, but I did admire him from afar. In fact, I was one of those guys who had gone out to try to find him when he went down in the Pacific. His Air Force navigator couldn't find the island they were going to, and they ended up in the ocean in 1943. This, however, is 1949, and he says, "You're cheating Eastern Airlines." I said, "I'm not cheating anybody." He said, "Let me show you. You take the hose from your truck and put it in the airplane. The gas goes into the plane and your meter shows how much gas went through the hose and then into the plane, right?" I said, "Yes." He said, "Then, you defuel that hose." We would turn the pumps on backward to suck the fuel that was in the hose back into our tanks. I suddenly realized what he was getting at. "There are 40 gallons of gas in that hose, and they don't subtract from the meter. I want a credit." I thought to myself, "My God, that's why I have a surplus in my tanks every month." We couldn't figure out why we were having hundreds of surplus gallons every month, and we didn't know what to do with the damn fuel. I put some tanks in the ground and had all my employees bring their cars down every night and fill them up with aviation fuel. The cars ran like gangbusters, and they all had free gasoline. Eastern corrected that situation.

In the meantime, my partner Stan Rumbough and I had gotten interested in politics because we had gotten screwed out of Willis Air Service. We decided to run somebody for the presidency, so we started Citizens for Eisenhower in 1951. At that time Eisenhower was the most honored person in the world. He had been the head of NATO and was now the president of Columbia University. I organized half the states, and Stan took the other half. I took the South because I was originally from Texas.

*

I was born in Beaumont. My father worked for a shipbuilder, and I was only down there for a year because he got a job with the Baltimore Drydock Company. When I was thirteen I got rheumatic fever and was sent down to Mobile, Alabama, to live with my aunt. The South was supposed to be a better climate for my health. I went to high school in Mobile and then got my degree at the University of Florida. I majored in psychology because I couldn't think of anything else to do.

I graduated in 1940, and I don't remember at that time thinking in terms of this country going to war. I gather now, from reading the books that were written in those days, that a lot of people in this country didn't think there was going to be a war. I know that most of my friends thought we were going to stay out of it.

I had always been interested in flying, and the Navy was looking for college graduates. I enlisted and was sent to what they called then an elimination base. I went to Anacostia right here in Washington. They would take groups of ten and put you in a trainer. If you soloed in ten hours you were sent on to flight training, and if you didn't you were eliminated. It was that simple. It was a plus if you hadn't flown before, because the Navy didn't like anyone to have other training. They wanted you to do it their way. I will never forget this instructor, Major Parker. He was a Marine Corps pilot from World War I and he said, "Well, it's time for you to solo, Willis. If you live, I'll be amazed, and if you do make it you're going to be the worst goddamn pilot in the Navy." Maybe that was just his psychology, but he scared the shit out of me. I went around the field twice, and when I landed he was waiting for me. "Goddamn, you're still alive."

I was sent down to Jacksonville, spent a year there, and got my wings and commission in May of 1941. The day I got my wings I thought I had gone to heaven. The Navy asked us what we wanted to fly, and everybody wanted to be a fighter pilot because that was the hot thing to be. They divided the class up, and I was sent to PBY school. I was the most disappointed guy in the whole world. I thought, "My God, what a way to end my life, flying those old pigs."

I went to VP-11, which was forming a PBY squadron. We trained and had a blast for eight months. The Navy at that time in Hawaii was "King Shit." You got in your whites every evening, went downtown, and you'd have to fight the women off. We flew only two hours a day because gasoline was rationed, and we were only allowed two bursts with the guns on each flight. There was no feeling of crisis as far as we knew. The big headlines that I remember were about the fact that the Japs had sent two big emissaries to Washington to work out reconciliation, and we were shipping tons and tons of steel to Japan from the West Coast. Roosevelt wanted a war. He needed a war, but I think he got more war than he bargained for.

★

In 1951 Eisenhower didn't want to run for president, but he came to look at what Rumbough and I had done. He wanted to meet these two guys who had started eight hundred clubs all over the country. We had millions of people involved in Citizens for Eisenhower. The first question we asked him was, "Are you a registered Republican?" He said, "I don't know, I don't think I've ever registered." We found out that just before he was twenty-one years old he had registered in Kansas as a Republican, but he never really got into Republican politics, and I think he was the greatest president outside of George Washington. Of course, I'm prejudiced, but when you look at all the things he did, he was great. Ike stopped the Korean War, and we didn't have a war during the eight years he was president. The budget was balanced the whole damn time, and he desegregated Washington. I mean, you could go on and on. The national highway system, he put that in, and that's the backbone of this country. He was a quiet, unobtrusive leader and fantastic to work with. He had only fifteen people on the White House staff, and now there's over five hundred.

After he became president, he asked me to come to the White House and join his staff. At that time the school and Idlewild were going huckley-buck, and I had started operations in Miami, Ft.

Lauderdale, and Tampa. Eisenhower had a rule that everybody on his staff had to sell anything they had, not like this blind trust crap today, which is a big phoney. As if the trustee doesn't talk to the guy. I had to sell everything, and I didn't get anything compared to what it was worth. I went into the government as special assistant to the president.

He told me that I was to handle all presidential appointments. The Republicans had been out of office for twenty years, so we had to restaff the whole government. I got a computer expert to come in and set up a system: what jobs were open, what jobs weren't open, and what jobs would come open in the near future. We appointed 53,000 people in four years. After four years with Eisenhower, I couldn't take it anymore. The heat was terrible because everybody who got appointments deserved them, and the ones who didn't couldn't hate Ike, so they hated me. I still get people who will swear at me at cocktail parties. "Son-of-a-bitch, Willis, I didn't get that job." Drew Pearson started running terrible articles about me once a week. Everybody said I was wrecking the civil service system in the United States. Hell, I didn't do anything without the president's approval. Finally I told Ike, "I want to get out. The appointments are all made, the system is in place, and I want to go back into business." Ike said, "O.K.," and gave me a beautiful sendoff.

I went to work for Charles Wilson, "Electric Charlie," who had been the head of General Electric. He was going to become the chairman of the board of W. R. Grace Company, and he wanted me to be an administrative assistant and do his legwork. He was a giant of a man, and when Charlie spoke people knew he was serious. I was there for one year when Wilson got teed off at Peter Grace and quit. He actually just walked out the door, period.

In the meantime, I had been approached by the directors of Alaska Airlines. They were in a terrible mess; in fact, the government had indicted them for mismanagement and misuse of government funds. It was a public company, and they had taken their airplanes over to Europe to take Jews from Europe to Palestine. It's in the book *Exodus*. The president of the airline was in jail in Damascus for smuggling gold. He would take fingerpaint and write Mid-East Airlines on the planes. When they unloaded the Jews in Palestine, they would wash the writing off and put Arab writing on the airplane so they could go down into the Arab countries.

I went out and toured Alaska for about two weeks, and it looked like a tremendous opportunity to build a transportation system in a large part of the United States that basically had no transportation. No roads or railroads to speak about. I told them I would take the job if I could buy control of the company from the people who had it. The government said, "We want you to do it, and we will help you because we have to get rid of these crooked people." I put up a couple of million that I didn't have. I borrowed most of it. It was 1955 when I went and got a bill through Congress to give the airline a permanent certificate. That was also when I lost wife number two. I bought a house in Alaska, and when she came up there she announced that there was no way she was going to live in a wilderness. I asked her what she was going to do. "I'm going back to Washington." I told her, "Go." When I got up there the only people who rode Alaska Airlines were drunks and people who didn't know any better. We turned that around and it became very successful, and I built up a big business.

I brought the airplanes back from Europe to where they belonged, and I went down to look at a couple of DC-6s that had been ordered from Douglas before I got there. They were beautiful, except they had no interiors. Like a tin can inside. I said, by golly, I'm going to make these airplanes work. I took a bunch of surplus seats, put them on pallets, and secured them to the floor. Then I took two Jiffy Johns, those things you see at construction sites, and put them in the back. We had an electric piano and a little open bar in the front of the plane. A guy would be playing rinky-dink tunes, and there would be a singer on those flights. The damn airplanes were full all the time. We had bingo games where we gave away an ounce of gold. Fashion shows with models from Seattle. TWA claims they were the first airline to have movies, but we were the first. I put in a 16mm projector and a regular screen. Home-cooked food. Our stewardesses were—how can I say it? Stacked.

When the oil was discovered in Alaska, we created an airlift. We hauled more freight to the North Slope than they did during the whole Berlin Airlift. This one tiny company. I bought huge Hercules aircraft to carry that stuff up there. We had competition with Western, Pan Am, Northwest, and Wein-Alaska. We were able to outmaneuver and outproduce all of those companies. We had the highest load factor of any airline up there, and we showed projections of tremendous profits. With those projections I made arrangements to finance a whole bunch of new jets, and by that time we had 1,500 employees.

The last, and most memorable, thing I think I did was to get the Russians to give us the right to go to Siberia. Those trips were 100 percent sold out for four years. Four thousand miles each way and congressmen, senators, everybody was going there. Everybody paid, too. There weren't any freebies. It was one of the most profitable airlines in the history of air travel, and then my lawyers stole it from me. I had planned to spend some time out of the country, and so I signed some papers that gave them power of attorney. That's when and how they decided to get rid of me. The banks I was working with said I had to get rid of some people, and these people found out and they decided to unload me first. It's still in the courts and, looking backward, if I had planned ahead, I could have had safeguards all over the place.

After that happened I took ten fishing trawlers to Africa and set up a commercial fishing business. My third wife left me at that point because, she said, "Anyone who lives over here is crazy." The business did fine until the president of Ghana was killed. I left the country because I didn't want to get shot. I've done a lot of things since Alaska to try to survive and keep money coming in to pay the lawyers.

My new project is a rehabilitation center for people with alcohol and drug problems. We have one of the biggest markets in the country between New York and Washington. It's unlimited. We are buying a woman's seminary that was built in 1876, a beautiful place right near the Patuxent Naval Air Station in Patuxent, Maryland. There are twelve nuns who live in the school. When we go to visit them, they all sit there and every once in a while two of them get up and go to the chapel and say another prayer. We have a camp down there that can handle five hundred people. A 500-foot waterfront, swimming facilities, tennis courts, an Olympic-size swimming pool, you name it, we've got it. We're going to have kids down there, government people, all kinds of people getting help.

My weakness is that I shoot first and then take aim. But it would not be me if I did it any other way. I would not have stayed in combat. I would have gotten my ass out of the Pacific and gone back like almost everybody else to the States and said, "My God, I made it." Not ask for it over and over again. I believed in what I was doing then, and I believed in what I have been doing ever since. I think that is what makes things really work. You have to have something to believe in. I did what I could during the war. I think most of us did the best we could, but there was so much waste. The population of this country is completely cold and immune to the sacrifices that a lot of young men went out and made. I don't know how much time you've spent in a veterans hospital, but it's enough to drive you nuts. To see these fellows who never even started to live. Most of us were so dedicated and angry during World War II that we didn't realize what we were getting into. I thought it was an honor to serve in the war, and it was also an honor to work for Eisenhower in the White House. I'm afraid I'm going to die with nothing on my tombstone but honor. You could take my medals and a nickel, and it won't get you a cup of coffee.

FLYING TIGER

The war began for Edward Rector at the same time that it did for Charles Willis, except that he was so far east, in Burma, beyond the international date line, that it was December 8. He was having breakfast in the mess of the legendary Flying Tigers, the unusual "private" air force created by Gen. Claire Chennault before America entered the war. Its purpose was to help a China then being overrun and close to defeat by Japan. You would have had to hunt for a more faraway battleground.

You would also have to look hard for Ed Rector's house today; even though it's in suburban Arlington, Virginia, it's lost among the trees. The inside is a comfortable, easy bachelor hall, full of aviation souvenirs. One collects a lot of them by the time one becomes a retired Air Force colonel, as Rector is—precise, military, but not intimidating. The weekend of our discussion, it was a bonus that he had a houseful of old friends—real-life former Flying Tigers.

The Flying Tigers were a unique fighting force at a special crisis moment in history. The Axis was riding high, America was legally neutral, and China was close to total defeat. We had, however, a leader, Claire Chennault, who was an exceptional man. And President Roosevelt allowed us to be released from the Air Corps, Navy, and Marines to serve in that "private" air force. Chennault had thought up the idea of such an interim force that could stem the Japanese advance until the Chinese could rebuild their force. He sold that idea to FDR. I'm sure that Chennault knew that someday the United States would be fighting the Japanese, but he never used that as a selling point when he was recruiting pilots and ground personnel. He told us our job would be to help China defend the Burma Road, period.

The Japanese had taken all the port cities, so the Burma Road had become the lifeline for those Chinese not yet conquered.

We were a relatively small group of about three hundred. There were just under one hundred pilots and the rest were administrative, medical, ground crew, and technicians. We had an occasional Australian or New Zealander, maybe two or three, but everybody else was an American. I was recruited by a reserve naval commander at Christmas of 1940. At that time, I was a naval aviator flying off the old USS *Ranger* and *Yorktown* doing naval exercises and neutrality patrols in the Atlantic. Looking back at my naïveté then, I thought this country would never get into that war. When I was told we were going over to defend the Burma Road I didn't need any more motivation. I had read about that part of the world in Kipling since I was a kid, and the word Burma excited my imagination.

We were given what was then a very handsome salary. The base pay for pilots was $600 a month and an additional $500 for each confirmed victory. Compare that to an ensign's base pay in the Navy at that time, which was approximately $220, plus $93 flight pay a month. We all signed on as wing men in the AVG [American Volunteer Group]. The next rank was flight leader, which paid $675. Vice squadron commander was $700 and squadron leader paid $750. We wore Chinese Air Force insignia, khaki slacks or shorts, and tan shirts. The original idea was to recruit only fighter pilots, those with fighter or dive-bomber skills, but by the time the AVG program was under way, war clouds were looming for the United States and the recruiting standard had to be—I won't use the word lowered, but let's say, altered. We had any number of bomber pilots, instructors, and seven or eight Navy patrol plane pilots.

★

I grew up in western North Carolina. An older brother was in the Marine Corps and he told me, "What you ought to get into, young fellow, is aviation. That's going to be the coming thing, you just watch." I must have been ten years old when he told me that, and I thought it sounded pretty exciting. By the time I was twelve, I was spending all my money on pulp magazines like *Battle Aces*, which had stories about the famous First World War fliers. I had stacks of them and knew all the aerodromes and the types of airplanes. I never walked around a corner when I was a kid, I banked.

I think we all turned out pretty good because my mother was a

Ensign Edward Rector, left, and his crew chief stand in front of an SB2U dive bomber. The year was 1941 and a few months later Rector would be in faraway Burma, a member of the Flying Tigers.

saint. She was a very kind and understanding person. On the other hand, my father had a good heart but was stern, demanding, and unforgiving. He was a lawman and also first deputy sheriff of Madison County. Cars would pass through town—remember, this was during prohibition—on their way from Detroit to Miami with loads of Canadian whiskey. Every once in awhile you'd see one listing with a negative rake, and my father would tell his colleagues, "There's one, let's get him." The sheriff's department had a couple of Ford touring cars, and we would all hop aboard and give chase. Sometimes the whiskey runners would abandon their car and I would run after them on foot, and I can still recall sitting on a guy until a fat, out-of-shape deputy came panting up to me and said, "That's the way to do it, boy."

The cars would be sold at auction, and my father would break the whiskey bottles in the public square. In a town the size of Marshall, everybody knew the two or three local sots, and I can remember seeing the tears rolling down their cheeks when they saw that Old Crow and Green River whiskey going down the grate into the French Broad River.

My father sent my sisters to college, nursing school, or normal school. He told us boys, "If you want to go to college, get out there and earn it. Do it on your own." I was an athlete in high school and was fortunate enough to make all-western North Carolina center playing football. I had scholarship offers from several of the big schools, but I'd already checked to find out what was required to become an aviation cadet. Football scholarships at those big schools were only good for your freshman year. If you made the squad, then you were good for the next three years. That's not what I wanted, because your education depended on making the damned squad. I needed two years of college to qualify for the Army Air Corps and, if not selected, four years plus a degree to qualify for Naval Aviation.

Catawba College in Salisbury, North Carolina, guaranteed me four years of college, team or no team. Catawba is a little Yankee school that's located down south. It was run by the Dutch Reformed Church. I enrolled there, and at the end of two years I took the Army Air Corps physical exam at Langley Field near Norfolk, Virginia. That was early 1937, and there were thirty-three guys taking the exam. After a full day of tests, they told thirty-one guys to go home. Another fellow and I were the only ones left. They told us to come back the next day, and I went back to my little dollar-a-night rooming house and allowed myself to get excited for the first time. I thought, "They wouldn't call us back if we hadn't made it."

The next day a flight surgeon examined us and said to me, "I'll have to turn you down. You've got chronic rhinitis." I said, "What's that?" "Inflammation of your nasal passages." I told him that it was February, and I had just hitchhiked for a day and a half in the slush and snow to get to those tests. In another day or two it would be gone because I never had any problems like that. Nope, they took the other guy. I hitchhiked back through the slush to Catawba, went to school for another one-and-a-half years, and qualified for naval flight training. I realized later that if I'd passed that physical, I could be dead because I'd have been out in the Philippines, or somewhere like that, when the Japanese hit.

★

I took my initial flight training at Anacostia Naval Air Station in Washington, D.C. You had to solo in ten hours unless you were like a guy in our class whose father was an admiral. He got thirteen hours. Then I went to Pensacola in August 1939, and after I received my wings in June 1940 I joined the fleet and qualified as a carrier pilot. I was assigned to Bombing Four, flying SBTU-2s, on the USS *Ranger*. There's nothing more interesting than carrier operations, and I think it's the most exacting flying in the world. This was the good old days with a straight deck, a landing signal officer, and nine arresting cables. That's where the AVG found me.

The majority of the AVG personnel left from San Francisco during July of 1941 on two Dutch ships, the *Bloemfontein* and the *Jaegersfontein*. I sailed on the *Bloemfontein*, and our group numbered 29. Another 120 men departed earlier on the other ship. The rest came in driblets of fours, sixes, and tens on other ships. We went over under assumed professions so the Japanese wouldn't get word of our intent. I became a construction engineer and others were salesmen, oilmen, or newspaper reporters, and one guy, Eddie Goyette, went as a baseball player.

Twelve hours from Hawaii we were met by a cruiser that escorted us into Honolulu. We were there for two or three days and learned that the Japanese had moved into French Indochina. When we got back on the ship the captain told us we'd be sailing to Brisbane, Australia, under wartime conditions, blacked out and no smoking on deck. From Brisbane we threaded our way up through the Great Barrier Reef and then into Manila. Next we went to Batavia, in the Dutch East Indies, spent ten days ashore, and were then picked up by the *Jaegersfontein*, which took us to Singapore. We then boarded a little Norwegian coastal trading vessel and sailed to Rangoon, where we were met by representatives of the AVG. That afternoon, we boarded a train and took the five-hour, 180-mile trip to Toungoo, where the AVG was based on an RAF reserve base and where Chennault began preparing us for our role.

Our later success in combat was due to his teachings. We had a very good success rate if you look at what was happening to the Air Corps in the Philippines, New Guinea, and the Dutch East Indies. Our official record was 296 Japanese aircraft destroyed, but it was later confirmed to be actually higher. After the war the British found the wreckage of forty or fifty airplanes in the Martaban Bay between Burma and Siam. The Japs didn't have self-sealing tanks, we'd riddle them, the fuel would leak out, and they would never get back to Bangkok. We didn't go back and try to claim those planes, that's just a fact we found out later. During the eight months we flew as the AVG, we lost only six pilots in aerial combat.

Chennault taught us how to utilize the attributes of the P-40 against the Japanese aircraft. The Zero could out-turn the P-40, because it was a very agile aircraft. Every fighter pilot, from the First World War on, has been taught that if you're in a fight, and you have to do a lot of turning, the plane that has the best turn rate can always get on the tail of the other guy. Chennault took that fact, drew on his great knowledge of aerobatic flying, and came up with his thesis. First of all, you might not outturn a Zero in a P-40, but you had him outgunned. Chennault told us to never hesitate to engage in a head-on pass because we had two .50-caliber machine guns firing through the prop and four .30-caliber guns, two guns in each wing. The Zero had two 20mm cannon in the wing and two 7.7mm machine guns firing through the prop. Secondly, we were faster than he was. If a Zero turned with you, you didn't try to turn with him. We'd stick the nose down 10, 20, 40 degrees, whatever was required to get out of his way. The in-line, liquid-cooled engine in the P-40 gave the airplane less resistance than the Jap with his radial engine. He had a lot of frontal area slowing him down, and once you pulled away from him, you'd climb back up and join the fight again. Chennault was proven right because the Zero and other Jap fighters couldn't keep up with us.

The Japanese pilots were very good, and they knew how to use their airplanes. The way they got most of our guys was with their quick maneuvering ability. However, Chennault also made the point that if you had more speed than the enemy fighters they couldn't run home. You could overtake them and they would have to turn and fight. Then you could use your superior firepower. Those were the attributes of the P-40 that he taught us to utilize, and he told us to never stray from them. After our first fights, Chennault wrote a twelve-page letter to Gen. Hap Arnold, chief of the Army Air Corps, and outlined all of the things that were proving successful. He told me later that none of the information he sent was ever passed around, and there were P-40s in places like Java, New Guinea, and elsewhere still trying to turn with Zeros and getting shot down. I've discussed this with others, and we've wondered how many lives would have been saved if that information had been passed out and Chennault's methods put into practice.

★

We'd get up at six o'clock in the morning, have breakfast, and by seven we were in the classroom. We went to class every morning for two or three weeks, and after an hour of that, we'd go up and practice the tactics we'd just gone over. Our flying would be finished at one o'clock, and then we took the rest of the day off. This was central Burma, and we arrived just after the monsoon season. It was hot as hell! We got in the habit of taking siestas because there was nothing else to do in that heat. In the evening we'd have dinner and then either go into town or go bicycling around the countryside. Burma was a wonderful place to wander around. If you recall your *National Geographic* magazines, there were photographs of native women who wore silver bracelets on their elongated necks. A tribe of those people lived eleven miles from our base, and we would take a Sunday trip up there to see them. They were very friendly and when the women took those bracelets off, they couldn't even hold their heads erect. I was taking pictures with a Brownie box camera and sending them home to show my family the fantastic things I was seeing. It was as fascinating as I had imagined it would be.

We were having breakfast on December 8, 1941, when we got the word that Pearl Harbor had been attacked. Chennault immediately put four airplanes in the air, and we went on 24-hour alert. In concert with the British and Chinese he worked out the best way to deploy the AVG. The Hell's Angels Squadron was based at Rangoon with the RAF, and the other two squadrons, the Adam and Eve and mine, the Panda Bears, were sent to Kunming, China, to help defend that city, which the Japs had resumed bombing. We arrived there at about 5:30 in the afternoon and flew our first combat mission the next day at 8:00 A.M.

The Japanese had bombed Kunming the day before and came back that morning for another go. We went up to intercept them. My airplane was scheduled for a periodic check, and when I saw the other planes taking off I ran to the flight line and told the crew chief to get the cowling back on. They had just started to work on it, so they got it back together in a hurry and I took off and caught up with the other airborne pilots. I can recall thinking to myself, "This is it. Finally, combat."

The bombers were flying in a beautiful V-formation, and I picked out the last plane on the left side of the formation and started a curve of pursuit from a high-perch position. I had heard about target fascination, and it happened to me during that first sortie. You become mesmerized, and some pilots have been known to fly right through the target because they would lock on and not shake themselves loose. I was closing in on the bomber, firing all the while. I can still see all of it in my mind today, crystal clear. It was at the last second, no, the last split-second that I shoved the stick forward and went under the bomber. I don't know how close I actually came, but I can still see every detail. The camouflage paint, the rivets on the wings, and the tail gunner slumped over his gun with his jaw shot away. As I climbed up for another pass, I looked down and saw that the bomber was still in formation, but streaming flames and smoke. He slowly dropped his nose and finally went straight in. Once again, I remember thinking, very calmly, "So that's the way it is."

I learned a lot that day. First of all I had experienced target fixation. Second, I held the trigger down and overheated the guns. When I started down for another pass, I had only one little .30-caliber firing. I tried to clear the other guns but couldn't get any more action, so I went straight for the lead bomber from a head-on position with that one little gun going pop, pop, pop. Finally, even that gun stopped firing, so I decided I'd better return to base.

This was my first trip over China, and all we carried were primitive little maps. I figured that the bombers were going to fly directly back to Hanoi, where they came from, so I flew alongside, just out of range. After I got their heading, I did a 180 and flew the reciprocal, thinking it would get me back to Kunming. What I didn't know was that the Japs were heading east-south-east, instead of south, because they were going around some clouds. I ended up passing east of Kunming and force landing 90 miles away.

★

After I finished Ernest Gann's book, *Fate Is the Hunter*, I went back and thought about my flying career. If you've flown enough (I've got over 10,000 hours), every pilot has had one or more dicey calls, especially if he's flown combat. I've recalled seven times that I should have been dead, except that fate was not seeking me. Coming back from that first mission was one of those times, trying to find an auxiliary field on my primitive map. I ended up in a river canyon whose sides gradually became sheer cliffs. The sky was overcast, with a ceiling of 400–600 feet, and suddenly the canyon narrowed to less than a mile in width. I was pulling 90-degree turns to keep from crashing into the sides of that canyon. Then I ran into a straight stretch of about two miles and just floorboarded the throttle and started to climb into the overcast. There I sat, climbing at 140 miles an hour, expecting to run into a mountain at any moment. Suddenly it started getting light on the top of my canopy, and I realized I might make it. I broke out into beautiful sunlight with mountains sticking up all around me. I turned the airplane around and headed straight back toward a little village I'd seen before I went into the canyon. By that time my red light was on, indicating low fuel, and I knew I had to get that bird on the ground. It was a pretty soft belly-landing, wheels up, flaps down, because I used my carrier-landing technique and landed in a plowed field. At this point I didn't know if I was in friendly or Jap-occupied territory.

The village was located on higher ground, and it looked like an avalanche of people was coming down on me. Thousands of people in a human wave. I reached in my shoulder holster, took out my .45, and crouched on the wing, looking over the fuselage. Then I decided that was pretty silly, put my pistol back in the holster, and stood up on the wing. They turned out to be friendly Chinese, and I was the first American they had ever seen. The Chinese government had told the people that the Americans were there to help defend them against the Japanese. They told them to treat us kindly and do anything to assist us. I had my flight jacket with the "blood chit" on the back. We didn't call it that, but I've found out since that's what other people called it. It said, in essence, "This is an American flier here to help us. Do anything within your power to assist and accommodate him and return him to his unit." It was signed by Chiang Kai-shek. We also had the Chinese Air Force insignia on our planes.

The people from the village ended up taking me into their town and treated me to a very lavish dinner. I ensured the ground observer net knew I was down safe and spent the rest of the day with some local auto mechanics who helped me take the guns, ammunition, and anything else that I could salvage from the P-40. We put it all in a truck so it could be brought back to Kunming. Chennault told us to retrieve everything possible if we went down. Later on, the Chinese picked that airplane up, and we saved the whole damn thing. They even retrieved airplanes that were lost under water.

When I got back to Kunming and told my story, I found out that I was the first member of the AVG to shoot down a Japanese plane. Later we learned that only one Jap returned to Hanoi. I went to Chennault's office and explained what had happened, about the map and how I got lost. He said, "Well, Eddie, the only thing I can fault you for is that the other guys got back, but they barely got back because they were lost for three damned hours." Then he asked me why I came home before the others. I told him that my guns wouldn't fire. He said, "You should have stayed in there and made passes to draw their fire so the other guys could get a shot in." I said, "Huh?" The old man was something else.

You don't know what scrounging and living without things is

like until you've lived like we did. The Chinese provided us with bed and board, and I've since learned to appreciate what epic efforts they made to keep us happy, especially with the problems they faced. Later, in the 14th Air Force at forward locations, you'd put on your khakis and they'd smell like hell. Then you realized they had been washed in a damned rice paddy because it was the only water available. We never got beer, booze, Cokes, or extras, because everything had to be flown over the Hump [the Himalayas] and Hump tonnage was too dear to use for amenities. Sometimes we'd spend a week or ten days without fuel because the transports didn't get us enough fuel to mount a mission. Ours was a hand-to-mouth existence. It would take five months for gasoline to reach us from the time it was off-loaded in Calcutta until it reached our bases. You can imagine how we treasured that fuel.

When I was commander, 23rd Fighter Group, I was driving around one morning at a forward field, checking things out, when I saw a master sergeant kicking a guy in the tail. I stopped and asked him what the hell was going on. He said, "Well, sir, look here. He was preflighting this airplane, and he let damn near a gallon of gasoline spill out on the ground when he was draining the pet cock." I took the sergeant aside and told him that I appreciated how he felt but that was a little extreme. He said, "Sir, he'll tell the new guys that I kicked his ass and they'll be more careful."

Our early success had a terrific effect on morale because we were the only Americans that the newspapers and government could brag about. We were losing our hat, ass, and spats everywhere else. Here we were, the AVG, downing eight Japanese planes on our first day of combat. Then over Rangoon on Christmas 1941, we destroyed twenty-seven Japanese airplanes. Two days later, on the 27th, another sixteen destroyed. I think that our early success and the fact that we were the only people doing anything was a big factor in terms of the aura, if you will, of the Flying Tigers.

The shark mouth also added to our mystique. Somebody in our outfit had seen a picture of an RAF plane that was fighting in the African desert that had a shark's mouth painted on it. Again, being innovative types, some of our guys cut out some stencils and put a shark mouth on one of our planes. It looked so good they painted every one of them and by the time we went into combat, every P-40 we had was painted that way. They were eye-catching, and we became known to the Chinese as the American Tigers.

Once the United States was in the war, we realized that the AVG couldn't go on as a separate, special entity. Chennault had been appointed a brigadier general, we knew that the salary we were being paid had to end, and we had to relinquish our elite position. Each of us had to make a decision as to what we were going to do—go back to our former service, stay on, or whatever. When the AVG went home, we became the China Air Task Force. There were five pilots and twenty-eight ground crewmen who decided to stay on, and we became the core of the 23rd Fighter Group. The pilots were Tex Hill, Frank Schiel, Chuck Sawyer, Gil Bright, and myself. At the time, I was holding the fort out east in Hengyang, China. I was Hill's deputy squadron commander, and we were fighting and raiding, the usual bit, when Tex came back from a ferry trip. He took me aside and said, "Chennault talked to me and told me to come back and give you his pitch. Somebody has to stay on and show these new, green pilots what the problems are, or they're going to kill themselves. The terrain, the fact that the maps are 20 miles off, navigation, things like that." He told me who was staying, and then he said, "Chennault said I should ask you personally, Ed." I said, "Damn! I want to go home." Tex said, "So do I, but hell, the old man asked us to stay." I knew I didn't have a choice, so I stayed.

Most of the AVG went home to the States and joined their former services. Some, like Chuck Older, joined another service. We were classmates at Pensacola and he was a Marine pilot before he joined the AVG, and when he returned he joined the Army Air Corps. When I came back on my second tour in China and took over the 23rd Fighter Group, Chuck was a lieutenant colonel and my deputy group commander. I think staying out there was the smartest move I ever made. Here I was, a major in the Army Air Corps, and I wasn't quite twenty-five. By the time I was twenty-eight, I was a full bird colonel.

When the 23rd Fighter Group was created, Tex Hill became the commander of the 75th Fighter Squadron, Frank Schiel the 74th, and I was designated commander of the 76th. Col. Robert L. Scott, who wrote *God Is My Copilot*, was the group commander. I was in Kweilin, China. Tex Hill was 200 miles away from me in Hengyang, and Frank was doing air defense in Kunming, 400 miles away. We were really spread out. When I was given the squadron I went looking for Maj. Johnny Alison, Army Air Corps, recently arrived in China. I took him aside and said, "Johnny, I need advice. I can handle the Japs, but Christ, what about all this paperwork? I don't know anything about Army Air Corps regulations and procedures." He said, "Eddie, forget the paperwork and don't worry. You've got an adjutant and a first sergeant and they will do the morning report and take care of everything. You just continue fighting the war."

Chennault also sent me a safe. Believe it or not, before we got Air Corps codes, he made up a code of his own and sent me a safe to keep it in. And, you know what else he sent me? Ten thousand U.S.

greenback dollars! I didn't want to sign for it because I didn't want the responsibility for that kind of money. It was like a million dollars. I ended up putting it in the safe, and later on I found out the old man knew what he was doing because I lost a couple of pilots and had to arrange to buy caskets and take care of burial expenses. When Bruce Holloway took over the squadron, I was the happiest person in the world as I signed off on that money.

I never felt that things were too desperate out there at that time, because the enemy wasn't doing that well and, to be honest, we were cleaning their plow. We knew that if we got into a fight, we could pretty well wax the Japs. That's just the way we looked at the situation. I don't think that being a Flying Tiger ever hurt my career. I eventually had ten-and-a-half confirmed kills in combat, and in terms of the jobs that I held subsequently, that didn't hurt either. While we were out there, the Army Air Corps units started coming in. The 11th Bomb Squadron, the 51st Fighter Group, and a year and a half later the China Air Task Force became the 14th Air Force.

When we finished our first tours, Tex and I came home and I ended up at Walter Reed Hospital for about three months. A parasitic sheep liver fluke had lodged in my liver while I was in China. It had been dormant, but with all the fanfare of returning and being wined and dined, it weakened my system and I damned near died. A gifted man, Dr. Rogliano, found out what I had and my recovery was spectacular. I went on to Eglin Field in Florida and started doing test work. I was flying the latest aircraft, but I could see the war was ending and, to be honest, I wanted a bit more of the action. The hospital said that since I had picked up that parasite, I was barred from overseas duty. Lo and behold, Chennault requested me to return and I was on my way. Pretty soon I became the commander of the 23rd Fighter Group. That's the job I held until I sent them home at the end of 1945. We were flying P-51 Mustangs, the finest World War II fighter. In terms of taking care of your ass, and the enemy, the P-51 was something else. I'm not denigrating the old P-40 because it was a great airplane for its time, but the P-51 belonged to the next plateau of capability. I've flown over one hundred types of airplanes, including jets, but you'll hear most P-51 pilots say the same thing. From Yeager on down, everyone who flew that airplane says it was the best of its time.

After the 23rd went home, I joined Brig. Gen. J. P. McConnell (later Chief of Staff, USAF) who was the chief of the Air Section of the first Military Assistance Advisory Group (MAAG) that the United States organized in the post–World War II era. We worked with the nationalist Chinese air force at headquarters in Nanking and with all units in the field. I was director of operations, air section, until I returned stateside in mid-1947.

I have lasting respect and admiration for the nationalist Chinese people. I think we did everything within our power to help the nationalist Chinese save China, but it just wasn't in the cards. The peasants wanted to change the old pattern, and because communications were slow, Chiang Kai-shek never got the word out that he was going to create a new order. The groundswell of support for the communists was too great, and we all know how they won. Everything fell apart, and the nationalists were eventually shoved off the mainland in 1949. It was just an uncontrollable flood tide that couldn't be stopped.

On return I was assigned for two years to the Old Continental Air Command Headquarters at Mitchel Field, Long Island, in the initial planning for an air defense system for the continental United States. These first gropings resulted eventually in the present-day North American Air Defense Command (NORAD). I was next selected to attend the Armed Forces Staff College in Norfolk, Virginia, and from there was assigned to the Air Staff, Pentagon. I was chief of the Air Defense Requirements Division. We were responsible for stating all the requirements for the air defense of the United States. Radar, both airborne and ground, guns, missiles, and aircraft. We worked very closely with the Canadians and British. I had that job for eighteen months when my name came up again. The United States was forming a new MAAG for Taiwan (following the North Korean invasion of South Korea) and since I had been with the Chinese twice, my name continued to come up. I fought it until the end—I really liked what I was doing in the Pentagon. I was finally ordered to go as chief of the Air Section. Of all my twenty plus years in the Air Force, this was the most rewarding tour I ever had. When we arrived, the Chinese were virtually destitute. You wouldn't believe how little they had on Taiwan. When I left, after two-and-a-half years, there were three fighter wings equipped with late–World War II P-47Ns and one wing with P-51Ds and P-51Ks. In addition, we converted one wing to F-84 jets, upgraded five air fields, established a Combat Air Command, and put in radar. The Chinese Air Force continued to grow. Today Taiwan's air force is one of the most efficient and combat-capable in the world.

My next orders rather upset me: I was posted as commander of the Pilot Instructor Training Wing at Craig Air Force Base, Selma, Alabama. I sought out Lt. Col. Ken Rosebush, my deputy Air Section chief, and asked him what the hell was going on. It looked to me like they were taking the "old fuds" and putting them in training command because they had no other place to put us. He said, "Just wait a minute. I know you fighter jocks. You get the idea that people in the training command aren't producers. When it rains or snows and the runways become icy, do you know what TAC [Tactical Air Command] and SAC [Strategic Air Command] do? They stand down for a few days until they get everything squared away. You know what the Flying Training Command does in the same situation? They fly because they are the only command in peacetime that has a daily commitment." Then he asked me how many pilots I thought they trained a year. I said, "I've got no idea." Ken said, "They train 11,000 a year, and do you know what it means when you've got 210 guys flying that have to graduate by four o'clock today because, day after tomorrow, you have another 210 coming in? Some of them have wives and they have to have quarters, they need airplanes to fly, everything has to work and you can't afford to stand down in flying training." I began to get a new appreciation of the post and took over the wing on December 18, 1951.

★

Later I attended the National War College and was assigned to the Pentagon and retired from the Air Staff in 1962. But I wasn't at loose ends; I had my postservice life all planned. My first position was with a company doing business in India. We were handling engine and air frame repair and overhaul, later getting into contract airlift. Later I went to North Africa and was involved in the same endeavor for the same company. Next, two other guys and I set up an aviation and communications consulting agency in Brussels, Belgium. Europe was ten years behind the United States in terms of the detailed requirements of the International Communications and Air Organization (ICAO), an arm of the UN. This is the worldwide organization that sets (among other things) the standards for all airports around the world. Eventually, I sold out to my two partners and moved back to the States nine years ago. I'm still involved in the consulting business and work out of my home. I've never married, and a lot of people have asked why. I reply I'm too damn selfish, and after all, it's my life. When I want to travel I want to be able to depart in 20 minutes. My life has been very enjoyable, and I've done virtually what I wanted to do since I was twelve years old.

CITADELS AT SEA

In the vast sea war with Japan, spread out over the largest ocean on earth, the aircraft carrier became the key ship for both contestants. It was the major target for its rival clouds of planes, despite the fact that these floating airfields, unlike the dreadnoughts of earlier times, never came within sight of each other in battle. Japanese carriers created havoc at Pearl Harbor, where the only good news for the United States was that the three Pacific Fleet carriers were out at sea and escaped. It was just three carriers—*Enterprise* (CV-6), *Yorktown* (CV-5), and *Hornet* (CV-8)—that turned the tide of the war at Midway in June 1942, but it was sometimes touch-and-go until mighty feats of shipbuilding brought the new fleet carriers of the *Essex* (CV-9) class into action at the end of summer in 1943. With them came lighter carriers on cruiser hulls, the CVLs, and the scores of little escort carriers, or CVEs, originally built on merchant and tanker hulls. They won battle stars in both the Pacific, destroying the mighty Japanese fleet, and the Atlantic, where their planes finally put the U-boats on the defensive.

A great carrier task force at sea is a sight never to be forgotten, the great flattops escorted by their ring of defending battleships and cruisers, destroyers darting about, the combat air patrol high above scouting for the unexpected. Tens of thousands of men at sea made it possible for a few hundred to strike the enemy. Life aboard the carriers was a maze of new technologies, procedures, and skills, with comfort and good fellowship dwelling side by side with danger and death. To some who served aboard them more than forty years ago, the experience still seems unforgettable and, in a way, beyond belief.

An F6F Hellcat ready to take off from the U.S.S. *Yorktown*, June 1943. National Archives.

GERRIT HUBBARD ROELOFS

SQUARE CIRCLES AND SMITTY

The late Gerrit Hubbard Roelofs, distinguished professor of English at Kenyon College, in Gambier, Ohio, was a big man in tweeds, bow tie, and elbow patches—a quintessential scholar. Commenting on his "lucky" career, he told us, "Here's an unhandy type of guy who went off to Amherst and did pretty well. I then went into the Navy to become a pilot because, in fact, it was the toughest thing I thought I could succeed in. Obviously my friends had the same question in mind. They'd say, 'You are going to be a naval aviator and land on one of those carrier things?'"

Roelofs fought his war mainly from the decks of the little escort carrier Rudyerd Bay in the Pacific, and his deep voice echoed affection whether he was talking about his Grumman Avenger torpedo plane or the hidden rhyme in Milton's prose. It saddens us that he died before this book could come out.

Something I've noticed increasingly over the years is that the war separates me from other people, or at least those too young to have been in it. I spent four years in the Navy at a critical time in the life of the country. We were fighting desperately for our salvation and our survival, and we were up against formidable powers. We had a cause we could believe in absolutely, there was no question about it, and everybody was involved. With this sense of purpose, also, came the discipline of mutual responsibility, which the Navy taught us.

That discipline remains with me to this very day. I did a lot of antisubmarine patrols from our aircraft carrier, often in some of the foulest weather you can imagine, and sometimes in seeming calm—even more dangerous because you can be deceived by the gentleness

Gerrit H. Roelofs in the cockpit of a TBF Avenger. Flying from the deck of an escort aircraft carrier taught useful lessons to a future English professor.

of the ocean. While I was out, usually about five hours, the life, safety, and security of my ship and the tankers we were shepherding depended on my vigilance, my fidelity, and my discipline. It was a responsibility imposed on me *by* me, and only by me. Not by somebody else. I was given a sector to fly and it was my duty to fly it, fair weather or foul. Furthermore, we had to maintain radio silence. I would navigate off my watch, compass, and air speed indicator, constantly checking my position on my small-area plotting board. If there were any wind changes, I had to spot and record them and change my heading. You looked out the cockpit window at the whitecaps to see which way the wind was blowing. I got so I could estimate the velocity as well as the direction of the wind by the whitecaps. I'd look out and say something like, "Well, I think it's 14 knots, at 21 degrees southwest." Then I'd check if that was what the air combat intelligence officer had sent down to us when we took off. If it had changed, I had to make those corrections and rework my navigation.

When I came back to the ship, the roles were reversed. Everybody on that ship was involved in getting me safely aboard. The protector became the protected. They had to be *faithful* (to their duty, as I had been to mine) to get me in. The whole system was built on the principle of mutual aid and organization. The fighters' first obligation was to protect the bombers. The only time they could go off on their own was when they went out on a fighter sweep. But, even then, the wing man had to protect the tail of the gun, the lead plane.

One time, after the war, I was out plowing a field at my parents' farm and happened to see a crow being driven to the ground by swallows. They were coming in like this and that, scissoring back and forth—the pattern called the Thach Weave in the Navy. Always watching out for one another. The same as with Wildcats attacking a Betty, the standard Japanese bomber.

My students here at Kenyon College find World War II unbelievable because it is so far away from them. It's now 40 years ago. A lot of them have even forgotten Vietnam. But, if they do think about war, it is in relation to Vietnam: a much different war, a war that was a terribly misguided effort. The government wasn't honest with itself, the troops, or the American people. The discipline of mutual responsibility is the most important principle as far as I'm concerned.

And this goes back to the kinds of things you learn when you are flying in the Navy. You have to watch over your wing man. The wing man has to count on you to do the navigating, because you can't fly wing and navigate at the same time. You don't have the freedom. You can't stick your head in the cockpit and work out the problem. You are watching out for each other all the time. And the ship has to watch over both of us, by radar, and be ready for us when we return.

If I say so myself, by the end of the war I had become a very good dive-bomber pilot. I could handle the Helldiver, known to Navy pilots as "The Beast." Although it ultimately turned out to be a remarkable dive bomber, the SB2C was so called because the early models had a merciless history of killing pilots. The whole tail section would pull off in a dive, the wings would fold in flight (because there was no lock to hold the levers in place), or the split diving flaps would close down on one side and stay open on the other when the pilot tried to close them on pullout after a vertical dive. Hence "The Beast."

There were plenty of times when I was scared. Most of the flying I did was off a jeep carrier, the *Rudyerd Bay*. All the ships built by Henry Kaiser were named after bays and inlets in the Pacific Northwest. Our carrier was named for a little bay near Alaska. Jeep carriers were little ships that couldn't have been more than 450 feet long, and about 60 feet wide. They'd bounce up and down like corks. The *Rudyerd Bay* would list heavily when it turned into the wind for a predawn raid, and you'd be looking down off the side of the deck, right into the ocean. When you taxied up to the catapult, the wheel of the TBF was only a few inches from the coaming. You'd creep forward with the brakes squealing. It was what you had to do, and you just went ahead and did it.

When we were dive-bombing with the SB2C, I'd have the gunner in the rear seat call out the altitude. We'd start off at about 17,000 feet, and he'd call off every thousand feet in the dive. The closer to the ground we got, the higher his voice would get. When I got to 2,500, I would always have to make one last correction before I made my drop. The last thing I would hear was the screaming of the gunner, and then I'd pull out and black out. We were pulling eight to nine Gs and we didn't have G-suits in those days.

The TBF, the Avenger, was the first plane I flew on the *Rudyerd Bay*. When I sat in that airplane the first time, I wrote to my parents to tell them that it's like sitting on top of a hay wagon loaded with hay. How on earth was I going to get that thing into the air? Actually, sitting up there was one of the great things about the TBF. You could look over the nose of the plane. It sloped down like a Saab automobile.

The TBF was a lovely airplane. But it was, however, a heavy ship; and if you got over 150 knots, say up around 180, you would have to put both hands on the stick, the pressures were so heavy. I had a gunner in the turret behind me and the radio man had a little area behind the bomb bay. There was a little door on the right side that he used to get in, and he had a bench that he could swing out to do his work on. His instruments, radar scope, and radio were all down there with him. The radar was very primitive and was only good for 15 miles, if it was working at all. He also had a stinger gun that pointed toward the rear of the plane, which was his battle position. The radio man also had access to the after end of the torpedo, so he could set the depth that it would run. If you were going after a big ship, a carrier or something like that, you'd want to set the torpedo to run at 20 feet so it would hit below the armor plate. If you were going after a destroyer, you'd set it for 8 feet.

When I was working on my qualification trials at Glenview, north of Chicago, the TBFs we were flying were stripped down. No guns, no armor plate, no radar or turret, nothing. They were really like big sailplanes and handled differently from the operational aircraft we would be flying later. We'd had a lot of bounce drills on the fields around Glenview (cow pastures, really) and then they sent us out to this tiny carrier on the lake to make our six landings. It was actually a car ferry that had been converted into a "carrier." We'd come around and make our approach. The first landing, that was the one. You'd hear about it as *the* ultimate experience, and it was. When you hit there was a big boom, lots of noise, and you literally dangled in the crash harness. The human body can stretch a lot, even when tightly restrained. So this is what it's like. Why, it's easy!

By my fourth landing I was feeling quite confident. I got the cut from the LSO, or landing signal officer, eased back on the stick, and waited for the big jerk when the hook grabbed. I was sitting there fat, dumb, and happy. Then I heard the crash klaxon blowing; people were running and diving into the catwalks. I looked up, and there was all of Lake Michigan in front of me. Then I hit the barrier. I was terribly embarrassed and ashamed. A ten-thousand-dollar propeller ruined. I was hauled out of the cockpit to stand on the catwalk, wondering what on earth had gone wrong. Nobody came over to talk to me. Finally, a sailor came up and said, "You're to get in that plane over there and make two more landings." This was about 10 minutes after smashing up. So I got into that plane and nearly did the same thing again on my fifth landing. I wasn't flying the plane down to the deck because it was so light and had a tendency to float. The LSO came over to me and told me what I was doing wrong, and I made the last landing. It was fine.

On your approach to the carrier you're in a nose-high turn and all you see is the LSO. You can't see over the nose. When you get the cut, the nose drops; then you can see the deck. Everything depended on Smitty, the LSO, and when he signalled "cut," it was mandatory. I had to chop the throttle, no matter what happened to the plane or the ship. Smitty had all the gifts of an actor and a dancer, as well as those of a skilled LSO. He was the best I have ever seen because he was so dynamic. He was also a superb instructor. When we were ashore, he drilled us in the difficult and dangerous art of simulated carrier landings, and then he gave us detailed individual criticism after each session.

What still amazes me about Smitty is his unfailing capacity to project his perception of my attitude over 800 or so yards of heaving water, when all I could see were the spots of color of his paddles. Few actors can project that far and be vibrantly animating. Smitty, perched on the platform at the very end of the deck, also had to stand unperturbed by the heaving and pitching. At first, all I would be able to see was a roger (both hands outstretched), which meant I was O.K. Then a signal to steepen my rate of turn; now one to slow down (I had to be two knots above stalling speed); now one that tells me I'm too high. At all times, Smitty is holding out his arms to me, *willing* me to come aboard. Even though my heart is leaping out of my mouth, I know that Smitty will bring me aboard. After nearly 40 years, I can still see him across the gray-green swells and whitecaps of the Pacific, arms spread wide, confident and smiling.

In 1945 we were training for the assault on Japan, and at that time they wanted to simplify things by having only two types of aircraft on a carrier. The bomber squadron was doing dive bombing as well as torpedo bombing.

I read a book recently that stated the SB2C never dropped any torpedoes. Well, I dropped a torpedo just after the war on a target destroyer while on our shakedown cruise on the new carrier *Franklin D. Roosevelt*. The only way they could get a torpedo in the Helldiver was to stick the tail part in the bomb bay and close it part way. There was the plane, the torpedo sticking out of the bomb bay at a very obscene angle. They had never experimented with catapulting a Helldiver with a torpedo because they were afraid the torpedo would break free on the catapult shot and go right back through the gunner and out the tail, so they decided we should make a full deck-length launch. We had 860 feet of flight deck to get that plane in the air. I had been opposed to our flying this sort of thing, so I got my group to two-block their jockstraps on the radio masts. They got the *Roosevelt* up to about 30 knots, chasing little wind gusts all over the Caribbean. That ship was just booming along, and I started howling down the deck with that jock streaming from the pole.

I later heard that Admiral Marc Mitscher said, "Hey, what's that plane doing out there? It's grounded!" When a plane wasn't fit to fly for some reason and was grounded, they'd put a small flag on it. The assistant navigation officer knew me, and he said, "No, that's Roelofs and his division. They've two-blocked their jocks."

I got to the end of the flight deck and the old plane wasn't even airborne. I just trundled off into space, got the wheels up, and then began to inch the flaps up. I had that throttle wide open, and they say they could see my wake in front of the ship for five miles.

In true Navy fashion, we'd been following the book with regard to what a torpedo squadron should do on a shakedown cruise. You are to drop one torpedo, and so we did just that. But our tired planes had a year of combat training service in them, and after that long full-power exercise, they had to replace most of our engines. Fortunately, we didn't have any accidents. When the most junior ensign in my division came back, he made his usual bad landing and bounced right over the barrier. By chance there were no airplanes parked forward. He put on the brakes and managed to stop his plane. All they had to do was tell him to fold his wings, and he was parked exactly where he should have been. That was an absolutely incredible piece of luck.

★

October 25, 1945, was Navy Day, and the *Roosevelt* was commissioned that day. We came down from Hyannis and landed at Floyd Bennett Field in New York. Our second flight that day was to fly a huge "FDR" letter formation over the ship as Mrs. Roosevelt spoke the ceremonial words and swung the champagne. Letter formations are terribly dangerous because there's no place to move. Once you get into them you can't get out, because if you move you will run into somebody else. Then, in the afternoon, we joined in with all the air groups that were located up and down the East Coast. There were twelve hundred naval aircraft over New York City that afternoon. It was a wild day. One of those wonderful fall days. The fleet was in, and President Harry Truman was going up and down the Hudson in a destroyer reviewing the ships. The battleship *New Jersey*, the *Enterprise*, all the great ships. Destroyers, cruisers, the lot. It was a sight I'll never forget. Together, we were the Argonauts, Ulysses, Aeneas: we had endured and finished, and home was ours.

By this time we were tired; it was our third flight of the day and my wing man fell asleep. I was watching him (we were over Wall Street), and his head went down and his plane was sliding into me. I couldn't get to my radio fast enough. He woke up in time; otherwise I wouldn't be here. Then we made a big circuit of New York and some F4Us got into a tail chase. One after another, they went looping up and down the Hudson River, and I think some of them went under the George Washington Bridge. Then we went back to Floyd Bennett. Ten hours in the air, and I've never been so tired in my life. But it was one of those days you never forget, especially seeing it from a pilot's perspective.

We were then transferred to the *Roosevelt*. The first time I saw her at sea, it was off New York. There was a heavy sea running and the

Roosevelt was all by herself. The escort destroyer was astern, and this great ship was just sort of disappearing every now and then in the heavy weather. At a thousand feet, she didn't look much bigger than the *Rudyerd Bay*, but as I made my approach I realized the sheer bulk and size of the ship. After I landed, I could feel the deck moving up and down with the sea. The *Rudyerd Bay* would just bounce around, but the *Roosevelt* had this massive feeling. When they started to bring me up the deck, I really had to work the plane because the deck was coming up and impeding my forward progress.

To come aboard a big ship like the *Roosevelt* was just as difficult as coming aboard a CVE like the *Rudyerd Bay*. It might be larger, but it had one hazard that the CVE did not have. When you have a piece of machinery that enormous size going through the water at 28 knots, you are moving a lot of air. That air rushes along the gun sponsons and underneath the overhang of the flight deck, catwalks, and so forth. It creates a great deal of turbulence right at the ramp. This is right where you are the slowest in your approach; and, particularly in the Helldiver and the Corsair, you could actually swing the stick back and forth and nothing would happen. You are just hanging there, and if that rough air gets hold of you, that's trouble. What I didn't want to do was hit the edge of the deck—the coaming—with the bomb bay. Sometimes I would have four depth charges in there, and that's 450 pounds of torpex in a tin can.

I stayed with the *Roosevelt* for a whole year after the war ended. At that point I realized that if I didn't go back to school I'd always be an Airedale without much intellectual achievement. I couldn't get anywhere in the Navy unless I left flying and went into some other type of work. I didn't want to do that, so I left to study English literature at Johns Hopkins and prepare to teach.

I had no idea that the war had taken such a toll on my nervous system. I didn't anticipate what a shock it would be coming back to school. I would be sitting eight hours a day in a chair in the library, whereas for four years I'd been leading this violent, nonintellectual life aboard a carrier. I guess what I missed was that excitement and frenzy. I lost a lot of weight and couldn't sleep. I felt as if I didn't know anything and was starting all over again. The Ph.D. program at Hopkins had a kill rate that was higher than that at Baron Field in Pensacola. There were twenty of us who started in 1946 at Hopkins, and only three of us finished our degrees. I was still up in the air until my second year, when I began teaching and realized that this was my vocation. Everything settled down after that.

My first job was at the University of New Hampshire. Once again I was very lucky. Nobody was hiring at that time. I just wrote to them and was picked for the job, unseen. To start off at a school like New

Hampshire was a wonderful experience. I'll never forget those kids who came out of the hills of New Hampshire to scramble for an education. It allowed me to see what the state university does for people, all kinds of people. After six years there I came to Kenyon, where I've been ever since. That was in 1957. It's the best teaching job there is, and I wouldn't exchange it for any other. The geographical location of the school, Kenyon's isolation, takes me back to the carrier. You are a self-contained unit and you have obligations, and those obligations are made quite obvious to you, both in your failures and in your triumphs. The triumphs range from finally getting a struggling student to have some self-respect, to having an accomplished one write a prize paper or win a fellowship.

From my Navy experience, I bring images to the classroom. Tremendous images. Seeing the Third Fleet for the first time, in the morning sunlight and the mist. We were heading for a rendezvous and I was in the first flight. My job was to send back a message when we spotted the fleet. Ships stretched from one horizon to the other. It was absolutely immense. Another time I was off Ulithi and I watched forty escort carriers steaming out of the lagoon in a column of twos. I looked back, and for a moment I could see the whole Fifth Fleet and elements of the Seventh. I said to myself, "I am a part of this." I was an infinitesimal part, but of something that was overwhelming. All you had to do was to see the fleet and to know that one of those ships was yours. You weren't just a solitary individual.

There were other things, like storms. We saw some beauts. We went through the great typhoon of December 1944 that crippled Admiral Halsey's fleet on its way to the Philippines. That was the worst disaster our Navy ever suffered in a storm. Three destroyers rolled over and sank. Over 180 planes were blown off carrier decks. The *Hornet* had part of its flight deck ripped off by winds that gusted up to 165 knots! Our ship was blown to a standstill, and you couldn't stand on the deck. To be in the grip of a storm like that is something that you will never forget. You realize that there is something pretty big out there and that your ship is just a little speck on the ocean.

On another occasion we were operating off the Philippines in some oily, wet weather. I say oily because the sea looked like oil, dark and heavy, and there was a mist rising from the water. Visibility was very poor. We were cruising along at an extremely slow speed, making a fleet change of course, and suddenly I saw this huge, great thing appearing near our stern. It was the bow of an *Iowa*-class battleship, a huge arching bow with its Pacific camouflage markings. It looked like a sea monster coming upon us, and bit by bit the rest of the ship appeared. It was terrifying and wonderful at the same time.

I try to use the sights, sounds, and experiences that I've had as illustrative material to make a point in class. Very often it works because it authenticates something that is highly abstract. The immediacy of the action, the vividness of the sights, and the sharpness of the sounds are so ingrained in my memory that I can convey them to students. When I teach Milton's *Paradise Lost*, I point out that when Satan comes to the outside of the created world and peers down through the hole, what he's looking at is what I was looking at through the bombsight in my dive bomber. Looking straight down that hole at the world.

Another example. Wordsworth, in *The Prelude*, describes how he'd been ice skating and stopped abruptly on his heels. He talks about watching the world whirl around.

> yet still the solitary cliffs
> Wheeled by me—even as if the earth had rolled
> With visible motion her diurnal round!

That's actually an experience you have when you're night flying. All of a sudden you are the one who is motionless, and everything else is moving around you. That's when you start to have trouble. If you stare at one star, for instance, that star will start to whirl around you. The trick is to look at two stars.

At examination time, I instruct my nervous class in the art of flying square circles. In the Navy I was taught to fly a square search pattern whenever I could not find my ship. You can't stop your plane and ask the nearest whitecap where you are. And you must maintain radio silence. You can't afford to panic.

Twice I returned from a long antisubmarine patrol to find that the carrier was not where I had predicted it to be, not where it was supposed to be. My God, I'm lost! I was scared silly. I had to take stock of my situation: Both wing tanks are empty; I have forty-five minutes of fuel left; the rudimentary radar shows only "snow" because of the heavy sea; visibility is two miles, the ceiling is 700 feet, and rain squalls blot out patches of the horizon. There are thousands of miles in all directions to go before I can reach land. The Pacific is a monstrous ocean. Just the thought of being swallowed alive by this immensity is appalling. Fear makes me rigid and numbs my mind. But I remember the search pattern: square circles.

The expanding-square search is simple to work out and very practical; though numbed by fear, even my nonmathematical mind can quickly solve the problem. Fly into the wind for two minutes, then do a 90-degree turn to the left and fly two minutes on that course; then turn 90 degrees again to the left and fly four minutes, and so on, increasing the time every second turn. Maintain the record on your plotting board. After doing two—or at the most three—squares, reverse the pattern. Fear subsides somewhat because I am doing something sensible and reliable. Panic is stilled, and the ship is found.

So I tell my students to translate the expanding square search into a search for Shakespeare. Make a list on the first page of your bluebook of all the plays for which you are responsible in this examination. Opposite each title, list the names of those characters who come quickly to mind. Titles and characters should expand your memory, making you recover the argument and the basic metaphors of the plays. Next reread the quotation; in other words, navigate through the speech, locating the checkpoints. Go through the checklist by rereading the instructions: "Name the play, act, and scene; identify the speaker and the character spoken to; determine the situation, context, and action; note the key word or metaphor." To get aboard, you must show understanding and a capacity to respond to word, character, and action.

Students often consider taking an exam to be a kind of warfare, or at least a contest in which the instructor has all the advantages and is on the other side. The truth is that more than anything, the instructor wants each of them to come safely aboard, not to spin in on the crosswind leg.

An examination is as much a matter of trust as is flying a patrol and returning for those last hair-raising minutes of the carrier approach. I once told this exemplum to a former student who was terrified about taking a final exam in another English department course, and she used it well. My Christmas card from her contained this message: "I flew square circles and came aboard like a Navy fighter pilot." And indeed she did!

CHARLES MOUTENOT

A FINE FRATERNITY

*Retired from the senior ranks of New Jersey's civil service, Charles
Moutenot now spends much of his time in Florida and the Bahamas. The
sea, as it was during the war, is still a major part of his life. Vigorous and
athletic, he looks far younger than his sixty-eight years.*

*At one point our talks took us aboard his World War II ship, the
aircraft carrier* Essex. *Tied up in Bayonne, New Jersey, the forgotten
vessel was littered with debris. Charlie looked around the gloomy hangar
deck. "You should have seen the activity that went on down here
during the war. The planes, the men, the action. For me, it remains
unforgettable." A week after our visit the* Essex *was towed to Philadelphia
and scrapped.*

I was kind of a wild-haired guy, and the only reason I went to school
at Catholic University in Washington was to play football. I never
finished up my last year. I went into the Navy. If the war hadn't
happened, I don't know where the hell I would have wound up. I
had nothing in mind about what I wanted to do.

I grew up in Edgewater, New Jersey, and I went to LaSalle Military Academy for a year, and I couldn't take it. I didn't like the
regimentation, and I never got passes to come home on the weekends. I was always getting demerits, and spent most of my weekends
marching. However, it helped me out in the service. When I went
down to Jacksonville for training, anyone with any knowledge of
marching was ahead of the game; so I became a platoon leader.

I actually joined the Marines. A friend of the guy I was rooming
with had just completed the Marine training program. He came over

to see us and had that sharp uniform on. We got to talking and I liked what I heard. The next day I went down to enlist in the Marines, took the physical, and they said, "We'll let you know." I got the notice that I was accepted and went down to Anacostia Naval Air Station in Washington. I soloed, and then they told me that it would be a long wait until I could continue with my training. Rather than wait, I switched into the Navy and went down to Jacksonville. We were flying the N2Ss and N3Ns. They had open cockpits, and you always had to be sure you had a rag in the plane to reach out and wipe the oil off the windscreen.

I don't think there was a better era in aviation than the one I grew up in. I started flying in planes that were fabric-covered biplanes. At the end of the war they had the Corsairs. The first radio I saw was a crystal set. You really have to sit back and take a look at progress, because you are living and moving right along with it.

When I finished at Jacksonville, I went to Opa-Locka, which was a fighter training base. While we were down there we flew the F2Fs and F3Fs. The F3Fs had weak oleos [shock absorbers] on the landing gear and they'd sag on one side. You'd walk out to the flight line looking for one with the wings level. You were brand new in the plane, and you didn't have much flying time. It's hard enough to take off with the wings level, let alone with them slanting as you're going down the runway. The mechanics knew what we were looking for, and they'd stand next to the plane holding the wing up. You'd pick one out and think, "I've got a good one today." Then you'd get in the plane, crank up the engine, the guy would walk away, and the wing would droop.

After Jacksonville, I went through advanced pilot training at Norfolk. In total, flight training took about nine months. The Navy's requirements were pretty high, that was 1941, and you had to have a certain number of college credits. There was no rush to put guys through, even with the war on. As a matter of fact they were bouncing out quite a few, and some of the guys I knew who didn't make it went to Canada and signed up with the Royal Canadian Air Force.

They had a rule that you couldn't get married until you were in the Navy for three years, or something like that. A couple of guys were killed at Norfolk on New Year's Day. They checked and found out that one of them was married. Of course he had tried to hide the fact and in doing so, he didn't have his wife down as the beneficiary

Charles Moutenot fought his war as a gung-ho fighter pilot on the aircraft carriers *Ranger* and *Essex*, without (at the time) any second thoughts. This photograph was taken after the war at Floyd Bennett field.

for his insurance. That caused a lot of trouble. One morning we reported to muster and the Old Man was sitting there with a big list. You'd be called up and he'd say, "Are you married?" It was just one straight question. They found out that so many guys were married that they changed the rule. I got on the horn and called my girl in Washington, and she made all the arrangements. I think her parents and my parents worried more than the two of us. They thought we were crazy.

The skipper gave me a couple of days off, and I flew to Washington in an SNJ and we got married. Then we came up to New York and spent the night at the New Yorker Hotel. The next day I went back to Norfolk and went out on the *Ranger*. That was the first carrier actually built as a carrier, not like the *Long Island* and the *Santee*, which were just oil carriers. They put a deck on the damned things and called them aircraft carriers. I loved the *Ranger*. It was a real homey ship, and I could have stayed on her for the rest of the war. The Atlantic was cold, and you'd come down off the deck and get below and it was nice and warm. The smell of coffee and the chow cooking. I'll always remember that feeling. On the other hand, the *Essex* was a big, cold ship with over three thousand guys running around on it. It took a week just to find out where everything was.

We had a hell of a good squadron skipper both on the *Ranger* and on the *Essex*, Jack Raby of Fighter Squadron (VF) 9. I don't think there was a better skipper in the whole fleet at the time. He was an Annapolis graduate, but he had such a way about him that everybody just loved the guy. When we first joined the fleet we were flying Brewster Buffalos. They were hot little planes and I loved them, but at 10,000 feet you had nothing. It was strictly a sea-level airplane. There were only about five pilots in VF-9 at that time because we were still building up. One day the skipper said to me, "Put your gear on, we're going for a flight." He took me up to find out just how proficient I was. It was unbelievable. We did all kinds of stuff in the air, and when we came down he offered a critique. He said, "You could fly a little closer," or, "When you did that slow roll, you were dropping your nose." He checked everyone out that way. I thought it was great. It gave you a little added confidence in your flying, and you also felt closer to the Old Man. That's the way it always was in the Navy. Proficiency. They were always striving to be better. If you reached a certain level, that wasn't good enough. You had to go up to the next step. Your flying was always getting better and better.

We sailed the *Ranger* to Bermuda and then joined a convoy and went on to North Africa, where we were part of "Torch," the 1942 invasion. We were gone for about a month, and when we came back to Norfolk the *Essex* was just about completed. We went out on a shakedown cruise and when we came back, we took off for the Pacific. In the meantime, my wife became pregnant and my oldest child was born. I didn't see her until she was about fourteen months old.

I know my wife and family were worried, but I never had any thought about anything happening to me. I still think, to this day, that if it's going to happen, it's going to happen. Just be ready, that's all. It's that simple. There were a couple of guys who had a problem with combat. One guy was sent to Attu Island in the Aleutians, which was probably the worst duty you could get. He ended up flying seaplanes. The weather is so lousy up there that I think that was going from the frying pan into the fire. However, I could appreciate it if you didn't feel comfortable in combat. That's one hell of a place to be, and you'd better get out of it and do something else.

The actual flying of an airplane is a very simple operation. The difficulty comes when something goes wrong and you have to make a forced landing, things like that. Emergencies take experience and expertise. If you had an engine failure on takeoff, you had to have some experience to be able to handle things properly. However, if everything is normal, flying isn't a real problem.

Actually, a carrier landing isn't a real problem, either. At least I never found it to be a problem. I think a carrier is the safest place to land a plane, especially if there is something wrong with it. Say you couldn't get the landing gear down. If you had to land on a long runway, that damn thing could start to cartwheel, something like that, and you'd be done for. You just have to wait until you stop rolling. On a carrier, you are caught by the arresting gear and that stops you in a hurry. During the period of time that I was on the ship, there were many cases when a guy would come back with his plane shot up, and he would be brought aboard safely. Landing was always good, especially on the *Essex*.

When you'd come back to the ship you would get the clear to come aboard. They knew the approximate time we were due back, and the decks would be cleared. A flag would be raised for the all-clear, and we'd start our approach. You'd always be in a turn on your landing run because your view over the front of that big cowling was nil. You were really cocked up and just about keeping the thing airborne with engine power. Your flaps and wheels were down, and you would keep the propeller in low pitch with a lot of power on so that you were actually just hanging on the prop. You'd stay in that turn all the way so you could keep the landing signal officer in sight. Your eyeballs were right on him. You'd be getting your altitude squared away and he'd signal you, "You're high, you're low, you're too slow," and when everything was all right, "You're O.K." The roger, as we called it. You'd come in over the fantail of the ship and as soon as you received the cut signal from the LSO, you would chop the throttle and the plane would come down on the deck. You'd catch the arresting gear with your tail hook and that plane would stop in a hurry. Then you'd give it full power and go steaming up the deck to be spotted. This whole procedure had to be done with speed and precision so the landing pattern would not be held up. A lot of times guys would get back low on fuel, and you couldn't wait around to land or you'd end up in the water.

Up forward of the arresting gear they had what they called barriers. These were large cables that were about two inches in diameter on steel arms. Normally they lay flat on the deck. If a plane missed the arresting gear, the barriers would be raised and the plane would hit them and stop. This was to prevent a plane from crashing into the planes already spotted forward on the deck. If you did hit the barriers, it would usually wreck the prop, but little other damage would be done unless you flipped over. That did happen, and if the plane was badly damaged, they would just throw it over the side. If there was a crash, there wasn't time to do much about it with the rest of the planes waiting to come in. Expediency demanded that it go over the side so you could keep things going. There are plenty of planes down at the bottom of the ocean.

I remember a mission that I flew when we were in Africa. When they were pulling me out to the takeoff spot, they released the wings and the starboard wing got away from the crew and swung down and hit the deck. The pitot tube was mounted on that wing, and it looked like a pretzel when they got the wings up and locked. When I took off, my airspeed indicator read 40 knots, and it never changed for the duration of the flight. Forty in a climb, forty in a dive. I really had to fly by feel. We spotted two enemy cruisers and a destroyer trying to make a run out of the harbor, and we started strafing them. At this time we were pretty green, and this was our first shot at anything that would shoot back. The three ships were in a line, and we would line our planes up head on to them and fly over them, strafe the first one, pull up, strafe the next one, and so on. By the time a few of us had done that, the ship's gunners had a hell of a bead on us. We should have been coming in from different directions and using evasive tactics, not just flying a straight line.

I felt this terrific crash and a sting in my leg. I had taken a hit from a 40mm and I didn't know how much damage had been done, but I sure as hell knew I was hit. We had instructions on what to do if we got hit and had to make an emergency landing. There was an area on shore that we were supposed to land on; supposedly there would be people who would take care of us. The ship wasn't too far off the beaches, something like 30 or 40 miles, and I decided that I'd rather take my chances getting back to the ship. I got back O.K. and got aboard with no problem. Besides the damage in the front of the plane, the shell had gone out the back end and hit the tail. Part of the vertical stabilizer was missing. They threw that airplane over the side.

The Grumman planes could take pretty good hits. Both the Wildcat and the later Hellcat would take a hell of a beating and still be flyable. When we went up against the Zeros we found that if you could get a shot into their tanks, they'd go up in flames. Our gas tanks were rubberized and self-sealing. We could actually take a hit and get away with it. Also, we had a lot of armor on our planes.

When they commissioned the *Essex* and we were assigned to her, it was in the books for us to get the first Corsairs. Eight of us went up to Connecticut to familiarize ourselves with the plane, but they were having trouble with the hydraulic systems and there was going to be a delay getting them. A few weeks later we wound up going to Bethpage, Long Island, where the Grumman plant was located, and picked up some Hellcats. It was a much better plane than the Wildcat, which we had been flying. First of all, it was faster than the Wildcat, and second, you didn't have to crank up the landing gear. You can imagine taking off from a carrier and having to lean down, take your hand off the throttle, and crank away. Twenty-seven times you had to crank it to get them up. There was a lug that stuck out, and that fit into a hole in the frame and would lock the gear up. A lot of times you wouldn't get that lug in there securely and the gear would drop down, causing the handle to spin around. I don't know how many guys had their wrists broken by that handle. The Hellcat was also a much better plane to fly because it had more power. But it didn't handle better than the Wildcat. It couldn't turn as fast, for one thing. It was like going from a Chevy to a Cadillac. The instruments were laid out nicer and the cockpit was more comfortable. They made a lot of changes on the planes as time went by.

We had what I thought was an unnecessary accident when we were coming back from Africa. We had been practicing bombing and strafing on a sled that was towed behind the ship. This fellow came in and when he hit the arresting gear, he still had the power on and the plane angled across the flight deck and went over the side. The plane settled down in the water, and I was looking right down at it. You opened the canopy on the Wildcat with a crank, and there was a pin that would lock it open when you were landing or taking off. The pilot was O.K. in the plane—I could see him trying to get the canopy open—but the jolt from hitting the arresting gear or water had caused the canopy to partly close. It was evidently jammed, and the plane went down and he was lost. That caused a real commotion, and they started checking out canopies. The result was that we had the machinists drill holes in the track that the canopy rolled on, and we had a good-sized bolt on a chain that we would stick through that hole so it couldn't slide and get jammed.

We used to do a lot of work on the planes ourselves. We'd wax the wings, put putty around the gun cells where the machine guns came out of the wings, anything to cut down drag on the plane. It's amazing on an airplane what you can do to make it go faster. For instance, take that rough pad you step on to get into the cockpit. Get rid of that, you could pick up 10 miles an hour. We used to try and keep our planes nice and clean just to get that little bit extra out of them. You didn't know when you'd need it.

We had a good outfit on the *Essex*. We had the airplanes and we knew what to do with them. The Japanese pilots we ran into were from excellent to awful. When we went into Truk, I was on the fighter sweep that first morning. We had no information on Truk, but we did know it was a fortress. We took off and went to the target, flying right off the water so they couldn't pick us up on radar. As we approached the island, we started to climb to get altitude so we could start our strafing run. The best climbing rate of the Hellcat was about 140 knots, and that's just about what we were doing because we still had our belly tanks on. The next thing I notice, tracers are whipping by me. I looked up and here were four Zeros making a high side run on us. Everybody just nosed over and scattered. We all got separated, and I found myself back fairly low off the water. Every time I'd start climbing up again, I'd spot some enemy planes and have to change my course. I finally got back up to a fairly good altitude when two Jap planes made a run on me. There was a nice big cloud close by, and I jumped into that and made a turn inside of it and came out. There was a Zero off to my starboard side. I continued on course, and he came around and made a run on me. I kicked the rudder and put the plane into a skid, and it slowed down abruptly. He went charging by me and I slid on his tail, and here was a case where this enemy pilot didn't really do anything right. I had a good shot at him and there was an explosion. I ran through the smoke and some debris. They just didn't seem to do all they could in some situations.

I don't like to think of it now, but I hated the Japanese. I shot that guy down and one other plane, and I hate to think that I killed anybody. I didn't see any 'chutes so I don't know if they bailed out or not. That bothers me now, but it didn't then. In fact, I'd be pissed off if my wing man would get a shot at something and I didn't. We knew enough about the war by that time and we heard some of those tales about the things the Japs were doing to our guys.

★

I wanted to stay in the Navy and make a career of it. I loved the Navy. After the war I was the executive officer with the Red Ripper Air

Group based at New London, Connecticut. I used to get a plane and fly down to see my wife and kids in Newark on weekends. At that time I had two children and my folks were after me, "Get away from that flying, you have a family." Also, every time I went down to see my family, it got harder to leave, so I got out of the Navy.

When I came out of the regular Navy, I did go into the reserves. We were flying Corsairs and Hellcats at Floyd Bennett. Just before I left there, they got jets and I got to fly them. I had to leave Floyd Bennett because I was commanding officer for three years, and you could only hold a command for that period of time. I took a run down to Lakehurst with a friend of mine, and there was a group there flying antisubmarine missions with S2Fs, and that was terrific flying. I hadn't flown any twin-engine planes up to that time, and it was like being commander of a flying destroyer. You had everything aboard that plane. Torpedoes, bombs, rockets, it was a fantastic plane. However, after a period of time they started cutting down the number of hours that you could fly. You could stay in, but you didn't really have anything to do. Not only that, every Saturday they had inspection. They made you put on the goddamn whites, and it was the peacetime Navy once again. I tried it for a while and finally just packed it in.

My parents had a French dry-cleaning business that my grandfather had started in 1898. The plant was in New Jersey, but our clientele were all over the country. Very select, you know. For instance, we had all the museums, and people even sent cleaning from Europe. My parents took me in as a partner, and I stayed with that for about 10 years and then we sold it. Next I bought a liquor store and lounge, but I couldn't take that business. God Almighty, that was really awful. You'd see the same people in there all the time with the same stories. A guy and his wife, or a guy and his girlfriend, would spend the whole damn weekend in the bar and think that was great. I only stayed in that for about three years, and then I had enough.

I went through the state police academy training course in New Jersey and became an investigator in the federal investigation section. I operated there for a while, and then I was transferred to Newark and became an investigator for the securities bureau. I put in 22 years there. I don't have any regrets. I would have loved to have stayed in the Navy, but you never know what is going to happen. My life has been very nice, and I've got a hell of a nice family. I've never had any trouble with any of the kids, so I'm a very fortunate guy.

My son Lee flew a gun ship in Vietnam. That's a very fast helicopter loaded with weapons. He originally wanted to go into the Navy but didn't have enough credits. I guess he took the next best thing. I was happy when I thought he was going in the Navy, but when he ended up in the Army, I didn't like that so much. At that time, all you'd hear on the radio in the morning was that we'd lost fifteen helicopters, five helicopters, nine helicopters. When we talked about it, I think there were a lot of things that he felt and I felt, as flyers. For instance, he was on a mission one time over an unfamiliar area, and the weather closed in. I'd had that same experience and knew how he felt. He had that same closeness with the guys in his unit that we had. It's all the same. However, some things were quite different. He was living in those huts and every night they used to get bombarded. They'd have to all run out and jump into trenches. I had a nice bunk with sheets on it. Very comfortable.

That guy was in another world when he came back. I'm not blaming that on Vietnam, although it could have been just that. He came home from a whole different war than we did, as everybody is well aware of by now. He just sat at home and never did anything. I really think those guys had a question mark of their own, not just because other people thought it was wrong. They were thinking on their own, "Christ, are we doing the right thing?"

I used to go to retreats with a guy from Yonkers. We'd go to Loyola House in Morristown, which is run by the Jesuits. I brought Lee with me a couple of times, and although at first he didn't seem to get much out of it, I think that was a turning point for him. It started him thinking, and he got the call. He accepted it and he's now a Jesuit. That's a brainy outfit. He's getting his doctoral degree at the University of Toronto, and he's as happy as can be. That's the main thing. He rarely talks about Vietnam, and I don't think any of his peers up there even know he was a pilot. At this point in time he doesn't think much of that effort.

I've taken my kids on the *Intrepid*, the carrier that's now a museum in New York, and they wanted to know about my experiences on the *Essex*. How did it work? How did you land on something that small? What does arresting gear mean? But I never really talked to any of them about it. As a matter of fact, I kind of dislike people asking me about the war. You always have the feeling they're waiting to hear some gruesome, hairy story, and you don't have one to tell. War stories, you know. I have an old Navy buddy who has a nice little Piper Cherokee Six that we go flying all over the place in. We were down in the Bahamas a while ago, and we were in a place talking about different things that happened to us during the war. There were some civilians sitting with us. They were terribly interested in what we were talking about, but it's so much easier when you're talking to people who have some idea about what a war is really like.

HOOK DOWN, WHEELS DOWN, FLAPS DOWN

As Charles Moutenot and Gerrit Roelofs have both made very clear, the landing signal officer (LSO) was a very important man in a carrier pilot's life. Baldwin Smith, the Smitty of "Square Circles and Smitty," was for a time on the same ship with Roelofs.

Our talk with Smith was conducted at his idyllic summer place south of Buffalo, New York. He still has his landing paddles, and he demonstrated how he'd bring a fighter aboard a heaving deck. Smith is built like an athlete, displaying perfect posture; his voice exhibits that valued Navy quality, "command authority."

In the modern Navy, the LSO's paddles have been replaced by a system of digital lights. But in the war years the LSO was a pilot's only way home. "I can still see Smitty," Gerrit Roelofs said, "across the gray-green swells and whitecaps of the Pacific, arms spread wide, confident and smiling."

The phone rang last summer, and a woman wanted to know if this was the Baldwin Smith who was a landing signal officer during World War II. She said she was Gerrit Roelof's sister and that Gerrit had been trying to find me for quite a while. I couldn't believe that any guy from that time was still thinking about me. I hadn't seen him since the last time I landed him aboard a carrier. He wrote me a letter and sent along a copy of his school magazine with an article he had written about me. When I found out he was ill, I phoned and talked to him, and he didn't sound good. About two or three days later I called again, and he seemed much better and got into some of the stuff about the old days. His wife said he was working again and doing better. When I called the next time I found out he had died five days earlier. His wife sent me a very nice letter, and I'm sorry that we hadn't been able to get together. In the letter his wife said that he had talked about me way back in 1946 when they first met. She said he said I'd saved his life. I think that an LSO became sort of a father to those men in that you turned them into real naval aviators when you taught them how to land on a carrier. There was something there, a bond built up.

Gerrit was a dedicated pilot, and he just wanted to do the best for me and the best for the squadron. He wasn't the greatest pilot in the Pacific, but he got the job done. He knew what you wanted and he did it. He wanted to learn so much and, when he was coming in, his head was always way out of the cockpit. He was so intent. He was a neophyte when I met him, with four or five hundred hours, and that doesn't make a carrier pilot. Gerrit was part of my first squadron. I went out to California to pick them up, and I couldn't believe it. Those guys were all over the sky. I gave them the signal that means "go back and land at the air station." When I got them back to the base I told them, "Look, I'm not a naval aviator, but I can fly. You guys better shape up or you'll be shipped out because I'm not going to take you on as a squadron the way you fly carrier approaches. I'm not trying to be harsh, but you fly like a bunch of clowns. You are going to have to cool it and do what I tell you to do, when I tell you to do it." I ran through all the signals, high, low, fast, and the rest, and you should have heard the grunting and groaning out of that group. I told them how to turn and how many seconds to wait until they broke off, and they went out like little soldiers and shaped up.

I ended up taking them out to a carrier that was in waters off Catalina to qualify. The skipper of the ship was one of the fellows who was all for having nonaviators doing LSO work if they had the qualifications. I didn't know that at the time, and my fellows were circling around and they started coming down, stepped down as nice as you please. I think there were fifty or sixty of them, and they made their eight landings each and didn't break a wheel. Fifty guys, eight landings apiece, and they didn't even blow a tire. It was gratifying to me, naturally, and I got a letter from the skipper of that carrier that was a heartbreaker. It was sort of a commendation, and I'm still very proud of that today.

Later on, when our ship was out in the Pacific, we often seemed to get our boys aboard first. They really learned how to fly a pattern, and we were getting them down at about 25- or 35-second intervals. That's landing—taxiing up the deck and getting the barrier back up. They'd give me a green light up on the bridge, which meant the deck was clear. I had two guys up front with me. One would yell, "Hook

Baldwin Smith, carrier landing signal officer, gives a pilot the "roger." Father and mother to all returning pilots, he got them back aboard safely.

down, wheels down, flaps down." If any of the three weren't there, you'd have to wave them off. The other guy was my talker. He had two instruments. One showed the wind velocity over the deck and also indicated to him what direction it was coming from relative to the ship's course. The other was a telephone to the bridge. To get into the vernacular, I'd tell the talker, "Tell the captain to get the fucking ship into the wind." He'd call the bridge, "Mr. Smith requests that the captain please get the wind four points off the port bow instead of the starboard bow because we're getting a slip stream from the island and these guys are going to have trouble getting down."

You would get very casual out there on that platform. A plane would be coming in, I'd cut him, and the wing would be coming directly at my head, and I would just sort of duck down and he would sail over me. There was a net back there but it wasn't something you would want to jump in if you didn't have to. It was a ways down. I went in that net a couple of times. One guy was flying a TBM, and he had it wrapped up too much. I knew that if I waved him off he wouldn't be able to do anything with the airplane. I kept signaling him to speed up, get it down, and his wing scraped the ship. The next thing, he was upside down in the sea. There were two crewmen in there with him, and the destroyers came and picked them up. That was a close one, but I am proud of my record. I never killed a pilot; in fact, I never maimed one either, except with rhetoric. At mess we'd discuss their landings. I wouldn't lay into them, they'd ask me how they'd done. We'd have a nice pleasant discussion and try to correct the problems that somebody might be having.

There was one torpedo pilot that they wanted me to flunk, but I wouldn't do it. I saw his potential and it worked out all right. He flew like the Army guys. He'd start letting down way out there, and in the meantime I could get three guys down who were coming around the corner. I told him, "If you ever get away from me, buster, you look down and find the biggest deck you can land on." One night he didn't come home, and the next morning a TBF came over the horizon and rocked his wings. The whole bloody fleet had to turn into the wind to get him aboard. After he landed I dropped my paddles and ran up to him. "Where the hell have you been?" "Well," he said, "I had a little trouble getting home so I did just what you told me to do, Smitty. I found the biggest carrier I could find. The only problem was that they had a fire up forward of the barrier." It turned out he landed on the *Saratoga*, which had been hit by a Kamikaze. He had gotten right in the traffic pattern with the fighters and they didn't know it was a TBF, he was going so fast. He was so proud of himself because he had done just what I told him to do. The poet type. Blond, nice-looking guy, and calm, very calm. One day while doing field carrier landings he got a little slow and spun in and everything sort of crunched. I went over and he was leaning against the airplane smoking a cigarette. You don't stand there and smoke a cigarette when you've just cracked up an airplane. We had a few words about that, and I told him, "One more of these little episodes and you're going to be washed up as a carrier pilot."

★

I'd do all kinds of tricks on that platform. Roelofs said in his article that he thought I must have gone to dancing school. If they weren't lined up, I'd walk them over toward the center of the deck. I'd be off my platform and they'd have to move over to see me. They were always looking at me, not their instruments. I'd walk them into line, and when everything was okay I'd run back to the platform and cut them. They have to have confidence in you in order to obey you. If you give a command of any kind and it's given in a lazy, lackadaisical fashion, the response will be the same. When you want a guy to cut his throttle, you want it right now. The pilots agreed with me. My shoulder was black and blue all the time from hitting it with my arm giving the cut.

There were two mandatory signals. One was the wave-off, which meant you had to go around again. The other was the cut. Pilots had to take those two. If they didn't want to come in slower, for instance, there was nothing you could do but send them around to try it again. A wave-off meant that something was out of whack and there was no way to get down on this pass. They were skittish when they came back from getting shot at, and all they wanted to do was get home. They were coming in at 100 knots with the engine developing about 45 inches of manifold pressure. The prop was holding the airplane in the air, and once you cut that fan it dropped like a brick. They were burning up a lot of fuel in the last hundred yards, and when you're running low on gas you don't want to go anywhere. At Iwo Jima there were days when the birds were walking. Fog and cold. I was bringing them in almost too fast, but I wanted them down on the deck. There were a few barrier accidents, but I'd settle for that instead of losing my guys.

I was much more frightened during the typhoons we went through than I was at any other point during the war. Our anemometer went straight up into the air at 120 knots. Just took off, gone. I had three pilots for roommates and our quarters were way forward in the forecastle. We would have to go to the hangar deck, climb up a ladder, and there, at the end of a narrow companionway, was our room. We were quite competitive and used to fight a lot, especially during bridge and poker games. The word would get around the ship that the roommates were playing cards, and everybody knew it would end up in a catastrophe. We'd get SRO crowds for those games. During one of those typhoons we were playing poker and I was winning more damn money. I was taking terrible chances because this was the last go-around and what the hell, there's no tomorrow. I've sailed in a lot of craft, and when the books start falling out of the bookcases, that's the sign of a real sea. There are guardrails along the front of the shelves to keep them in. Pretty soon we started to get little leaks here and there. Hello there! I'm sitting on a beautiful hand when the other guys decided that I should go up and find out what was going on. They felt I knew the skipper better than they did. I put my money under the edge of the table and started up to the bridge. I went up the port side, and the bridge was over on the starboard side. Getting across that mother-loving deck was an experience.

I finally got to the bridge and went up the ladder. There's the skipper sitting in his swivel chair smoking a big cigar. No helmsman at the wheel, nothing. I said, "How's it going, skipper?" He said, "Well, I don't know, Smitty. I've tried everything. Flank speed forward, flank speed aft, right rudder, left rudder, nothing happens, so we're just rolling with the punches." I said, "What about the other ships?" He said, "Oh, they're around here someplace." He was a great skipper, and he wanted to know how the game was going down below. I said, "Fine. I just made a lot of money and I'd better go back and see if it's still there."

We were in two bad typhoons, and in the first skirmish with the weather we lost three aircraft. We didn't know anything about a typhoon. The second one was much worse, but we didn't lose an airplane. They were wiggling around, but none went over the side because we'd learned how to lash them down. You can't see a bloody thing. It's not raining that hard, but the wind is blowing at 120, 130 knots, and it blows the top off the waves. I had joined the Navy because I didn't want to fight in the trenches and all that jazz. I wanted a clean white tablecloth, Queen Anne silver, and busboys. After that typhoon we had a couple of feet of water in the ward room, and we had to eat cold food standing on the dining table. It worked out fine, but we weren't used to cold stuff. The Navy had it all, and I always felt sorry for those Marine pilots who flew off those islands. We would train them, and they really enjoyed the food while they were aboard our ship.

One more thing about those storms. They would last for several hours, and when they stopped the wind would just quit. But the sea would continue to boil. We had four destroyers in our screen go belly up, and we sent our planes out to search for survivors. There was one

CITADELS AT SEA

guy who was holding on to a hunk of wood with one arm and his friend with the other. He'd been out there in the water for a day or more just hanging in there. Unfortunately we didn't have helicopters. As I said, when the wind quit, it really quit. I'd have to bring those guys back aboard that bloody ship with 19 knots of wind over the deck, which was as fast as our little carrier would go. You wanted 30. The ship would be going up and down and also in a corkscrew motion because of the sea, and that gets a little sticky. You couldn't cut a guy when it was coming up because his wheels would go right through his teeth. All of this had to be timed. I had to anticipate the ship's motion so that when he hit the deck it would be more or less level. If you cut him with the stern up in the air, he would just roll down the deck and into the barrier because the hook wouldn't grab a wire. The typhoon wasn't the problem, it was getting those guys in afterward without busting everything wide open. You got used to that and like any other sport—hockey, golf, tennis—you got a sense of timing.

★

I grew up in Montreal and played every sport I could get into. Soccer, English Rugby, cricket, baseball, you name it. I also sailed at the Royal St. Lawrence Yacht Club, and I think all of that helped me when it came to the Navy. I was born in Buffalo, but my mother and father were divorced when I was about three, and my mother married a Canadian. He was a fellow who had a hell of a First World War record in the Canadian army. His father had been a general in the Boer War, so military training was in his blood. I went to school at Selwyn House in Montreal and then to Bishop's College School in Lenoxville, Quebec, which was a very strict military boarding school patterned after the English public schools. I then went to the University of New Brunswick and didn't major in a hell of a lot. I played hockey and was on the swimming team, things like that.

After college I went to work at a lumber camp in northern Quebec owned by the E. B. Eddy Company, and then in a paper mill owned by the same company. It was located in Hull, Quebec, which is right across the river from Ottawa. I was what they called a "broke tender." The newsprint machines were going about 1,500 feet a minute, and when the paper broke I had a stick and was supposed to shove the waste down a hole in the floor. My God, can't you see me with 1,500 feet a minute of paper coming off that machine? "Where is he?" I'd be buried down there. I enjoyed working at the paper mill, but then the company decided to turn me into a salesman. My first assignment was in London, Ontario. I would call on retail stores, and my main product was toilet paper, which was rather embarrassing.

That's really starting at the bottom! I had friends in Toronto, and we used to go on weekends to the Muskoka Lakes, north of Toronto. We would play exhibition tennis for the tourists. The four of us went to a dance one night at the Royal Muskoka Hotel, and I ended up sitting at a table where the conversation was about Buffalo. Even though I'd left as a child, Buffalo was still on my mind because I knew my real father lived there. My name was Smith but I grew up as "Drury." My mother changed the monograms on the silver that I had been given when I was a baby. She even changed the name on the inside of my Bible. I wasn't supposed to know any of this. I asked this man who was talking about Buffalo, "Do you happen to know a fellow by the name of either Richard or Harold Smith?" He said, "I know Richard Smith very well. In fact, I played golf with him last week." I asked him if Richard Smith was first married in about 1914. "Yes he was." "Did he have a son named Baldwin?" He said, "Yes, in fact we were talking about Baldwin while we were playing golf." "Well," I said, "I'm Baldwin Smith. My name is Drury now, but I was born Baldwin Smith. If you would be good enough to tell my father that you met me and if he cares to see me, that's fine. If he doesn't, that's O.K. too. I'm doing just fine."

I came back from my holidays and the first thing I saw on the hall table was a letter from my father. My mother recognized the handwriting and she was quite upset. "What are you doing behind my back?" and all of that. I told her I wasn't doing anything behind her back, and that I wanted to meet my father and that was that. I met him in a hotel lobby in London, Ontario, and you talk about fear and trepidation. Every time the door opened, I'd say, "Oh, no, that's not him. That can't be him." When he finally walked in there was no question. We were identical in mannerisms, and it just had to be him. Talk about the argument of heredity or environment, I have great proof about heredity. He liked sports, tennis, golf, hockey, just the same pattern that I followed. He owned a company in Buffalo, John E. Smith's Sons, that manufactured machinery for the meat processing industry. All the big companies, Armour, Swift, Cudahy, and Wilson, used our equipment. I had gotten married in 1939 and we had one child, so I decided my best bet was to go to work for my father. We moved to Buffalo and I went to work assembling machinery.

I joined the Navy in 1942. I'm sure I could have gone back to Canada and joined the Canadian army, because I had gone to a military school. My Canadian friends were being killed like crazy, and I thought, I'm an American and all that stuff, but I owe something to those guys and I had better get with it. I wanted to get in the service in this country, but I didn't care to get drafted. My father had a friend in Washington named Hamilton Gardner who was a four-striper. He told me to write to the Navy Department and tell them my qualifications. There was a program called the AVS, Aviation Volunteer Service, and it was set up for executives who might have something to offer the Navy. I wrote an account of my experiences, what I had done with various companies, and I guess I'm sort of modest by nature so I didn't blow it up enough. Hamilton told me to try it one more time and give it a real good shot. I gave it the works the next time and got my orders and commission. I was told to report to Quonset Point, where they ran the hell out of us for three months. It was quite an intensive little program they had there.

Next I went to Norfolk, where I got into air-plot training. That had to do with directing aircraft to and from the carrier, and there was a lot of radar work connected with it. It was the most fascinating thing I could think of at the time. Strangely enough, I was assigned to Buffalo, which was ridiculous. Usually the Navy sends the guy from Buffalo to San Diego and the guy from San Diego to Buffalo. I went on the USS *Sable*, which was a paddle-wheel ferry boat that had been converted into an aircraft carrier for training purposes. It was beautiful for carrier landings because it was so stable. A sidewheeler doesn't have the corkscrewing effect you have with a propeller-driven ship. We took the ship to Chicago, and we were anchored inside the breakwater by Navy Pier with a sister ship, the *Wolverine*. The air-plot officer's job was to get the planes from Glenview Navel Air Base to our ship, and that wasn't very difficult. You just gave them a vector and that was that. Sometimes I'd give them a vector and they'd say, "What are you talking about? We're right over your head."

We trained thousands of pilots, and it was a terrific program. Each pilot had to have eight landings to qualify as a carrier pilot. I had a lot of spare time, so I started hanging around like a bum near the platform where the landing signal officer stood. It was on the port side, aft, and that's where the action was. I got to know a guy named John Paul Preston. He was a trade school boy, a naval aviator who had gone to the Naval Academy. He had been on the old *Yorktown* (CV-5) in the Coral Sea, and he took a liking to me. He saw my interest in this activity back there on that platform and asked me, "How would you like to be an LSO?" I said, "I'd love it." He told me that he had a classmate who was on the detail desk in Washington, and he was going to give me a chance. "You're a natural athlete and that's what we need back here. We're running out of pilots to do it." I think there were two other LSOs in the fleet who weren't naval aviators. My interest was there and if you want something bad enough, I think you can always get it. I guess that's been my philosophy of life.

My orders for training took me to Glenview. That's when I learned how to fly. Most of my teachers were off the old *Yorktown*, *Hornet*, *Saratoga*, *Enterprise*, ships like that, and they knew what the hell they were doing. The Navy wanted to put them out to pasture because they had been through enough. I didn't get wings, I never soloed a plane, but I knew how to fly so I'd know what was going on up there. You had to know about manifold pressure, how the flaps affect the airplane, and I think a person like me was more cognizant of it than the pilots because it was second nature to them. I was learning it for the first time, and I had to hang on to every piece of knowledge they were giving me. Those pilots were great guys and very patient.

They would fly me out to these little outlying fields where they were doing carrier landing practice, or what was called "bounce drill." You'd bring the planes in just the way you would on a carrier, and I'd stand behind the LSO for hours. It's actually more dangerous than being on a ship because if a plane spins in, it's bye-bye birdie. You have no place to run.

We were landing every kind of plane the Navy was using at that time, because you had to find out the characteristics of each one. Some would come down quick, others would float, and another might bounce. I liked any airplane with the name Grumman. The F4Fs, F6Fs, TBFs, they just seemed to be better airplanes. In retrospect I feel sorry for guys like Roelofs who had to fly those Curtiss SB2Cs. You could feel the weight of that airplane just holding the paddles. I did that for three or four months, standing behind those knowledgeable LSOs, and I learned the code. There's another guy writing it down. DID, dive in deck. LWDOA, left wing down on approach. F and F, flat and fast. You know the number of each pilot's plane, and when you saw him afterwards you'd go over every landing and show him what he did wrong.

Then they took me out to the ship, and I stood behind the LSO for another four months. They would send those pilots out in flights of six. That's forty-eight landings, and you would do about ten groups a day. You got the feel of how it was done. Then, one day, the guy hands you the paddles. "Okay, you're on. Front and center." You quiver a little bit, but you stretch your arms out and pretend you know what you're doing. He stands behind you. Everything went fine! The next day I flew out to the carrier, and he left and it was just me. Nobody behind me, and it was my shot. I had to perform over five or six hundred carrier landings before I was qualified. It was a long procedure, and I really felt I knew what I was doing when I got my own squadron.

I joined the *Rudyerd Bay* at San Diego near the end of 1943. We made a couple of runs back and forth with Jap prisoners from Kwajalein to shake the ship down. They built a barbed-wire compound down in the hangar deck, and I remember one big Japanese soldier who didn't like the way the other guys were acting. He really put them in line and shaped them up. They were a tenacious enemy. Once you get that samurai code in you, or what have you, God tells you what to do and you do it. Tough and very well-disciplined people. Look what the hell they've done since the end of the war. Who really won the war? I've got a Japanese camera right here with more goddamn equipment than I need. Look at all these Sonys, Toyotas, and Hondas. There's one right outside now. I thought I'd be the last guy to buy one, but I succumbed.

We had our winter flight gear issued after Iwo Jima, or perhaps it was Okinawa. Next stop, Honshu. Then dear Harry Truman dropped that beautiful thing. All of those people today who say that we shouldn't have done this or that weren't out there to see what was happening. Thousands of guys, including myself, wouldn't have come back from an attack on Japan. It was supposed to take a couple of weeks at Okinawa and it took ninety days.

The Japanese didn't always play by the rules of war. I was on Truk just after it was liberated, and this guy and I decided to take a walk in the country. We walked up this road and there was a little hut with a couple of bedsprings in it. I started bouncing up and down, you know, how you bounce on bedsprings, and on about my third bounce, while I was in midair, I looked down and there were four pineapples—grenades—connected to those springs. I thought, "Oh, Jesus, let me down easy." We got the hell out of there and went back to the ship. The hell with the nature studies.

You'd hear this stuff on the intercom. Kamikazes bearing zero-nine-zero, closing twelve miles . . . closing six miles . . . closing three miles. There was a shelter off the catwalk below my platform, and I'd go down there and think I was safe as a clam. It must have been made of steel a quarter-of-an-inch thick, and I think a .22 rifle bullet could have gone through it. The Jeep carriers were Mr. Kaiser's transport ships made into carriers, and there was no armor-plate steel to speak of, just flimsy stuff.

One night off Iwo Jima, the ship off our port side, another Jeep carrier, was burning from stem to stern from a Kamikaze hit. Nothing but flames. The *Saratoga,* which was up a couple of miles, you could see her burning too. I had to bring four night fighters aboard that night. They were off the *Saratoga* and since she was on fire, the admiral said, "Give them to the *Rudyerd Bay.*" I had never brought anything aboard at night, let alone an F6F. I just remembered what some guy told me; he flew off the *Lexington*. Keep them up there as if they are going to land on your head. Your sight is different at night and you think a plane is at a certain point, but it's really in a different place. They were good pilots and I hardly had to give them a signal. The only thing you had to do with an experienced pilot like that is maybe line him up a little bit, but you still have to give him the cut. The first guy came in, and I thought I'd blown it. It seemed an eternity from when I cut him until I heard the wire go out. He got the fourth wire. The rest of them caught the second or third wire.

While I was getting those guys aboard, I looked down and a fish, a torpedo, went right past the ship. I could see the phosphorescence in the water. I looked down and said, "Hello there." Then a Betty went by. That's a two-engine Japanese bomber. Its experienced pilot would lead the Kamikazes down and point them at the fleet. I felt I could almost touch the plane, and I could see the outline of the pilot. I got out my .45 and unloaded it at him. Nothing happened, but I had the great gratification of shooting at a Japanese plane at least once during the war. You have to forget that sort of thing, all that stuff going on around you, and concentrate on the job at hand. It wasn't a matter of bravery because you were so intent and you just did what you had to do.

After they were down, I went in to see the pilots. I had all this gray stuff on my face that was like cold cream. It was to protect me in case of fire and I was thinking that I was the bloody hero of the fleet. Those guys were so casual. "Your name is Smitty, isn't it? Thanks Smitty, thanks a lot. We couldn't get down because of the fire but I guess you knew that." The next day they were gone. Those naval aviators were something special. It was Christmas day, I don't know what year it was, and I looked up at this torpedo plane coming in and there's a big beard flowing out of the cockpit and a big red hat. It's Santa Claus in that airplane. That's the humor of the American soldier, the kind of thing that brought a little break into the war and helped morale. Even the captain had to laugh. It was a wonderful team to be on, all cooperation and goodwill. They had a big ceremony in the ward room at one point. I'm not blowing my own horn, because this is what happened. They gave me the "green weenie with the mud cluster." It was a little cocktail-sized hotdog on a ribbon with the cluster on it, and they pinned it on me. They said it was for getting them in safely, and it was beautiful. That became my CB name, "Green Weenie."

One night we went into Ulithi Lagoon. It was like a great big inland lake, and it used to take us three days to get all of our ships in there. Task Force 58. Once we got in there everybody would go nuts.

First you would get the enlisted men and all the beer that would fit into whale boats. You get them set up someplace ashore and then make for the officer's club. That could get a little horrendous. The All-American football players would be half-loaded, and they would get out there with a coconut. You wouldn't believe the crunching. Honest to God, it was carnage. At night everybody would go to the movies on the flight deck, and that night we were just forward of the *Franklin*. All of a sudden we hear an aircraft engine and we look up and—Jesus! There's a kamikaze about 100 yards aft of us. The Japs had assembled a couple of aircraft on some island and then brought them in close by submarine. The first plane hit the *Franklin* right in the middle of the flight deck. The second Jap pilot must have thought he saw the biggest aircraft carrier in the world. He hit the airstrip where I used to train pilots. He went to his maker thinking he did the samurai thing, and all he did was put a big hole in a runway.

After Okinawa, I got orders to report to Pearl Harbor to train night fighters. We dropped in at Pearl, and the whole ship's company and my squadron were going home. Everybody except me. I got off with two parachute bags, and I thought they were a little heavy when I went down the gangplank. I got down on the dock and found out that those pilots of mine had put two ingots of zinc in each bag. I looked up and they were all laughing at me. I got so mad I threw those ingots at the ship.

When the war ended I came back to the States on a heavy cruiser. That was terrible. A carrier is flat and steady, even the *Rudyerd Bay*, and I don't think I could have taken the war on a rolling cruiser. We got to Los Angeles, and when a few of us got off the ship we saw a bunch of girls in a convertible. Transportation was tough to get, and we must have looked pretty salty so they took us aboard and gave us a ride to the airport. I had orders to go to Floyd Bennett Field in Brooklyn, and I didn't do much while I was there because I was just waiting to get the hell out of the Navy. I left just as fast as possible. When they got busy with that Korean thing, John Preston called me up. By that time he was a full captain or admiral, I don't know which, with the Navy Department in Washington. He said, "Smitty, I just called you because I think we may have to put the first team back in." I said, "You got to be kidding. I'm not on the first team anymore, nor will I be again, ever." I figured that it was time for somebody else to go to war. I remembered the plaques that were put up after the war with all the names of the men who were killed. While it was going on and right after, everybody was patriotic. After a few years they took those plaques down and everybody forgot about the war except the people who were in it.

JAMES T. BRYAN, JR.

TO SAVE A LADY

Like Charlie Moutenot's Essex, the first of the new fleet aircraft carriers of the war, her sister ship Yorktown was also scheduled for scrapping. But this Yorktown, listed as "CV-10" in Navy style, meaning Number Ten in the grand roster of fleet carriers that goes back to the Langley as Number One, was a lucky ship, luckier than her predecessor of the same name, CV-5, which was sunk in the great battle of Midway, in 1942. In June 1975 she was towed away to new glory at Charleston, South Carolina, for preservation as the centerpiece of a naval museum. She has become a handsome memorial to all who fought aboard her, living or dead, and, increasingly, to all the Navy's carrier crews and airmen as well—a latter-day relic as moving as the frigate Constitution or Nelson's flagship Victory.

What is astonishing is that this feat of preservation was accomplished by one man. It was, also, a feat of leadership, organization, and persistence, the same traits he showed as aviation ordnance officer on the Yorktown during her World War II battles. As the planes came aboard to reload with bombs, rockets, torpedoes, and ammunition, with speed and care essential, the man in charge was Lt. James T. Bryan, Jr. In The Fighting Lady, a documentary film made on the Yorktown during the war, you can see him loping across the flight deck with his rearming crews and loaded bomb skids, and he has to this day the tall, lanky look of the young man in the movie. A retired insurance executive, Bryan lives in Laurel Hollow on Long Island, New York, with the U.S. Navy captain's daughter he married during the war.

James T. Bryan, Jr., elegant here for the camera, was the busy armaments officer for the carrier *Yorktown*, the famous "Fighting Lady," whose preservation he masterminded after the war.

We had the first *Yorktown* reunion in 1948. I learned that Ruppert's Brewery in New York City was making its famous taproom available to veterans' groups and serving a free steak dinner and "all the beer you can drink." My wife and I sent out invitations to 500 of my former shipmates, and the turnout was extraordinary. We had 250 men, including the first and third commanding officers, the first air group commander, and a torpedo plane pilot (and his two crewmen) who had survived 24 months as POWs. We talked about the war, laughed a lot, and remembered some friends who didn't come back.

The reunion turned out so well that we decided it should be an annual affair. The ensuing year Pat Garvan, *Yorktown*'s 1944–45 ACI (air combat intelligence officer), and I incorporated the USS *Yorktown* Association in New York state. I served as president until 1951 and then for the next twenty-five years as secretary-treasurer and unofficial executive director.

In 1970 we held our annual reunion in Boston and sadly participated in the *Yorktown*'s decommissioning. She was then towed to Bayonne, New Jersey, and placed in the mothball fleet. In 1973 I was in Florida on vacation and just by luck took along a copy of *Naval Aviation News*. There was an article about the Navy's starting to scrap the *Essex*-class carriers, with the *Essex* the first to go in 1974, and then the *Bunker Hill, Randolph,* etc. One of those etceteras was going to be the *Yorktown.* I decided that wasn't going to happen, if I could help it, and immediately started to find out how much time we had and what we had to do to save her.

I knew all about Admiral Halsey's attempts to save the *Enterprise* in 1957. It was very disheartening because, although he raised half a million dollars, the Navy only gave him six months, which was absolutely impossible. Not only did he have to raise the money, he had to find a location that would take the ship and guarantee the additional millions of dollars to berth and maintain her. When the time ran out, the Navy said, "Tough luck, Admiral Halsey," and "The Big E" became razor blades. That was tragic because she was the only prewar carrier that managed to survive the war.

I immediately called on various members of our association to see whom they knew who could help. Peter Dierks Joers, an Annapolis graduate, who had served on *Yorktown* in 1944–1945 as the communications officer, called John Warner, secretary of the navy, and inquired what we needed to do to save CV-10. Shortly thereafter, the undersecretary, Frank Sanders, sent us pages of specifications that spelled out everything and advised us that the ship had been put on a temporary "hold list," and that her scrapping date was now mid-1974. We had twice as long as Bull Halsey had with the *Enterprise* fifteen years before.

Our 1973 reunion was at Virginia Beach, and there was a good turnout. I put the idea of saving the *Yorktown* to the members, and it was unanimous to do it. For the next nine months I conducted practically a one-man campaign trying to get the Commonwealth of Virginia to acquire the ship and moor her in the York River near Yorktown. In November, Rear Adm. Raoul Waller, CV-10's first X.O. [executive officer], and I went down to Yorktown and Williamsburg to try and assure the city fathers that a World War II carrier was not going to ruin their image as a Revolutionary War showplace. We weren't very successful locally but had better luck with state legislators. We appeared before the Virginia Advisory Legislative Council in Richmond, which resulted in a bill being introduced in the House of Delegates. It would have established a commission to acquire and operate the *Yorktown* as a tourist attraction in the Yorktown-Norfolk area. In addition, $100,000 was appropriated for a pilot study.

Obviously, all of this was very encouraging but was going to take a long time, and the date to start scrapping CV-10 was April 1. I contacted the Navy Department and they said, "Look, we'll give you a few more months, but that's it." I'm sure they thought we were just a bunch of guys with an impossible dream.

In late March the president of our association called and said, "Jim, I've just heard that South Carolina has formed a state authority. They've appropriated $4,000,000 to establish a naval and maritime museum in Charleston to be called "Patriot's Point." As South Carolina didn't have a namesake battleship, like Alabama or North Carolina, to preserve as a state memorial, the state had asked the Navy if they could get an aircraft carrier. The Navy told them about the *Yorktown* and our association's ongoing efforts to save our ship. Another thing in the ship's favor was the fact that she had been decommissioned for only four years and therefore was in excellent shape.

The *Yorktown* was known as "The Fighting Lady," and was one of the five large carriers to receive Presidential Unit Citations. We had a hell of a ship and were always competing against the other carriers. The first six months we operated in the same task group with the *Essex*, and she was usually only a mile or so away. We could see her planes landing and taking off, and they could see what we were doing. Our battle cry was, "Beat the *Essex*." You had several hundred men working on the flight deck, and they were breaking their butts to land and respot the planes coming back from a strike. At the same time they had to get the bombs and ammunition up from the magazines and loaded on the planes, gas the aircraft, get the pilots in the cockpits, and bring each plane forward for takeoff. If we got all our planes off first, before the *Essex*, there would be a big cheer from the flight deck.

After hearing what Charleston was putting together, and with time running out, I figured our association and South Carolina should join forces. Virginia graciously passed its claim to the *Yorktown* over to Senators Strom Thurmond and Fritz Hollings, and in September of 1974 I went to Charleston and met with the Patriot's Point Development Authority's board of directors. I said, "O.K., we're going to be partners. You get the ship down here and we'll bring in our association with all of our memorabilia and give the ship the personal touch your staff hasn't had any experience with." The board accepted our support with open arms, and the Navy extended the scrapping date to July 1975.

In May 1975 I went to Washington to witness the Navy turn "The Fighting Lady" over to South Carolina in Strom Thurmond's Senate office. The *Yorktown* cost South Carolina only one dollar, but there was a stipulation that she had to be a museum, not a glorified restaurant or amusement park.

Within 25 days of getting the contract signed and sealed, we had tugs hooked up to the ship and she was being towed from the pier at Bayonne. The *Essex* and *Hancock* were tied up at the same pier and shortly thereafter went to the scrap heap. A large delegation of Yorktowners was on hand to see CV-10 off, and some of us followed her out to the Verrazano Bridge on a police boat. The towing company turned down our request to ride the ship to Charleston, saying it would be too dangerous and their insurance wouldn't cover it.

I followed her trip in the Charleston papers, which daily showed the ship's progress down the coast, and knew exactly when she was due to arrive. I flew down and went out on a Coast Guard cutter to greet my old ship, along with everybody else in the Charleston area who had anything that would float. There were over seven hundred boats of all sizes, from canoes up to huge yachts. A photographer took a picture of my profile with the *Yorktown* in the background, just coming into the harbor. He has said since that it is one of his prize photographs. "Here you are, Jim, seeing your dream come true." He was right; it was an unforgettable moment.

By late afternoon they had worked her into a place where she was going to lie, and in a short time the sand filled in around the hull. I don't think a 150-mile-an-hour hurricane could budge it. The ship was in good shape, but the hangar deck looked like a warehouse because it was filled with radar units, anchors, chains, anything they didn't know what to do with. There was a lot of work to do to get it cleaned up and ready for the dedication at our next reunion, but we were just tickled to get our ship. Several of us were walking around the deck and I said, "Here we are and this is what we've accomplished, the first part of our plan."

My great-grandfather and namesake, James Bryan, emigrated from Scotland in 1859 and settled in Savannah. He joined the Savannah Guard, and when the Civil War broke out the Guard was mobilized, and he ended up getting killed in 1863 at Battery Wagner at the entrance to Charleston harbor, two miles from where the *Yorktown* is now located. His brother emigrated to New York and joined the Merchant Marine. Soon after he was taken into the Union Navy, and assigned to the ironclad *Monitor*. He survived the epic battle with the *Merrimac*, but later on, when the *Monitor* was caught in a storm off Cape Hatteras and overturned, he was one of the eighteen men to go down and be entombed in her main turret.

My great-grandmother was left in Savannah with three young children, so at the end of the war she went back to Scotland. Ten years later, at age sixteen, my grandfather decided to come back to North America, lived in Canada for a short time, and then moved to Chicago. He quickly became very successful in the commodities and securities business. Unfortunately, he and my father, who was a partner, lost most of their money in the 1929 crash, and finally had to liquidate the firm in 1933. I grew up as a wealthy kid living on Long Island's Gold Coast; I went to prep school at Hotchkiss and ended up waiting on tables for my last two-and-a-half years as a scholarship boy. I managed to work my way through Yale, and when I graduated in 1939, I decided to go to work for American Surety, the insurance company where my other grandfather had been president and then chairman of the board. Figuring I'd be spending the rest of my life working on the corner of Broadway and Wall Street, I took the summer off and passed the final couple of weeks up at our camp on Tunk Lake, 50 miles northeast of Bar Harbor, Maine.

That Labor Day weekend I was having lunch with my family and Adm. Richard E. Byrd, the famous polar explorer, who was our neighbor on the lake. In the middle of our meal someone on the radio announced that Hitler had marched into Poland. Byrd, who was usually a jolly sort of fellow, suddenly became very serious and said that this meant another world war and the United States would probably be in it in less than two years. At the time I can remember thinking that what Hitler did in Europe didn't have much to do with us.

I went back to New York and worked for American Surety for thirteen months. All of a sudden it appeared Admiral Byrd was right, and we were getting closer to war. President Roosevelt and Congress decided we were going to need a draft, and being twenty-four years old, I knew I'd be prime material. I sure didn't want to go in the Army, and since I had always been interested in swimming and sailing, I decided to look into the Navy.

At that time they had a program, entitled V-7, to train college graduates as Naval Reserve officers, the so-called ninety-day wonders. There were only 150 spots open when I got my papers in and Admiral Byrd was a great help, sending a telegram recommending me highly. I was only worried about one thing. My eyes were borderline—closer to 20/30 than the 20/20 the Navy insisted on. I went to see an eye doctor, and he gave me some exercises to strengthen my eyes. I did them religiously for two weeks, but I was still worried. Lo and behold, when they took me into the room where they were going to give me my physical, the eye chart was about 10 feet away. I quickly memorized the last two lines and steamed through the test. Shortly thereafter I was accepted in the U.S. Naval Reserve.

Less than a week later the lottery for the draft was held in Washington, and damned if my number wasn't the second one FDR picked out of the big drum. I became an immediate "celebrity" and reporters called my home and then came to my office. I still have the clipping from the *New York Times* stating that "James T. Bryan, Jr., the holder of the second number drawn, was out to lunch, but fellow employees said he wasn't at all concerned."

My first naval experience was a 30-day midshipman cruise on the new heavy cruiser *Vincennes*. We got only as far as Norfolk, where *Vincennes* and her sister ship *Quincy* tied up at the base for several weeks. We were treated like seaman recruits and introduced to everything from gunnery, navigation, and engineering to swabbing decks and cleaning heads [latrines]. All of this was designed to wash out 25 percent of us, and at one point they were going to give us another tough physical. I thought they'd get me this time for sure. Lady luck came to my rescue again.

A good friend of mine became ill and ended up in the sick bay. As soon as I learned this I sent him a note, "Fred, if you're near it, please copy down the last couple of lines on the eye chart." A day later a note came back with the *whole* chart written down. I found out that everywhere I went, San Diego, Norfolk, wherever, the same eye chart always came up. To this day I carry that note and chart in my wallet as a reminder of what helped me get in, and then stay in, the Navy.

In late February orders came, sending me to the decommissioned battleship *Illinois*, renamed the *Prairie State*, anchored in the Hudson River. My four years at Yale had been spent more on athletics, fraternity functions, and such matters, than on studying. My marks were mostly Bs and Cs along with too many Ds and a few Fs. However, from my first day as a midshipman I started to apply myself, and my family and Yale contemporaries nearly fainted when I ended up in the top ten of our entering class of five hundred.

About a month before graduation we were asked what kind of

active duty we'd like. There was no question in my mind. I wanted to be a PT boat skipper because Preston L. Sutphen and his wife were my family's closest friends on Long Island. As general manager of the Elco Naval Division of Electric Boat Company, now General Dynamics, he supervised the building of over three hundred PT boats. The Navy told me there were already too many PT skippers but if I was interested, I could put in for torpedo school and in October there might be some openings. I put in for Newport, Rhode Island, as it was the only torpedo station I'd ever heard of, and I was dating a girl from Boston. Well, I got my orders to torpedo school all right, but they read Keyport, Washington. I, along with twenty-four other guys, figured it must be a typographical error and marched down to see the executive officer. He informed us that it was no error, and we would be spending the next four months on the West Coast.

After I'd been in Keyport three weeks, an officer came down to the area where we were learning the intricacies of torpedoes and asked if anyone would like to play tennis after class with the commanding officer. His regular opponent, the X.O., was out of town. Fortunately, I had brought along my racket from home and, in fact, for the past two weeks had been eyeing the court. I quickly put my hand up, and we had an enjoyable game. I was asked back. On July 17 I was swimming in the lagoon when I saw a blonde girl dive off the dock and quickly surmised this must be Norma, the C.O.'s daughter. It didn't take me long to introduce myself as the reserve ensign who had been playing tennis with her father. We were soon playing tennis and ping pong, going fishing, and dancing at the "O" Club in Bremerton, with transportation furnished by the C.O.'s official car and driver.

After Labor Day, Norma left to attend the San Francisco Ballet Company school, which left me with a kingsized dilemma. What seven weeks earlier started out to be an enjoyable summer infatuation had developed into something much more serious. Fate helped again when I received orders as torpedo officer at the Naval Air Station, North Island, across the harbor from San Diego. Most of my classmates were assigned to destroyers and light cruisers, and at least six of them would be killed within the first six months of the war.

With two weeks to report to San Diego, I flew to Oakland, then took the ferry to San Francisco, where Norma was waiting for me in the terminal. Ten days later I gave her an engagement ring, although we both agreed that marriage would have to wait for a year because of her serious interest in dancing. Leaving San Francisco I was the happiest man in the world, but soon came down to earth when I inspected my first naval command. All I found was a large concrete building equipped with an overhead traveling crane and some storage racks. No compressor, no overhaul and testing equipment, no torpedoes, and worst of all, not one enlisted torpedo man. When I questioned my boss, the first of the long line of regular Navy officers I would be butting heads with for the next 45 years, he curtly told me to relax—the equipment was on order and my job in the meantime was to sell war bonds. I kept after him to expedite my equipment and pretty soon he became really annoyed and said, "Look, Bryan, you're in the Navy now, you do what you're told and if I tell you to sell war bonds, you sell war bonds. I don't want to hear any more about your torpedo shop, or I'll transfer you out of here." Not anxious to end up in the Aleutians or Espiritu Santo, I kept my mouth shut.

On December 7, 1941, I was swimming with a couple of friends off Coronado Island when someone came running down the beach shouting, "The Japs have bombed Pearl Harbor." We were told to return to our base immediately. Where do I go? My torpedo shop is just a naked building. The next day I was still high and dry when I got orders to report to the office of Capt. Ernest Gunther, the commanding officer. "Bryan, I understand you're our torpedo officer. We have to prepare to meet the Jap fleet. Can you load torpedoes on our patrol planes?" I replied, "I'm sorry, Captain, we don't have anything. We just have a bare building." He blew his top and said, "You've got the green light to do anything that's necessary to get that torpedo shop in operation as soon as possible. You can go to the destroyer base and demand that they give you compressors, any equipment you need. Find torpedoes wherever they are and get them in here. I insist that this be given top priority and want you to report to me when you are ready to load."

This was what I had been waiting for, and I could now go anywhere. I took advantage of it and found out I liked operating that way. In less than a month I had forty-five men working in the shop and had enough torpedoes, so we could use some for training as well as against the Japs. Toward the end of February, Norma and I were married, and after a five-day honeymoon we moved into an apartment in Coronado.

In early 1942 everyone connected with carrier aviation was eagerly awaiting the delivery to the fleet of Grumman's new 200-knot TBF Avenger torpedo bomber along with the new Mark 13, Mod 1 torpedoes. For over 45 years Pearl Harbor has been the symbol of the U.S. Navy's woeful lack of preparedness, and millions of words have been written about Japan's very successful sneak attack. On the other hand, only minimal publicity has been given to the fact that we had so many weapons that were grossly inferior and inadequate. My December 7 barebones torpedo shop and war-bond salesman duties were only the tip of the iceberg of our incredibly substandard capabilities in carrier-aviation torpedo warfare. Our carrier magazines were stocked with torpedoes designed in 1929, which could be dropped at altitudes no higher than 50 feet, at speeds no faster than 110 knots. They had effective ranges well under 1,000 yards. Until the Battle of Midway, in June 1942, our five carrier-based torpedo squadrons flew the short-range, obsolete Douglas TBD, known as the "Devastator"—the most ironic misnomer of the war!

On March 23 the first Avenger landed at North Island, flown by Lt. Cmdr. James Taylor, a famous test pilot and the father of a good friend of mine. Norma served him her first dinner-guest meal. A few months later I received a telegram from my mother with the grim message, "Jimmie Taylor was killed yesterday testing an experimental plane." I never in my wildest imaginaton could foresee that 45 years later I would have the honor of helping to perpetuate his memory in the Carrier Aviation Test Pilots Hall of Honor on the *Yorktown*.

The day after the Avenger arrived I decided to find out how to load one of my torpedoes using the brand-new equipment designed by BuOrd (the omnipotent Bureau of Ordnance) and distributed to all aircraft carriers, torpedo squadrons, and air stations. The principal items were a portable bomb hoist, designated the Mark 7, and a universal bomb-and-torpedo hoisting band. I was crouching under the bomb bay, watching the hoisting process, and just after I moved out from under the aircraft, the hoist broke and dropped the 2,000-pound torpedo exactly where I had been. Not only did the cast-aluminum pulley of the MK 7 hoist have to be redesigned, we also had to redesign the "universal" band—another dream child of some aviation ordnance specialist whose only practical experience was sitting behind a desk in Washington.

After the war I talked with a Grumman engineer and asked him, "How did you guys get a torpedo into the Avenger?" He said, "We used a concrete dummy torpedo and a large forklift truck." I said, "Did you ever give any thought to the fact that there are no forklift trucks on an aircraft carrier?"

During those eight months at North Island, getting one air group after another ready to go to sea, we were trying all sorts of things. I didn't have an engineering background and I'd never even fooled around with a car. But as soon as I got around those airplanes and torpedoes, everything seemed to fall into place. I would think something up and was lucky to have a great crew who had the knowledge and skill to carry it through.

By early December, however, I was ready to move on. I had fallen in love with carriers and wanted to work with their torpedo squadrons under combat conditions. I shot off a letter to a Yale classmate, Eddie Collins, Jr., son of the great baseball player, who had just been assigned to the detail desk at BuPers [Bureau of Personnel]. I asked him if he could get me on one of the new *Essex*-class carriers. Ten days later I got a clipping of Eleanor Roosevelt christening the new *Yorktown* and a note from Eddie: "This is your new ship. You'll have orders before the end of January."

I reported to the *Yorktown*'s commissioning detail in Newport News on March 6, 1943. With my year's training in aerial torpedoes, and my other experience, I couldn't imagine that they wouldn't need somebody like me. Nothing doing. The exec said, "I'm sorry but we already have a chief warrant torpedo officer and rearming officer, so we will have to put you in the gunnery department." I spent two weeks in gunnery training on the battleship *Wyoming,* and when I got back to Newport News I was more determined than ever to get on a carrier. For the next month I reverted to my November 1941 war-bond salesman days, badgering the top brass. To shut me up I was given orders to report to the *Yorktown*'s air group (AG-5) at the Naval Air Station, Norfolk, for "temporary duty" until the ship went on her shakedown cruise to Trinidad. AG-5's commanding officer was the legendary Jimmy Flatley, one of the Navy's two top fighter pilots and the finest officer I've ever known.

Flatley and I hit it off right away, and everything I wanted to do he would back me up on 100 percent. Now I had another green light and was able to get to know, train, and form the rearming crews. I also found the type of chief petty officer I knew was an absolute necessity if this thing was going to work. Charles E. Murray was, in fact, still a first-class petty officer and not even nineteen years old, but he had graduated from the aviation ordnance school in Jacksonville, was an electronic and mechanical expert, and a born leader. I put him in charge of my fledgling rearming crews, and he became my right-hand man. Chiefs like him keep the Navy going.

Charlie and I immediately made one major change in carrier rearming practice that eventually was universally accepted as standard procedure. Since the days of the *Langley** back in the 1920s, ordnance men attached to, for example, a torpedo squadron had nothing to do with the bombing and fighter squadrons on the same ship. This would often result in a large number of "spectators" when a rearming drill did not include more than one type of squadron. We started out at Norfolk having the torpedo and bombing crews practice loading each other's aircraft. Eventually we also brought the fighter rearming crews into this team effort. This innovation helped give the

Ed. note: The Navy's first aircraft carrier, converted from an old collier and named for Samuel Pierpont Langley, an aviation pioneer and secretary of the Smithsonian Institution.

CITADELS AT SEA

Yorktown by far the fastest rearming division in the fleet in the last two years of the war.

When I ended my "temporary duty" and returned to the *Yorktown*, I was finally assigned to the Air Department, but under the aviation ordnance specialist. This was all right for the time being, as I had a feeling his inexperience and attitude were going to be his downfall. Besides, with Flatley's backing I was in an excellent position to take over when he fell on his face. Well, that's exactly what happened. The day of reckoning arrived when the Plan of the Day called for a full-scale rearming drill. That was the biggest and most pleasurable snafu that I ever witnessed during my six years on active duty. After three hours some planes on the flight deck were still not fully armed, and needless to say, Jimmy Flatley was fuming. Upon our return to Norfolk, I was overjoyed to learn that Flatley had arranged to transfer the other fellow off CV-10 and give me full responsibility.

When I officially took over the arming division, I encountered problems and challenges that made my earlier North Island experiences pale in comparison. Traditionally, the gunnery department controlled all of a ship's magazines; as a result bombs were stored in specific compartments without their tail vanes or hoisting bands. When bombs were needed we had to find the gunner's mate with the keys and have him muster a crew. In half an hour or so bombs would begin arriving on the third deck, where our assembly crews had to start putting them together from scratch. Again, with Flatley's backing, we took over the magazines using muscular aviation ordnance man "strikers." We stored the bombs with their tails and bands attached, and we rearranged compartments so that 500-pounders, by far the most frequently expended, were stored right next to bomb elevators.

Bomb, rocket, and ammunition-loading equipment was grossly inadequate or nonexistent. As a result Charlie Murray and I adopted the "do it yourself" principle and during the next 15 months designed over a dozen pieces of rearming equipment, almost all of which were eventually approved by BuOrd and placed aboard new carriers. Fortunately, CV-10 had a terrific machinist mate, Mike Cintola, who welded together our prototype designs and eventually turned out our necessary requirements.

Another thing, "ready storage" was a term unknown to U.S. carrier aviation as late as the fall of 1943. However, when we began steady, day-after-day strikes during the Tarawa invasion, and came under day and night attack during the raid on Kwajalein, it was obvious that the flow of bombs, and later of rockets, from magazine storage racks to the flight deck had to be speeded up dramatically. It became a must to keep a percentage of bombs, depth charges, and rockets on skids in the magazines around the clock. Gradually we removed the storage racks so we had space for several dozen loaded skids, which could be moved to the flight decks as fast as the two-stage bomb elevators made their round-trips. This procedure was the forerunner of "universal bomb storage," which we designed and then forwarded in blueprints to Bremerton Navy Yard. They were installed aboard the *Yorktown* during our 1944 overhaul. From that date on all carriers got this new improvement in bomb and rocket storage.

The *Yorktown* sailed from Norfolk on July 8, 1943, and went through the Panama Canal and straight to Pearl Harbor. We weren't there more than a month when we went into combat off Marcus Island. J. J. "Jocko" Clark, later an admiral, was the skipper of the *Yorktown*, and he was known as the "Patton of the Pacific." He got us from shakedown to combat in record time. It was always "go, go, go," because Clark wanted to get out there and mix it up with the Japs. His motto was, "Get the job done and to hell with regulations." He rubbed some people the wrong way because he was so aggressive, but I've heard it said that "if we had three or four Jocko Clarks, we would have won the war a lot sooner."

"Pop" Condit was shot down on the Marcus strike. Lt. James Condit was an old man of twenty-six because he had been in the Navy before the war, and he was the gunnery officer in the torpedo squadron. Condit was another guy that I saw eye to eye with right from the beginning. He was flying a TBF and he, his gunner, and his radio man all ended up in a rubber boat 75 miles off Marcus Island. We thought they were goners, of course, and didn't find out until after the war was over that they were picked up by a Japanese fishing boat and taken to Marcus. The Japs hit Condit with a baseball bat, beat the hell out of him. He was lucky to live through it because the *Yorktown* and the *Essex* were the first new carriers operating in the Pacific, and the Japs tried to get him to tell them about the state-of-the-art equipment on those ships. Later on he was taken to Tokyo, and that's where he spent the rest of the war.

Looking back on it, I think the loss of Condit was one of the incidents that got me interested in creating a memorial for the people that were lost during the war. One of my ordnance "partners in crime" gone, just like that. Shortly thereafter, a series of things happened aboard ship where people I knew were killed, and I came within a split second of being killed myself.

Before our first combat mission I was standing next to a steel stanchion that helped support a safety chain around the open bomb elevator. I was looking at my clipboard, assigning rearming crews, when the brakes on a taxiing SBD dive bomber locked, and the plane veered directly at me. All I can remember is somebody yelling, "Look out!" receiving a solid push, and ending up between two bomb skids with that huge prop spinning six inches above my back. Afterwards I noticed the stanchion was cut in half; but it wasn't until one of our reunions that I learned from Tan Gannon, one of my 1943 ordnance men, that he was the one who knocked me down. He said, "Do you remember me? I was only a second-class petty officer and I had to knock down a lieutenant."

During the Tarawa invasion, in November 1943, I lost one of my men. Four F4F Wildcats couldn't find their own ship, the *Liscome Bay*, and asked permission to land on the *Yorktown*. We got three of them down and Joe Coppi, one of my top rearming crew leaders, was up on the wing of one of the planes making sure the guns were not armed. After my earlier brush with oblivion, I never again took my eyes off a taxiing or landing plane and noticed that the exhaust flames of the last plane were high enough to clear the barrier. I screamed a warning at Joe and literally jumped out of one of my shoes toward the island. The "bolter" landed on top of Joe, burst into flame, set fire to a half-dozen parked planes, cooked off their .50-caliber ammunition, sent flames 100 feet into the air, and for a few minutes we thought our ship might be destroyed.

Then Elisha "Smokey" Stover was lost. He was a pilot, a farm boy from Eureka Springs, Arkansas, and my best friend ever since I was assigned a room across from his. I really admired his most prized possession—a piece of wing fabric with part of a big red meatball painted on it. It had been lodged in the damaged wing of Stover's Wildcat after, in a head-on crash, he had downed his fourth enemy plane while based at Guadalcanal's Henderson Field. Grounded for battle fatigue, he had talked his way into another tour of duty with us. He led the *Yorktown*'s first fighter sweep on Truk, and I think he had a premonition that something was going to happen to him. The night before he was lost, I was with him and he was wrapping his gun in plastic and making sure it was watertight. He also took off his good shoes and put on an old pair. He said, "The Japs are never going to get my good shoes." He was last seen floating in his raft, not far from the entrance to Truk's harbor. What actually happened will never be known, but he was probably picked up, tortured, and beheaded the next morning with six other pilots from Task Force 58. I waited until I knew he wasn't coming back to write his mother and dad, thus starting a 40-year series of remembrances in his honor.

In the fall of 1944 I was taken off the *Yorktown* and transferred to Jimmy Flatley's Fleet Air Training Command at good old North Island. By the time I reported, Flatley had been recruited by Mitscher to be his operations officer but his replacement, Capt. John Crommelin, was certainly in Flatley's league in every respect. Recruiting a draftsman and several ordnance men, I immediately began to refine all of the rearming equipment and bomb-and-rocket-magazine storage ideas that we had developed aboard CV-10.

In late January 1945 we received a new rocket called the Tiny Tim, which was 11.75 inches in diameter and could do the same amount of damage as a cruiser firing a 12-inch gun. They were delivered to us in wooden crates, and we had to learn how to store and handle them on our own. In short order we designed a method of assembling one of those rockets in 30 seconds. The head weighed 500 pounds all by itself, so the trick was to put the motor on one skid and the head on another, move them together, mate the threads, and screw them together with a long-handled spanner wrench.

I made out all sorts of reports and suggested how these rockets should be assembled and stored. Rockets are worse than a loaded gun because they don't just blow up if a carrier is hit, they go shooting down the deck and when they hit a bulkhead, explode. The carrier *Franklin* (CV-13) was the first ship that would get the Tiny Tims, so my boss—Adm. Alfred Montgomery—sent me up to the naval air station at Alameda to teach the *Franklin* ordnance crews how to store, assemble, and load them. I took along some of my rearming equipment and when I went aboard, I was delighted to find that the division leading chief was P. P. Day, who had worked for me on the *Yorktown.* He was glad to see me, and invited me down to the mess hall, where he got all of his ordnance men together to hear what I had to say. I started explaining our 30-second assembly method and told them about other rearming equipment. The meeting had gone on for about an hour when, all of a sudden, the *Franklin*'s aviation ordnance officer burst in and asked me what the hell I was doing there. I showed him my orders and told him P. P. Day could certainly vouch for my credentials. He was some rich guy who had somehow gotten in the Navy and didn't have any experience to speak of. Without listening to a word, he told me to get off the ship. When I refused, he stomped out and 15 minutes later was back with the air officer, who was a full commander. He threatened to have the master-at-arms throw me off the ship bodily. I very reluctantly left, steaming mad, and went back and reported to my boss how I was treated. But nothing was done, and the *Franklin* sailed a day later. Within a month, the first time they were using the Tiny Tims, she was hit by two 500-pound Jap bombs and 791 men were killed.

What went wrong? They brought the Tiny Tim motors and heads up from the magazines to the hangar deck and took hours putting them together, using a single-assembly jig designed by the ordnance officer and his division instead of our half-minute procedure. Eighteen assembled rockets were then loaded on F4U Corsair fighters spotted on the hangar deck until they could be brought to the flight deck following the launch of the first strike. So here you had eighteen times 500 pounds of TNT, ready to go off and race up and down inside a big enclosed deck packed with gassed planes and many hundreds of men in chow lines, a holocaust waiting to happen. On the *Yorktown* we had a cardinal rule, *never* keep bombs, or rockets, or loaded planes on the hangar deck, no matter what. The flight deck was made of wood and a bomb could go right through it and explode below. When an *Essex*-class carrier was hit, the death toll would rarely be 100. The largest number was *Bunker Hill*'s 350. Even if you use the latter number, you have 450 more deaths on the *Franklin* than on any other large carrier, and a great many of them I blame on the ego and stubbornness of that ordnance officer. I knew all about what happened because P. P. Day survived and several months later came to North Island to work for me.

After a heroic struggle, the *Franklin* finally limped back to New York. No one knew much about what I have just described, and the Navy said, "Look at the damage this ship sustained, and yet her crew saved her." So they gave out medals instead of court-martials. For years the records of a Senate investigating committee were kept secret, but now they have been declassified, and I think somebody should dig into it and tell the real story of those officers' blatant negligence. The disaster with the space shuttle brought it right to mind again, except that there was no whitewash this time. They have pinned it on the top brass who made the decision to overrule the engineer who told them something was wrong and through the night kept saying, "We shouldn't launch this shuttle." Nobody listened.

Immediately after the *Franklin* tragedy I got orders to go to Pearl Harbor and meet with supposed experts from the Bureau of Ordnance, the Bureau of Aeronautics, and Commander Air Pacific. Then I was sent to Washington for another high-level conference to discuss bomb and rocket storage and handling on all classes of carriers. As a result of those two conferences, all my rearming equipment and magazine storage plans were made standard. Last year I went out on the nuclear carrier *Eisenhower* and found they were still using many of the same ideas we originated back on the *Yorktown*.

After the war ended I stayed in one year longer. I was thinking about a career in the Navy, but when I talked to Adm. Ralph Jennings, the new skipper on the *Yorktown*, he recommended against it. I wasn't an aviator, and it was going to be an aviator's navy after the war. Also, I had been handling the real thing in combat. Rockets, bombs, ammunition, and all the excitement that went with it. They would go back to dropping little practice water bombs, and he thought I would be bored as hell. The Navy was starting to put almost all the large carriers in mothballs because at that point no one dreamed a carrier would ever be able to handle nuclear weapons. In the summer of 1946, Norma and I took a trip up the West Coast to Seattle, and we saw the *Yorktown* and six other carriers moored side by side.

When I left the Navy I went back into the insurance business in New York. I retired in 1986 so I could spend more time working for the *Yorktown*. If I had utilized all of my salesmanship on insurance, I know I could have made a lot more money. I did well enough, I suppose, but I always tell people that when I left Frank B. Hall, Inc., hell, I just left an office. Who is going to remember what I've done as an insurance broker? But I know damn well that 200 years from now, that great ship will still be down there in Charleston. When I started out in the 1950s, I wanted to do something for a few of my heroes who had been killed. Maybe just in a small way. Things like bringing the Stover family to a reunion in New York; giving the Crommelin family a plaque in memory of Charlie, our second air group commander. Once I got the ship, that all changed. How many guys have a 1,000-foot-long aircraft carrier to play with?

After the ship was opened to the public in January 1976, we started to work on the Stover Theater and the Coppi Room. By October we had the theater opened, dedicated, and began showing the documentary film *The Fighting Lady* three times a day. To help finance the theater we started selling "chairs" to people who wanted to honor or memorialize their husbands, fathers, shipmates, and squadron mates. Of the 240 chairs, 235 have been subscribed to.

Pilots started coming to me at one point and saying things like, "I left the *Yorktown* after a year and ended up in another air group on the *Essex,* or the *Lexington.* I lost my wing man and can't I do something for him?" I resisted the idea for a year or so because I thought, let them get their own ship. However, it became obvious they weren't going to get any. So, in 1979 we proclaimed *Yorktown* "Naval Aviation's National Memorial to Carrier Aviation" and opened her decks to her 143 sister carriers. Of these, 108 suffered casualties in one of the three wars.

Unbelievably, the Navy has no lists of those killed on these ships, let alone in which war, so I have had four different researchers working in the National Archives the past eight years. Sometimes it takes as long as six months before we come up with a list we feel is 99 percent perfect. If we miss a few names, and we invariably do, they can be added later, as they do on the Vietnam Wall. We now have 5,465 killed in action (KIA) names on fifty-eight individual ship plaques out of an estimated ten thousand. A widow, son, brother, or what have you can come and say, "After 45 years, someone has finally remembered. The last time I heard from the Navy was when they delivered the 'killed in action' telegram." There are a lot of families who don't even know that the *Yorktown* is in Charleston, or that it has a plaque with their relative's name on it. When we do locate someone, such as Butch O'Hare's* daughter and four grandchildren, the whole family will come down and walk around in awe. They can get a feeling of how he lived and where he fought during the war.

This is my life's work, and if I live that long, one of these days we will have 108 carrier plaques and every KIA's name on the *Yorktown*. Then she will truly be the "Arlington of Carrier Aviation." I'm the one who stayed up at night and wrote every word that appears on the thirty-six Carrier Aviation Hall of Fame plaques that are mounted on the flight deck. Men like Forrestal, who built the World War II Navy, John Waldron, heroic leader of Torpedo 8, Jimmy Flatley, all of them. I'm not being boastful, but I know for sure that our "Fighting Lady" would be scrap, and the thousands of carrier aviation heroes and KIAs would not be remembered by a lasting, tangible memorial if I hadn't appointed myself to do this job.

Ed. note: Lieutenant Commander Edward H. ("Butch") O'Hare won fame by shooting down five and damaging a sixth of nine enemy bombers attacking the old carrier *Lexington* in 1942; President Roosevelt personally presented him with the Congressional Medal of Honor. He was lost in a night battle off Makin in the Gilbert Islands in 1943. Chicago's big airport carries his name.

DAVID QUINN

NEVER A DULL MOMENT

The business of rescuing downed airmen was brought to new levels of daring and success in World War II. It involved whomever and whatever was at hand: PT boats, occasional submarines (one of which rescued carrier pilot George Bush), destroyers, and airplanes capable of landing on the water, from little float planes to huge flying boats. Rescuing was always a dicey business, especially in heavy ocean seas or under attack in enemy waters.

At heart a small-town lawyer, David Quinn is still fit at sixty-four. He keeps an office over a drugstore on Main Street in Katonah, New York. It's a comfortable place with rows of leather-bound volumes lining one wall. He speaks quietly and modestly about his career and the notable women in his life—his wife, Newsweek *and* Washington Post *columnist Jane Bryant Quinn, and their daughter Martha, a video disc jockey for MTV. On one side of the room is a table displaying a glass-enclosed model of a Martin Mariner, the flying boat he piloted during the war. It takes a leap of the imagination to grasp the fact that this mild-mannered man once flew his plane into Japan's hostile Kobe Bay to pick up a Navy flyer who had been shot down.*

Several years ago I got word that a PBM newsletter was being published. I sent in my $15 and started getting the thing and found out that there are a lot of PBM nuts around. Among other things, they gave the dates and locations of squadron reunions and the person's name to contact, etc. I saw the name of somebody who was in VP-214, my old Atlantic Fleet antisubmarine patrol squadron, so I dropped him a line. I've never corresponded with anybody in my life,

David Quinn was in primary flight training when this photograph was taken. Three years later he was a full lieutenant rescuing downed flyers from the waters off Japan. Today he is a lawyer.

but this thing has blossomed, and I now hear from all sorts of people in the squadron, including one guy I sold my 1939 Mercury convertible to in Norfolk in July 1944.

I'm sure it's a combination of age and nostalgia, but it is nice to hear from people who were part of what I now realize were the most fantastic years of my life. I think that about 98 percent of them would agree. Me from the Bronx, another guy from Peoria or Kansas City— we were from all over the place but we hadn't really been anywhere. It certainly radically changed our lives. If somebody asked me, "What were you doing in May 1959?" I couldn't tell him. But each month of that four-year period of the war is etched in my mind. I can tell you where I was, what I was doing, and what the people with me were doing. I can give a fairly good summation of what the weather was like and what the ocean was doing. Most of the rest of the experiences in my life are one confused memory.

I used to deliver the *Bronx Home News* in the summer of 1940. I was sixteen years old and making the grand total of $8.40 a week. I would hitchhike to Ridgefield Park, New Jersey, and take flying lessons in Piper Cubs on floats. We flew off the Hackensack River. Then I got a job with the New York Central Railroad putting timetables on the trains when I was seventeen. I did that until my eighteenth birthday, when I went into the Navy. I took the physical and mental tests when I was seventeen, and they held me in abeyance until I hit my eighteenth birthday in July 1942. The change the Navy made, which was helpful to people like me, was that in May of 1942 they lowered the requirements from two years of college to a high school education. The Navy's pilot losses had been unexpectedly high. That opened the door for me.

In September they sent me to Syracuse University under a program they called Civilian Pilot Training. The Navy paid your room and board and taught you how to fly. Then, in January 1943, I was sent to preflight school at Chapel Hill, North Carolina. If you've seen the movie, *An Officer and a Gentleman*, you've seen what preflight is about. They did everything possible, physically and mentally, to get you to quit. Pressure upon pressure; push, push, hoping you would break. That was one thing the Navy did and still does, to my knowledge, during training. They put incredible pressure on you, and if you survive that training experience, you will probably survive in combat. At least you won't break down. That was the purpose of that kind of training, and I think it worked. In all the time I flew in the Navy during World War II, I never met, or ever heard of, any pilot who ever said, "I've had enough. I'm not going to fly anymore." In truth, we often sat around the Officer's Club on Saipan and devised comic ways to get out of the war. One of the group declared he would see the psychiatrist, who would ask, "Is there anything wrong with you?" and the pilot would say, "No, everything is fine," while urinating in his pants. What ingenious things we planned! We would fly to Vladivostock, land, and be there the rest of the war. Then, after all that talk we would go out and fly our usual missions.

Things were thrust on you. I was a naval officer, an ensign at nineteen, a lieutenant junior grade at twenty, and got a field promotion to full lieutenant at twenty-one. When I was twenty-one I was squadron operations officer, third in command of 150 men. It wasn't considered that big a deal at the time. I never thought anything of it.

★

When I arrived at Chapel Hill preflight school they lined us up and asked if there were any 135-pounders in the group. Two of us raised our hands, and we were instantly put on the boxing team. After boxing three hours a day for three months, I was 152 pounds of very mean cadet. After preflight we went to Squantum Naval Air Station near Boston, where we took our primary flight training. We flew the N3N, the famous "Yellow Peril." It was an absolutely marvelous airplane, the slightly bigger brother to the Stearman. It could do anything in the book, and nothing will ever be as much fun as flying biplanes. The old-timers who were at Squantum told us that Boston night life was similar to Rome's under Nero. They were right. In three weeks I was, again, a 135-pound weakling.

I left Squantum in July 1943 to go to Pensacola. We flew the Vultee Valiant, also known as the Vultee Vibrator. Three weeks in them and then on to Whiting Field to learn instrument flying under the hood in SNJs. At Whiting we got to choose the kind of plane we wanted to fly with the fleet. Fighters, of course, were the most desirable, and I always thought of myself as a single-engine type. However, I chose multi-engine patrol planes. We heard all the news from Barin Field where they trained fighter pilots. It was called "Bloody Barin," and the rumor was that every afternoon they scraped bodies off the runway. I was just nineteen, but for some reason I had enough maturity to realize I would prefer to live through the war. It may have been a life-saving choice. Also, I was familiar with float planes, and I had enjoyed that type of flying immensely.

One thing certain about choosing patrol planes was that you got them. Everybody wanted fighter planes, and the Navy usually got its patrol pilots from the rolls of excess fighter pilot applicants. Anyone foolish enough to sign up for flying boats was welcomed with open arms. We were sent to Bronson Field, where we flew the PBY. I spent the next 288 hours I was in the air flying that crate. I'm sure you've heard the same stories I have—the PBY was the backbone of the fleet during World War II, it was an intrepid and rugged plane, etc., etc., and the truth of the matter is that the PBY was a bomb. The really useful thing about it was the consistency of its air speed. It would climb at 90, glide at 90, and cruise at 90. Actually, to be truthful, cruise speed was 103, but that's close to 90. If anyone has political ambitions, he should locate the flack who created and perpetuated the PBY myth. His career would be made.

We soon discovered the airplane to be slow, lumbering, noisy, and uncomfortable. The low interior caused us to walk in a perpetual stoop. Two million years from now, an archaeologist will excavate the bones of difficult-to-catalog beings with apelike postures. Ex-PBY pilots.

We flew PBYs for three months, and I received my wings on November 2, 1943. At graduation, an admiral asked how old I was. I said, "Nineteen, sir." He looked at me and said, "Wgrumph." I took this as a compliment because how many nineteen-year-old ensigns get a "wgrumph" from an admiral?

Then I was sent to Jacksonville Naval Air Station for operational training. We flew PBYs for three more months and would take turns being plane commander, first pilot, and second pilot-navigator. Then I got a break. I was sent to Norfolk for fleet assignment. Some guys went to the Pacific Fleet, some went to the Atlantic. You had no choice and no idea where you were going to be sent. For some unknown reason, two of us stayed at Norfolk, flying antisubmarine patrols with VP-214. Our job was to go out and escort convoys or to find specific targets that had been seen by other aircraft or ships. We would now be flying the PBM, the Martin Mariner, and it was the difference between night and day. The first night we got to Norfolk, Hal Russell and I walked over to the hangars and gazed at our first living PBM. It was absolutely the most beautiful airplane I'd ever seen. It had a big, deep hull and graceful gull wings. Long after the war, I reverently showed my wife a photograph of a PBM. She looked at it and said, "Its mother must have loved it." Furious, I tore the picture from her hand and looked again. She was right. But how can you tell anything to a teenager in love, especially with an airplane?

I started flying with VP-214 on March 1, 1944, and that was the most boring flying in the world. Long, dreary flights. We'd take off at three o'clock in the morning, and Norfolk is just as cold as New York at that hour. There were twelve men in the crew, three pilots and nine enlisted men. Two pilots were always in the sack. Same with the enlisted men; four would be on duty and the rest sleeping. We'd fly out two or three hundred miles and pick up a convoy, and then stay with them for nine or ten hours. We would fly at 1,500 feet and make an hourglass pattern over the convoy area. The plane was on automatic pilot, and you would simply twist the dials to make your turns. Your job was to look. We never saw any submarines, but I think the fact that we were there kept the subs down. Some of our flights were 13 hours long, none less than 9. Just reviewing those flights in my log book still causes my eyes to close.

I did that until September, and then the squadron was transferred to Guantanamo Bay, Cuba. We flew more boring antisubmarine patrols. About October 1, six of us volunteered to go to Corpus Christi, Texas, to act as PBM instructors. I arrived in Corpus Christi only to discover that they did not want ensigns as instructors. Two of us were ensigns, and they told us we would be transferred to the Pacific. That wasn't exactly what I had in mind. In 1944, Atlantic Fleet duty might be boring, but they were shooting at people in the Pacific.

At that point the Navy lost us. Ensigns Huddleston and Quinn were transferred from the Training Command to Operational Command, and one let us go and the other never picked us up. Happily, we still got our checks from the same source. Two months went by and we religiously checked the board twice a week to see if we had been assigned. I think we'd still be there if we hadn't shot our mouths off in the officer's club. Someone turned us in, and I was immediately assigned as a first pilot in an air-sea rescue crew.

We trained our heads off in PBM-5s. I went out to the Pacific in June of 1945 and joined VH-3, which was stationed at Okinawa. That was great flying because there was always something going on. Never a dull moment. We'd be picking up guys who had gone down in the ocean, and that was exciting work. Completely different from patrol flying, especially when you were flying over Japan or enemy-held islands. Landing and taking off in the ocean is always difficult. In order to pick somebody up, you had to cut the engines. You never knew if the engines were going to start again, and we had heard prisoner-treatment stories coming out of Japan. After the war, I was working in Troy, New York, where I met a professor who was teaching at Rensselaer Polytech. He was a visiting professor from Japan and had been educated in this country before the war. During the war his job, in Japan, was to interrogate American pilot prisoners. He said it was hard for him because he knew that during the last part of the war, prisoners were often beheaded.*

I recall seeing Japan for the first time from 1,500 feet and it did look menacing. We had a little toehold in this tremendous Japanese-controlled area. I was on the first plane to actually make an air-sea

---

*Ed. note: American prisoners were beheaded throughout the war.

rescue in Japan itself. We landed in Kobe Bay, which was like landing under the George Washington Bridge in New York. Earlier we rendezvoused with the Third or Fifth fleet, I don't remember which, and we were circling the area. Sixteen Corsairs approached us, and since we were observing radio silence, they indicated with hand gestures that we should follow them. When sixteen Corsairs suggest you follow them, you do it. We had no idea where they wanted us to go. We followed them toward Japan, and they were on top of us and under us, just like a blanket. We flew right to the Inland Sea, and they gestured that one of their men was in the water, in a raft, right in the middle of the bay. Every time a Japanese boat came out to pick him up, a couple of Corsairs came down and shot the hell out of it. We landed and cut the engines. On our landing approach, we could see people walking on the Kobe waterfront. We did not spend a great deal of time on the water. Of course, our prayers were that the engines would start again because they were very tired engines. We got them going, took off, and were at about 900 feet when I saw from my side of the airplane that a Val, a type of Japanese dive bomber, was making a run on us. All kinds of shouts for help were made over the radio, and our escorts came and shot that fellow down. Then, on open mike, they congratulated us on doing a wonderful job and told us that they had to return to the fleet. They wished us good luck on our trip back to Okinawa, which was about 500 miles away. We had to hug the coast of Japan, and the Japanese-held islands, at about 800 feet. We landed at about 9:30 at night at Okinawa.

I knew the war had to be close to being over because any sort of Japanese military plane could have shot us down. The Japanese knew we would eventually invade the homeland, and they were stockpiling their remaining first-line planes for the big day. I assume they didn't think we were worth going after. At any rate, they didn't get us, and back we came. When we returned, the base at Okinawa had given us up for lost, and since they had no idea where we had been, they refused to believe us when we told them what we had done. Then, everybody got on the bandwagon. In fact, the operations officer claimed that he had ordered us to go on the mission.

At Okinawa, there was always an awareness that you were in a war, which I had never had prior to that. It was 24 hours of being alert. At Kerama Retto, a group of small Japanese islands near Okinawa, the Japanese had an interesting habit of swimming out to moored aircraft and dropping in a hand grenade while you slept. Every night, one of the copilots and three enlisted men stayed on the airplane. We always had an especially alert guy sit on the wing with a machine gun. After Kerama Retto, we were transferred to a large seaplane tender, the *Pine Island*, which was stationed in Chimu Wan off Okinawa. The planes would be moored around the ship and routine maintenance was done by mechanics in boats at night using flashlights. Major maintenance, engine changes and so forth, would be done right on the deck of the tender after lifting the planes out of the water by crane. Most of the routine work was just to get the engines turning the next day. No one paid the slightest bit of attention to ordnance. If you tilted the machine guns, rusty water would come out of the gun barrels. Just get the engines going so you could go out and pick guys up. That was our job.

We always had escorts when we were on our missions. We preferred Marine or Navy escorts because they would fly tightly around us. If we had an Army Air Forces escort, we would usually see them as dots at twelve or fourteen thousand feet as we were flying along at fifteen hundred. We did not appreciate that.

One time we had a particularly sad experience. We were flying off Sasebo, a seaport in the southern part of Japan. Every operational pilot knew each day where the air-sea rescue plane would be flying at a particular time, and we were called by a B-25 that was shot up. He got in touch with us, verbally, and told us he was coming into our sector. He had only one engine running and couldn't make it much further. We calmed him down and said, "Hey, listen, don't worry. We'll get there and pick you up. Relax." We asked him where he was and he told us. We never heard from him again. We spent over three hours combing every inch of that sector and never found a trace of the plane. It was very disheartening to know that there was somebody that close and you couldn't help him.

But we saved far more than we lost. Our executive officer, Jim Blumenstock, a former All-American football player at Fordham before the war, landed off Kikai in the open sea. Kikai was a small Japanese-held island, about 150 miles north of Okinawa. When you land in the open sea, especially if it's rough, it's like landing on concrete. It jars the fillings out of your teeth. The water was so rough that when he hit, the engines broke loose from their mounts and tilted down. With his engines in that position, he couldn't take off, so he picked up the pilot and proceeded to taxi his PBM back to Okinawa. There was a ceremony a few days later and he was pronounced the "PBM Taxi-Champ." They had to junk the plane, but he got back. That was the capability of that airplane. Just marvelous.

In July of 1945, a typhoon came up and hit Okinawa. Just prior to the storm we flew our PBMs to Saipan so they wouldn't get damaged. There was such a crowd of planes and crews from all over the Pacific arriving at the island to avoid the storm that they ran out of room at the seaplane base and sent us to Marpi Point, a fighter base. The next day I went out to watch the fighters land and take off, but no flying was evident. I wandered into the operations tent and was told by the duty officer that there had been a party the night before and nobody felt much like flying that morning.

Suddenly, I had what could best be described as a Grinchlike thought. I knew the engine on a Hellcat was the same as on the PBM, and therefore I knew the power settings. I said to the guy, "Would you mind if I flew one?" He asked if I had flown one before. I said, "Sure, I flew one at Corpus." This was, of course, a lie. He said, "Well, I guess there's nothing wrong with that. I'll give you number seventeen. It doesn't have a radio, but the tower will give you a green light for takeoff." I said, "Fine, I have no problem with that." He drove me out to the plane in a jeep. I said, "It's been several months since I've flown one of these, will you check me out on starting the thing?" I got in the cockpit, and he showed me how to start it. Then he drove off, I taxied out for takeoff, got the green light, and poured on the coal. Before I know it, I'm at 400 feet and accelerating. I put the gear up and flew out to sea. I'm doing 165 knots and can't believe the speed. I was sure blood was pouring from my nostrils. I was in seventh heaven flying that thing around. After about an hour I decided to come back and land, go back to the base and tell everybody about it, and come back and fly again in the afternoon.

I opened the cowl flaps, put my flaps down, put the gear down, made my approach, and got a red light from the tower. Now, since I didn't have a radio, I said to myself, "Maybe my approach was bad." I put everything up, circled around and came in a little higher and wider, but got another red light. Again, I think, "What's wrong? Maybe there's an admiral coming in." So, I put everything up again and went out and flew around for a while, came in and did everything again, red light. Now, I see an ambulance coming down the runway and there are a lot of guys running around.

I decided that the only possibility was that my gear wasn't locked, although the indicator on the panel said it was. I knew there was a hand pump down to my left, but I had the shoulder harness on and didn't know how to release it. We didn't wear shoulder straps in a PBM, just seat belts. I strained forward and got hold of the thing and managed to give it four pumps. The next thing I know, there's another Hellcat flying wing on me and the pilot's making all sorts of gestures, none of which I understood. I follow him in and I land, a good landing, incidentally. I got out of the plane and found out that I had a hydraulic problem and the gear had dropped, but not locked. I looked like a wasp trailing my gear on each approach. Those four cranks on the pump locked them in place.

That was my first and last flight in a fighter. The word was passed around that they had let a patrol pilot fly a fighter. It was sad, because I would have loved to fly that plane that afternoon. I didn't have any problems of my own making, so I think it proved that a patrol pilot could handle a Hellcat. I forget who it was but some famous pilot said, "A man wearing gold wings can fly anything." That's the way we felt. I would have put any World War II Navy pilot against any RAF, Luftwaffe, or Japanese pilot. There is no question that Germany turned out some superb pilots, as did England and Japan, but man for man, Navy pilots were exceptionally well trained, and I think the best of the bunch.

Life was crowded on the *Pine Island*, but it wasn't uncomfortable. We had a ship's newspaper, actually two mimeographed sheets, and on August 6 a special edition told us that a new bomb had been dropped on Hiroshima with the power of 20,000 tons of TNT. We all knew they had made a mistake, by several zeros, at least. Later that night, however, they issued gas masks to all of us because they expected the Japanese to come down that night and drop gas bombs on us. Nothing happened, but we didn't sleep much that night. On August 8 we were covering an air strike against Shanghai, and on the way back we were diverted over the southern coast of Japan because of a report of a downed pilot. Late in the afternoon we were just off Nagasaki, and since we were only flying at about 1,500 feet, we got a good look at the city. I remember thinking what a lovely city it was. The next day it was gone.

Even when the European war was over, I thought it would go on in the Pacific for at least several more years. I never thought about what I was going to do after the war. I thought Roosevelt was going to be president forever. You were locked into the present—your next assignment, what squadron you might go into—never into the future.

And then it did end. It ended with the speed of light, and we didn't know what hit us. They surrendered, and the next day we were on our way out of Okinawa. It was astonishing how fast it all wound down.

★

In the summer of 1946 I got a job as a pilot for Long Island Airlines. We flew Grumman Widgeons, twin-engine amphibians, with one pilot and five passengers. One passenger sat in the copilot's seat, and we made five round-trips a day between the Hamptons and Twenty-third Street and the East River in Manhattan. I did that all summer, and then I went to Florida and flew more Widgeons for Sarasota Flying Service. I was in Havana in September, and I flew back on a Pan Am DC-3. Almost immediately after takeoff, the pilot came back to go to the john or something, and I introduced myself. I'd never been in the cockpit of a DC-3, and I asked him if I could come up and take a look. He said, "Sure, come on up." When I got up there he said, "Get in the left seat." I flew that Pan Am flight back to Miami and then I surrendered the seat and he landed the plane. He said, "Why don't you get a job with Pan Am?" I said, "Why not?" He took me in to personnel, and I told them I was a plane commander, twenty-one years old, with a green card. That meant I had very advanced instrument training and 1,000 hours of multi-engine time. They greeted me with various secret Pan Am handclasps and embraces. There I was, practically hired as a Pan Am pilot, which delighted me. Then, I went in to fill out the paperwork with the personnel guy and he said, "You're a college graduate, aren't you?" I said, "No, I've never spent a day in college." Even though they were desperately looking for pilots, you had to have at least two years of college before Pan Am would hire you. That was the beginning and end of my career with Pan Am.

I started at Columbia in February of 1947, and after graduation I received a faculty fellowship at Colgate University. I went there for a year and then spent three years at Albany Law School. I practiced law in Troy, New York, for about one and a half years and then was appointed an assistant attorney general of New York state. I did that for three years and resigned to join a law firm in New York that specialized in aviation law. We were all pilot-lawyers, ex-service men. Did that for five years and then, with one of my partners, founded a business, the Airways Club, which was sort of an AAA for airline passengers. We sold our shares in 1966, and I went into private practice, where I remain today. Incidentally, that company we started is now called the Airline Passengers Association.

I joined the Naval Reserve right after the war and stayed in until 1969. In the very beginning in 1946, reserve flying was haphazard. You'd fly on Saturday afternoon at three, or something like that. That all changed, and it became a very well-run outfit. I was very flexible, being a lawyer with my own practice, and the Navy knew they could call me up at any time. I was always ready to go.

I became commanding officer of VR-834, a reserve transport squadron, in July of 1965. That was the month President Johnson radically increased the number of military personnel in Vietnam. They didn't have the supplies to sustain those fellows, so each naval air station that had C-118s (a Navy version of the DC-6) had to supply one reserve crew and one plane per month to fly 15,000 pounds of cargo out to Vietnam and bring seventy-five people back. It was fascinating to be back in a war zone. I was interested in the Vietnam War and wanted to see it for myself. But not in a hawkish way. I thought it was an absurd and ridiculous war, and still do. But I wanted to get a feel for it, and it was my job. I didn't duck it. My friends told me I was crazy, and when I was making those landings at Da Nang I would ask myself, what is a forty-two-year-old lawyer doing flying to Vietnam during the height of a war? Why don't I stay in New York where I belong? But the next time it came up I volunteered again.

I've got one son who is an ex-Navy pilot and a Piedmont Airlines captain, and another son who is a lawyer. Awhile back my daughter Martha went to Tokyo to do some promotion work for MTV. She asked me if I'd ever been to Osaka. She knew I'd been to Japan. The only time I'd seen Osaka it was burning, and Tokyo was almost completely destroyed. I told her, "Just don't tell them what your father did for a living in World War II."

TARGET GERMANY

At first it was twenty-five missions. With 10 percent or more of the bombers being shot down on the raids over Germany, it was more than flesh and blood could stand without a final goal at which, maybe, you could come home. A man must be given some hope of survival, the generals reasoned. Later, as fighter cover became available and the Germans weakened a little, it became thirty, then thirty-three. That was the Eighth Air Force, from English bases. From Africa and the southern flank of the Axis, it was fifty.

The British went by night in their big bombers, Lancasters, Halifaxes, and Stirlings, and by day the Americans followed them in armadas of four-engine B-17s and B-24s. This was the centerpiece of the air war in Europe, constantly increasing in fury and in the havoc it wrought on the cities and people of Germany—even though, until toward the end, it did not seem to slow down enemy war production. Other bombing campaigns sought changing enemy targets in Italy or German-held Eastern Europe, or followed the Allied armies, but the steady mass flights from England were almost a grotesque imitation of the peacetime commuter taking his daily train from his suburban home to his city job. Same route (more or less), same comfortable base (more or less), a long vacation or even retirement glimmering in the future (maybe less than more)—a very different war than that conducted from the ever-moving aircraft carriers and airfields of the Pacific, where nothing stayed the same.

To have done these things and survived is something no man can ever put behind him.

A B-17F, "Martha 2nd," after returning to base at Essex, England, from a mission, December 15, 1943. National Air and Space Museum, Smithsonian Institution.

KENNETH CARLSON

BORROWED TIME

A retired New York businessman, now youth advocate, Ken Carlson spends a great deal of time at the Asphalt Green, a center for disadvantaged children located in Manhattan. A man of dedication, Carlson is helping save youngsters who are running out of hope.

During the war he served as a navigator on a B-24 Liberator based near Norwich, England. He seldom speaks of the one mission he missed in April 1944. Carlson had been severely wounded and was in the hospital when told the rest of his crew had perished in the flak-filled skies over Germany. The memory of those young men is always with him.

Some of my other memories are sort of mixed, but I'll never forget anything about our first mission over Germany in the "lucky" *Judith Lynn*. Getting up at 2:00 A.M., having breakfast, then going down to be briefed. Listening to an intelligence officer tell us where we would get antiaircraft fire and where we were going to pick up fighters, it seemed unreal. It was like something out of the movies, except there I was. I had a real feeling of detachment. The worst part of any mission was waiting to see if you were really going to fly that day. It was the middle of the winter and the weather was usually bad. We sat in the airplane, waiting, for what seemed like hours, and then we were going. Heading down the runway, one after another, meeting above the clouds and forming a squadron. It worked so well we couldn't believe it. Here we were with hundreds and hundreds of airplanes, all in formation, heading for Germany.

The first time I saw an airplane shot down was another thing I won't forget. It looked—again—distant, unreal. A fighter was just

Kenneth Carlson, standing, far right, was responsible for the whimsical name of his crew's B-24 Liberator. Standing, from left to right, are Lieutenants Frank Caldwell, bombardier; Thad Johnson, copilot; Joe Roznos, pilot; and Carlson. Kneeling, left to right, are sergeants Charles Waldmann, Hal McNew, Ed Miller, Frank Dinkins, Corporal Cleo Pursifull and Sergeant John Rose. Radio operator Sergeant Henry Vogelstein replaced Pursifull on the final mission, April 1, 1944.

falling with a slight trail of smoke. A parachute came out, and the plane continued down. There was no sense of feeling or sound. Once again, it was as if I was at the movies, not really seeing the real thing. We were almost over the target when all of a sudden we saw these black puffs, which were, of course, flak. But it really wasn't that close, and we made our bomb run and nothing really interfered with us. We had a fighter attack coming back, but that also was much easier than I thought it would be. The first fighters I saw coming after us looked a lot different than I expected. You knew from the flash cards what they were supposed to look like and how fast they were going to come in. But when you actually had a gun in your hands, they were coming so fast you didn't have time to be scared. The first fighter that came in blew up and I thought I got it, but it wasn't me. It was the turret gunner on top of the plane. I probably didn't come near it because I had a handgun. They would come in as a rule—when I was there—from twelve o'clock [dead ahead] on, and they would fly as close to the formation as they could to break us up. Our fighters would give us good cover, but at that time the P-47s and P-38s couldn't go with us all the way to the target.

There wasn't any real fear on that first mission, just a long day. We came back, landed, and each of us was now one of the boys. We were able to hold our own in our Quonset hut full of veterans. After you came back, you had your debriefing and you'd find out if you were flying the next day. If you weren't, you'd be in a jeep and heading for Norwich as fast as you could get there. We'd go in a pub, mix with the RAF, the free Poles, drink beer, listen to the piano, and play darts. I think that's the real reason the war was so unreal for me. If you made it back, two hours after you'd finished fighting a war, being shot at, dropping bombs, you were back in England getting drunk as a skunk if you felt like it. Singing and having a good time, knowing that you weren't going to have to fly the next day. We never discussed the war. Once we were over there and in combat, the only things we discussed between ourselves and other crews were things that might be useful in the air. How the Germans attacked, where they would come from, how to handle a plane if it was crippled.

It was so different from what I had expected to do during the war. I wanted to get into a fighter plane and kill Japs. I was listening to the Giants football game on the radio when I heard about Pearl Harbor, and I decided to enlist the next day. I'd never been in a plane, didn't know what it felt like to fly, but I had read so much about Lindbergh, about Billy Mitchell, about the airplane. My father took me out to see Lindbergh take off in the *Spirit of St. Louis,* and that really made an impression on me. I knew there was no question that if we wanted to win the war, we were going to have to do it with airplanes.

When I got to Nashville to be classified, I thought they were going to make me a fighter pilot the next day. They gave us a battery of tests, and although I qualified to be a pilot and I wanted to be a pilot, they needed navigators. I didn't have the slightest idea of what that was. What I did know was that I was going to be in a bomber, not a fighter plane. Navigators flew in bombers. The only bomber I knew about was the B-17, the Flying Fortress. I didn't know what a B-24, or Liberator, was. I enlisted to be in a fighter plane, to control my own destiny. To be an ace and shoot down the bad guys, who were Japs. And here we were, seven months later, lumbering along in a big tank of a B-24 at less than 200 miles an hour, loaded down with fuel and bombs, bombing German cities for eight or ten hours. Add to that it's 40 degrees below zero and people are shooting at you. That's not what I had in mind December 7, 1941. You do that once, and come back—that should be enough of an experience for anyone. But you had to come back and do it the next time, and maybe 5 percent or 10 percent of the planes went down on each mission, and you didn't have to be a mathematical genius to figure out your chances of making your full twenty-five missions.

When we left West Palm Beach, Florida, in 1943, we still thought we'd be bombing Japan. Our first checkpoint was Port of Spain in Trinidad. We weren't supposed to read the orders until we were airborne, but Joe had opened them by the time we were going down the taxi strip. The orders said we were to report to the Eighth Air Force in England. I think that most of us were disappointed. We had bought knives and machetes, and we were on our way to get Japanese. The fact that we were going to England changed our discussions at night, and we had to rethink what we were doing and who we were fighting.

It took us 45 days to get to England. We flew from Trinidad to Guiana and from there to Brazil, then to Africa, and finally to Scotland. They had been having heavy rains in Africa and Dakar was one of the stops. They had steel-mesh runways which had sunk into the mud and they couldn't do much about it. The planes had to wait until they could get the runways fixed, so we spent some time in the different places on the way over. We saw things which none of us had ever seen before. For instance, the tremendous poverty in South America and Africa and the terrible shock of young kids, ten or twelve years of age, pimping their sisters who weren't much older. I came from New York and I'd been working for Household Finance as a loan investigator and bill collector in poor neighborhoods. I'd seen a lot more than some of the other guys, but I'd never seen anything like that. When we finally got to Dakar, they took our passes away. They didn't want us to go into the city itself, but we found a way to get off the base. I think the thing I remember most about Dakar was the absolute filth of the people walking down the streets. They would go to the "bathroom" on the streets in front of anybody, anywhere, anytime. All of this just seemed to be beyond anything a bunch of young guys from the United States had expected to see.

We flew from Dakar, French West Africa, across the Atlas Mountains into Marrakech, Morocco. By this time I had started to like the B-24 for a number of reasons. Foremost was the fact that I didn't get sick. When I was training, in smaller planes, I was always sick to my stomach from bouncing around in the air. But, from the first time I got into a B-24, I was never sick again. The other reason was that it was easier to navigate in the bigger plane. It felt more comfortable and stable.

Of course, when we got to Marrakech we headed out to see the Casbah. We'd wrap ourselves up in sheets so we could explore the real native habitat. I had bought some solid ivory bracelets in Dakar from somebody who assured me that they came from an old elephant tusk. I was looking at some silver bracelets in the Casbah and this guy looked at my ivory and said they weren't real. I told that Arab that he didn't know what he was talking about. Of course they were real, they were made from an old elephant tusk. He asked me if he could light a match to them. I told him, "Of course." He did, and those solid ivory bracelets went up in flames. It turned out they were some kind of Japanese cellulose.

We knew we were getting closer to combat and we were getting reports all the time about how many planes the Eighth Air Force was losing over Germany. We knew the days were getting numbered, but we were also learning how to fly together as a team. There wasn't anything we couldn't do in that airplane and we felt very comfortable about that. We arrived in Prestwick, Scotland, and the weather was bad. They put us in a holding pattern, and we were concerned about the amount of gas we had. A plane that came in before us ran out of gas on the approach and crashed, but we landed without a problem. I believe everybody on that other ship was killed. One navigator made an error in plotting the course and his plane came in right over the coast of France. They were shot down and had to ditch in the English Channel before they ever arrived. The crew were all saved, but the plane was lost.

We were assigned to the 93rd Bomb Group, which was located near a little town called Hardwick. This was in the East Anglia section of England, just south of Norwich. The four of us, the officers, were put in with three other crews in a Quonset hut. They were already operational so we would hear the horror stories and try to imagine what it must be like. We were the new kids beginning to learn this business. They took Joe Roznos, our pilot, a terrific guy from Hollywood, and put him with other crews to fly as a copilot on training flights. This way, he could become familiar with the tremendous number of air bases that were in that part of England. They did the same with the rest of us so we'd know what to look for and how the group operated. Then they put us back together as a crew, and we flew training flights on our own. The ten of us got along together extremely well.

When we arrived in England, they took our plane away from us and gave her to a crew that was already flying in combat. I had named the plane *Myrtle the Fertile Turtle* before we left the States, and that was probably the biggest disappointment that we could have had, other than being split up ourselves. I think they had misled us into believing that airplane would be ours. We all felt we would make it together, all of us, including the plane, or none of us would make it. What we didn't know was that we were losing the war at that time. Every time our planes went over Germany, we were losing an awful lot of them. *Myrtle* was a brand-new plane and had a nose turret. They wanted to give her to a crew that had already flown a number of missions so they would be as effective as possible. It would be impossible for them to leave that airplane on the ground while we went through indoctrination training. That's what happened to all the replacement crews that went over. What we got to replace *Myrtle* was an old, beat-up airplane that didn't have a nose turret, just flexible guns in the nose. However, it had survived many early raids and the crew who flew her had made it and gone home. Therefore, it was considered a good plane. That was the one we flew, the *Judith Lynn*.

I won't go through the individual missions. However, we did make the first three over Berlin in March of 1944. Those were very important to us because everybody wanted to go to Berlin. We felt that once we got to Berlin, the war was going to turn in our favor. On the first raid we went straight in over the Zuider Zee and straight out. That raid was called "Bloody Monday." The papers reported that we lost over sixty airplanes. We actually lost more than that because a lot of them were crippled and were damaged when they landed.* There were so many enemy fighters, so much flak, but we really did a good job. Everywhere you looked, Berlin was on fire. Everywhere. I think it was reported afterwards that after those three raids we established

Ed. note: Sixty-nine of 658 attacking aircraft were lost.

dominance of the air. After that, it was only a matter of time before we would be able to land our troops in Europe.

On our eighth mission we flew to a town called Friedrichshafen, which was on the Swiss border. Our target was a secret rocket or jet plant, and we received more fighter opposition than I'd ever seen before. It might not have been more, actually, but they were more effective while we were going in. The Germans were all over us. The flak was also more accurate than I had seen it before. We came up to the target and were able to make our run. Just as we dropped the bombs, I felt as if somebody had hit me with a sledgehammer. I didn't even know where I'd been hit. I just felt numb, no pain. There were big black pockets of flak all around the plane and we were bouncing all over the sky. I looked down and it was my right forearm, or what was left of it. It was hanging by one bone. I was wearing a heated flying suit and the piece of flak had taken out part of the arm, wires and all. It was just sort of missing. There was blood, but no big gushing stream. I held my arm and announced to Joe that I'd been hit and when there was an opportunity, it would be appreciated if somebody could come down and put a tourniquet on my arm. One member of the crew came down with his portable oxygen bottle, took one look and fainted. Then "Dink," the engineer, came down and he put the tourniquet on my arm and wrapped up what was left of it and put me in one of those big fur flying suits to keep me warm. He stayed with me most of the time while I endeavored to locate where we were. We had been hit in a number of places and the plane was now on fire. By this time, we'd also dropped out of formation, and were lagging behind the squadron. Many disabled planes force-landed in Switzerland.

The arm was no problem on the way back. I was able to find out where we were and Joe flew that airplane back with one engine out. The fire extinguished itself somewhere along the way. We shot the red flare which meant, "We've got wounded aboard," and got clearance to come right in. We lost a second engine on the approach and after we landed they counted over 150 holes in that airplane.

That was the end of my flying career. I was taken to the hospital, not really expecting my arm to be part of me when I woke up, but they operated on me and patched it back together. They told me I was in the operating room for eight hours and unconscious for over 72 hours from an overdose of pentathol. The nerve was sutured and the doctors told me there was always the possibility it would regenerate. Within five years, after constantly working with them, the full use of my right arm and hand came back. In 1970, I was having a problem with my hand. I went back to the doctor who had been taking care of me for years and he thought it might be the result of the war wound.

He sent me to the best orthopedic man in New York. When I got there, it turned out to be nothing more than contractions that happen to some people as they grow older, but the doctor, Dr. Theodore Himelstein, was the same doctor who set the bones and sutured that nerve in England. We couldn't believe it, but sure enough, he was the orthopedic-neurological guy who put me back together with the possibility that my arm would come back. Every single day he was faced with people who had horrible wounds. An amazing man.*

Anyway, they put me in the hospital and everybody was feeling sorry for me. My crew came to visit me and Joe brought the piece of flak that hit my arm. He found it buried in the instrument panel that was behind me in the plane. He knew it was the piece because it had blood and wires of the electric flying suit caught in it. Then my crew got a leave to London because the plane was so shot up. It was in bad shape and so were they. Their next mission was to Ludwigshafen in April 1944. They took a direct hit right in the gas tank and the men who were flying next to them reported that the plane blew up in hundreds of pieces—like the shuttle did on my sixty-fifth birthday. Only two 'chutes were seen coming out of the plane, and because of those 'chutes they were carried as "missing in action" for, I think, a year before they were declared officially dead. Their bodies were never found.

I was recovering in the hospital and of course nobody wanted to tell me. A group captain finally came to tell me what had happened to them. There's always been the feeling, would it have been different if I had been navigating that airplane? They didn't even have a navigator on that mission. There wasn't a spare so they had to fly without one. But, once you wash that out, these are questions that aren't worth asking anymore because there is no way you can go back and relive them. It was the roll of the dice, and that's why I've carried that piece of flak in my pocket for forty-five years.

I was in the hospital with over twenty people, all officers, in our ward. It was located in Lincoln, England, and there was a cross section of men in that ward. Second lieutenant or full colonel, it didn't matter, you were there. It was so morose and sad. Everybody was missing arms, legs, or testicles, or had holes in their stomachs, or head wounds, or third-degree burns. Depressing. You had to do something to laugh, so I organized what was called "Carlson's Raiders." Since we were officers, we were allowed, if we were ambulatory, to go occasionally into town and have some fun. I took this group of guys and made them do this and that and it worked. You

*Ed. note: Dr. Himelstein is interviewed in chapter 6 of this book.

couldn't just sit around and feel sorry for yourself. One guy, a B-17 pilot, had lost his left leg and he had nothing but a stump. I taught him how to ride a bicycle, and he could zip along with one leg like you never saw in your life. We'd have a few drinks at night and come back on our bicycles and he'd forget he had one leg and hop off the bike on the stump and open up the skin graft. There'd be hell to pay, but that was Carlson's Raiders, and we had a hell of a good time, in spite of what had happened to us.

I remember lying in the ward, when we heard a wonderful roar starting about midnight, June 5, 1944. It sounded like every airplane in the world was up in the air. We knew that was the beginning of the invasion of Europe, and when we looked up in the air in the morning, every conceivable type of airplane was flying back and forth. That day it was announced that our troops were landing in Normandy. Three days later I was sent back, in a hospital plane, to Mitchel Field, New York. When I came back people acted as if I had done something heroic. Family and friends were proud of the fact that I had been in the Eighth Air Force and that I had come back. But many people I was in rehabilitation with felt as I did. We hadn't done much. Not when you thought in terms of what you had gone through to become a navigator, bombardier, pilot, whatever. The horror that I had to live with for a long period of time, besides losing my crew, was all part of the same thing. We may have won the war, but I felt like I was a loser. In fact, I never talked about it for years. When I met my second wife I was able to talk about it, but up until that time I didn't feel there was anything to share with anybody. When I was shot we were still losing the war so somebody else won, I didn't. I think that's why I'm not interested in going to group reunions, that sort of thing. It's very difficult for people like myself who lost their crew to go back and relive those wonderful experiences that other people have who went through their twenty-five and came back and feel that they did accomplish what they set out to do.

I was sent to a convalescent home in Pawling, New York. The sponsor of the home was Lowell Thomas and he was a terrific guy. He would bring his softball team, "The Nine Old Men," and they would play our team, all of whom were disabled in some way. He flew in people like Colonel Stoopnagel, Gene Sarazen the golfer, all kinds of wonderful people. I played and I couldn't use my right arm. We had one-armed guys, one-legged guys, but again, it took our minds off what had happened to us.

After I was there for awhile, I was sent to learn how to be a navigation instructor. You couldn't just go and be an instructor, you had to go to an instructors' school. It was located in Monroe, Louisiana, and we had everything: lieutenants, captains, majors. We were all going to be instructors of one kind or another. The poor guy who had to teach us had never been overseas, and he was a captain. We had people who not only outranked him, but had been in combat. He would get up on the podium and start to say how the first thing you have to do is such-and-such. One side of the room would start to light matches and throw them up in the air and say, "Flak, flak!" The other guys would make paper airplanes and throw them at someone else and shout, "Here come the fighters!" It was absolute panic. How we ever got through the instructors' course, I'll never know. We never really learned a hell of a lot, but we were all assigned to bases in Texas. I went to San Marcos Air Force Base, which was near San Antonio.

Everybody wanted to know what it was really like in combat. That's the first thing they'd ask you. I don't think anybody could tell them. I sure couldn't. The only thing I could do which was really productive was to revise the tests that navigators took to eliminate the emphasis on celestial navigation. It's a wonderful thing to know, I needed it to get the airplane to South America, Africa, and up to Scotland, but after that, no. The people who were going to the Pacific didn't need it that much, either. What you needed more than anything else in one of those bombers was the ability to read instruments, know what those instruments were telling you, dead reckoning, things like that. You had to really know how to read a map; that was the most important thing for a navigator. You had to learn to figure fast and on the basis of things that were continually moving. Nothing stayed still. In a navigation training flight everything was great. Fly to the Grand Canyon and back again. You could take your time doing everything and it wasn't hard at all. You weren't dropping a thousand feet in turbulence, bouncing around in flak. Fighters weren't coming at you from every direction, going in and out of clouds, all of the things that really happened to you in combat. Many times you'd lose your bearings because your mind was on other things besides navigating the plane. There was no way to pick them up again unless you could read a map well.

I was discharged in September of 1945, and came back to New York City. I tried hard to get into an advertising agency, but I couldn't get a job. I only had one year at Cornell because my father died in 1939 and I had to go to work to help support my mother and grandmother. Agencies wanted college men, so I went back to Household Finance and got my old prewar job back. My boss told me how lucky I was. He also told me that I would have to adjust to lower pay and I wouldn't have that nice uniform with the wings on it. I'd have to start where ordinary people start. I worked there for awhile and ended up becoming the youngest manager in the company. At thirty years of age I became assistant to the president, in Chicago where the company's headquarters were located. Then, I decided to try, a second time, to do what I always wanted to do, advertising. I moved to New York, without a job, and three months later I was working at McCann-Erickson, now Interpublic, one of the largest international advertising agencies, with accounts like Exxon, Coca-Cola, Westinghouse, National Biscuit, and General Motors. We also handled Nelson Rockefeller's campaign for governor of New York—but that's another story.

I think the reason I gravitated to the advertising business was to learn about people and find out why they do certain things. How you motivate people. That's where I spent the rest of my business life, in advertising, public relations, and marketing, and I feel that I became successful at it. Selling any kind of product or service. I also learned that the "Truth Well Told"* can be the biggest lie in the world. Also that drugs had become a part of the entertainment industry and that I could hire *anybody* to write or say anything I wanted. That was in 1956!

The war experience helped me in the business world. As I said, I was always interested in people more than things. The war was the most intense way to find out, not what people say they're going to do, but what they will really do. Though I was scared many times during the war, I have never been afraid of anybody since. Things have happened to me that have been unfortunate, but I never had anybody tell me what to do and make it stick if I didn't believe it. We had a major client that was having trouble with its new brands. The guy I was dealing with was a bully and could get away with anything, even with the president of my agency. They introduced me to him, and I went back to our office and worked up some ideas. I brought the layouts over and presented them to him. He tore the ads up and threw them on the floor. "Take this junk out of here and get me something good." I closed the door and walked over to him. He was a big guy and I looked him in the eye and said, "Don't you ever do that again." From then on he acted like a gentleman. The point is, that there's a time, if you've been through certain things, when nobody is going to do something that compromises you. If you want to be the richest guy in the world, you're going to have a problem. But if you want to make a living, do what you want to do with your experiences, you don't have to be anybody else's man. That's what's good about my experiences in the war. As I look back on it now, it changed my whole life. It was worth the price of admission.

After McCann, I went to J. Walter Thompson, and in December

*Ed. note: McCann-Erickson's slogan.

of 1965 I started my own agency. We did quite well, in fact. We introduced BMW automobiles and motorcycles into this country in 1966. They hadn't been able to sell their cars here. We found out that there was already a reverse thinking about the war. It was behind us. There was a large group of young people who were on the way up. You only had to present the car as a great piece of machinery, German machinery, and it certainly was that. If you were driving a BMW, you were noticed. You would be saluted by someone driving another one. The guy I signed the contract with was a former German officer. I didn't know it at the time, I found out later that BMW made a lot of the parts for the advanced German rocket program.* When I went over to Germany to see him, he asked me where I was during the war. I told him that I was in a B-24 bombing Germany. He took me out to the edge of Munich and stopped at a park. He said, "This used to be Munich, but we had to bulldoze it over. This is what you did." I took out the piece of flak that I carry, showed it to him and asked, "Do you know what this is?" He said, "A piece of German 88." I said, "They took that out of my right arm and another just like it went in my crew's airplane while I was in the hospital and they're all dead." He looked at me and pointed to his ear. "You see this missing ear lobe? That was an American machine gun bullet." As we sat in the Regency Hotel in New York many times after that, he concluded that we should have been on the same side and gone after the Russians.

Some of the people who served in the war, at least the ones I've maintained any contact with, feel we lost the war we fought to win. It seems, as I get older, that whatever it was we were supposed to do, didn't get done. That's a frightening thought to live with, especially at sixty-eight years of age. That's why I got involved with dealing with young people.

In 1973 I bought an old boathouse in Camden, Maine, to keep it from being torn down. I discovered it was the oldest boathouse in America, registered it with the National Historic Trust, and named it "The American Boathouse." Since I sold my business I live up there six months of the year. There were a whole bunch of kids using and peddling pot, coke, and pills, and nobody was doing anything about it. The worst influence came from the wealthiest families who were just there for the summer. Their kids would come in with all kinds of money and expose the local kids to drugs. Here was this old boathouse and that was where they were hanging around, dealing drugs. I bought it and with the help of George Martens, another retired businessman, turned it into an outlet for youngsters. We cleaned up the park, helped the public library, ran restaurants and

*Ed. note: BMW also made aircraft engines, notably for the Folke-Wulf 190.

retail shops, put in a photographic and art studio, and supported a new Shakespeare company. I saw that you could make a change, but it was absolutely the most frustrating experience I've ever had and it still is today. If you measure results the way I measure business results, you never see them. You lose many more than you win. And you get the cooperation of very few people. Everybody talks about drug abuse in this country but few do anything about it. All the problems were up there in Camden. The school board was unaware that the kids were in the woods smoking pot in the morning instead of going to class. Unaware of why kids committed suicide, good kids. It was all there. I knew it. The kids knew it. The town didn't want to know.

I was a part-time lobsterman when up in Maine, and I took the kids out fishing. We built boats, fixed up old boats, and made lobster traps. There were trips out to the islands for survival weekends and some of them got involved with community service. I decided at one point to try and develop an interchange for inner-city kids from New York. The young people from Maine could bring their lobsters down to New York and market them. Their counterparts from New York could come up to Maine and see what life was in another environment, away from the pressures they face. That was over ten years ago, and the deeper I get into it, the more I believe in it—"learning by doing." I'm a lot younger dealing with these young people than I am dealing with people my own age. They're a hell of a lot more stimulating and more up to date than the people who are out playing golf every day of the year.

At one point I saw a television show about a priest who was working on 42nd Street. He was saving kids from prostitution, crime, and drugs, getting them off the streets. I thought to myself, "My God, I have to go down and take a look at what he's doing." I went down and met Father Ritter, got shown around, and ended up submitting an idea. I told him I'd come down and set up a messenger service. I started as a messenger boy for a bank after my father died. You have to start someplace. I said, "I'll teach these kids how to show up on time, how to develop good work habits. I'll buy them Adidas uniforms and find the clients and they'll walk and run all over New York." They sat on the idea for a year and then an outstanding young man who was on loan from Citibank, who happened to be white, and a dedicated young black man who was in charge of vocational training at Covenant House, which was Father Ritter's organization, called me in Maine and we got the program going in 1982. I told them to give me four typical young people and we started "Dove Messenger Service," which now has many clients and has processed hundreds of kids. We did it, and I'm in touch with those four original kids today.

We also started the "Eagle Squadron," after the first Eagle Squadron of volunteers who fought with England to save freedom before this country ever committed itself. When my father took me to the movies, it was easy to tell the bad guys from the good guys. The villains wore black hats. I don't think, if I were young today, that I could find a compelling reason to volunteer to fight for the freedom of America, because there are so many powerful Americans who don't have our best interests in mind. The bad guys aren't all Russian. There are a lot of them here and some of them are in pretty high places.

I show the kids my pictures from the war years. They're always interested in World War II and what it was really like flying in those planes. Each of those first four messengers had a number. They knew my number in the plane was number four. The pilot was one, copilot two, and the bombardier, three. They moved me to number five. The Old Navigator, that's what they call me. My whole pitch to kids is, you can be number one, but you can still be happy if you're two, three, or four. I wanted to be number one, I became number four.

It works. However, you have to be with them. You have to go fishing with them, run a restaurant with them, run a messenger service. You have to expand it. That's how I met Dr. George Murphy in 1977 and got involved with the Asphalt Green project here in New York City. I was working with the Ninth Police Precinct and the Boys Brotherhood Republic on the Lower East Side. The community affairs officer of Exxon, which had been a client when I was in advertising, told me about a quixotic doctor who had taken over an old asphalt plant in Manhattan and was trying to "grow grass" on it. I went to see him at Cornell Medical School where he taught pathology and fell in love with him. He was as persistent as I am. I helped arrange some of the corporate support, and today we have a fabulous facility for young people. Sports, photography, theater, art, and a communications center. You name it, it's there. We also took over the old fireboat pier and Mill Rock Island from New York City. The pier is near the Asphalt Green and the island is in the East River near Hell Gate. The fireboat house is used as an environmental center, and Mill Rock Island has become an outdoor training and activity center. The facilities are not enough, however. It is still a tremendous struggle to get kids to come and participate in a positive experience since drugs and AIDS have decreased our educational possibilities. It's a lot of work, a lot of fun, depressing sometimes, yes, but when they make it, it's worth the effort. Dr. Murphy died of cancer July 15, 1987, but the

Eagle Squadron is alive and the spirit that powers it will never die. His last words to me were "we must help youth learn by doing."

Recently I received a letter from one of those first four messengers. He lived with a relative who believed in killing goats and drinking their blood. Cults, drugs, pimps, homosexuality. I mean, this was the background. He lived in one neighborhood and never went anywhere else. They call it the Minnesota Strip, 42nd Street to 46th Street on Eighth Avenue. Peepshows, whores, that was his life. When I met him he couldn't even read a map. The first time he was sent to Central Park West, he didn't know how to get there from 42nd Street. He spent three hours running around Central Park and couldn't get through it. Well, he learned how to read and write well and was making it when he went back on drugs, stuck a pistol in some storekeeper's face, and went to jail. I remember him sitting in the lobby of my building at one point and I asked him, "Number One, are you going to make it?" He said, "I'm going to make it, Old Navigator." I went back up to Maine, and he didn't make it. He wrote me a letter from prison and it said, "Have you given up on me? I didn't make it." I wrote back and told him, "You didn't make it the first time, but you didn't tell me you were going to make it the first time. You just told me you were going to make it. Let's make it the second time." That's what we're working on now, the second time.

ROBERT GERAGHTY

A BIT OF A BUM

Robert Geraghty is a hard-nosed Irishman of the old school, a much-decorated, retired New York City police officer who still lives in his native Brooklyn. A New York cop gets to see a great many terrible things, yet nothing in that life has quite matched the day when, at nineteen, as ball-turret gunner of a B-17 bombing Germany, he had to bail out of his burning plane, or the eighteen months thereafter he spent in a German prisoner-of-war camp. It was a rather ghostly experience at a model airplane show in the peaceful precincts of Rockefeller Center Plaza, duly reported in the New York Times, *that led us to him.*

I work just about every Saturday at Rockefeller Center. I went there after I retired from the police force, and I've been there 15 years as an investigator. Most of the security people are ex-cops. One of the men that I work with told me that there was going to be a model airplane show outside in Rockefeller Center Plaza. He had seen the show the year before, and there had been a B-17 there. He told me that it was quite a model and that I should see it. So, sure enough, the next day was Saturday and I went out looking for it. There were a lot of models out there, but I couldn't miss it. It was pretty big, and I could see that it had a black "L" on a white triangle. That was the 381st Bomb Group, which was my group. The guy who built the airplane was there, and I asked him what the name on the nose was. I'd left my glasses back in the office. He said, "Hilda." Well, I'd never heard of a "Hilda" in our group, but I thought I'd take a picture of it all the same. I have a little Minox camera I take everywhere with me, and I bent down and tried to get close to frame the nose—and all of a sudden I see "Winsome Winn." My legs just turned to rubber. That was the name of my plane.

123

It was such a spooky feeling, and I thought maybe I was in a real twilight zone. All of a sudden I was thinking about things I had no control over, because that was the first time I had seen that name in forty years. For a minute it was only me and that model airplane out there. Everything else kind of faded away.

I asked the guy who built it why he chose that particular plane, and he told me he'd found a picture in a book and liked the way it looked. The *New York Times* heard about this and wrote it up. Simple as that. When you think of how many B-17s were built, how the hell he picked mine out of all those airplanes and I come looking for it! It was the damndest thing. My pilot's wife's name was Winnie, and when he was assigned to that plane, he had the name put on. One thing I do know, I never saw "Hilda" on that airplane and nobody saw her in one piece after me, because I saw it crash into a German hillside.

We'd only flown ten missions when we were shot down. Our number one and two engines were gone and we were on fire. There was a sheet of flame coming out of a hole in the wing all the way back to the tail. A couple of times the flames would come back and just bathe my turret. At one point my ammunition started to explode because of the heat. The pilot came on the intercom and told us to prepare to bail out. After that, something must have gone wrong because I never heard the command to bail out. The next thing I know, I'm sitting down there in my turret and the pilot, copilot, and navigator come out of the bomb bay. We had been hit over the target and the bomb doors were still open. They just jumped out. I said to myself, "Oh, my God! The plane is on fire, the crew's gone, and I don't have my parachute!" I used to put all that stuff in a big canvas E-4 bag and leave it in the plane. I was too big to fit into the turret with a 'chute on. I also had my shoes in the bag. We wore heated flying boots which wouldn't have lasted very long if you had to walk in them, so I had a pair of shoes in there in case I had to bail out so I could walk out of Germany. It sounded good at the time.

Now, I'm down in that turret and it has a safety strap around the back and two locks on the door to get back into the plane. My microphone is plugged in, my oxygen is plugged in, my heated suit cord is plugged in, and my foot is jammed in the range pedal that adjusted the sight. All I had to do now was get those two hooks and the safety straps off, pull those three lines out without getting tangled in them, open the turret, put my 'chute and shoes on and bail out! We were flying at 28,000 feet that day, which is about five miles up. What a horrifying time that was for me. Falling five miles in a burning airplane. If I'd been in a B-24, I would never have gotten out because of those skinny little wings. But the B-17 had a big wide wing, and when

Brooklyn's Robert Geraghty, ball turret gunner, stands fourth from left in this standard group portrait before his crew left the United States for England in September 1943. Front row from left: Joseph Connolly, navigator; Arden D. Wilson, pilot; Donald J. McDonald, copilot; and Harry Ullam, bombardier. Standing, left to right: Jack Embach, Arthur Homer, Wally Sussek, Geraghty, Dick Nisbet, and Tony Greco, the tail gunner killed when these men were shot down. Homer and Nisbet had been transferred to other crews by then, but were killed on other missions.

it went into a dive, it would pick up speed and then stall out before it started to dive again. I was lucky it didn't go into a spin because then you had no chance. Every time it stalled, I got a wire off me, unhooked something. When it was diving, I'd be pushed down into the seat, couldn't move a muscle. I finally got everything pulled out and climbed out of the turret. I got to my bag and put my 'chute on. I had already decided to skip the shoes. Then I had to crawl up the side of the plane, hand over hand, to the waist door.

Out I went and all I could think about was how quiet and peaceful it was. You can't imagine the roar that plane was making on the way down. I was in that roaring, crashing, burning atmosphere and all of a sudden, I'm floating down and it was so still. Then I was so happy, just glad that I was alive. Happy for my mother and father and family. And then I started feeling a little sorry for them. I knew they were going to get a telegram that I was missing in action. How long after that will they find out that I'm still alive? Everything that was going to happen was going through my mind.

I really wasn't in the air for very long because I had gotten out pretty close to the ground. The last German fighter circled me and actually waggled his wings at me before he took off. I didn't know if I was coming down in France or Germany. I saw that it was a mining area, and when I landed, there was a group of men waiting for me. One of them came up to me. I had some high school French so I put my hand out and hoped for the best. "Français?" He pulled out a piece of firewood and said, "Nein, Deutsch!" I then noticed that everybody had a piece of firewood in their hands. Now I knew where I had landed.

They held me until a truck came and picked me up. I was taken to a prison camp and put in a cell all by myself. I have never felt more alone in my whole life. Here I was, a kid from Brooklyn, in the middle of Germany, in a prison cell, in the middle of a war. I guess they were waiting until they rounded us all up because after a few hours, they came around with another truck and the rest of my crew was in the back. Oh, God, was I happy to see someone else! When I got up in the truck, I had to step over Tony Greco's body. He was our tail gunner and never got out of the plane.

I've always felt bad about Tony. When the crew was assembled at Walla Walla, Washington, I was the first one to show up. This guy walks up and says, "Hi, my name is Tony Greco and I'm going to be the tail gunner." Just like that. I said, "Hey, I'm the first man here and I'm going to take the tail; you can have the ball." We went around and around, and I found out that Tony had gone through four months of training and then they broke up his crew for some reason and sent him back to start over. I felt bad when I heard that, so guess who ended up in the ball.

I didn't mind it as much as I thought I would. It was really a safe spot because you were surrounded by the whole airplane. In fact, I got to love it after a while. I didn't mind being separated like that from the rest of the crew because I'm a bit of a loner, anyway. I guess that's why I'm still a bachelor. It was completely different in the turrets than the other guns because you didn't actually hold your guns. I didn't even touch the guns. They were mounted on the sides of the ball, and I moved the whole thing around with two handles. It was synchronized to a Sperry K-4 gunsight. It worked pretty well if you could track a plane for awhile because it took a couple of seconds to set the proper range and line up the sight with the guns.

You figure now, we were going 180 miles an hour in our plane, the German fighters were doing maybe 350 or 400 miles an hour in the opposite direction. They'd come rolling through the formation going like a bat out of hell. It was a horrendous sight. Your asshole really puckered up. You were lucky if you could get your sights on a plane the way they would come swinging through there at us. The first shots out of our plane were actually fired at an American! This P-47 came straight at us, and Jack Embalk, the top turret gunner, thought it was an FW and let go at him. That guy saw those tracers go by and he stood right up on his tail to show us his wings. I don't think he did that again, fly right at a bomber. We had a saying, "Little brother never sticks his nose at big brother."

I had a right and left gun, and I think about 650 rounds of ammunition. You always fired in short bursts of maybe ten or twelve shots at a time. If you held the thing down, you'd melt the barrels. Once in a while my guns would jam, but I usually could get them going again. The flexible gunners, like the tail and waist, could actually take their guns apart, and they had piles of ammunition. I just had what was loaded in mine. Sometimes that flak would come up and go "whoooooomp"! It would force me right out of the seat when it burst. I'd get so mad that I'd sometimes turn the turret down toward the ground and "boom, boom." I'd put a few rounds down at the gunners. You weren't doing any good, of course, but it made me feel better.

So, I was in the ball and Tony Greco got the tail gun, which he wanted. And God bless him; he was twenty years old when he died, and I've lived another forty years. I often wonder why me and not him. One man would get sick and another man would fly in his place and get killed. It didn't make any sense, and I guess there's no way to try and figure it out now. Combat over there was strange. You'd be having a drink in a bar with your buddies and having a great time. The English women would be there, and they were just wonderful. I'm Irish and I always was taught that the English were just terrible. We couldn't have been treated nicer by the English people, and we'd been thrown in their laps. We'd go home from the bar and go to sleep in a comfortable bed and get up for breakfast and a briefing. A few hours later you'd be in a mad raging battle a couple of hundred miles inside Germany, five miles up in the air. Flak, fighters, all noise, and planes being shot down around you. Then, a few hours later, you'd be back in the pub having a drink with the ladies. The next morning you'd be off again.

There were eight of us from my plane in the back of the truck and one P-38 pilot. He had tried to give us cover, and they had shot him down. Our radio man had also been killed. The Germans had salvaged everything they could out of the plane, and I suddenly realized that I was sitting on my E-4 bag. Remember, this is seven at night and we had last eaten at four-thirty in the morning. After all the excitement started to wear off, we realized we were starving. I knew there was a chocolate bar in my escape kit which was inside the bag. There were four Germans facing us with rifles, but I managed to get the kit out without them seeing me and stuck it in my flying boot. They put us in a cell after they searched us, but they didn't find the kit. I could have had a revolver in that boot.

The escape kit was a plastic case with a couple of chocolate bars, phony I.D., a cloth map, Benzedrine tablets, and things like that. All I was interested in was that chocolate. I pulled it out and goddamn it, we couldn't get the case open. It took us about an hour and a half. We used to call our right waist gunner, Wally Sussek, "Piano Mouth." He could open bottles of Coke with his teeth. That's how we finally got it open. We had just gotten all the stuff scattered around, and the chocolate bars broken up, and the German guards came back, searched us again, this time good. We never did get a piece of that damn chocolate.

The Germans never got rough with us. In fact, some of them were almost friendly. I talked to a couple of them who had been prisoners of the English in the First World War. They had been treated well and were returning the favor. With the Russians, it was different. I remember one day I was sitting in the latrine. The latrine in Stalag 17 was just a long wooden bench with holes. Underneath there was a concrete pit about 10 feet deep. I was sitting there reading *Der Adler* when all of a sudden something scratched my ass. I thought I had been bitten by a rat, and I jumped about four feet in the air. I turned around and an arm came out of the hole. A voice said, "Cigarette, comrade?" The Germans would throw the Russians down in that pit to shovel, excuse the term, shit. They weren't conducting the war under the Geneva Convention, and I guess neither of them treated the other too well. I'd see six or seven of them being brought out of their barracks every morning and being thrown in a ditch. They were dying of all sorts of things, and the Germans weren't doing a thing. I woke up every day damn glad we signed the Geneva Convention.

They took us from the military prison to an interrogation center in Frankfurt. All Allied airmen shot down were interrogated. We'd been told ahead of time by our intelligence people what to expect. For instance, the phony Red Cross man. This guy came in with a blue uniform and arm band that had red crosses on it. He would ask you to fill out a questionnaire, and he'd tell you that they'd see that your people would get it. Then you'd see the questions—the name of your plane, your squadron, their location in England, the types of bombs you carried, what was the initial target, and so on. This is the Red Cross? I gave them my name, rank, and serial number. At one point we were startled to hear one of them say, "We're not going to ask you anything about the B-29s because you don't know anything about them." They really did their homework—probably had one stashed away someplace.

We spent seven or eight days there, and then they shipped us out in boxcars. We were packed standing up—six days and six nights with no food. If you wanted to take a crap, they let a few out of the car at a time. You'd go right in the middle of a station, children, women, and everything else walking right by. That was really demeaning, but you had to do it.

We ended up in Stalag 17, which was about 24 kilometers from Vienna. I was there for a little more than a year and a half—January 7, 1944, to May Day, 1945. For a while, it began to seem like there was no other life. I had never lived a life before the camp, and there was no life to live after. That camp was my whole life. That television stuff you see on "Hogan's Heroes" is stupid. I get a laugh out of it. You couldn't get away with stuff like that with the Germans. To begin with, nobody escaped. Oh, they were building tunnels all the time. I never got into a tunnel. We were near Vienna; the Army hadn't landed on the Normandy beaches yet; what the hell were you going to do for food all the way across Europe? The only men who planned escapes were the ones who didn't smoke or gamble. They saved their cigarettes and bartered them for food. We used to get Red Cross parcels from home. They had a certain amount of food in them, but the Germans would punch every can so you couldn't store them. If you had an unpunctured can, you were rich. They'd come around and check your nails and hair for dirt when you were in bed. They'd find the tunnels and just fill them up.

But they'd keep trying, the prisoners. You take 4,100 Americans, you're going to get a few of everything, including some mining engineers. They had air-conditioning in there. Fit the one-pound dried milk cans together and run them up to the front of the tunnel like a pipe. Have a bellows pushing air in there so they could dig without fainting. They even had electric lights and little cars which could be pulled back by a rope. A railroad, lights, and air-conditioning. Leave it to a bunch of American airmen.

I don't think any of us thought we'd lose, never for a second. At least I didn't. At the beginning, when we first got in the camp, the Germans thought they were going to win. They were pretty cocky. But toward the end, especially after the Russians entered Vienna, they realized that they had a good chance of losing the war. When holidays came along, we tried to make them different. We'd put together a special meal for Thanksgiving and Christmas. Fourth of July was a big deal because we had to show the Germans we were Americans. There would be parades and boxing matches, all sorts of things. We even had a theater. It was in one of the barracks. It was called the "Cardboard Theater" because the walls were covered with cardboard from the Red Cross parcels. Some of the guys had backgrounds in the theater. I remember they put on *The Man Who Came to Dinner*.

After the war, Don Bevans and Ed Tivdzinski got in touch with me. They wrote the play *Stalag 17*. I'd met them in the camp, but didn't know them that well. The play was being presented for the first time at the Lambs Club. They invited a few of us that were in the camp to see it, and after it was over, we went out to the bar. "How did you like it?" I told them I liked it, but I didn't think it was going to be a hit. Shows you what kind of theater critic I am. It just seemed too bland to me, not real. I guess if you couldn't smell the place, I didn't think it was the real story.

The cold and the hunger, that was the worst. Food was practically nonexistent. When we first got there, the Germans gave us potatoes and rutabagas, similar to a turnip. Horrible! We never got any meat, except in the Red Cross parcels. We did, one time, buy a cow. We wanted to taste meat, and by trading things to a German farmer, we actually got a cow. Like I said, American ingenuity is something.

We lived on those Red Cross parcels. Not only food. The beds were stacked three high, and the pallets were stuffed with wood chips. You laid on it once or twice and it was like sleeping on a board. We used to take the bailing wire from the parcels and make springs— stretch them across the bed. Then we could burn the bed slats. Anything we could use for firewood, we would, because the Germans only gave us a few pieces of coal. It's pretty tough to be cold *and* hungry for weeks on end.

All of a sudden one day, the Germans got us all out and off we went; we knew something was up because they were acting funny. We were on the road for 28 days. What the Germans intended to do, it turned out, was for all the German forces to march all of the prisoners of war to one central place. They were going to put us in the middle of a circle and hold us as hostages and fight to the death. Ours, too! The Germans that were guarding us were all old men from the home guard, or young kids, and I don't think they saw any reason to fight to the death. We got the feeling they were just marching us to some place where they could give up. We actually started doing business with the farm people along the way. George Smith and I, both being from New York, were the hustlers. The guys from the Midwest would give us their extra cigarettes, chocolate, something that we could hustle for food.

As we marched, we used to pick up newspapers, and we had maps with us. We weren't supposed to, of course, but we knew exactly where we were because we had radios. We picked up military reports as we went. As I said, the Germans weren't being too pushy because they knew we were marching right into the hands of Patton's army. One day on the march we passed this German airfield. They had heard we were coming and came out to see what we looked like. We'd seen each other's airplanes, but never seen each other's faces or talked to each other.

I weighed 112 pounds the day we were liberated. The Americans sent two tanks and a couple of truckloads of men. The Germans still had their rifles. Our people just filed off the trucks, took the guns away from the Germans, and threw them to us. We were free. They landed some C-46s near us in a field and flew us back to Camp Lucky Strike. That was outside of La Halle, France. It was a rendezvous point for all prisoners of war being repatriated. We were all in bad shape, and I was like a twig. They wanted to know if you knew of any brutalities or war crimes. We were there for almost a week, and I wanted to be alone and free more than anything else. I was sick and tired of being with men.

I walked out of the back door of the camp and went into the town. I spoke to someone in the street and told him I wanted a room. He sent me to a butcher's shop, and I told them I was a former prisoner of war and that I wanted to sleep in a bed by myself. They took me upstairs, and there was a bed with a huge mound in the middle. It was a down mattress. I had never seen anything like that in my life. I climbed up on top of that mound and woke up 12 hours later. I think it was the sweetest sleep I ever had in my whole life.

They fattened us up and loaded us on a ship, and I came back to New York. We went to Camp Shanks, near West Point. I had broken my tooth and figured I'd been gone that long, a few more days wasn't going to make much of a difference because I didn't want to go home looking like that. I called my folks and told my mother that for the last year and a half, all I had been thinking about was her strawberry shortcake. I said, "Ma, I'd just like one little shortcake." My father picked me up at the subway station and when I walked into the house there was a huge table with a snow-white Irish linen table cloth, and right in the middle of it was the biggest strawberry shortcake I'd ever seen. I ate the whole goddamned thing!

Maybe it's because I'm Irish that I wanted to get into that war. I don't think I had any soaring degree of patriotism. I firmly believe in my country, believed it was right, but I think it was just a chance to get into the biggest fight around. I grew up in a section of Brooklyn called Ocean Hill. I went to school at St. Matthew's and then to Brooklyn Tech. It was a tough neighborhood, and I learned to take care of myself. I graduated in 1941 and got a job at E. W. Bliss in Manhattan as a lathe operator. They were making torpedoes. After the war, I didn't want to go back to a lathe. I went to NYU for a while at night and worked as a bank clerk during the day. I had this thing about being a journalist, a would-be writer. Then a friend of mine was taking the test for the police department, and I went with him. I took the test and passed it. It was a good move because it was a fabulous career, a marvelous time. But I think the war absolutely and completely changed my life. Having come that close to death's door, all I wanted to do was live and enjoy life. I just didn't give a damn for anything but living. I drink and eat more than I should, I'll be the first to admit it. I still feel the same way, just to live is enough. But I know that it cut my ambition, my driving force. If I had studied and applied myself, I could have retired as an inspector. I came out a patrolman. The war made me a bit of a bum.

It certainly was the greatest thing in my life. The 338th Bomber Group has a memorial association. There is a man in Pennsylvania who is directing it. He called me to tell me that my pilot, R. D. Wilson, had sent him a copy of the *New York Times* article about me and the model airplane. He got a big kick out of it. I called my pilot two years ago, and he was very surprised to hear from me. That was the first time I had talked to him since 1944. We weren't that close because we'd only been together for four or five months. There were only enlisted men in Stalag 17; the officers were taken to their own camp. If anybody goes to see everybody in the crew at some point, it probably will be me. I'm footloose and fancy free. If I get a chance, I'd like to see my pilot again. I always thought they had a particular kind of guts. We'd be opening the bomb doors, and the Germans would be throwing everything they could at us. The sky would be full of flak. There was no place to go except straight ahead on the bomb run, and they'd just go into all that crap. I was just along for the ride, but that pilot had to take that plane right into the worst of it. That was a special kind of courage.

When we were in the camp, a bunch of us started a thing called the "Legion of the Broken Wings." We had a book the Salvation Army gave us with blank pages. We had the names of over four hundred men from the tri-state area. I was the one who was supposed to call everybody when we got back after the war. When we were marching, I had a bout of the runs and everything I couldn't carry, everything I didn't really need, I dropped along the way. If I had that book today, we'd have a hell of a party each year.

Oh yes, one more thing. I went over to Europe in 1969 and went back to visit Stalag 17. I went to Paris and then took an express train to Vienna. Then I rode a little train up to the nearest village, Gneixendorf. Nobody in the town would tell me anything about Stalag 17, where it was. I don't know if they didn't know or just weren't talking. We never knew exactly where we were when we were in the camp. I finally had to go to the chief of police. I told him I was a New York City policeman, and he got out a map and pointed out where the camp used to be. The next day I got myself a limousine with a chauffeur, who happened to be an eighteen-year-old Austrian blonde with a miniskirt on. She drove me up to Stalag 17, or where it had been. I stood in the middle of a cabbage patch where my barracks had been, where I had spent over one and a half years of my life. There wasn't a thing around that would remind you of the place—nothing. And I remember the trip back to Paris. I'm sitting there in that beautiful train with a nice glass of wine, looking out of the window. And I'm remembering the time I walked over those very same Austrian roads, hungry, cold. It is something that will always be with me, my whole life.

A DEAR OLD FRIEND

Distinguished, articulate, Robert B. Parke spent over 30 years with
Flying *magazine, the last 10 as editor and publisher. Now retired, he*
pursues a career as a New York–based freelance writer and editorial
consultant. This is a long way from the young man who was working at
Life *magazine, as what that company called a "CBOB," or College-Boy-*
Office-Boy. Graduate school for Parke, as for so many others in those
precarious years, was the Army Air Corps. His classroom was the cockpit
of a B-17 Flying Fortress.

The grounds surrounding his house in Bedford, New York, are
magnificent, a mini-botanical garden. "Don't look at me," he protested,
"my wife Margaret's responsible for all this." It was obvious that this was
the first time Parke had spoken at length about his war experiences. He
repeatedly got to his feet and walked around the room, as if the flood of
memories wouldn't let him sit still—a gentleman talking about a violent
time he is still trying to understand.

Generally speaking, I'm not the kind of person to go back and relive
the past. For instance, I have never been back to my college. When I
graduated in 1939, that was the end of it. I don't think I'd seen more
than two or three B-17s since the war and never had the urge to get in
one. Then in recent years, when people were starting to get more
interested in World War II, the staff at *Flying* magazine had the idea of
my flying a B-17 again and doing a story on it. I wasn't particularly
keen about it, but I wasn't going to resist either. One week when we
were down in Texas at a dealer meeting, they called up the Confederate Air Force and arranged the thing. We landed there late in the

Robert B. Parke, pilot of a B-17 Flying Fortress, and some of his crew pose in England with their newly awarded Air Medals. Parke has his under his arm, still in its box. Top row, from left: Lieutenant James T. Kilkelly, bombardier; Staff Sergeant Wallace W. Phillips, engineer; Sergeant Joseph A. Basciano, top turret gunner; and Parke. Bottom: Sergeants Vincent Barbaria, tail gunner; John A. Swett, ball turret; and John S. Bogner, waist gunner.

afternoon, had a few drinks and dinner, and sat around talking. They told a few war stories and the next morning we went out to the hangar and there was the old B-17. Actually, it was a pretty handsome airplane, but I must confess that I didn't feel any palpitations.

The nose crew entered a B-17 through a hatch underneath the fuselage. It looks impossible, particularly with a parachute, but when you do it right, it's amazing how easy it is. However, if you do it wrong, you end up just swinging and you go no place. I had no intention in the world of doing anything embarrassing like that and was going to go in through the back door and walk up. That's how the rest of the crew got in. The pilot, copilot, navigator, and bombardier usually went up through that hole in the bottom. It was really an escape hatch. Somehow Dick Collins had learned about it and kind of challenged me. "Come on now, let's see you swing yourself up the way you used to do it." I was even wearing a suit coat but I decided, what the hell, and reached up; it happened so fast and easily, I couldn't believe it. Everyone was cheering and clapping. I climbed up to where the pilot sits. Sure enough, there it was, just as it always had been, that absolutely monster control column and huge, massive wheel. I don't know why, but the actual column must have been a five-inch pipe. One thing it certainly did was give you the feeling of stability. I also realized how tiny the windshield was. You'd never get it certified today with that small amount of glass.

I looked around a good bit and then sat down and made myself comfortable. What really made that airplane for me were the throttles. You actually used those throttles to fly the plane because the rudder wasn't much use. The rudder pedals were huge; I think they were made for Big Foot. Nothing powered in those days. There was a big long cable, and if you leaned into that rudder long enough, you might get a little action back there. You had the engines and ailerons to play with, and you used them for most of your flying.

Now the guy from the Confederate Air Force got in the right seat, and I started to go through the checklist. He finally got a little bit impatient and took over. I'd forgotten just how you did the mag switches, fuel, stuff like that. Next thing you know, the first old engine was turning over. That was a very comfortable sound. The only sound I've heard remotely like it nowadays is one of those huge Peterbuilt trucks. A kind of hollow, resonant, empty sound. Pretty soon all four engines were running and the takeoff went fine. The tail came up so easily, and we just about jumped into the air. It was so light with just three people and a couple of hours' worth of gas. During the war, you wouldn't think of going anywhere without a full load of fuel. Every bloody tank was filled because that damn thing used a lot. Today I suppose it would cost $50,000 to fill it up. These guys must have chipped in to just get enough gas in it for an hour or two. We got up and started flying around, and it really did feel good. I was interested in seeing how it actually did fly by today's standards. It's very slow and heavy compared to what you might expect today, but on the other hand it's solid and very easy to fly. For its time, it was quite a responsive plane.

I remember one problem I had learning to fly the B-17, and that was formation flying. That turned out to be the most difficult phase of the entire flying experience for me. At one point I can recall feeling quite sure I could never, never learn how to do it. Right from the first day they put you into the left seat you flew formation, and you flew formation, and you flew more formation. You never flew alone, just your plane by itself. Flying that big bumbling thing in close proximity to another airplane is terribly, terribly hard initially. Those instructors would be in the right seat, and they'd be flying close formation with absolute, consummate ease. They'd sit there and light a cigarette while they were doing it. A perfect relationship, both with their own planes and the other ones in the formation. Finally I figured that it could be done if they were doing it, and like so many things it just began to come. It wasn't as much the controls as the power. As I told you, the rudder wasn't the way you moved that airplane around. All of a sudden you begin to get this familiarity with the plane and you feel that you can do anything with it. As anyone who flies a lot will tell you, the more you get to know an airplane, the more you feel like that. Land it anywhere, take off on short strips if you feel like it. Cross winds are nothing but a nuisance, you don't worry about it, just do it. Just fly it.

They were always on our backs about flying a good formation, and I had a couple of experiences that showed there was something to it. The first fighters I saw were on my fourth or fifth mission. I think we were going to Augsburg, a ball-bearing plant. I was still flying rotten positions, where they always put the new guys. You're in the back and get all the prop wash of everybody else. Every movement of every airplane in a formation is like the wagging of a snake. You're always catching up. To fly a good formation if you're in the back, you're working all the time. Everybody's farting on you. On this mission I was in the high echelon but way back, and, God, I was working my ass off. You could lose four or five pounds on a long mission just sweating. I'd drifted back, there was no question about it. I was a bit high and back and had allowed us to get into a dangerous position. The German fighters would select the sloppy-looking formations. That was what everybody told you. I suppose that's true because usually they'd try to pick off the planes that were the farthest out or in a particular position in the formation. Trying to avoid as much of our firepower as possible. Sometimes, however, they'd come barreling in dead ahead to pick off the lead plane or the deputy. So much for theory. The Luftwaffe had its own systems, and to us it didn't make a damn bit of difference because it was all so terrifying. So there we were, a little high and behind and I heard somebody cry, "Bandits!" As soon as I heard that I tried to catch up with the formation, and went to high power, and nosed down. In a matter of seconds from the time I spotted the fighters, I was aware of a thumping sound and the flash of an airplane going by and then another. I couldn't see much except one of the fighters, it was a 109, coming in from the front, and you could see the flickering as the guns shot through the propeller shaft. I remember thinking it looked very pretty. Strange thing to think at the time, but that's what I thought.

By this time I was back in the formation, pulled in tight and flying well. I wasn't aware of anything wrong with the plane until the tail-gunner called up the copilot and told him our tail had been shot off! Those fighters had indeed had us as a target because we had drifted out of formation. Our butt and rudder had just about been shredded. Those Germans had been shooting perfectly right behind us, and if I hadn't nosed down a bit, they probably would have blasted the airplane. The airplane just got a little sluggish because we didn't have the tail surface anymore, but we got back without any trouble. It looked as if someone had taken buckshot to us.

One other thing about flying tight formation I learned after the war when I was talking to a former German fighter pilot. We were in Germany doing an article for the magazine on a German airplane a few months after I flew the old B-17, and the designer turned out to be an ex-fighter pilot. Now it always seemed to us that the German fighters were having a ball. They had those great airplanes. They would be weaving around and flying fancy stuff while we were just plodding along in those clunky B-17s. You just felt that you were walking stark naked down Third Avenue and people could line up along the curb and throw stones at you. You couldn't even run, you had to walk. We figured they had all the guns they needed, and all they had to do was barrel in and knock us down. And he looked at me in some astonishment and said, "I never knew you felt that way. We always felt as though we were little naked men rushing up against a stone wall and people were dropping tons of rocks down on us. We really had to get up our courage to do that at all, attack those bomber formations." It was a real surprise to hear things from his standpoint.

After about the first four or five missions I began to get this savvy feeling that there was just so much you could do to stay alive, and the rest of it was luck. It had nothing to do with how much skill you had as a pilot, or whether you were virtuous, or a good guy. It was about 87 percent luck. You weren't allowed to do anything fancy, just very minor evasive things. By the time we were getting to our twentieth trip, we'd get those damn Berlin missions. They knew we were coming. No deception. We were almost saying, "We're going to bomb your capital," and they were saying to us, "The hell you are." So we'd go shoving off to Berlin and they had more damn flak than you can imagine. You'd look ahead on a clear day and see this big black cloud, 50 miles away. You'd get closer and that black cloud was made up of thousands of flak bursts and that's what you were going to fly through. The closer you got, the more apprehensive you were, actually the more terror-struck you were. Then, it was always curious, as you got into it, you could hear the individual bursts all around the plane. Each a little change in tone. I usually concentrated on flying the airplane because I hated to look around at all the damn antiaircraft surrounding us.

On the very first mission when I saw those clouds, puffy black wavy clouds, it was gruesome-looking, but I didn't know enough to be frightened. The first indication I had of danger was the copilot shaking me. He pointed to a guy opposite us, and I saw that he was on fire. His whole goddamn wing was on fire. I could look right into the cockpit and see that the pilot was trying to get his door open and the airplane, just like slow motion, began to lift up and turn over. Then flame came out everywhere and it just vanished. Gone! Afterwards was when I really started to think, "so that's what it looks like." And it was that guy's first mission, too. He had total combat time of maybe two hours and fifteen minutes, something like that.

As I said, you felt your life was simply in the hands of fate. Everything was out of scale, and it was very easy to get enormously apprehensive and also terribly superstitious. I inherited a piece of armor plate, about 18 inches square, from another pilot. I put it on the seat and got to the point where I wouldn't fly a mission without it. You'd always put your parachute on in a certain way, carry your helmet under your left arm, begin to do all these idiotic things.

This business of superstition reminds me of something funny that happened about the naming, or should I say the non-naming, of our airplane. I wanted to be a writer when I first went to school. When I got out of college, I was quite excited to get an office boy job at *Life* magazine. I felt I was part of the literary world. When it came time to think about naming my airplane, I had made up my mind that I'd have this portrait of Eustace Tilley, the *New Yorker* magazine character, monocle and all. I thought it would make a great contrast with those voluptuous women on so many bombing planes. I had picked up my crew in Salt Lake City, and we were on a train going to Sioux

City to do our operational training when it first came up. The crew all gathered around and they were all lieutenanting me. "Well, lieutenant, what should we name the airplane?" This one guy wanted to call it *Buffalo Maiden,* or something like that. The copilot was a patriotic type, and he was all for something like *Flagwaver* or *Old Glory.* Finally, I tried to introduce this Eustace Tilley idea by saying, "Well, there's a curious fellow who's in this magazine, the *New Yorker,* you may not have seen it because it's mostly read around New York." I was apologizing all over the place, and finally I could see this look of absolute horror on their faces. I could see them thinking, "What a real dud we got for a pilot. What is this guy talking about?" There were a couple of tentative sympathetic questions. "Is he smiling?" "Is it funny, like a clown?" "Top hat, hey, top hat? What's a monocle?"

For one reason or another we drifted into other matters at the time, and it didn't really come up again until we were on the way to England. Somebody would say, "Well, Jesus, let's call it Parke's Crew," or something like that to test the water and see if I was still pushing this Eustace Tilley idea. I suppose if they had all come to me and said, "Look, we want to name it, 'Bat Out of Hell,'" I would have probably gone along with it, but, thank God, no two could agree. But then an interesting thing happened. When you first started to fly missions, you weren't handed a new airplane like everybody thinks. What you did get usually was some old clunker that somebody else had left behind. You ended up with the worst plane on the field. When you turned the engines over, you could hear all the rods and things clanking around; outside it would be pretty tattered looking because when there was flak damage, they would just put a new piece of aluminum over the hole. The plane usually looked speckled all over and you'd fly three, maybe six or seven, missions in that junker before you'd get an airplane assigned to you, which theoretically you would have until you finished your tour or got shot down. As I said before, everybody by that time had gotten terribly superstitious; you could be just as logical as you wanted to be, but you didn't take any chances. When we finally got our own plane, we didn't want to change anything. It didn't have a name, so we left it without a name. As far as I know, there was no B-17 named *Eustace Tilley.**

By the time you got to twenty missions you began to feel like a real veteran. The guys who were hitting their thirty missions were going home, and you became part of the group that had been around

---

Ed. note: Bob Parke contacted the *New Yorker* magazine after the war. They knew of no airplane named *Eustace Tilley.*

awhile. We'd been flying pretty hard and the pressure of the missions, the tempo, seemed to be increasing. Of course, we didn't know what the hell was going on everywhere else in the war. You could almost say in retrospect that the war was on the wane, but it didn't seem so to us at the time. The military newspapers tried to inform us about this or that, but we didn't pay much attention to it. It all seemed so remote from what you were doing. Combat flying was such a consuming activity that it was hard to think about anything else. Everything that you were doing day and night had to do with flying. Who got killed or shot down? Will the airplane fly all right tomorrow? What happens if I don't remember what to do about this or that? Who cares how a campaign in Africa is going or how MacArthur is getting along? You just seemed so terribly isolated. It was another world. Your world was on that little military base and inside that airplane, that's all there was to it.

After a certain point everything started to focus on that thirty-third mission. We finally got there without too much difficulty, and everybody was pretty happy. We didn't buzz the field as they did on "Twelve O'Clock High," that sort of thing. They had so many guys buzz the base and run into the ground or a hangar, maybe kill themselves, that they decided that was not a good idea. I wasn't one of the buzzer types anyway. I do, however, remember I was taxiing in after landing, and I'm looking out the window and being 99 percent sure that my wing tip was going to miss this hangar and also feeling that I don't care if it doesn't. Sure enough, it hit the hangar and hung us up. There were fifty airplanes behind me waiting to taxi by and who's this ass on his last run who's got everybody backed up? Then I remembered this hot-shot little pilot that I had way back in Columbus, Ohio, teaching me formation flying, showed me how to back up a B-17. You'd hold the right brake and run up the number four engine so you're pivoting on the right wheel. Then you'd do the same with the left brake and run up the number one engine and pivot on the left wheel. So to the wonderment of everybody, I backed away from the hangar and taxied out.

We got back to the States and had some R&R. It was a much more difficult adjustment than I had imagined it would be because everybody thinks of you as some kind of hero when you don't really feel very much like a hero. Mothers are quite adoring, wives and all are quite proud, and friends' wives are trying to get you to lay them. I was sent to Sebring, Florida. It's so easy to get bored in the military, and one of the smartest things I ever did was start to volunteer for all sorts of additional courses. The first one I took was the Bryan Instrument Training School in Bryan, Texas. This was the first instrument flying school in the world. This guy, Colonel Duckworth, had devised the flying practices that are still in use today. You flew all the time. Unless there was a thunderstorm right over the base, you flew. There was a lot of simulator time, which was unheard of then. It was a great school. I came back from that, and the next course I took was in C-54s, which were the biggest four-engine transports they had at the time. That lasted for five months. What I was really doing was just filling up time before I could get out. I wasn't really thinking about going into commercial aviation like a lot of guys.

I faced the sort of thing that literally thousands of others did. When I left for the war five years before, I was a senior office boy at *Life*. Now I was a captain in the Army Air Forces with 5,000 hours of flying. I was accustomed to making decent money and having a position of some importance. I hadn't really had time before I left *Life* to establish myself as a writer they would want to hire when I got back. They did have to hire me back as something, the government had taken care of that for everybody, but they were not about to hire me in the job I wanted. For me Time, Incorporated, had very cleverly devised some ridiculous task that had the aura of importance to it. It was a merchandising, marketing kind of job that had something to do with peddling *Time* and *Life*. Quite clearly it was something that I wanted nothing to do with.

So there I was with this job I didn't want and my marriage was also dissolving at this time. I had some friends in Philadelphia, and that seemed like a pretty good place to get a divorce and a new job at the same time. I moved there, got a job with Campbell Soup in promotion and put flying completely out of my mind. I was doing the usual bachelor things and having a rather jolly time. Things were going along pretty well for about five years, and then I got this letter one day saying, "Would you care to volunteer to go back into the Air Force?" Of course I wouldn't care to volunteer so I didn't bother to answer it. I thought they were crazy. Something they clearly didn't know was that I hadn't looked at an airplane for five years. The next thing I got was, "*Thou shalt* report to Fort Dix on such and such a date for a physical regarding resuming your duties as airplane commander, C-54." So I thought, I'll go down there and they'll take one look at me . . . I was a very heavy smoker at the time and thought I was quite over age. I had all these good reasons. Anyway, I got up there and walked in and, Jesus, I passed. It was incredible, just like the movies. If you were breathing, you passed.

This was the time of the Cold War. They were building the DEW line across Canada, and they didn't care if you smoked or anything else. Could you fly a four-engined airplane, that's all they wanted to know. You didn't have to run a mile to do that. So I asked myself, what am I doing at Campbell Soup that's so great? And I said good-bye to Philadelphia and went back to flying airplanes. It's funny how these curious little things in a person's life begin to make sense in the overall flow when you look back. It all seemed pretty unrelated at the time, but it turned out to be the kind of interruption that so often redirects you.

That flying turned out to be an absolutely extraordinary experience. We went out to Great Falls, Montana, and they put us through the entire airplane command course again. They weren't as dumb as I thought. Navigation, systems, everything, and then, zip, on to Springfield, Massachusetts, and we were flying to Greenland. We didn't know it at the time, but they had actually hollowed out a mountain and put all their secret gear in there. You'd look back in that airplane and see the oddest-looking things. They'd cut up these huge cranes, we'd carry them up there, and then they'd weld them back together. Big long derricks, Caterpillar tractors, trucks, it was just amazing.

When we started flying up there, it was 24 hours of darkness; by June it was daylight all the time. We almost got lost once. If you did get lost, you were dead, no doubt about it. The major navigation aid was a weak little omnidirectional beeper. You'd start toward that and if you'd miss it by, say, 50 miles, you could just go on sailing forever. Another thing, too, these were ancient airplanes. Sometimes you'd see marked on the insides of the hull, "Berlin, here we come."

My tour lasted 18 months, and I was really in a quandary. I was still a captain because you couldn't be upgraded and be a line pilot. A major could do some flying, but he also had to do desk duties. I had no great desire to push military papers around, and absolutely no desire to go back to Campbell Soup. I had always wanted to try this writing thing so I decided that was what I was going to do. I rented an apartment in London Terrace apartments down on Twenty-third Street for three or four months, locked myself up with a typewriter, and started to write. It was a wonderful experience. In three months I made $75. One thing I learned was how nice it is to have a quick reply from a magazine and also a quick check. It was a good lesson about what it's like to be on the other end of the editorial stick. One of the stories I wrote was about my flying experiences. We call them "I learned from that" stories now. I had never read any aviation magazines, didn't know anything about them. I got the phone book, and the first magazine listed was *Airfacts*. That was run by Leighton Collins, who is, of course, Dick Collins's father. Dick took my place at *Flying* when I left. I walked up to *Airfacts'* offices and said, "Look, I've got this story and I'd like you to have a look at it." Leighton, he was so patient, a real gracious gentleman, read it and said, "It's a nicely written story but I don't think this is the kind of thing that will do aviation any good." He was against adventure, danger stories as a matter of policy. Leighton felt that kind of story turned people off from flying. "I can't buy your story, but my advertising manager just left; how would you like the job?" I took it. That was the end of my writing.

One thing more about that article I did about flying the B-17 again. I felt that the story I wrote was really pretty true, accurate, and very much the way I wanted to have it come out. While it was a dear old airplane, I don't think, from my standpoint, it deserved to be treated as something more than that. Something mysterious and profound. A great piece of my life caught up in that airplane, that kind of thing. Certainly there are lots of stories to tell about the war, and it's true that flying changed my whole life. After flying the plane, I was very pleased that I did it, but I don't have a great yearning to go back and do more of it. It had been a stirring experience—like meeting a dear old friend. But we didn't have all that much to say to each other. Some of the other *Flying* people thought I had lost it, the warlike mood. One even said I couldn't face the emotion of the thing and just had to withdraw. That's the way he would have been, you see. A lot of people like that find it very difficult to appreciate that everyone isn't like them.

MARTIN L. BARON

SUCH GOOD GUYS

Martin Baron is an attorney, working for a large corporate law firm in New York City. We talked in his office. The walls are covered with the expected certificates and diplomas, along with a framed photograph of ten young men in front of a Liberator bomber. Next to the photograph is his "Lucky Bastard" award, conferred on any bomber crew member who managed to live through the war.

At one point he took a weathered leatherbound diary out of his desk. In it is listed every combat mission he flew. Date, target, type of ordnance and sometimes a few pertinent notes. The last entry is dated August 15, 1944. "That was the beginning of what I call the rest of my life."

I think my family is interested in my World War II flying to a limited degree. A very limited degree. Sometimes I tell a story, or start to tell one, and I can see my kids have turned off and I stop. Maybe they've heard it before. They'll ask me questions, geographical questions, things of that sort. However, as far as what my day-to-day experiences were like, they're really not terribly interested. I think that I talk about the war very little, but apparently my wife realizes that it was a very important part of my life. She had a surprise party for my six-tieth birthday at the Wings Club, the restaurant located at West-chester Airport. I'd never been there, and she picked it because of the flying motif. There were Snoopy and Red Baron dolls, and even the cake was decorated that way. We took photographs with airplanes in the background, that sort of thing. My bombardier, who lives on Long Island, presented me with a blow-up of a photograph of my crew in front of our plane. Curiously enough, two people presented me with a book about military aircraft in World War II. I must say, I'm

145

fascinated just looking through them. So, even though I don't talk about it much, somehow my feelings must make themselves known.

I enlisted on December 8, 1942. I was eighteen and I picked the Army Air Forces because I was interested in flying. When I was five years old, my father took me on a demonstration flight. We flew around the Travelers Insurance Tower in Hartford, Connecticut. I've been a bug about flying ever since then. I wasn't that anxious to get into the war, but if I was going to be in it, which seemed almost certain, I wanted to go as a flyer. I didn't want to be a foot soldier and I'm a lousy sailor.

I'd already completed three years of college. I grew up in New York and went to Townsend Harris High School. It was located in the City College building on Lexington Avenue. It was a liberal arts high school that was geared for the student on a faster track. I graduated from there when I was fifteen and started college. The high school was organized as a preparatory school for City College, and I was so young, I never seriously considered going anyplace else.

I was called up three months later, and went to basic training in Atlantic City. Basic lasted for about three months, and then I was sent to a college training detachment at Syracuse University. This is where you learned camouflage, mathematics, things like that. You had to spend time there in inverse proportion to the amount of schooling you had. I only stayed there the minimum time, about five months. At the conclusion of that, they sent me to San Antonio, Texas, for classification. You had to select what kind of flight training you wanted to get into—pilot, navigator, or bombardier. My thinking at the time was that I would really rather be a pilot, but I wasn't sure I could make it. I had the background and felt without a doubt I could be a navigator so I made that my first preference. After we made that choice, all of us were brought into a big room and were told by an officer that we had opted for something other than pilot training. He said, "We need pilots." Then he gave us the choice of changing our first preference. Well, I'd been in the Army for over six months by this time, and we all knew the Army was tricky when it came to that kind of thing. If you said you wanted something, and then decided you wanted something else because of what they told you, this would indicate to the Army that you really did not have your mind set on your first selection. Nobody in the audience made a change. I would have liked to change to pilot training, but I was afraid if I changed my mind I'd get nothing. The next morning they posted a chart on the bulletin board. Two-thirds of the people in that room were GDOed. Ground duty only. They had been disqualified from further candidacy for flying training. It was devastating for them. Absolutely devastating. They took only those men who were highly qualified for

Martin Baron, newly minted navigator and second lieutenant, AAF, wears the smile of one who survived all the tricks and traps of training. His reward was to navigate a B-24 over Germany.

what they had selected. I was one of the lucky ones, and I got my navigation training. I didn't know, and neither did anybody else at the time, just how highly qualified we were for what we had selected. I happened to find out later that I had a 999 classification, signifying the highest aptitude in each category.

I went from the classification center to San Marcos, Texas, for training. That took about five months. We took a lot of math, astronomy, dead reckoning, Morse code, things like that. At the same time we were learning all of this, we were flying and putting it all into practice. We flew in AT-7s. They were twin-engined Beechcraft trainers. Good little airplanes, and at that point we were flying missions in the neighborhood of 200 to 300 miles. We would have three or four trainees along with an instructor in each plane. I completed navigation training in February of 1944 and was commissioned as a second lieutenant. I got my navigator wings, a two-week pass, and was assigned to an operational training facility. None of us knew what job we would get, but most of us ended up in operational units being trained for combat.

I went to Colorado Springs where I was assigned to a crew. We trained together for approximately two months and started to fly longer missions. We were flying larger airplanes, but I don't remember what type they were. This was the crew that I would go into combat with, and we were being trained to function as a crew. Fortunately, I was with a pilot, copilot, bombardier, and others with whom I was very compatible. I don't know what searches of our psychological backgrounds had been done, if at all. I have no idea if they did that during the war, but I know that our crew fit together quite well right from the beginning. We trained for about two months and then we were sent to Lincoln, Nebraska, to pick up a B-24. I'll never forget my pilot, Ray Landtroop, signing his name for that $250,000 airplane as if he had the money to pay for it if it got messed up.

Then we got our sealed orders. The only thing they told us to do was fly from Lincoln to West Palm Beach, Florida. The next day we got another set of orders which we were told we couldn't open until we were one hour out at sea flying in a certain direction. We found out that we were assigned to England. That was the first we knew where we were going, when we were in flight, heading out to sea. I can't say what every man's emotional reaction was, but I think we wanted it. We felt there was a job to do. We were trained for that job and that job was combat. Rather than flying around the so-called American Theater, the Caribbean, that sort of thing.

We flew to British Guiana, and from there to Belem, Brazil. Then, across the South Atlantic to Dakar. This was the first real long over-the-ocean trip I had ever made. It was scary, but it turned out to be a pretty good experience. Ray knew some navigation because pilots had all been given a certain amount of navigation training. He didn't know how much confidence to place in me. Although we had been together for over two months, he decided that instead of following the course I had given him, he would follow his radio compass. I explained something to him that he should have known. On long over-water reaches, the radio compass was not accurate, and would take us on a curved path instead of the straighter one, the course I gave him. I made a quick calculation of the amount of gas we had and decided it would be better not to push the matter, but just to let him see how it would work out. The way the radio compass works is that it always brings you to the point from where the signal emanates, but as I indicated before, not on a straight path. We went on a more northerly course and by the time we were a couple of hundred miles from Dakar, we were going almost at right angles to the course we had originally followed. We got there, without undue difficulties, but without too much of a gas reserve. After we landed, Ray said to me, "I should have listened to you." It was good for both of us, because he knew that what I told him was right and he could and should rely on me.

Now we had to go through the Atlas Mountains to get from Dakar to Marrakech. As we approached the mountains, the ceiling got lower and lower. We were not equipped at that time for high altitude flying. I don't remember if we didn't have oxygen or what it was, but we just couldn't get above the clouds on that trip. There was no way the pilot could see his way, so we had to navigate our way through. If we hadn't picked the right path, we would have cracked up in the mountains. I think this was when we really melded as a crew. From Marrakech, we flew several hundred miles out to sea on our way to England because the Germans were flying out of Spain and they were picking off some of our bombers. It was quite dark when we got to England, and we were very happy to get there, especially when they told us the Germans had rigged up the western tip of France to look like an English airfield. Crews had actually landed at that field and been captured.

We were then assigned to the 389th Bomb Group, 565th Squadron. This was heavy bombers, B-24s. The airplane we were assigned to was designated "O-Bar." In other words, an O with a bar after it. That was the plane we flew on almost all of our missions, and we never named it. Now, thinking back, it's funny that we didn't because Bob, the copilot, was quite an artist. He painted a Bugs Bunny character leaning against a bomb on the back of our brown leather jackets. He also put the state from which we came. It was beautifully done and I had that jacket for years. Then, when I moved from one apartment to another, I left it and couldn't make the trip back to pick it up and the jacket was lost.

Each of us was very proud of being a member of that crew and that Bugs Bunny character. By that time, we all knew each other quite well, and we were well trained as a crew. We had gained a great deal of confidence in one another. Ray, the pilot, was an uncharacteristic Texan in that he was the quiet type. If he said something, he generally meant it, and it pretty well stuck. Bob Farris, my copilot, on the other hand, was a much more adventurous type, and he had a very good sense of humor. He was from Idaho and given to very wry outbursts of one sort or another. He'd say something and have everybody laughing. It was unusual to have two fellows from the same city on the same crew but Bill Rodman, the bombardier, was, like me, from New York. The crew chief was from Michigan, the radio operator was from California, one gunner was from Oklahoma, another from South Carolina, and another from Texas. Am I leaving somebody out? Oh, another gunner was from Michigan. We were all pretty diverse. I think we represented a cross section of youth in America at that time.

I'm still in touch with all but one of them. When I say "in touch," I mean that I send some of them Christmas cards. I have visited Ray and Bob, and Bill, the bombardier, and I are still quite friendly. We see each other a few times a year. The crew chief, something happened to him. I don't know what. I managed to find out where he was located ten years ago. I called up and spoke to his son and was unable to make contact. It was complete lack of interest on his part.

There have been very few people I have been closer to than my crew. There is no question of that. You developed so much esprit with them that the very thought of their flying without you was devastating. You could not accept the possibility that they could go on a mission and get killed and you would still be there. It would be terrible that they would be killed and unthinkable that you wouldn't, if you can understand what I mean. There were two occasions where this really hit home. I'd been up all night planning a mission. I was an experienced navigator by then and occasionally was called upon to prepare mission flight plans. I was too pooped and, by regulation, not allowed to go on that mission. My crew went and came back, and I never sweated out a mission like that one.

I kept a diary at that time, and I put down that we arrived in England, May 1, 1944, and we flew our first mission on May 15. We knew that the Eighth Air Force had taken tremendous losses, prior to the time that we arrived, but we felt that things were turning in our favor. I guess we always looked at the optimistic side. I never thought

150

we were going to lose. I don't know if that was characteristic of the Air Force or not, but I felt that we had such great industrial capability that we just couldn't lose. It didn't seem possible that we could have all this airpower and not come out the victor. Of course, I might have lost my life, but the country would win. At that time we were getting more fighter support. More American fighter planes were available, and perhaps there were fewer German fighters in the sky. The formations we were using were more effective by this time, and I must say that I never got the feeling that we were being sent out and told to "Go bomb Berlin" and maybe you'll come back. These were not suicide missions.

We were well trained; I know I certainly felt well trained. There was adequate preparation and reconnaissance before each mission. We also had excellent weather briefings. I felt that we were given targets that were necessary to bomb and that every effort had been made to find out as much as could be found out about the targets and what kind of antiaircraft protection there was. Also, the probability of fighter intervention, where'd we pick them up, that sort of thing. All of these things I found to be pretty much as briefed. Often we got jumped at a different place than we would expect, but we were never told not to expect it. Coverage by our fighters was spotty. Sometimes it was great and sometimes it just wasn't there. One time that it really did make a difference, we did have pretty good cover. On our twenty-seventh mission we aborted because we had one engine out and a hydraulic leak in another. Ray turned back over Germany and we were a sitting duck. We couldn't maintain our altitude and kept going down, down, down. Three P-51s showed up and escorted us back to the Dutch border, and then one of them took us to the Channel. The name on that fighter plane was "Linda" and it's no coincidence that my first daughter's name is Linda. I feel that I never would have been here had it not been for that P-51.

On most missions, I actually dropped the bombs. We were pattern-bombing, and everybody would toggle when the lead bombardier dropped his bombs. In some cases that type of bombing was successful, in other cases, totally unsuccessful. I would feel particularly good if we hit a military target and there was tremendous property damage. We were told what the targets were and what they were producing in those particular factories. One of the targets we bombed was the plants that were producing the rockets that the Germans were launching at London. I listed it in my diary as a robot-manufacturing plant. We thought of them as a type of robot at that time. I had experienced plenty of V-1s while I was in London and saw what they could do. Ball-bearing factories, it goes without saying, you know what they are used for and why you wanted to bomb them. I felt very differently when the target was socked in and we could not bomb visually. They'd say to go ahead and bomb using the rudimentary radar available at that time. We did on one occasion, it was Hamburg, and I must say that not only did I get no satisfaction out of that mission, I was very concerned. I felt that we might be hitting civilians and the thought was very bothersome to me.

Not only was I dropping the bombs, I could watch them hit. Most of the crew couldn't see down, but I could always see where those bombs went if the weather was clear. Also, we always had the photographs taken after the target was hit. The most interesting target photo that I saw was the bombing of St. Malo, which is a group of little islands off the coast of France. They had been heavily fortified by the Germans. There were U-boat pens, artillery, and whatnot, with a tremendous concrete top. We used very heavy bombs and blasted the place to pieces. I don't think anything survived that attack. If we missed the target, which we did on occasion, the brass would complain, but we always felt that we had one up on them. Even though they were senior officers, we knew we were on the firing line. They were reading pictures. Nobody was going to tell us what we did was bad, wrong, or indifferent if we were putting our lives on the line and doing the best we knew how to do.

Our first mission was scary as hell. Probably it was just because it was the first one, an honest-to-goodness mission. We went to an aircraft factory in France, dropped eight 1,000-pound bombs, and flew home. We didn't see any flak or fighters. It was as easy a mission as you could probably have, and yet, it was the most harrowing. The fear of the unknown. The first time we hit the marshalling yards at Saarbrücken, we did get flak and we got shot up very badly. It was so bad that, although we got back to the English coast, we couldn't get to our own airfield. They ended up taking off our entire wing and then putting on a new one. Actually, they pirated it from another, older plane. Our plane had never been painted and had a silver finish. The wing they put on was olive drab and it was pretty ragged-looking. However, our plane was easily identifiable, I'll tell you that.

As I said, that damage was caused by flak. The Germans were using a form of radar to aim their guns. In order to fool them as much as we could, we would throw what we called "chaff" out of the plane. It was nothing more than aluminum strips. Very thin, almost like aluminum foil. The idea was that the "chaff" would reflect on the radar as would a regular plane, so that the radar operators would be unable to get a fix on the altitude we were flying. If they got our altitude, you could be sure they would hit something because we filled the sky. If we could fool them by changing our altitude during the mission, we would, but we had several problems with regard to that. If we approached at a certain altitude and stayed there, the German radar stations in France, Holland, or Denmark, whichever way we came in, would have a long time to get a fix. Then they would warn the antiaircraft batteries. If we decided to go higher during the mission, we would lose a great deal of airspeed. That might be 10 miles an hour, which was considerable when we were only going 160. Once we leveled off we would have to calculate our bomb drop for a slower speed. We would also have to make sure that we reached the new altitude as a group in order to bomb at the correct altitude. So, as a general rule, we came in at a certain altitude and pretty much maintained it. We hoped to fool them with the "chaff."

We did get attached to that plane, *O-Bar*. We knew it. Even with that heavy damage, we knew it would bring us back. I think the B-24 was at least as good as the B-17. I've seen them shot up as badly as B-17s and they seemed to limp back, so I think they were damn good airplanes.

On D-day, we went to a big briefing room about eight o'clock the night before, and the doors were closed behind us. We were told that we were not going to be let out under any circumstances, for any reason. The next day was going to be the invasion. They told us we were going to take off at three o'clock in the morning, the only time we took off in the dark. Then, we were going to circle over Scotland, form up, and hit the beaches not later than six-thirty. If you didn't make it by then, you couldn't drop your bombs. They didn't want to take any chances with hitting our own troops. Each group put every plane in the air it possibly could. Everybody was rah-rah-rah! You couldn't stop anybody from going on that one. We formed O.K. and dropped our bombs about four minutes after six. There was an undercast so we couldn't see the ships coming across the Channel, but when we got over the beaches, it was clear enough to see to bomb.

When we got back, the weather was getting worse, but we were told that if we wanted to, we could go on a second mission. I don't know of anybody who didn't volunteer to go on that one, too. Half of us hadn't slept the night before, but it really didn't make any difference. We were really hyped to go. I have visited those beaches since the war, and I have no idea how they did it—I don't know. Visualizing those guys coming out of the water facing German artillery of all kinds. What we did was dangerous enough, but that other kind of bravery down on those beaches—I just don't know.

We had a harrowing experience on the second mission over Normandy. We came through the cloud cover over England—"we" meaning our entire group of seventy or eighty planes, in formation—and found ourselves on a collision course with another group coming out of the same clouds. There were several mid-air collisions, and planes went down. Our plane made a violent turn to avoid another plane, and we went completely over on our back, then down into a spin. Down we went and eventually the airspeed indicator hit 320 miles per hour. The wings are supposed to come off at 275, and I'm sitting there looking at all the instruments. I'm watching the altimeter and I know how high we are, but the fellows in the back didn't. All they could do was rely on what they heard on the earphones. What they heard was that Ray couldn't get the plane under control. Then my copilot, who was really a fighter plane–type, starts talking on the intercom and he says, "Stay with it. I think we can hold it." The nose gunner had come out of the turret and had his feet out of the nose wheel well ready to parachute out when I grabbed him by the collar, literally, and told him to stay with the airplane. He held on and we pulled out of the spin without a lot of altitude to spare. By this time we were too low to get back into formation so we jettisoned our bombs and came back and landed. A spin in a B-24 is not the most pleasant experience, I'll tell you.

Toward the end of June our plane had been heavily damaged again. Because of the damage, we were not scheduled to fly and the rest of the group went to Berlin. We lost three crews on that mission. Fellows whom I had trained with at Peterson Field in Colorado. It was absolutely a traumatic experience for me because these were people whom I had known longer than anyone we were flying with. Two of the men were in my particular squadron when I was in navigation training. In the Norwich library—Norwich was the largest town near our base—there is a memorial that was put up by the people of that town for my particular wing, the Second Bomb Wing. The names of those men who were killed are on the memorial. When I was there several years ago, I looked to see if those names were listed. Sure enough, they were there, as against the thought that perhaps they went down and became prisoners of war. But the names were there.

When I started flying combat, you had to make twenty-five missions. At the time, that was considered the point at which a flier's fortitude, the rate of attrition, and the needs of the Air Force approximately met. Just before D-day, the number of required missions was raised to thirty. Disturbing as the increase was, the attrition rate was somewhat lower than in earlier years, and we had no alternative but to adapt our thinking to a longer tour of duty.

I flew my thirtieth mission on August 13, 1944. I went with another crew because I had to make up the one mission I had missed. I sure hoped we wouldn't have any problems on the way back and when we hit the runway it was heaven, just heaven. You didn't feel like an old veteran, but you knew damn well you were. You were still very young, but you were experienced. I was an eighteen-year-old

154

when I went into the service, and I grew up in the ultimate graduate school. My older children are girls, but I can gather from their male acquaintances just how much more mature I was at twenty, let's say, than the boys of today who don't have that experience. Being thrown into the army, dealing with new conditions, new circumstances, and a great deal of stress in those airplanes over Europe imposed a lot of responsibility. But if push came to shove, I think there would be boys to do it again today just as well as we did. I don't think they're any less able, it's just that they haven't had to do what we did.

After I finished combat, I became a navigation and briefing officer with Air Transport Command. I was preparing crews for problems they might encounter flying over the North Atlantic. When the war was over in Japan, I had accumulated a lot of points and was among the first groups to go home. I flew back in a B-17 using the same route we followed on the way over, but the trip coming back was very different. For one thing we flew directly over Spain instead of having to go way out to sea. I was mustered out of the service, and went back to City College and graduated in August of 1946.

I worked in accounting, on and off, for the next four years. Finally, in 1950, I realized I wasn't that interested in accounting, and started to go to law school at night. In fact, I became so interested in law that I quit accounting and went to work as a law clerk. The pay was still low, but it was much more satisfying. Then I switched to full-time day law school when the Korean War broke out. I was recalled for a B-29 bomber group but ultimately I was deferred. I had no desire to go into combat again and have another interruption in my career. I felt I was finally making progress, and I certainly didn't want to lose more time navigating B-29s around Korea. If I had been twenty years old, it might have been different, but it was somebody else's turn, not mine. I had seen my share of war.

I finished law school, worked for two years as a single practitioner, and then accepted an offer from the New York State attorney general's office as an assistant attorney general. I did that until 1969 when I went to work for the firm of White and Case, and in 1983 I came here to Morgan, Lewis and Bockius.

When I came back from the war, I had a very positive feeling. I felt that we'd made the world safe for democracy. There weren't going to be any more wars. It was a very idealistic view. I also felt invulnerable, but on the other side of the coin, I always carry around a terrible feeling that a lot of good people had been killed and why had I been spared? A picture remains in my mind. I used to see the Catholic priest, Father Beck, who was a wonderful man, saying Mass for all the Catholic boys before a mission. Dressed in those weird flight suits, ready to put on their oxygen masks, they knelt down to pray. A few hours later, I saw many of them go down in a fiery dive. Such good guys. Faithful, straight, why them and not me? It is something that I'll never know the answer to, but I can never get it completely out of my thoughts. I never stop seeing those boys.

ARTHUR ARTIG

NO VISIBLE MEANS OF SUPPORT

Arthur Artig flew in a B-26 squadron that followed the army during the reconquest of Europe. The twin-engine bomber was officially called the Marauder, *but was known to the men who flew it as* The Widow Maker, *or* The Flying Prostitute. *It had indeed a reputation as a killer; however, Artig disagrees. He is himself a small, intense man, and his voice and manner are pure New York. He tells you exactly what's on his mind, however uncomplimentary it may sound to the current generation and its work habits. An engineer with Grumman Aerospace, now retired, he worked on many different airplanes since the war, but we doubt if any of them meant as much to him as* The Widow Maker.

I figured if I was going to go, I didn't want to walk to the war. It's a fact, I was never in an airplane before the war. I graduated from pilot's school and I couldn't even drive a car. I grew up in the Bronx and went to Syracuse University—engineering. When the war broke out, I was working in a defense plant and had a 2B classification. That meant I was draft-deferred because I was working on essential programs. Everybody was gone from the neighborhood; I was just hanging around, so I volunteered for the Air Force.

When the war ended I went to work at U.S. Plywood. They were trying to devise new methods of making production parts for airplanes out of plywood—parts like bulkheads, floors, wing ribs, things like that. During the war that would have been important because of the shortage of steel, but this was after the war and it didn't pan out. I left there and went to Republic Aviation. While I was there I worked on the F-84 and the F-105. From Republic I came here

157

to Grumman. I was doing armament design on things like the Gatling gun, the 20mm cannon installation on the F-14. I also worked on the F-14 pylons, which are under the wings and hold the missiles, bombs, and extra fuel tanks.

I got tired of that a few years back and went into production engineering, quality engineering, which is what I'm doing now. Still involved with airplanes after all these years. I try to get the different subcontractors, as well as my own company, to make better parts—make sure the parts have the same specifications and tolerances as the drawings. I'm not on a specific program right now. I'm sitting in the office where I handle our vendor work, and I'll tell you, it's no fun working anymore. It's the people, really. They have no morale. Make a lot of money and don't do any work. It's tough even trying to teach them, so you get to the point where you say the hell with it. I was always quick to help someone, to show them the best way to do the job. No more, because they resent your doing it. "You're over the hill, old man, and I'm just out of college, and I'm smarter than you." You just don't get any satisfaction any more. It's not just me, sour grapes or something. Most of the old-timers will tell you this, the real workers.

That's why this whole country is going downhill. There is no such thing as quality because the young people don't want to take the time to learn, and the old guys are getting out as fast as they can. Everybody wants to start as the president of the company. And the young engineers—they know it all.

They have a lot of new equipment at Grumman—computer graphics, for instance. You sit there, push buttons, and design. It's beautiful and it works. You can blow things up to different sizes and it will show you tolerances, just about everything you want to know. Quicker than sitting at a board and laying it out. That's the kind of thing that's happening in engineering. But you need the people who can run the machine and people who understand what it tells you. The machines get better and the people get worse.

Now, after saying all that, the airplanes fly. They work. Knock the people, knock the design, knock everything, but they work. So, what the hell is the moral of this story? I just think it could work a hell of a lot better. You wouldn't have the scrap rate and the re-work we have. It isn't just the parts either. The design itself can be a joke. A guy who I work with, Bill Phillips, who incidentally was a P-51 pilot in World War II, called me over one day. He was doing the configuration of an airplane. That's the overall outline of the plane after you fit all the parts into it—what it's actually going to look like. He said, "Art, look at this. This guy has designed this canopy for this ship." I said, "Why the hell do you want to get me involved? I have enough

Arthur J. Artig, far left, first pilot of a B-26 Marauder, poses with his crew at Lake Charles, Louisiana, in July 1944, just prior to leaving for Europe. From his left: Thomas E. Speer, copilot; John Kokos, bombardier; Ray C. Leighty, flight engineer; Lonnie Brauner, radio operator; and John E. Bailey, top turret gunner. They flew more than forty missions without a casualty.

problems of my own." Bill told me he wanted me to see what this coconut was doing because he thought it was wrong. Bill was fighting the canopy design. The designer had chopped the canopy right behind the pilot's head to put in a bulkhead. That meant the pilot can't see back. I asked the designer how the pilot was going to see behind the airplane and he said, "Oh, that's no problem, I've put a mirror up here." It was like a rear view mirror in an automobile. Now, in a fighter plane, your head's going all the time, especially when you're in combat. You never look at one thing. That's one of the first things they taught you, keep your head going. This designer is asking a pilot to focus on a mirror in the cockpit and then focus on a distant object and back again. Well, the result of all this was that they left that mirror in there, but they made the canopy so the pilot could swing his head around. You're a pilot, you want to see. The guy who was designing that canopy had never flown an airplane, much less in combat. On top of that, the director of the whole project's claim to fame was that he built model airplanes. Beautiful!

There were windshield wipers on the B-26. We got into heavy rain, I switched them on, and they did a beautiful job of smearing the window. Couldn't see a thing. You can take those wipers and throw them in the garbage. The water hits the windshield and naturally goes up in rivulets and you can see. The guy who designed them thought we were going for a ride on the Long Island Expressway with that airplane.

When I was working in armament at Grumman, one fellow asked me why I put the gun along the center line of the airplane. I told him that when the pilot is using that gun he's flying the gun, not the airplane. I knew what I was talking about because when you're hot under the collar, trying to hit something in combat, you don't know what the hell the airplane is actually doing. You haven't even got the gunsight on, you're flying that gun. On the B-26, we had four package guns, two on each side, that the pilot fired. For a while, there was also a fixed machine gun in the nose fired by the pilot, but they took it out. That thing scared the hell out of the bombardier, and the ejected shells would hit him in the head—another beautiful design. I had a sight for the package guns, but it was a pain in the ass. Not only that, you were afraid of it. It was a healthy piece of glass, and if anything happened in the air and you were thrown forward, you'd get it right in the head. There were always pilots walking around with stitches across their foreheads.

Four German Me109s hit our group one day. Most of the 109 pilots would roll over after they made their pass so their bottom was toward you. For some reason this one guy rolled toward me with his cockpit facing me. He broke right and went in front of me. I just held the button on those guns and in the excitement, I started following him down—not using the sight, flying the guns. He started smoking pretty good, and suddenly I realized that I'd left the formation. You've always got two wingmen and you weren't supposed to leave that formation, ever. I pulled back up and a Peashooter, a P-38, followed him down and finished him off. When I got back, this major came down with a big magnum of champagne for me. I think I was the only one in our group that got an Me109 with the package guns.

★

I didn't know much about the B-26 when I was going through flight school. We had heard the nicknames like *Flying Prostitute*, that sort of thing. They called it that because it supposedly had "no visible means of support." I went through twin-engine school, and before I graduated, they asked me which plane I would like to fly. They actually acted like you had a choice. I asked for a P-38. They said I couldn't have it because it was a fighter. I said, "Doesn't it have two engines?" They said that wasn't the point, it was a fighter. Typical military thinking, ass-backward. I also asked for the A-20, the Havoc. No chance, they were being replaced by the B-25. I said that would be all right, but they said they didn't have any B-25s, so I could fly the B-26. Some choice!

I reported to Del Rio, Texas, and I saw two columns of smoke at the end of the runway. I asked a crew chief what they were, and he told me it was the plane I was going to learn how to fly. Two of them had gone in that morning. I walked down the flight line and looked at those planes and they looked like monsters. I'd graduated from twin-engine school in a AT-17. That was like a Piper Cub with two engines. Each engine had 225 horsepower with a two-bladed prop we used to call butter paddles. You could get that plane down to about 10 miles an hour in the air and its top speed was 110 in a dive. In the B-26 you went from 450 HP to 4,000—like going from kindergarten to graduate school with nothing in between. You looked at that goddamned thing with those 16-foot, four-bladed props, and you were scared shitless. The more you found out about the airplane's reputation, the harder it became to get into the cockpit.

The first couple of landings scared the hell out of me. Hotter than anything that was around at the time, and for some time after that. You'd land that plane at 145 MPH, with an approach speed of 160. Now, you ask, why did you come in so hot? After you learned how to land it, the instructor would take you up to about 10,000 feet to do stalls. We used to do stalls in the AT-17, and you'd lose a couple of hundred feet. We took this B-26 up to 10,000 feet, cut the power, pulled up the nose, and started flying again at 3,000 feet. Couldn't do a thing with it; she dropped like a rock. That's why you came in smoking. Never get near a stall with that airplane, no way.

Landing wasn't a problem after you got acclimated to the speed. You'd groove it in. Beautiful, smooth landings. The problem with the B-26 was taking off. You'd sweat it out because they had those Curtiss electric props. If you got a runaway prop on takeoff, you'd had it. That airplane wouldn't get off on one engine, not even light. Forget it with a bomb load. We lost a lot of guys right on takeoff. You were always told not to go around. Just pull the gear up and go straight in on your belly. That's the sort of thing that caused the plane to have a bad reputation. However, they changed a lot of things during the war, and by the time they finished with that airplane, it was a hell of a piece of equipment.

For one thing, it was built like a tank. We used to fly two parallel runways in training. One runway was for planes taking off, and the other one was for landing. Besides us, we had commuter airplanes, navigation trainers, and stuff like that using the field. It was real busy, and one day a couple of guys got confused and landed the wrong way in a trainer. A B-26 clobbered them and drove their airplane right into the ground. Killed them both, destroyed that airplane and all that 26 had was a dent in the wing.

The only real trouble I had in basic was with an instructor, not the airplane. This guy was a freckled kind of little guy; a real California type, anti-everything from the East. People from New York, but especially New York Jews. To put it bluntly, I guess he was anti-Semitic. He used to hit us on the knees with the stick when he didn't like the way we were flying. We got smart after awhile, and we'd fly with our legs spread apart. He wanted me to wash out and he wanted my roommate to do the same thing. My roommate's name was Arnold Randolph Benson III, and Arnold used to tell Jewish jokes. He'd imitate Lou Holtz, the Jewish comedian, accent and all. He'd have the whole squadron in stitches and this instructor didn't like that at all; he put us up for washout rides three times. Finally Captain Allen, the squadron commander, said, "I don't know what the hell is the matter with you two guys. You can fly. Leave me alone. You don't have an instructor anymore, you're on your own." After Benson and I graduated, we got into this B-26 and went looking for that guy. We were going to fly him right out of the air. We couldn't find him and it probably was a good thing. Oh, yeah, the crowning touch. This guy was a big hero-type, right? He'd say all the time, "If I'm going to be killed, I want to be killed in combat and not be killed by some student." Just about that time, they were short of pilots in Europe, and they put a notice on the bulletin board asking for volunteers. Not only did he refuse to volunteer, not one of the instructors in the whole damn squadron wanted to go. So much for those heroes.

Everything changed so drastically when you went into combat. It had nothing to do with rank, what your religion was, where you were from, anything like that. All that crap was forgotten. Now you were fighting for your life, and everybody was in the same boat. You were always scared. You didn't admit it, but you were—let's say nervous tension. You were always wet. No matter what time of year it was, your back, rear-end, legs, they'd be soaking wet with perspiration. Your hands and feet would get so cold. There was a heater, but it was useless because if you put it on, you'd get carbon monoxide in the airplane. Jesus, it was cold in that airplane. Those poor guys in the back would be freezing because those turrets were wide open— the slots for the guns. It would be thirty-five below and it might have been colder than that because that's as far down as the instrument went. It would actually snow inside the cockpit; I mean actual snowflakes coming down on you. We tried everything to keep warm. Gloves were no good because you couldn't hit the switches. We finally ended up with a French design. It was silk, very thin, with a thin leather glove on top of that. It worked the best. On our feet we used a white cotton sock, a gray woolen sock over that and a combat boot, then a flying boot, sheepskin lined and all. But, like I said, those guys in the back had it the worst with that wind whistling through those slots. They bitched like crazy and finally the Air Corps gave them these electric flying suits. So, now, they're going to be nice and warm and we looked over the whole airplane and couldn't find a single outlet to plug in those damn suits. Another great design job. But everybody had an ashtray. You couldn't smoke in that airplane because it was so full of fuel vapor. There's an ashtray at every crew member's station, and I'm thinking how some guy's getting fat and rich making ashtrays for an airplane that you can't use them in.

I think the only way we got through that war was that we were young and dumb. Flying combat was very intense. You spent almost three years of your life doing the same thing almost every day and you really got pretty good at it. The one thing that amazes me, looking back, was that you'd get shot up one day, sometimes really bad— the airplane would look like hell—it wouldn't even dawn on you not to get back in the airplane and go on the mission the next day. When you were taxiing out, you'd see the guys standing on the ground who weren't going, and you'd wish you were there with them, but this is the strange part. When you were standing down, not going on a mission, you'd see those planes heading out and you'd wish you were going with them. Try and figure that one out. If your airplane was shot up and couldn't fly, you'd borrow another airplane so you could go.

I did that one day, borrowed another airplane, and when I pulled up the gear, it was just barely flying. I couldn't get that plane to climb, no matter what I did. I actually had to hop over the fence at the end of the field, that's how low I was. I followed the contour of the ground in order to build up air speed and she's finally going pretty good and I got up into formation. No problem after that, flying the mission or landing. Then they told me I was to report to the colonel. I'm standing at attention and he raked me up and down. "What in the hell are you buzzing for?" I had kind of a reputation for low flying so he was really laying for me. I wanted to fly under the Eiffel Tower after the war ended, but my crew wouldn't let me. I told the colonel that I couldn't do anything about it, the airplane wouldn't climb. He said, "Did you pre-flight that airplane before you flew it?" I told him I hadn't. He said, "Let's go look at that airplane and see why you had to fly so low." Now, I'm really sweating and I'm hoping that the ground crew found something wrong with that airplane. Well, we climbed inside that plane and there were thirteen heavy, lead-lined flak jackets in the back end. The gunners had lined the fuselage with flak jackets. Every time an airplane would crack up, the crew would run and clean out the flak suits. They figured that all that lead would make a much safer airplane. You take thirteen times 100 pounds, that's a lot óf weight in the ass end of an airplane the size of a B-26. The regular pilot of that plane knew about it, and he'd compensate for it when he was taking off. I didn't know about it and almost bought it. The next day the order came out that there would be one flak suit, per man, per plane. You should have seen all of those suits coming out of those airplanes.

They said if you're in the Air Force, you live like lords. That's because of all that Hollywood crap and the Eighth Air Force in England. You talk to a B-24 or B-17 guy who was in England, and you'll know there was a big difference from the way we lived on the continent. I tell that to people today, and they say I'm full of it. We were always moving up with the infantry, and we lived in the mud in tents. At one point they moved us into some captured German barracks. They were worse than the tents. The latrines had parts of guys that had been killed because they were using them for bomb shelters, and they stunk like crazy. You wouldn't even go in there. They put three guys in a room that was just about right for one guy. Terrible. We were the last airfield up the line from the Red Ball Express, which trucked up our supplies. By the time they got to us, the food was terrible because they were selling the good stuff on the way. We got C and K rations. If we got movies once a month, it was a lot. Entertainment was at a minimum. We didn't see Bob Hope and his USO show, nothing like that.

Right after the war, the summer of '45, we got a message that we were supposed to pick up the Don Cossack Choir in Frankfurt and bring them back so they could entertain us. We were in Venlo, Holland. They were old men at that time, some of them were sixty-five and seventy. We took three airplanes, just two of us in a plane, no navigator or anybody else. We get down there and I see this mob. It looked like an army. Each guy has two big bags because they had been picking up souvenirs and what not. I break it down and we've got to divide all of these guys up into three airplanes. We wind up with about twelve guys in each plane, which is kind of heavy. I was the last guy in because I wanted to see if everybody was all set, and this one guy is sitting in my seat. I said, "Can you fly this airplane?" I had a hell of a time getting him out of that seat. We didn't give any of them parachutes because we didn't have enough, and you couldn't give half of them 'chutes and not the other half. We made out like they didn't need parachutes. We crank up the engines, my wing man is fine, but the other guy says he can't get one engine going. It was hot so we kill the engines and tell everybody to get out. They didn't want to get out. We said, "We've got to get all of you out of here or we can't get these airplanes going, and we're not leaving here without everybody." Told them to get lunch.

Off they went, and we took the cowling off to see what was wrong with the engine. We figured it was vapor lock in the front carburetor because of the heat, so one of the crew chiefs went and got a big rubber mallet, and here come these guys with their sandwiches and they see this guy beating the hell out of the airplane. You can imagine their thoughts. Well, we get it all fixed, start them up again, and loaded everybody up again. I'm going down the runway and all of a sudden, I hear this noise; I almost put that airplane into the ground. One guy decided to play the accordion at that moment. What a crew! We get into formation and fly back to Holland with no trouble. Those guys loved the flight. We took pictures of them sitting on the bombs.

Another thing, where we were, was the women. The French girls wouldn't talk to you unless you were properly introduced, which was a tough thing to fix. Not only that, the towns near the camp hated our guts because, before we moved there, they said we'd been bombing them and killing French people. The Belgians and Dutch realized we were just doing our job, and if something like that happened, it was unavoidable. But the Dutch girls, forget it. They're all built like cows.

Big muscles and they couldn't speak English. And Dutch is a very difficult language. With the German girls, you had nonfraternization. So that's what we had.

Our squadron was *small*. I think there were about three hundred in a squadron, something like that. Out of that, there's only ninety-six guys in combat. Everybody else was support. People don't realize that. We'd take guys along on a mission. They'd get permission and come along for the ride. We took infantry guys, armament guys. I had a Polish captain with me once. When we were in France there was a Mosquito squadron on the other side of town, and they were crazy—crazier than us. Czechs and Poles flying in the Royal Canadian Air Force, and you wouldn't believe what they used to do with those Mosquitoes. They would never ground-check the airplane or check the traffic control—just start the engines and go. They flew low! We flew low, but they used to go lower than we did and we were cutting wheat with our props. They would tear into anything because I don't think they had anything to lose. Most of them came from families that were gone. They were going to get the Germans, no matter what.

I think the advantage, if there was any, of being in a B-26 outfit was the fact that we flew such close formations. We flew between one and three feet apart—six airplanes—so it's close and tight. The closer you are, the more firepower you have. I think the German fighter pilots were very unhappy about attacking a 26 outfit. They would rather go for the heavies because they could pick on one guy. We were moving quick and they knew it. Lots of times we would say, "Gee, the heavies are up there, thank God."

The same with flak. They'd usually go for them because they had twice the bomb load we had and couldn't do the evasive maneuvers we could. The Germans fired their guns the same way—"boom-boom-boom-boom." Always in fours. No matter if they were firing visually or by radar. Four would come up, and the next four would never come up in the same place. We used to change heading and altitude every 15 seconds. The heavies couldn't do that. The only time you had to fly straight and level was from the IP to the target. That's the "initial point of attack" to the target, and that normally ran about an average of five minutes. We never gave the bombardier five minutes. Of course, he would scream like hell because he was working fast, calculating speed, wind drift, all of that. Two or three minutes seemed like an hour when you were flying straight and level and those guys on the ground were shooting at you.

On a couple of missions we were flying over the sites where they were firing the V-2s. We'd see the flash on the ground and you could see this thing coming up and you were watching and waiting—they never told us until much later what the hell the V-2s were—so we were watching and waiting for this thing to come up and let go. We thought they were some kind of giant flak. Then they'd go right by and they were gone. Some of the intelligence we got was not worth a damn. During the Battle of the Bulge they told us not to worry. "You won't be getting any flak." Well, those tanks were shooting at us with everything they had. We got seven-and-a-half minutes of solid flak going in and coming out. Do you know what seven-and-a-half minutes of flak is? FLAK!

Of course, we did some job on the Germans during the Battle of the Bulge. The weather was rotten at the beginning and we couldn't fly, but later on we gave them hell. We were bridge busters, my squadron. A lot of our missions were involved with cutting the Germans off by busting up the bridges and roads. One morning we hit the wrong target, and our mistake left the retreating Germans with no place to go. We were supposed to hit a target over some marshland near Bastogne. Instead we hit a bridge that was on a main road, and we got hell for it. We came back from that mission and got debriefed, and General Elwood Quesada chewed us out. After he finished giving us hell, somebody got up on the platform and read us a commendation from General Patton telling us that we had done a terrific job by cutting the road. So we still had to go out that afternoon and get that other bridge we had missed in the morning. On the way out, we see all of these tanks, trucks, what have you, and the P-47s are just flying back and forth shooting the hell out of them. If you ever read that story, that's how it happened. The lead bombardier just picked the wrong target, the wrong bridge, and we got hell and a commendation out of it.

Now, looking back on it, I think that most people thought guys flying B-26s were off the wall. Maybe they were right, but I really liked that ship. When I got out of the Air Force, I tried to get a job with the airlines. I went to Pan American, TWA, and Eastern. They all gave me pretty much the same line. "Oh, you were flying B-26s? You're either a crazy guy or a hot pilot, and we don't want either." They basically wanted four-engine transport pilots because they figured they were kind of stable and were used to flying straight and slow—kind of . . . conservative. I stayed in the reserves and flew out of Floyd Bennett for a while. They had a troop carrier group at Mitchell Air Force Base, but I didn't want any of that. I didn't like flying those C-47s. I tried it overseas. Terrible lump. Didn't move, didn't go. You get spoiled, and it's like a BMW versus a Volkswagen. Hop into a C-47 or C-46 and push the throttle, nothing happens.

I'd love to see a B-26 today. In fact, if I try, I can still picture all the instruments and everything else in that cockpit. At the end of the war, we flew our plane down to some depot in Germany, and they parked them nose to tail and blew them up. Didn't strip them or anything from what I remember—just blew those airplanes up. Jesus, that was some airplane.

REGINALD H. THAYER, JR.

A STATISTICAL ABERRATION

Thayer lives near the Hudson River, a few miles from the majestic Tappan Zee Bridge. Heavyset, congenial, he has attended several reunions of his two bomb groups, the 97th and 306th, and maintains contact with many of his World War II comrades.

During May of 1985, ABC's Good Morning America *devoted a show to the forty-fifth anniversary of V-E Day. Reg Thayer was a featured participant, along with John Kenneth Galbraith. The latter had been involved during the war with the Strategic Bombing Survey, which analyzed the results of European bombardment. Galbraith asked Thayer how many missions he'd flown; Thayer told him seventy-nine. Galbraith was taken aback. "You're a statistical aberration," he said to Thayer. "Completing the required tour of twenty-five missions was itself nearly impossible."*

When I was in the Aviation Cadets, I was twenty years old and hitchhiking into Los Angeles when a guy picked me up and noticed my uniform. He turned out to be a First World War Navy pilot and started telling me about his flying days. Well, it bored the hell out of me. I was twenty years old, ready to get into the "big" war and very sure that I was going to be another Eddie Rickenbacker. He was an old fogey. At the time, he was probably all of fifty years old and here I am sixty-five years old as I talk to you. I said to myself at the time, "I'm never going to do that to the younger generation when I get to be his age." That's why I never talk about the war unless someone brings it up.

169

I joined the 97th Bomb Group in North Africa in June 1943, shortly after the ground fighting in Africa had ended. All of my fifty missions with the 97th were flown from bases in North Africa to targets in Sicily, Italy, France, Germany, Austria, and Greece. The target on my first mission was some docks at Messina, Sicily, on June 25 and on my fiftieth it was an airfield at Athens on December 6.

I guess the thought crossed my mind that I might not make it, but I don't remember being nervous about it. Of course, I was quite relieved when it was over. Things were always going on that didn't sink in at the time, but thinking back now you wonder how we made it through. In the fall of 1943 we got a new group commander, Lt. Col. Frank Allen, who decided that if you didn't hit the target, it wouldn't count as a mission. There was this bombardier by the name of Jaskiewicz; we called him "Jabbo," and he flew his fiftieth mission. That's what we had to do in Africa. After the mission he got drunk to celebrate, but when they developed the target photographs they found out that they had missed the target. So Jabbo had to fly the next day. Came back, got drunk again, and they found out they missed the target again. He had to fly his fifty-second mission. Years later I bumped into him on a street corner in New York City. I said, "Do you remember that Colonel Allen?" He said, "Do I remember Colonel Allen? That son-of-a-bitch could have killed me! I had to fly fifty-two missions for him." I heard later that the Pentagon found out what he was up to and told Allen that he couldn't do that. Fifty missions was fifty missions regardless of whether the target was hit. Colonel Allen was a former airline pilot and he used to talk about "frontal penetration" and "weather fronts." He'd say that in the airlines, when you come across a front, you know how to go through it. Now, one airplane going through a front, that's one thing. Taking thirty-six loaded bombers through a front, when they're all flying close together, going into clouds, was risky. There could be collisions, guys could just spin out and go in. There were procedures for taking a group through a front when it couldn't be avoided but it was tricky business, and not as easy as Colonel Allen made it out to be. I didn't particularly like Allen at the time, but I have recently learned that the inexperienced bomber group commander that I knew him to be in the fall of 1943 went on to compile a distinguished combat record and voluntarily flew more than the required fifty missions. My all-time favorite commanding officer was Col. LeRoy Rainey, who preceded Colonel Allen as 97th Group commander. Rainey was an inspiring combat leader who also flew more missions than he had to.

I finished my fifty missions, spent a week in rest camp (a lot of hell-raising and not much rest) on the Isle of Capri, and then came home during February of 1944. They asked me what kind of assign-

Reginald H. Thayer, Jr., a bombardier in B-17s, did his required fifty missions out of Africa, and then volunteered for another tour of duty flying twenty-nine missions out of England. In this photograph, taken in Tunisia in the fall of 1943, he stands at the far right rear, next to (going left) copilot Drake, navigator Gordon Ruberg, and the pilot and commander of the 414th Bomber Squadron, 97th Bomb Group, Lieutenant Colonel Bela Harcos. Forty-five years later, Thayer can identify only two crew members in the front row: Ballard, second from left, and the tail gunner, Shiflett, far right.

ment I wanted and I told them I wanted to go to England in B-17 bombers. They said, "You can't do that, you just came back from combat." So, they sent me down to Midland, Texas, to a bombardier instructors' school. It was safe duty, I guess, but I didn't like it. There wasn't much to do except go into town and get drunk once in awhile. I knew they were getting ready for the Normandy invasion and I wanted to go over and help support that effort. The Air Force kept giving me the runaround and I said, "The hell with this," and did something sort of crazy, I guess, but it worked. I wrote a letter to General Arnold, the head of the whole Air Force at that time. I wrote it in longhand and dropped it into a mailbox on a street corner. A while later, a major general wrote back and said I would get the assignment I desired "on or about June first."

June came, the invasion, of course, was on June 6, and by that time I had been transferred to Hobbs, New Mexico, and was teaching pilots how to work the auto pilot in conjunction with the Norden bombsight. I was still bored so I went to my squadron commander and said, "Look, I've got a promise to go to England, and they didn't keep their promise, what do I do now?" He said, "Write another letter, but for Christ's sake, have this one typed." He instructed a WAC lieutenant to type my letter. Her name was Sylvia Falkovic and she was pretty. In a matter of weeks, I got a telegram ordering me to Langley Field, and I joined a contingent that was going over to England. Got there about September 14 of 1944 and joined the 368th Squadron, 306th Group at Thurleigh, about 50 miles from London.

★

I was a junior at Columbia when they hit Pearl Harbor. That night I wrote letters to the Army Air Corps, Marine Air Corps, and the Navy Air Corps. Then I started to worry that it might take a long time to hear from them so I went down to 39 Whitehall Street. I had to take a lot of examinations, but I finally got to enlist, December 30, 1941. I wanted to be a pilot (another Eddie Rickenbacker!). I went to pilot training and they washed me out so I ended up in bombardiers' school. Most guys thought they should be pilots, and most bombardiers were fellows who didn't make it as pilots. It really made me mad at the time, but I can understand it now. It was a matter of expediting. They could teach other guys to fly quicker than they could teach me.

Pre-flight bombardier training was at Santa Ana, California. After that they tried an experiment with some of us. The Air Corps was always trying ways to speed up training because air crews were needed so badly at that time. A bunch of us were pulled out and instead of sending us to regular bombardier school, they sent us to an established B-24 bomber group in Tucson, Arizona, that was already flying practice missions. The trouble with that was that the crew members of those groups weren't experienced instructors, and we were sort of a nuisance to them. They decided that the experiment wasn't working, and sent us to regular bombardier schools. I was shipped to Victorville, California. Bombardier school was at one time an 18-week course, but to save time they kept compressing it and my class did it in 11 weeks. The instruction was the same, they just lengthened the day. We had to get up at five in the morning. Those training programs were one of the miracles of the war. They always talk about building all those planes in a hurry; when I look back on it and see how they were able to train us in such a short period of time and how proficient we got, I wonder how they did it. Maybe because we were young and eager.

We'd have ground school and flying every day and finish up late at night. For 11 weeks we did nothing but drop bombs, bombs, and more bombs, and attend classes. We flew in twin-engine Cessnas. A pilot, an instructor, and two student bombardiers. We carried ten 100-pound practice bombs, five for each student. They were filled with about 100 pounds of sand and three-and-a-half pounds of black powder. We called them "Blue Blivets." (Until we started calling them that, the commonly accepted definition of "blivet" was unprintable.) During the day they would make a white puff and at night, a flash when they hit the ground. We'd always take a camera and when one bombardier was bombing, the other one would point the camera through the bomb bay and photograph where the bombs hit. We'd fly everywhere from 1,500 to 13,000 feet, and we had to have a certain average score to graduate. Your average bomb had to be dropped within 250 feet of the target.

We also learned bombsight maintenance and troubleshooting, in case something went wrong on the mission. The Norden bombsight was very reliable. If the target was missed, it was almost always the bombardier's or pilot's fault. It wasn't just a matter of the bombardier using the sight correctly, the pilot had to fly the airplane according to the bombardier's instructions. We always had to carry a .45 pistol, and if the plane was forced down in enemy territory we were supposed to put a bullet into a certain vital part of the sight. My understanding is that in the excitement of going down, not everybody did that. Anyway, it wasn't long before the Germans had one. When you weren't flying, the bombsights were kept in a vault on the base with armed guards around it. As soon as we landed, we had to take it right back to the vault. I've got one for which I paid $37.50 at an army surplus store around 1970. I read someplace that they cost the government $25,000 each when they were new in World War II.

After I finished bombardier school, I went to Salt Lake City to get my assignment. Then I went by troop train to Blythe, California. You went everywhere by train during the war and on that trip we averaged 17 miles an hour. I spent a month at Blythe, and that's where I met my crew. These were the fellows I flew my first fifty missions with over Europe. This was operational training, and it was divided into three different stages. We spent the first month in Blythe familiarizing ourselves with the B-17 and learning how to work together as a crew. I remember the first practice mission we flew as if it were yesterday. We were all trying to size each other up, see who we were going to fight the war with. I was very lucky because my first bomb hit the center of the target. The tail gunner, Woodie Lawless, said, "Goddamn, you hit that right smack in the center!" I said, "Yeah, that's what I'm supposed to do." I think my next bomb was 500 feet off the target! Then we went to Pyote, Texas, for another month. Longer missions, bombing from higher altitudes, getting better all the time.

Our final month of training was at Casper, Wyoming. We worked well together and had developed a lot of respect for each other by the time we finished up at Casper. The pilot of our crew was a guy named Tom Smith from Tyler, Texas. He was only about twenty years old, but he flew the B-17 like he'd been doing it for a hundred years. He was quite a gambler. He felt so sure about winning that he never gambled with his crew members because he said he didn't want to take our money. One night in Casper I saw Tom and a pilot named Powledge, who was from Atlanta, Georgia, win $1,800 shooting craps in a casino. Months later we heard that Powledge was killed on a bombing mission over Germany. In January 1944, shortly before we came home from overseas, Tom won $2,000 playing poker over a period of about a week, and on the boat coming home he won another $2,000.

Our copilot was a guy named Alexander Alvarado from San Antonio, Texas. His nickname was "Iggy." A real nice guy. Our navigator was Gordon Ruberg from Eltingville, Staten Island. His nickname was "The Barrel" because he was built like one. A hell of a good navigator. Our flight engineer/top turret gunner was Horace Pabst from Kenosha, Wisconsin. Very competent and very serious. He bought tools with his own money for use in maintaining our plane. Our radio operator/gunner was Warren Laucella from Lynbrook, Long Island. He was also very serious and very competent. We called him "The Squirrel," but I don't remember why. Our ball-turret gunner was Frank Sloat from Rye, New York. He was the youngest guy on our crew (about eighteen) but when we got into combat he had a lot of poise. One of our waist gunners was Paul Hamlin from Binghamton, New York, and the other was Dale Lavigne from Mansfield,

Louisiana. Our tail gunner was George Woodrow Lawless from Shreveport, Louisiana. We called him "Woodie" and at the age of twenty-seven he was the old man of our crew. Most of us were about twenty-one when we first got together.

I think we were pretty well prepared when we went to Smokey Hill AFB in Kansas to get our airplane to take overseas. From there, in short stages, we flew to South America, across the south Atlantic, and wound up with the 97th Bombardment Group in Algeria near a place called Chateau Dun, just a little airfield out in semidesert farm country. It was a bit desolate, but lots of sun and blue sky. We were living in tents. Sometimes to get away from the G.I. chow my crew teamed up with our ground crew and had a big chicken fry of scrawny chickens which we bought from the Arabs and plucked, cleaned, and fried.

We were kind of excited about our first mission. I don't want that to sound like bravado, but we looked forward to it. We had trained hard for it. There were fighters buzzing around and all I could think of during the bomb run was that as soon as I got rid of those damn bombs, I was going to get my hands on one of my machine guns and knock off some of those fighters. After I dropped our bombs we started to fall behind the group, which is bad because when you stay together, you have a concentrated bunch of machine guns going. The fighters picked on stragglers. Then one of the gunners told me that the bomb-bay doors were open. I closed them as fast as I could and we caught up with the rest of the planes. It was a very embarrassing experience, and I felt like a dope. I had been trained hour after hour, the first thing you do after the bombs go away, you close the bomb-bay doors because the drag slows you down when they're hanging open.

While we were at that base, we went on the first bombing raid to Rome. General Jimmy Doolittle himself came to our group and led the mission. We had special photos with all the Vatican buildings and religious buildings outlined in white. I kept one of those photos from that mission and recently gave it to the West Point Museum. Written right on there, "Vatican City, Must On No Account Be Damaged." Maybe five hundred bombers came over Rome that day and only one bomb hit a church. We hit railroad yards and things like that. They had avoided bombing Rome because it was such a great city, but they found out the Germans were taking advantage of it. The railyards were jammed full of war materials.

I flew with essentially the same crew for my first fifty missions, but with people getting sick and injured, there'd be temporary substitutions. On August 1, 1943, I was scheduled to fly on a plane to take someone else's place who was sick. After attending the briefing,

I discovered that I had a problem myself, probably from eating too much of an overripe watermelon sold to me by an Arab the day before, and I went to see the squadron commander, Captain Mode. He told me to wake up a guy named Frank Bigelow so he could take my place. I woke Frank up and gave him my target map and photo and away he went. He got shot down that day and spent two years in a German prison camp. I got into a crap game that day. It was payday and I lost all the money I had and all the money I could borrow, five hundred bucks. It was still one of the luckiest days of my life because I would have been shot down. I don't think I would have gotten out of that airplane because I was young and cocky and I didn't wear my parachute until later on in my combat career. Five of them got out, including Bigelow. I bumped into him at Fort Dix when we were getting out of the service and he wasn't mad at me. We still keep in touch. Great guy.

Another time I was scheduled to fly with a pilot named Steadman and somebody else got sick and I took his place in another plane. That day Steadman was shot down over Italy. Fighters got him. The plane was damaged and was unable to stay up with our formation. I remember seeing the German fighters swarming around his airplane like bees. He went down about 10,000 feet and exploded. A terrible thing to watch. That was the second time a last-minute substitution saved my life.

I told my crew at one point that we were all going to come back together. Well, we didn't. None of us were killed, but only seven of us came back the way we went over. Iggy ended up as a prisoner of war. He got shot down on the same plane with Bigelow. One of our waist gunners was injured in an explosion on the ground. A plane blew up next to him and they thought it might have been sabotage. They put a silver plate in his head and he was taken off flying status. Then, the other waist gunner, Dale Lavigne, lost a leg on a mission we flew near the Salerno beachhead.

That mission was on September 18, 1943. The Allies had just turned the tide at the beachhead, and we were told that the Germans were retreating. Normally we flew at 20,000 to 25,000 feet. This day they sent us in at 15,000 feet because they said we wouldn't run into any flak. The Germans were dragging their guns along with them during their withdrawal and couldn't set them up. Our mission was to bomb this mountain road between Battapaglia and Eboli and cut them off. So, in we come at 15,000, and they had their guns set up in the mountain, and sent up an awful lot of flak. Lavigne got hit in the leg, and we had to land at Catania, Sicily, to take him to the hospital to have his leg amputated.

When I got to England in 1944 for my second tour, it was a little different. They didn't maintain the integrity of the crews for some reason. I would fly with a crew for a certain period of time and then there'd be a reshuffling and I'd fly with somebody else. Most of the men I flew with were pretty casual about the fact that I had previously flown fifty missions from Africa. Nobody said, "What a great thing you're doing." Nothing like that, and I sure didn't expect it. A few of them just said, "You're nuts!" One man told me he liked flying with me because I had a charmed life and another guy said he'd rather not go with me because my luck would run out sooner or later.

By that time it was obvious that we were winning the war. The event that dramatized to me that we had air superiority was a mission to the Ruhr Valley toward the last weeks of the war. It was like the industrial area around Pittsburgh. Mile after mile of factories and mills. We had to hit Cologne and were in the lead plane of a thousand-plane mission. Everybody was supposed to maintain strict radio silence at all times in missions. There was cloud cover, and I conferred with my pilot, Dick Claeys, and told him we couldn't hit the target because I couldn't see it. So Claeys got on the air and he announced to the entire formation that we're going to another target instead of Cologne and he named it. The Germans down there heard every word of it, but there wasn't a damn thing they could do because at that stage of the war we had air superiority. It must have been terrible for the people sitting down there in that city. Everyone knew we were up there discussing where we were going to bomb. We went in and there was no opposition. We plastered them and got back safely.

Dick Claeys and Tom Smith were the two best pilots I ever flew with. Claeys flew seventy-one missions and stayed in the service after the war. The poor guy was killed when he accidentally flew a plane over Yugoslavia after the war and was shot down by a Yugoslavian fighter plane. It touched off a furor that made the headlines all over the world.

Nothing's good about war, but what we were doing made sense to me. We were bringing the Germans one step closer to surrender with every mission. The sooner that happened, the fewer Americans were going to die. It was that simple to me. Nuremberg, Ruhla, Schweinfurt, Cologne, Hamburg, Münster, Bremen. Merseburg is a name that maybe few people have heard of, but everybody in the Eighth Air Force knows all about it. That was a big oil refinery area that was heavily defended and we used to go over there time and time again. They used to tell us, "You'd better hit it good today, because if you don't, you'll go back tomorrow."

A few years ago I was in Europe on business. I was flying from London to Frankfurt on a Lufthansa flight with a client. I was looking at a map of Germany, the one that's in the back of the seat. This guy knew what I did during the war and started to ask me, "Did you bomb this city during the war?" He pointed to some place and I said, "Yes." He pointed to another one and I said, "Yes." There was a German lady in the seat next to us and she was listening to all this. I felt embarrassed, but she didn't say anything. I wonder if she was in any of those cities this guy was pointing out.

I finished up in England on April 6, 1945, shortly before V-E Day. It was a mission over Leipzig. I didn't know it was my last mission at the time. It was my seventy-ninth (twenty-ninth out of England), and I had one more to go because at that time members of lead crews were required to fly thirty missions while others had to fly thirty-five. But the war ended! We flew back to the States in a B-17, and, believe it or not, we got lost. We had a very experienced navigator, a guy named Wagner, who forgot to check his gyrocompass against his magnetic compass. One of them was off and we went way off course over the Greenland icecap. He finally realized his error and we recovered and flew to Bradley Field, which is near Hartford, Connecticut. There was a tremendous number of planes coming in there and we were one of the first to land. We didn't think it was any big deal, but when we landed we noticed there was a big crowd of people behind all of these ropes and it turned out they were there to greet us. That took us by surprise. They busted down the ropes and barriers, came through and were shaking our hands, kissing us; it was quite touching.

After I got out of the service I went back home to Yonkers and finished up at Columbia. Then I got into the insurance business in New York City. I went to a few reserve meetings, but they bored me. Those guys were too interested in building up their attendance records so they could get a pension 25 years later. So I became an inactive reservist. When the Korean War started, they called me and this time it was a whole different story. My wife was pregnant with our first child, but there was no way to get out of going again. I still think, even if I could have found a way out of it, I don't think I would. We were in deep trouble in Korea for awhile. I didn't look forward to it, but I felt I ought to do it. They sent me down to Waco, Texas, for refresher training and then to Denver for gunnery training and then to San Antonio for B-29 crew training. I didn't like the B-29. It was just big, not like the B-17. I really loved the B-17. At the last minute they took a third of us and made us instructors and sent me to Mather Field in California. By this time the war was winding down and I got out in June of '53. We liked California so much that I got a job in insurance in San Francisco. Three years later I came back to New York and I've been here ever since. So, that's it, 46 years in a nutshell.

Lord knows what I would have done if there hadn't been a war.

When I came back, I was four years older and a much better student. I think everybody was. I'll never know what would have happened. I often think of my grandson. I wouldn't want him to go through a war. I hope there's never another one, but I'm glad that I didn't miss the one we had.

PACIFIC ADVENTURES

The war in the Far East was not only half a world away but, to those doing the fighting, almost without any connection to the faraway struggle with Germany. It had a confusing, unfamiliar geography, different tactics and problems, and above all a fanatical, unpredictable enemy. It was difficult for the European-American to adjust to an enemy like the Japanese, to whom suicide was a perfectly acceptable tactic—just as it was hard for us later to deal with other inscrutable Asian enemies in the Korean and Vietnam wars, and to adjust to less than victory.

Of the two men in this chapter, one stayed in for all three conflicts, making a career of the Air Force. The other, after the defeat of Japan, chose not to, and still seems to regret the decision. For all its hazards and occasional disasters, flying exerts a strong hold over men who have once done it, perhaps more than all the other trades of war.

Despite damage from an antiaircraft shell, a B-29 Superfortress continues its bombing run over Osaka during an attack on Japan's largest industrial center, June 1, 1945. National Archives.

ROBERT RAMER

THE WHOLE WORLD WAS ON FIRE

Robert Ramer, a B-29 pilot who took part in the burning of Tokyo, is a big, self-assured man. Initially a reluctant interviewee—"I don't often wallow in my war experiences," he told us. "That's something I put away a long time ago," —he eventually came to enjoy our long taping sessions. Now retired from the building trades, Ramer lives in the Catskill Mountains, north of New York. At one point we took a trip to the Air Museum near Bradley Field, near Hartford, Connecticut, to see their restored B-29. He walked around the giant bomber, obviously moved by the encounter, his first since 1945. "When it's all said and done, I owe this airplane a lot. She got me there, and got me back all in one piece."

When we took off on a mission, they always gave us a camera. Intelligence wanted you to take a picture of any unusual event or anything you thought was important. We were over the target on one mission and my bombardier was stooped over the bombsight. He suddenly looked up and said, "There's a Jap in front of us." He was telling me so I'd take a picture of him. This Jap plane was following the formation in front of us but then he turned around and started coming back toward our plane. All of this took a lot less time than I'm taking to tell you. I can remember very clearly that I was taking pictures with one hand and at the same time tapping Clarence on the shoulder. I was telling him that he should stop looking in the bombsight and start shooting at the fighter. In the B-29, the bombardier also doubled as the nose gunner. I'm yelling, "Clarence, Clarence, get him!" And he's saying, "Wait a minute." He was the coolest man I have ever known in my entire life.

Robert Ramer, front row left, pilot of the B-29 Superfortress *Little Gem*, with his crew on the island of Saipan. Some of his crew members had flown in Europe with Major Robert Morgan, in the legendary B-17, *Memphis Belle*.

Now, two things happened. One, I was looking through the camera and started to lean backwards in my seat because the Jap looked like he was going to come right through the front of our plane. In doing so, I hit this fan we had behind me to keep the air moving in the cockpit. I did get cut, but mainly I had a lot of hair removed. At the same time I was doing that, Clarence looked up, grabbed the gunsight, and pressed the button. Poof! I saw two or three tracers go into the fighter's engine and he exploded and went right under us. Clarence went right back to the bombsight. When we got back from the mission I reported what had happened and they said, "Bob, you are entitled to the Purple Heart." I'm not proud of it, but I got it. That was my big war wound.

We used to take pictures of the "Baka" bombs.* These suicide guys would come up on a one-way trip. They had their funeral beforehand on the ground. One of my crew members went crazy because of them. I guess he was one of those people who let that kind of thing get to him. He started screaming, "Baka, Baka!" It missed us, but he had to be subdued and ended up going home with a Section Eight. I ended up taking a lot of pictures when we were over the target. At that point, I wasn't even flying the plane because it was on automatic pilot. I was like a passenger, and to tell you the truth, there were better things in life than just sitting there observing all the action. Watching that shrapnel coming up, you'd try to crawl inside your helmet.

I saved a lot of those photographs and brought them home with me. They were important to the Air Force at the time because our people could tell how close our bombs had dropped to the target, damage we had done, things like that. They were important to me because I had been there. I asked myself awhile back, why the hell am I saving this collection of pictures from the war that don't mean anything to anybody else? And I threw just about everything out.

My attitude changed over the years and I decided that's all gone, long gone. I've gone through a transformation. I was born at a time when everything was in its place. The United States was the greatest

---

*Ed. note: The Baka ("fool's bomb"), as Americans called it, was the "oka" (cherry blossom) to the Japanese, a murderous 4,700-pound bomb rigged up with small wings and a tail. In its tiny cockpit, a suicide pilot could fly it by rocket propulsion into a target at a speed of 600 miles per hour. A Baka had to be launched in the air from beneath a bomber that would fly it to within range of its target and cut it loose. One Baka pilot's body, dressed in a black funeral robe, was recovered when it hit the deck of an American ship off Okinawa. Bakas, against which there was little defense, were fortunately costly and less numerous than the ordinary kamikaze planes and small boats. that Japan deployed in 1945 with increasing and devastating fury against Allied forces closing in on her home islands.

nation in the world. In fact, it was just about the whole world, and the rest was just a tiny little area over there someplace. A policeman was a policeman. All the girls were virgins except for a few who were "bad girls." Packard built the best cars.

I think there's two of me. The one that was a very naïve young man that went off to war. In the last few years maybe I've become jaded, or maybe it's, as I said, another me. If I were nineteen or twenty, knowing what I know now, I would not do it. Just go down and enlist in the Air Force and climb in a bomber and kill Japanese just like that without a lot more thinking. I don't believe the president like I used to. Everybody rips off everybody else. I put my ass on the line for America and what do we have today? Was it worth it? It has to do with Kent State, Watergate, Vietnam. What did it really all mean? Today they are building Toyota plants in the United States and I drive a Datsun.

Take the Nuremberg trials. They were asking the Germans questions like, "Why did you do this and that?" And the Germans would say, "I had orders." We'd say, "You mean to tell me that's why you did those horrible things? Just orders?" I hated the Germans, but what if they had won the war? What would they have done? Put me on the stand and said, "Did they tell you to go over and fire-bomb Tokyo and help kill eighty thousand people?" I would have to say yes. And if they asked me why, I would have had to tell them I had orders. If I had stood up at a briefing and said, "Wait a minute, what is the purpose of this war? I don't know whether I agree with what you're doing and I really don't want to kill Japanese," I would have been carted away as some sort of nut.

I realize how different my attitude was about a lot of things. I don't think death, the real idea of dying, ever occurred to me. Now, when I say death, I'm talking about how I think about it today. Dead! When we would go to a briefing and see what they had planned for that day, we'd say, "Good God, they're crazy! They're going to lose a lot of men." I'd think to myself, "Hey, a lot of *those* guys are going to get it." There was some kind of protection around me. It was as if I were enclosed in some sort of plastic container for the war. We would joke, "Don't wear that expensive wristwatch on this tough mission. Give it to me because you might not come back."

We were like kids. We were worried about making the officers' club nicer. That there was a rumor some nurses were on our base. How we could get our hands on a jeep? What were we going to have for dinner? There was some lumber that came in that was supposed to be used to build a laundry. We stole it and put up a handball court. We did weird things, and these are the things I remember the most from the war. We had one ongoing project that took up a lot of our time. Saipan was a coral island and you would cut your feet up trying to get out to the water to go swimming. We got these 55-gallon drums and filled them with rocks and submerged them to make a dock. That's how we occupied our time. Planning dances and throwing liquor bashes. I don't think anybody was thinking about the overall picture of what we were accomplishing at our level. In the movies you see somebody like Gregory Peck lecturing a crew about the significance of what they are doing. Keeping the world free, part of the big picture, that sort of thing. I don't remember any of that at all. At our level we were into pranks and jokes. Things that to this day I'm ashamed of.

For instance, we had Quonset huts and each hut had only pilots, or bombardiers, or what have you. Each one was like a fraternity. In the morning you would walk to the shower and pick up a rock and throw it on top of the hut where, maybe, the navigators were sleeping. The rock would make a big racket and the navigators would come running out. "Who did that? Who threw that goddamned rock?" Someone else would say, "I think a pilot did it." The battle would be on. We got into terrible wars among ourselves that ended up with things like a jeep rolling into the front of a Quonset hut. We were young men who should have been in school and we did what young men will do.

Now, there were other people who were fighting the war on a different level and they were very serious about what they were doing. We had a party one night and the whole outfit got so drunk that the next day's mission was scrubbed as far as we were concerned. I can still remember how angry those officers were over that, and it didn't happen again. They were into the big war, but at our level, no, we were into our fun and games between these missions they had scheduled for us. They told us what to do and we were willing to do it.

★

I was working at a printing plant on Long Island when the war started and everybody who worked there went down and volunteered. It just seemed like the thing to do at the time. All of us took the exam to get in the Air Force and I was the only one that passed. I was called up in October of '42. I remember taking my sneakers, a change of undershorts, and socks. My mother gave me cornflakes for breakfast, and said, "Bye." I took the subway to Grand Central Station by myself and went off to war. Just like that. I don't think I had more than a few dollars in my pocket. To me, at the time, it was another adventure and it was better than working.

I went through ground school at Maxwell Field in Alabama, and then I went to Camden, South Carolina, where they brought us out to an actual airplane. I had never been in an airplane before that. I had seen them in the air, but I had no idea how they worked and I think that was an advantage. There were people who had previous experience, and they had to unlearn a lot. I think I soloed pleasantly and took to flying nicely. I graduated and then went to multi-engine school at Moody Field in Georgia. I was then assigned to Hendricks Field at Sebring, Florida, as a B-17 pilot. I hadn't been there long when they sent me to central instructors school at Columbus, Ohio, where I learned how to instruct pilots. Then, back to Hendricks Field where I began to teach. It was wonderful. There was a swimming pool, an officers' club, and someone to shine my shoes at night. It was great and I was doing just fine. I was really happy down there and would never have volunteered to go overseas. I'd go to the pool, play a little softball, and teach flying. Hey, the war was on and I was doing my part. We couldn't all be warriors.

One day my buddy and I were in the movie and a call came through the PA system. "Lieutenant Reeves, report to the base commander." What the hell, I was with him so I went along. He was inside with the base commander and I was sitting outside. The commander saw me and asked, "Ramer, what are you doing out there? You might as well come in here too." I said, "Yes, sir." He said, "I think it's time you two men went overseas." We said, "Yes, sir." That's how that happened. I didn't ponder on it at the time. It sounded interesting.

I went to Lincoln, Nebraska, and from there to Clovis, New Mexico, where I picked up my crew. Talking about how young we were at that time, I remember something specific that happened at Clovis. I think it must have been some holiday, Thanksgiving or Christmas, and everybody had their mothers and fathers in to see them. My tail gunner introduced me to his mother and she told me that she wanted to meet me because her son's life was being entrusted to me. Here was this woman telling me to take care of her son and I'm twenty years old. On top of that, he was older than me. What a blow it must have been for her to see me, the airplane commander. I said, "Don't worry, we'll get back all right." She must have gone home and gotten sick.

The first time I really saw a B-29 was at Clovis. We had heard about this new bomber they were working on, but it was secret stuff at the time and there were a lot of rumors. My first impression was that the thing was so goddamn enormous that I didn't know how it was going to get off the ground. We thought the B-17 was a big airplane, but this thing was tremendous. I had to get used to the idea that the rest of the crew was way, way back there somewhere. It was a magnificent plane to fly. We went first class. Warm and comfortable. We even had a food warmer. I'm talking about warming up whole dinners. When we were about an hour from the target, we'd plug in the warmer so when we got done with the bomb run and were coming home, we could eat our dinner. It was very important to us that it got plugged in. We were disgusting, I must say. The cockpit in a B-29 was like an office. There was more than enough room in there and the visibility was incredible with all that glass. There was a tunnel that went back over the bomb bay to the rest of the plane. They did that so they didn't have to pressurize the whole interior. Sometimes I'd go in there with a blanket and sleep like a baby. Remember, we were flying missions to Japan that went 15, 16 hours. Like I said, that airplane was very pleasant, especially when you compare it to what else was available. I had flown in B-17s enough to know what it could be like. The temperatures were horrible in those airplanes.

Another big difference between the B-17 and the B-29 was the way they were controlled. The B-29 had power-assisted control surfaces. It was hard enough to push that big barn door on the B-17, much less something as big as the rudder on the B-29. I think that was the first time that this was done. Motors assisting the pilot with the controls. At Clovis they had only a few B-29s, and we had to do most of our flying in B-17s—training where the crew could learn about each other. The only thing that I found really different was how to take off and land with that tricycle landing gear because it was a strange feeling to keep that tail off the ground. Everything I had been in before had a tail wheel and I wanted to just keep bringing the wheel back when I landed like I always had.

As I said, the crew was getting to know each other and I had some trouble with one of them. I had never been to school to know how to act as an officer. I came right out of a printing plant, no college ROTC, nothing like that. I became friendly with everybody. Our radio operator, an enlisted man, didn't know Morse code. Can you imagine assigning a man who didn't know code? I told him I would help him, and he'd come to the officers' club every night and I would work with him. In fact, I got him a promotion up to sergeant. It went from Lieutenant Ramer to just Lieutenant and then Ramer and finally Bob, right before my eyes. At the time, I thought we were doing fine.

One day we were on a training mission and we had an engine fire. I told him to call the base and tell them what was going on. The radio operator had to have his headset on at all times. If he went to the bathroom, he gave it to someone else. I yelled back when I didn't get an answer on the radio. Nothing. I yelled again, "Get that goddamn headset on and call the base." Something like that. We got the problem resolved, and when we got off the plane he comes over and grabs me by the throat. "Don't you ever curse at me like that!" Now, if one of the enlisted men walks over and grabs an officer by the throat, you know you've got problems. I had to get rid of him. Another officer who knew what had happened gave me some advice that's stayed with me my whole life. You give the order to the copilot and let him execute it. Let him do the yelling and cursing. From that time on I didn't have much contact with the enlisted crew, and for whatever reason it worked. I've remembered that, as I said, and it has come up any number of times in business when circumstances like that have happened. I learned a lot in the Air Force about being in command and being an executive. The pilot was an executive in a way. You can't get too close or those relationships are going to interfere with the job you have to do.

We left Clovis and arrived on Saipan, February of 1945. There was a very gloomy attitude at that time. We were losing a lot of planes, and not to the enemy. Most of them were operational losses, running out of fuel, that sort of thing. They were trying high-altitude, precision bombing as they did in Europe and it wasn't working. The planes would take off and fly a few hundred feet off the water in tight formation. You'd stay down low because you were loaded with bombs and fuel. Playing with those throttles, back and forth, keeping your plane in formation for almost eight hours, was some job. Your wrist would go limp after awhile. We'd fly that way until there was a signal to begin climbing to 20,000 feet. That was where we usually dropped from. I remember one day there was a cloud formation in front of us, a tremendous front. The leader takes the whole goddamn Air Force right into this cloud bank. Now, we're talking two hundred B-29s, wingtip to wingtip! I mean, we're talking stupidity; I couldn't believe it. Go underneath, go around, do something. All of a sudden you're in solid white with water streaking off the glass. You know there's an airplane on your left, your right, above and below you. I'm on instruments and trying to go perfectly straight and maintain my speed. I'm sitting there petrified and feeling any moment that an airplane was going to come up under me. Ten, fifteen minutes like this and I figure that every plane in the whole outfit . . . the whole formation is going to fall out of the sky. We came right through the clouds and sailed right out into the clear; nobody hit anything. I still, to this day, say to myself that couldn't have happened.

Once we were at 20,000 we'd head for the target, and if we could find it, we'd drop our load. It was a waste of time because it just wasn't working. There were always clouds and radar was no real help. We tried dropping on a lead bombardier and that didn't work. We tried dropping, each guy on his own—that didn't work either.

We weren't hurting the Japanese, and we were losing all sorts of planes at the same time. Losing a B-29 was like losing a ship. People were ditching all over the place. Everybody was getting very down and morale was terrible.

Then we went to a briefing and it was just like the movies. There was a blackboard and it was covered with a curtain. All the pilots and enlisted men were there, hundreds of men. "Gentlemen," somebody said, and we all rose and the general walked in. Then we all sat down. "And your mission for tonight is. . . ." I'm expecting Clark Gable any minute. He opened up the curtains and I want you to know, everybody was talking to everybody else. "Wow, is this guy crazy?" It was a whole new ball game. We were going to fly to the target, each plane by itself, and go in at 9,000 feet. Now, we had been complaining about being at 20,000 feet, but we didn't think we wanted to be at 9,000 feet, especially if they were shooting at us. Also, this was going to be a night run and we were going to be dropping incendiary bombs. We took off and we were 50 miles from the target, Tokyo, all alone in the sky, and all of a sudden we see this glow. We didn't know what it could be and it got bigger and bigger and suddenly we realized that it's Tokyo. It was one giant fire. I'm looking at the city on my left and it was like looking down into Dante's Inferno. The whole world was on fire. The fires were illuminating clouds at 30,000 feet. We were going right into black clouds of smoke, and the plane was actually picked up and thrown hundreds of feet in the air and then dropped again by wind currents caused by the heat of the fires. Guys were hitting their heads against the top of the fuselage. It was horrible and it was incredible. Our instructions were to go over the target and if we saw an area that wasn't burning move over and drop on it. When we opened the bomb doors, we could smell the buildings and flesh burning. It was sickening. We knew right away that the Japanese were panicked. The search lights would usually track after several planes, making a pattern in the sky. This night, however, they were all going after one plane and trying to get him. They weren't using their brains. While they were following that plane and throwing everything at him, we were going straight through. They got a few planes, but not enough to help them.

When we got back to the interrogation, it was pure exhilaration. We knew that we had dealt them a horrible, horrible blow. We were elated with our success. You didn't know what the hell you were doing at 20,000 feet, bombing through the clouds, but you sure as hell knew what you did that night.

In my opinion, from then on the whole thing turned around and the Japanese were finished. We went after one city and then another. All incendiary raids. Osaka, Yamaguchi, I can mention lots of them . . . Nagoya . . . they just became names. One by one going up in flames. We lost some planes, but minimal. None of those operational losses that we were having before. There was a period of time where we would go on a mission, come back, sleep, get up, and go out in the plane again. Out of my thirty-odd missions, twenty-five of them were fire raids. When we weren't flying, somebody else was hitting them. We were like truck drivers. Take a load from here and drop it over there and come back and get another one. I mean, how glamorous can that really be? Since that time, it's occurred to me that we were the truck drivers and the fighter pilots were the racing car drivers. Fighter pilots were into their weird paint jobs and war stories and all that stuff. All razzle-dazzle. They didn't have to stay on the road like we did.

I'll tell you, though, they were great to have along. You know in the movies when you see the Indians are totally surrounding the little group of pioneers and suddenly there's the music and here comes the cavalry? Those Mustangs, they were our cavalry! One mission, especially, we were going to Tokyo and there was cloud cover above us. We knew there were Mustangs above those clouds. The Japanese came up and went right up through the clouds so they could get above us and come down and give us hell. Suddenly it was raining Zeros! They were coming down smoking or had two Mustangs chasing them. Wow!

I always looked at the whole experience as almost a classic story of how beautiful it could really be for somebody. I was a Jewish guy from New York working in a paper factory and I went on to become an officer and a pilot. I came out with the wings and the whole shmear. At the time, I was decorated because I was one of the few pilots in the 20th Air Force who had flown thirty-five missions without an abort. I was a good pilot. In fact, a general by the name of Rosie O'Donnell contacted me and said he was going to form a group of pilots to fly the A-26 in the States and would I be interested? That was a great honor. You don't get invited by a general to go into a new outfit that's flying a new airplane every day of the week. I remember writing to my wife and telling her I'd like to stay in and fly after the war was over. But, when I got home, she and my mother-in-law weren't going to hear about it. The Air Force? My son-in-law the pilot? So, for the love of my wife . . . see? This is terrible, I'm blaming it on someone else. I just said I've had it and to hell with the whole thing. I went into business and did very badly. I had some second thoughts about going back in, but it was a couple years later and they had more pilots than they needed.

Yeah, I think I missed my chance. There's a great book that could be written by somebody, *What Could Have Been*. Everybody would have a chapter. If I had it to do again, I think I wouldn't have hesitated. It was the kind of life for me. In fact, I thrived on that type of atmosphere. Everything was done for you. Schedules are prepared, meals are laid out, and it's a very controlled environment. When I take a trip, for instance, I have to have everything planned and paid for in advance. I don't enjoy myself if I don't know where I'm going to be sleeping tonight. That's just the way I am.

Now it's funny. I started off by telling you how I feel that I was naïve, and have ended up by telling you now I should have stayed in the Air Force and been a pilot if I had been smart. Maybe I've separated the war and flying airplanes from each other. Let me see if I can explain what I mean. We had Marines on Saipan. To me that island was the war; to them it was their rest camp. We were in our cozy Quonset huts, with an officers' club, mess hall, and a booze allowance. We played our games. The Marines lived in pup tents out in the open, shaved their heads, and cooked their food. They were like mad dogs, and I think that was done intentionally. They were downright hateful. We came back one night to our hut, and there was a Marine sitting on a chair with a samurai sword. I'll always remember him because he was a horrible-looking young man. Lean, he almost looked cadaverous. His uniform, forget about it. He had shorts on with no socks and G.I. boots. He wanted liquor. You could feel he hated us. He didn't want to talk to us, just wanted to trade the sword for liquor. I had a feeling it would be a good idea, so we traded.

What happened to me and what happened to those Marines had nothing to do with each other. I didn't want to see anybody eyeball-to-eyeball. What I was doing was at least 9,000 feet down. I don't think I could have handled the Marines' war. Oh, hell, what do I know? Maybe, if they were playing *The Caissons Go Rolling Along,* I would have been just as gung ho. I don't think so, however. It just seemed repugnant to me. I don't know how anybody can get up and charge into almost sure death. I thought they were crazy. When the casualties were pouring in from Iwo Jima, they brought them to Saipan. There was a plane standing by to fly them right back to the States if they were in real bad shape. I can remember some of those Marines who were all shot up trying to get up and saying, "You're not going to put me on any airplane. I want to stay right here." Those guys had just come out of fighting hand to hand with the Japs, and they were afraid to get on an airplane! Is that crazy? Maybe my idea of what's bad is not what another guy's idea of bad is.

FRANK BOSCH

THREE WARS, THREE HOMECOMINGS

*You can't help but notice the framed squadron insignias on the wall of
Frank Bosch's family room in his comfortable home in suburban Virginia.
There are twelve different combat units represented, spanning three very
different wars. World War II: "We were a team, that's why we won the
war." Korea: "The* esprit de corps *started to suffer." Vietnam: "There,
we were the bad guys. Just a bunch of killers. Of course, that's changing
now." Compact and rugged, Bosch fought cancer with a combination of.
medicine and fortitude. He won that battle and now works with senior
citizens, trying to infuse them with the same never-quit spirit. "We didn't
use the word 'can't' in the Pacific and I don't let them use it here either."*

I've been skating since I was nine years old. I started with clamp-on
skates on sneakers and I've been at it ever since. High school and
amateur hockey, and in the service whenever I could find ice. A
couple of years ago I saw an ad in the paper. They were looking for
senior skaters. I called up and told them that maybe I could help out.
The woman at the county department of parks and recreation started
talking with me, and I told her I had my degree in health and physical
education. She said, "This is wonderful. We also have these body
shops for seniors [exercise classes]. Could you help us out with
these?" So, today, how many volunteer efforts am I involved with?
Sixteen. They call me and they know the price is right. I could make a
ton, but I don't want to do that. It's something I enjoy doing, and it
gives me a good feeling. The seniors know that I licked "the big C"
and I tell them we don't use the word "can't." I'm not paying anybody back, don't get me wrong, but let's face it, after all those years of

shooting at people, this is very rewarding because you see the good you're doing.

I'm also involved with the Vietnam Memorial. We went out to the memorial a few years ago and I saw some of those troops who were there and they were pretty shaggy and cruddy. They didn't impress me in the least. All of these horrible-looking guys that were representing the vets from Vietnam weren't what I thought should represent the people I had served with over there. Mardy, my wife, said, "Why don't you go down and do some volunteering?" I said, "I don't have the time." She kept insisting. I put it off until one day I picked up the paper and saw a story asking for volunteers. I called up and told them I could give them four hours each Wednesday. We have a directory with all the names listed, alphabetically. People will come in and they are so emotional they can't even read the book. We offer to help locate the name, explain about the memorial, help in any way we can. I find that people are appreciative. All of these efforts are very rewarding for me.

We all came back heroes from World War II and a lot of guys, in spite of what they say, were a little reluctant to take the uniform off when they came home. You'd walk along the street with your ribbons and feel pretty good about yourself. We'd won the war. That outlook has changed a lot between that war and Korea. When we came from Korea, we were entitled to wear civilian clothes, and you saw a lot of guys who knew you were in the service, but you didn't see the uniform. Then, coming back from Vietnam, that was something else again. You took off your uniform before you were anywhere near home. The reception was a little bit different, I would say. A lot of nasty things were said about us in the papers and the universities. I had two in college at the time so I knew that from what my own immediate family was telling me. Calling us bad guys, a bunch of killers. Also, the reaction of the neighbors. Mardy wouldn't tell people what I did for a living. She'd just tell them that I was out of town on business. We could shrug it off because we'd been around the horn a couple of times. However, for the young guy just coming back from a tough war, getting that treatment was very difficult. To this day, a lot of them can't cope with it.

Don't get me talking about politics and Vietnam. I keep reading articles that say the dominoes did not fall, and I think that's a bunch of bull. The dominoes might not have fallen, but a lot of people have died since we left that would not have died if we'd done our job. I think we should have let the military win it. During the Tet offensive I was flying all over the country. We could see what happened when Johnson stopped the bombing. We had them on the run, had them on the edge of no return. When he stopped the bombing, we could

Lieutenant Frank Bosch in 1945. Flying missions during World War II in a Black Widow night fighter, he would go on to fight in two more conflicts in the Far East, and retire from the Air Force as a lieutenant colonel.

watch them building along the DMZ. It was just like watching ants after a rainy day. They all came out of their holes. They were very open about it. Our fighters couldn't go in, our choppers couldn't go in, and the B-52s couldn't go in. It was like a condemned man watching them build the scaffold to hang him on. Then we went back in and it was too late.

The Korean war was the first where the military was controlled by the civilians. We saw what happened there. Then we got into Vietnam and we were totally dominated by civilians. The civilians even directed tactical operations. In World War II, they left the military operations to military men. Don't, for God's sake, give me a bunch of guys who are trained to be professional killers, be it on the ground, on board ship, or in the air, and when it comes time to use them, time for them to do their jobs, say, "Hey, you can't do that."

In the Pacific during World War II, we were at the tail end of the supply line. We had less of everything to work with, and terrible working conditions. The night fighters were new and, being individual squadrons, we belonged to nobody, but our morale was good. You had your name, the crew chief's and the pilot's names on the airplane. We felt we owned that thing. The government may have paid for it, but it belonged to us. In Korea, that started to change. The airplane no longer belonged to us. We'd go to the briefing and fly whatever plane came up on the maintenance schedule. No individual aircraft, no individual crew chiefs. They would assign whoever was available to work on the airplane and it became just another job. Also, in Korea, we had a lot of people who had been called back into the service because of the emergency. They hadn't wanted that. Homes were broken up, businesses went down the tube. Guys were pulled back into this new war who had had no time at all to really settle their personal lives. The *esprit de corps,* those feelings of closeness that we had in World War II, started to suffer.

★

I was born in Louisiana, but I grew up in New York. My mother moved us up to New York because she wanted us to have a New York education. I went through the school system in Brooklyn. I graduated from high school and went to work for Mergenthaler Linotype Corporation as a printer's devil. Ever since I could remember, I wanted to fly. I waited until my eighteenth birthday and got my former hockey coach to give me a letter of introduction to one of his old sergeants who was working at 39 Whitehall Street, the recruiting center in New York City. This was in 1940 before we got into the war. Out of the nineteen that were there that day, eight of us passed the physical. At that time, they would give you the physical first, and if you got through that, they'd sign you up. The pilot program at that time required that you have two years of college, minimum. Here I was right out of high school, but the deal that Coach O'Leary and the sergeant had cooked up would have had me assigned to the 19th Bomb Group, which was based at Mitchel Field. Everything was fine, and then the sergeant said, "Wait, you have to have your mother sign this. You have to bring your mother back here with you." I went home and my mother reluctantly went back to Whitehall Street with me, but she wouldn't sign the paper. Eventually I was able to get in, but it wasn't until 1942.

I went through flight training in the Southeastern Training Command and washed out of single-engine advanced training a month before graduation. I was at Spence Field, Moultrie, Georgia, at the time. I was capable, in fact I flew in the formation on our graduation day from basic, but what got me in trouble was my attitude. When I was sent to single-engine, I was elated. You talk about cocky and sure of yourself, that was me. "Boy, I'm going into fighters. I'm a hot pilot." Well, I guess I opened my mouth too much and wound up on the brown list. I said something one day and that was that. It was one of the worst days of my life. I left Spence Field at the end of May, and they sent me to Moody Air Base, which was also in Georgia, to join a pool of washed-out pilots. All we did at Moody was work details and then I went before the classification board. They said that I was qualified to go to bombardier, navigation, or radar night-fighter training. All I heard was the word "fighter." I didn't know what radar was, didn't have the slightest idea what night-fighters did, but I heard that word "fighter" and I said, "I'll take it." Looking back on my career, I'd say in the long run everything worked out for the best. I have no complaints.

I went to Boca Raton Air Field in August of 1944 for radar observer, night-fighter training. I graduated from there in November 1944 and got my commission as a second lieutenant. Next we went to Hammer Field, which was located near Fresno, California, for transition into the P-61. *The Black Widow* was the first plane actually designed to include radar from the beginning. One of the reasons the airplane was so big is that the radar at that time was very bulky. We finished our training in the airplane, then left for the Pacific, and ended up at Finschhafen, New Guinea.

The very next day we took off in a C-47 and the pilot left the automatic pilot on; we crashed into a hangar. Four guys were killed and four of us were hurt. I got burned and cut up and stayed in the hospital for a week. The hospital was run by two former missionaries, a husband and wife. He was the hospital commander and she was the head nurse. At the scene of the accident they got my dog tags mixed up with one of the dead men and notified my mother that I had been killed. She had two very bad days before they corrected the error. When I was released from the hospital I had to hitch rides to the Philippines. I looked like a bum because I had to scrounge some clothes. All of my stuff had been burned in the crash. One C-47 that I ended up on had nurses, engine parts, chickens, you name it and it had it on board. Finally I got to Lingayen Gulf with the 547th Night Fighter Squadron and started flying missions. We flew over North Luzon, the North China Sea, and Formosa. We flew two types of missions in the Philippines. One was the CAP, Combat Air Patrol; we'd go up and patrol a given sector. There wasn't much night activity because the Japanese didn't fly at night, so after we'd flown our mission, the ground controllers would give us a target of opportunity. We'd go in with napalm or bombs, and maybe shoot them up a little bit. The other type of mission was a basic night-intruder mission. We'd go and attack specified targets. Low-level night work. Air strips, refineries, troop emplacements, anything that they wanted to hit. We had regular nightly runs up to Formosa to shoot up Jap naval installations.

Taking into consideration the time and the existing technology, the P-61 was the state of the art. It was a good, steady airplane, very forgiving, reliable, and also had tremendous firepower. It didn't have the speed of some of the others, but as far as dependability and safety went, all who flew it or flew in it would agree that it was one of the best. When we got the SCR 720 radar, it was better than anything going at the time. They used that set in the F-82 all the way up until 1952. It was better than the German equipment or the British, although they had actually developed airborne radar. The Japanese were still using very primitive radar. In the Pacific, there were very few night-fighter kills. As I said, the Japs didn't fly at night and aerial victories were slim. The highest-scoring ace in the Pacific in night fighters was C. C. Smith. He got seven. The American Fighter Aces Association will not accept P-61 fellows. Their number one criterion is single pilot, period. Gunners in B-17s and B-24s and our guys are not accepted as aces even if they got five.

You were married to your crew. That was one of the things that I fought for in later years when I became an instructor. I'm a firm believer in crew integrity and I used that concept in teaching. They didn't have to think of what the other guy was going to do, they knew by instinct. I flew with one guy for six years, George Wacker. I like to think that we did everything better than anybody else. Wacker was a fighter pilot in P-38s. After we'd flown for a while, he wouldn't trade an RO [radar operator] for anything. In fact, he turned down the F-86D, which was a single-place airplane. He said he was spoiled.

A good RO can do that for you. He does your navigation, paperwork, radio work, all you have to do is fly the airplane. Most pilots also realize that those extra eyes are worth their weight in gold. When you're in bad weather, you've got your head in the scope. There are times you have to stay in there. But a guy who sticks his head in the scope and never comes out, he doesn't know what's going on around him. Coming into landing patterns, looking for traffic, for instance. We worked out systems with pilots. During heavy weather takeoffs, we'd call out every thousand feet as we were rolling. When we were in the air I'd tell the pilot what was behind him and what he could expect in front of him.

The technique that we used was that the RO would bring the aircraft to a position where the pilot could see the airstrip visually. The pilot had to trust us to be able to do that. A lot of them, however, would cheat. They'd be eyeballing for the strip, looking for lights or something before we were there. Same thing with targets. This one guy, especially. We later became good friends, but I'd flown with him a few times and I knew he cheated all the time. This one night we're flying an interceptor training mission. It was a really black night and we were in and out of weather hunting our target. All of a sudden he says, "Where is he, where is he?" I said, "I know where he is, but I'm not going to tell you. You've been cheating. You follow my instructions and I'll put him where you want him." Everything worked fine after that.

In Korea we flew basically the same types of missions that we had flown in the Philippines, but in the twin Mustang, the F-82. It was a trustworthy airplane and had a really good range considering that it was a makeshift. The airplane was originally designed as a long-distance day fighter for bomber escort work. The idea was that there would be two pilots so one could spell the other during the long missions. When the F-82 was converted to the all-weather configuration they had taken a lot of the dual controls out, but still left some of them hooked up. The rudder pedals, for instance, were still working on my side. The throttle quadrant had been pulled out, but the push-pull rods that operated the throttle were still there. We'd be on these long patrols and we'd be up there all by ourselves and it would be as black as ink. I was flying at that time with Dave Knight. I'd reach up and take hold of that little nut on the end of the throttle rod and move the rod just a little bit. The engine would go "arghhhhhhhhhhh" and Dave would say, "What was that? Did you hear that? That didn't sound right." When you'd been flying for several hours with the engines running the same way, if they made any kind of noise you'd really come to attention. He'd put his head down and you'd see him adjusting the throttle to get the engines in sync again. Well, I'd do that every once in awhile to break up the boredom, and I showed the trick to a couple of other ROs. They thought it was quite funny, and everything was fine until one of those rascals got drunk and told one of the pilots. They wanted to kill me.

As I said earlier, each war was different. My first, World War II, that was a ball. We were young and we didn't look upon losses the way you do when you get older. In Korea it was different because we were older, more careful, along with being much more proficient. We had better equipment. In Vietnam there was even a bigger difference. In World War II my squadron commander was a captain. In Korea he was a major. In Vietnam he was a lieutenant colonel. In fact, we had thirty other lieutenant colonels in the squadron. This makes a big difference. These guys were good and they really performed their missions. As a result, our particular squadron suffered the least amount of losses and we didn't get easy missions.

I was forced into combat cargo in Vietnam. I did everything I could do to stay out of it because I didn't like big airplanes. I never did. They sent me to school and I have to admit I was not very good because of my attitude. But I got through, and when I was sent over there and started working with those guys, it was a complete change for me. I'm not ashamed to say it, I had a complete turnaround in philosophy. We were flying the C-130, a great airplane. It had beautiful instrumentation and could really take a beating. Very good for lower level work and they had sufficient speed. The combat cargo crew's mission was getting everything in: people, supplies, mail, you name it.

We'd go into those strips in the morning with live, hale, healthy bodies and bring them out in the afternoon, shot to hell. Combat cargo, along with the helicopters, took on a tremendous amount of importance in that war. Yet you won't find us mentioned because there was no glory in it. I'll tell you one thing, there wasn't that much opposition in the air, but you could be assured that you would be shot at from the ground on every mission. You didn't have anything to shoot back with, except a stinking, lousy .38 revolver. We'd do most of our flying at above 2,500 to 2,700 feet and made these very steep approaches to the strips. We only got fighter support on the bad missions such as the Quesan operations and the Ah Shau Valley.

The air war took on a much different complexion. For one thing, the chopper came into prominence and they were doing things with it that people hadn't dreamed of. Before this, it had been used mainly as a life-saving device. We turned it into a lethal weapon and a major means of transporting troops in and out of the battlefield. The fighters were being used for ground support and things like that.

In Vietnam, as everywhere else, some people thought the crew was the pilot and that everyone else just filled seats. We knew different. You have to have a good team. Pilot, flight engineer, and navigator. A good copilot was essential too, but copilots were usually young guys being broken in to the squadron. After getting some experience, they would become first pilots. The load masters were a different breed of cat. There were no bad load masters because nobody would tolerate a bad one. A bad one could kill your entire crew. You don't just throw things into an airplane that big and expect it to fly. It's a very special talent. The pilot, engineer, and navigator tie in together. A bad nav can fly you into the rocks. You can misread the radar. The engineer, well, he's got all the heavy work and he's running the airplane for the pilot. The pilot just drives the airplane.

We'd fly in any type of weather. You'd delay them, yes, but I don't remember when we cancelled any missions for weather. Those tropical storms will come through there and they are vicious but would soon pass. We were going into this little strip at Sung Be. There was a typhoon in Vietnam at the time and the weather was terrible. These troops had field artillery and we were bringing them ammo. We contacted them and they said, "Please come in, we're hurting." They were down to their final rounds. I was using the radar and finding holes in that horrible weather. We kept getting lower and lower until we started to pick up ground fire. We still couldn't see anything. Finally I said to Dibrell Stowe, the pilot, "If you want to go in there, I'll bring you in." I made a radar approach using this little mountain on the north side of the strip as my fix. We got in and those guys on the ground just about kissed us. We were the only airplane in the sky, everybody else went home.

I flew with some wonderful guys in Vietnam. I had this very good friend, Bernie Bucher. We never knew each other before the day we walked into the squadron. There was that instantaneous magnetism that happens between some people. I soon felt as though I'd known him all my life. We were working around the clock at the time. We'd be on 15 hours and then off 12. Different crews would fly at different times and sometimes you'd go weeks without seeing some guys. Bernie and I weren't on the same crew, but we shared a locker. We kept a bottle of Cutty Sark in the locker and he would drink it when I wasn't there, and I'd drink it when he wasn't there. Those rare times when we were together, we'd get to sit down and bull and have a drink. Whoever got down to the bottom of the label would have to replace the bottle. It was Mother's Day 1968, about four in the morning. I was just getting off and he was coming in, all shiny and shaved. He said, "I just put a new bottle in there. When I get back we'll break it in." Well, he didn't make it back that day. Of all the guys I've known that didn't make it, that one hit me the hardest. He shouldn't have been in Vietnam in the first place. He didn't volunteer for it and he was getting ready to retire. We were checking our schedules and it would have been a couple of days and we would have both been off. We would have had that drink together, but he didn't come back.

You never got used to the losses. When I was an instructor, between Korea and Vietnam, we lost twenty-four people in one year at one base. That was 1954. Lack of training was responsible for that. These kids would go from flying big airplanes on day missions and then they were thrown right into the night program. That was sheer murder. They tried to correct it. People would be fired, but there's no substitute for good, solid training. Not when you're dealing with lives. The taxpayers never remember the names of the kids that went down in an airplane, they just remember that the airplane cost a million and a half at that time, or now, fourteen million dollars.

There is one thing they usually overplay in the movies, but they can never really get the true feeling of what it was like when you heard that somebody had gone down. The first thing the base would do was close off all communications so that someone didn't call the family before they were notified properly. It was roughest on the wives. In the movie, *The Right Stuff,* there is a scene where Gordon Cooper's wife is talking to a couple of other wives, and she says, "Our government spends millions of dollars to train these guys how to fly, but they don't spend one goddamn cent to teach the wives how to cope with the possibility of them not coming back." The first time Mardy was exposed to it was right after a Christmas party. I had my guys over; a lot of other guys from different flights came too. We had a great time. Dancing, talking in the kitchen, just having a ball. Two days later, Rex and Keene were dead. She asked me, "How can that be? Those two young, vibrant young men, how can they be dead?" She had never realized it before; wives never realize it until something like that happens. She looked upon me in a different light after that. From then on, when I left, she didn't know if I was coming back. Mardy said she made up her mind never to go to bed mad. The people you lived with and flew with on those bases became your family. They became your father and mother and uncles and aunts. Nobody can understand that kind of life who hasn't lived it.

Mardy kept our family together. When I was away she always set a place for me at the table. She would show them pictures, tell the children what I was doing. When I came back there was no transition. She's something special. Mardy's a very soft woman, but she also knew what the score was and she helped a lot of younger wives. During the course of my career we lived in thirty-one different houses. My daughter Bonnie went to three different schools for first grade. When I was going to school to get my degree, I counted up the schools that the Bosch family had been associated with, one way or another. Teaching, nine children going to colleges, high schools, what have you, there were thirty-one different schools. Yes, I do think my children are different. For one thing, they're far more sophisticated than children who haven't been exposed to what they saw. They lived in quite a few cultures and even to this day they still have friends they met all over the world. I think it gave them an entirely different outlook, and was actually beneficial to them in the long run. However, it didn't make me upset at all that none of them wanted to go into the service.

I prepared myself to leave the Air Force and flying. That was something I tried to tell the younger guys. We all have to do several things. One is that you've got to die some day, and the other is that you've got to leave the service. You can't stay around forever, no matter how good you are or what you're doing. I hung up my flying suit, put on my jeans, and went back to school as a freshman. I went to George Mason University, here in Virginia, and got my master's degree in health and physical education. I even graduated with honors, so it proves you can teach an old dog new tricks. Now, that's not saying there wasn't a shock. When I left the service, I had a pretty responsible position. I had some thirty-odd people working for me and I turned right around and closed the door and became Joe Nothing, a freshman. Way, way down at the bottom of the pole. Once you get over that, however, it's okay.

If I had to do it over again, all circumstances being what they were, I would choose the Air Force as a career. I looked upon the military as a calling, something that you believed in; it had to come first. You're not there to get rich, you're not there to get any acclaim. It's something a guy feels in his heart and in his guts. He's serving his country. If you look upon it as a job, get the hell out. I don't want you protecting me. I don't want you at my back when I need help. There is an expression I have always disliked: "Thank God it's Friday." No military flyer ever coined that phrase. We worked seven days a week, 365 days a year. How many people can say that they were being shot at on Christmas day? I hope I'm not being overpatriotic. I don't think you can be, but I love my country and I'm willing to protect it.

Looking at the Air Force today, if I were going in now, however, I'd think twice. Our flying was fun. Today everything is so standardized. The way you are briefed, debriefed. The missions are spelled out completely. Execution, time of flight, everything. You have somebody looking over your shoulder continuously because you are not running around with a couple of hundred thousand dollars worth of airplane, you've got something like fourteen million dollars worth of fighter. I have nothing but admiration for the young military aviator today. He's qualified because he has to be qualified. All units are evaluated periodically, and there are no old pals at those evaluations. It's a different type of outfit today. I'll tell you a story that may explain what I mean.

After the war was over, Bill Behnke, whom I flew with in the Philippines, and I were in Japan and they had some P-38s parked on the field. Bill and I got to looking at one and we decided that it was a pretty good-looking airplane. I asked him if he had any P-38 time and he said, "Yeah." I said, "Okay, want to try it?" He said, "Let's go." It had a double cockpit and I flew in back of him. Bill started looking around the cockpit and he said, "I'm trying to remember how to start this thing." He finally gets the engines going and we go rolling out and take off. We're going along and it's very nice. A good feel and very sensitive. We're looking around and all of a sudden, wham!, the engines quit. He forgot to switch from one fuel tank to the other. Bill gets the engines started again and gets us down in one piece. When we were on the ground, I asked him, "How much time do you have in a P-38?" He said, "Well, I sat in the cockpit of one once." That's the way it was.

FIGHTER JOCKS

Pilots lined up with their P-39 Airacobras in the 39th Squadron of the 31st Pursuit Group, the oldest fighting plane command in the Air Corps. National Archives.

Physical courage in battle, or in any other hazardous situation, involves overcoming or even putting aside the perfectly normal instinct of fear. Nearly every man going into combat will, if pressed, confess to fear. But if there is no such thing as a truly fearless man, there are obviously a handful who seem to be underendowed with that healthy instinct or whose adrenaline pumps faster than it does in most of us. We claim no survey or scientific authority for this comment and simply state that what seems like fearlessness appears to have surfaced very often among the flyers of all the nations in World War II. We present in this chapter three examples of this intrepid breed.

THOMAS G. LANPHIER, JR.

AT ALL COSTS REACH AND DESTROY

Talking to the late Thomas G. Lanphier, Jr., was like walking on eggshells. He did not suffer fools gladly, and you had to pay attention and get your facts straight. Lanphier was an ace Army Air Corps fighter pilot who flew 112 combat missions in the South Pacific, sank an enemy destroyer, and shot down seventeen Japanese planes. It was hard to get him to talk about his part in the famous secret mission that brought down and killed Japan's brilliant top admiral, Isoroku Yamamoto, for which Lanphier was given an immediate promotion from captain to lieutenant colonel. There is a controversy about who shot down which plane in the Yamamoto group that arose afterward through Lanphier's former friend and wing man, Rex Barber. Lanphier was saving some of his story, we believe, for the book he was writing, which was unfinished when he died in November 1987. We can only print what he told us, leaving the argument to others.

I met General MacArthur a few years after the war. My father knew him and he took me over to the Waldorf Astoria where the general was living at that time. They talked for awhile and then MacArthur said to my father, "Tom, I want to tell you something funny that happened during the war. George Kenney came in one day and showed me a communication that said something about Captain Tom Lanphier shooting down Admiral Yamamoto. I said, 'What's that old son-of-a-bitch doing flying a fighter plane at his age?'" MacArthur had thought my father was the one who shot down Yamamoto.

My old man was a West Pointer, and after he graduated from the academy, he was assigned to a post in the Panama Canal Zone. I was

Lieutenant Colonel Thomas G. Lanphier, Jr., shown here as a captain, was the son of a World War I flyer and the ace Army Air Force fighter pilot who shot down Japanese Admiral Isoroku Yamamoto, architect of the attack on Pearl Harbor.

born in Panama City on November 27, 1918. My father always referred to the moment as the week that Army beat Navy three to zero. At that time he was a second lieutenant in the 33rd Infantry and when the First World War broke out, he was sent to France in charge of a machine-gun unit. He saw action at Chateau Thierry and then managed to get transferred into the Air Service and ended up in command of flight training at Issouden, France.

In 1924 he took command of the First Pursuit Group at Selfridge Field, Michigan. Hap Arnold, at that time director of information for the Air Service, told my father, "Take that group and put it on display all over the North American continent, from Mexico to Canada. Dedicate airports anywhere they clear a pasture big enough to get a PW-8 in and out of. Enter the air races—and win 'em. Sell the Air Service to the American people." That's exactly what my father did. He trained aerobatic groups, he dedicated airports, his men won air races.

Growing up at Selfridge Field was an incredible experience for a young boy. There were aces from the First World War such as Strahm and Hunter. Airplanes were always overhead. I was the mascot for the 17th Fighter Squadron football team, and the captain of the team was an enlisted man, Tech Sergeant Emil Shatko. He was three-quarter Cherokee and a crew chief. Shatko took a shine to me, and between the two of us we convinced a young second lieutenant, Irvine Woodring, to take me up in the back seat of a Jenny trainer. Woodring and another guy, Bill Cornelius, started giving me what amounted to flying lessons, and I soloed before I was fourteen years old.

This had all been done on the q.t., and when I landed, feeling quite proud of myself, my father pulled me out of that cockpit and proceeded to flail me with a length of rubber shock absorber. He had come down early that morning for a spot inspection, and I'm sure he was more frightened for me than angry. That didn't lessen the pain, and after six or seven whacks, Shatko stepped in and said, "Major, the kid's had enough. Whip me, I sent him up." My father glared at him and then turned on his heel and left. Cornelius and Woodring told my father that they had helped, and they had to stay on the base for eight weekends, a godawful punishment for two young officers. I lost my mascot position and never soloed the Jenny again. Shatko wasn't punished. I never asked my father, but I would imagine he felt the officers were to blame, and I'm sure he also respected Shatko's sticking up for me; God knows, I did.

My parents were divorced in 1930 and my two brothers and I stayed in Detroit with my mother. We attended St. Paul's of Grosse Pointe where we were thoroughly and classically taught by Sacred Heart nuns. After high school I went to Stanford University and majored in journalism. It took me eight years to get through school because my father went broke in the market and I had to take time off for various jobs to pay my debts. One year I worked on a ranch in California; another year I hashed tables in a fraternity house and worked part-time at a race track. The last two years, I had a night job on the *San Francisco News* covering the labor beat and occasionally serving as second-string drama critic.

My father came to see me in the fall of 1940. He said the United States was going to be in the war and I should join the Air Corps and get a commission as a pilot so I wouldn't have to "crawl around in the mud." He also said, "Get in a fighter so you can zig and zag. Then you won't have to sit in a bomber like an unthinking hunk of meat."

"Christ, Dad," I said, "we're not going to get in any war. My roommate and I are the executive vice-president and secretary of the Head for the Hills Club."

My roommate, John Driscoll, and I thought my father was over-stating the case. Like most of our friends, we had continued to ignore the ominous events in Europe, and if I thought about it at all, I was sure that we'd remain neutral. Hitler was just a name to us. My father's fervent speech won out, however, and Driscoll and I signed up with the Air Corps. I picked transports because I wanted to get married, and transports meant you stayed in the United States and got a little better accommodations. However, upon graduating in November 1941, I was assigned as a "volunteer" to the 70th Pursuit Squadron at Hamilton Field, which was across the bay from San Francisco. John got killed the week before graduation in a training accident.

There were one hundred pilots and we reported to Captain Henry Viccellio, who had to pick forty of us to take to the Pacific, post unknown. We had one P-40 that we each flew once and he really picked us by watching us play poker. Viccellio wandered around for thirty days watching all of us play, with his eye out for the traits that would make a good fighter pilot. He appreciated recklessness, as long as it was occasional and outweighed by traits more conducive to longevity. I think it was as good a way as any to pick us, as long as we could get up and down in an airplane.

On Sunday morning, December 7, my father called me. "Turn on the radio, the war is on. They've leveled Pearl Harbor." He didn't give me any I-told-you-so. His final words were, "You'd better get back to your post. And keep the sun at your back. Carry on, son." We sailed on the liner *President Monroe*, landed at Suva Harbor, Fiji, and then moved to a grass strip called Nasouri. We took our P-40s out of their crates, assembled them, and soloed in them. Each pilot gave his crew chief a ride, sans parachute, to keep everybody on the *qui vive.*

We then moved to Nandi where we spent eight months training for combat. We went to Guadalcanal in December and discovered the facts of war. The day-by-day business of fighting off mosquitos, boredom, intestinal flu, malaria, torrential rain, burning sun, the nauseatingly sweet stink of dead bodies, bland food, loneliness, weeks without mail from home, and occasionally an almost welcome attack from the enemy in the jungle or in the air.

My first billet was Fighter Two, which was across from Henderson Field. We lived on a ridge near the runway. The Marines played hell with our sleep when they lobbed shells over the top of our tents onto enemy positions farther inland. The enemy's returning mortars were even more disturbing. Our creature comforts on the canal were, early on, afforded us by the Marines. Our flying operations were very primitive. We had no control tower and the only radio contact was a Marine installation you could talk to and hear, but which afforded no navigational aid. Our flights to and from the island, sometimes going hundreds of miles over the Solomons, were executed by guess and God. Since there was always a crosswind off the water, we would take off both ways on the runway. We were now flying P-39 Airacobras, and my wing man and I would wait for the two fighters coming at us to get airborne and then take off down the runway under them. We all landed the same way and didn't have any accidents flying this way. When we finally got a control tower, the accidents began to happen.

We would fly daily two-man reconnaissance patrols to see if the Japanese were bringing in any ships. We didn't have that many airplanes so most of our flying was over Guadalcanal. Occasionally we'd fly intercepts, escort B-17s, or dive-bomb various targets. This reminds me of the one mission, out of almost a hundred I flew in the Solomons, that still gives me nightmares. The others I closed out long ago. I was returning from one of those early recon missions and was flying up the beach when I saw a naked Japanese soldier running out of the surf toward the jungle. Without thinking, I nosed my plane over and began strafing the beach. He stopped and turned to face me, whether in fear or defiance, I don't know. I watched the puffs of sand kicked up by my bullets race across the beach, and he fell dead as I flew over him. When I wake up from the nightmare, I always rationalize that action the same way. We had a saying, "Every Nip that gets into the jungle can mean a dead Marine." It doesn't always help.

In late February we went down to Sydney and Auckland on leave and we really had the feeling that the people were glad to have us there. When we returned from leave, we went to Efate in the New Hebrides and checked out in the P-38, the Lightning, which was a huge improvement over the lowly Airacobras. The P-39 could reach

20,000 feet at best, whereas the new P-38 could fly at 40,000 feet, which was above the Zero's ceiling. Superior altitude is the most important characteristic of any fighter. First of all, it's the safest place to be, a platform where you can decide on your own terms where and how to fight. Superior altitude can also be converted into superior speed, the second important characteristic of a good fighter plane. Also, from the pilot's point of view, it had two fans, or propellers, which gave you double security against falling into the South Pacific. The Lightning couldn't turn with the Zero, but it could dive away from the enemy if all else failed and it certainly had firepower: four .50-caliber machine guns and a 20mm cannon firing straight ahead. We checked out in that marvelous airplane and went up to Guadalcanal in early March, where we flew top cover for B-17s and SBDs with very little Japanese resistance.

In March and April we flew a number of on-the-deck [low-level] strikes and shot the hell out of the Japanese. On April 2, we went out and set a freighter afire by skipping our wing tanks into him and then setting the fuel afire with tracers. When Admiral Halsey heard about it he sent one of his flamboyant messages: "Very neat use of heat. Your treatment hard to beat. Commander Third Fleet sends . . . congratulations on big hotfoot." Two weeks later we went up to Shortland Island, which was near Tahiti, and bounced a float-plane base.

Early in April, my brother Charlie shot down his first Zero. He too had gone to Stanford and graduated with a degree in engineering. He became a Marine aviator after Pearl Harbor. I was returning from a sweep up the Slot one day when I was surprised to hear my name called by the Guadalcanal ground station. When I answered, someone else interrupted me. When it happened twice more I yelled, "You son-of-a-bitch, stay off the air! Recon is calling me." The other voice said, "He's calling me, you bastard." It turned out to be my brother and he was at Fighter One, a jungle mile or so from where I was stationed. We did get to see each other a few times out there, and, several months after I left the Solomons, while he was flying a strafing mission on Kahili, he got hit by groundfire and had to bail out. The Japanese captured him and took him to a prison camp at Rabaul. He eventually died of gangrene and malnutrition. Over the years I've thought of him, time and time again. Men like Charlie gave their lives for their country without the recognition that has been given to the men who didn't get killed, myself included.

★

I found out about the Yamamoto mission on April 17, 1943. I haven't talked about it for years and now, in the year or so since I've been working on my book, I've talked about it so much I'm weary of it. I tend to speak quickly and I know I leave things out. I always end up apologizing to people if I confuse the issues but I've come to realize there is an interested audience. I'll tell you why I'm writing about it. A few years ago, I was feeling rotten and I was in the doldrums. I'd spent almost a month in the hospital when I got a call from Bob Baylor, who was an ace in Europe. "Tom, I hear you're not feeling too well. How about coming up and giving a little talk about your father, Billy Mitchell, and all of that. I think it is fascinating and a lot of people would like to hear you speak." I said I'd do it, and a few weeks later I drove up to a restaurant, the Nieuport 17, in Santa Ana. There were twenty-five or so fighter pilots in the audience, including my cohost, Ken Walsh, the Medal of Honor Marine fighter ace whom I flew alongside with in the Solomons. I looked down at a table and there, opposite me, was Curt LeMay, the legendary bomber pilot and leader of SAC. I'd known him for some time and he used to drive me up the wall. LeMay believed that fighters were fine for strafing, dive bombing, and that sort of thing, but the bombers didn't need them to fly cover; they could take care of themselves. I got up and gave a reminiscent talk about my father and his First World War times; it went over pretty well. Afterwards we were sitting around and Curt said, "Tom, you ought to write a book. You have a feeling for what you and a lot of other guys did. When a war is over, we are the villains in the public eye, especially the generals. Goddamn it, Tom, you talk about us as though we are human beings." What he was saying was an old refrain, of course, but coming from LeMay it was interesting because he's usually a laconic man about such matters.

★

That Isoroku Yamamoto was Japan's top admiral and naval strategist made an attempt to shoot him down exciting, but it started off as just another mission. You didn't think of epochal moments when you were out there because you just went from day to day trying to beat the boredom. We figured that we'd at least get a chance to fight some Zeros on the mission. To us, ignorant of the extent of American breaking of Japanese codes, it was a miracle that Yamamoto was there when we showed up.

I was due to go on leave when my C.O., Henry Viccellio, told me, "Tommy, we're going to hold you over for a couple of days."

"Christ, Vic," I said, "To hell with you. I'm on my way to Australia on leave!"

But he told me I had to stick around, even though he couldn't tell me why. It would be interesting, he said. We would find it interesting for the rest of our lives.

The next day Major John Mitchell, my relief, and I went into

Admiral Marc Mitscher's tent, called "The Opium Den" for the ideas dreamed up there. Mitscher was sitting in a chair off to the side and John Condon, the Marine operations officer, gave us a blue tissue TWX cablegram, the kind the Navy used for top secret dispatches. It said that Admiral Yamamoto, accompanied by six Zeros, would be arriving by air from Rabaul at Ballale Island, off Bougainville, on Sunday, April 18, 1943, which was the next day. It gave his itinerary and ended with:

SQUADRON 339 P-38s MUST AT ALL COSTS REACH AND DESTROY. PRESIDENT ATTACHES EXTREME IMPORTANCE TO THIS OPERATION.

It was signed "KNOX." Nobody present had ever seen an order like that. In fact, I had never seen an order before. We used to decide verbally where we were going to go and then just go.

Then Mitscher spoke up, "Lanphier and his people have been up in that area, and I want him to make the bounce." My flight, of Barber, Moore, and McLanahan, had successfully strafed the float-plane base there and had also shot up that destroyer. So they figured that we would be pretty good at hitting something on the surface. The navy plan was for us to catch Yamamoto while he was on a subchaser going from one island to another.

"Look, Admiral," I said, "There are several things wrong with that. Number one, I don't know a subchaser from a cruiser, and there will be hundreds of boats in that harbor. Second, by the time we make a pass, let alone a second one, they'll have killed us with their antiaircraft or fighters, because everything will be zeroed in to defend his ship. Third, our experience with that destroyer was that, while we were strafing it, most of the crew jumped off the boat."

Mitscher interrupted me. "Ship," he said.

"O.K., ship," I replied, "But I don't recall anything in that TWX that says Yamamoto can't swim."

"All right, kid, how do you people want to do it?"

What we decided was that we would try to get Yamamoto in the air west of Kahili Airbase on Bougainville. I doubt that anyone who took off on that mission, certainly not myself, dreamed we would actually contact the admiral's flight, especially when you considered that we would be approaching each other from 600 miles apart at a combined speed of two-thirds the speed of sound. Also, we had only eighteen P-38s, and we assumed that the hundred Zeros known to be at Kahili would be covering the admiral's arrival.

John Condon gave Mitchell the circuitous route he had plotted, low near the water to evade the enemy coast watchers. We figured

Yamamoto would be at 5,000 feet because the old man wouldn't want to wear an oxygen mask. Mitchell, who was leading the group, would take his fourteen fighters up to 20,000 feet to give us top cover, and the four in my group were supposed to go to 10,00 feet. That meant we'd be above our target when he arrived and the four of us would bounce him.

But I was still low at 1,000 feet, 10 miles from the island, when I heard Doug Canning, one of Mitchell's men: "Bogey, ten o'clock high." There the admiral was, just as the cablegram had forecast: two Betty bombers, escorted by six Zeke fighters. Mitchell started to climb ahead to his altitude, and I angled over and began climbing parallel to the enemy planes. Our tactical situation was by no means encouraging. Rather than waiting at 10,000 feet where we could dive out of the sun, we were below and in front of the enemy, with four to his eight.

The four quickly became just Barber and me when my number three man, Holmes, could not release his auxiliary fuel tank and chose to go off down the beach, out of the fight, attempting to shake it loose. His wing man, Ray Hine, went with him and died in the subsequent action over the sea.

In the ensuing five minutes or so I saw no one but my Japanese targets. First I set a Zero afire as it dived at me to fend me off the lead bomber, which had dived down and away inland when his formation spotted Barber and me. Then I flipped over and chased the lead Betty for a couple of minutes, finally catching up with it over the jungle treetops and, with a lucky, extremely high-angle volley, set his right wing afire, finally causing the wing to fall off and the Betty to explode as it fell into the jungle. Yamamoto's identifiable body was found the next day, by the Japanese, thrown out of the bomber.

Meanwhile Barber started to chase the wing bomber, which proved to contain Yamamoto's ranking staff officers, and he claimed in the combat report that he shot the tail off that plane. Then he went out over the harbor, saw another bomber, and shot that one down. He brought back parts of it in his air intake. After the war, it turned out there was no bomber with its tail shot off, anywhere in the area. The only bomber that went into the jungle had its wing off, as I claimed at the time. Barber undoubtedly got the one out in the harbor because three men who were in that bomber lived and described what had happened.

As far as the controversy raised by Barber today goes, he doesn't claim he got Yamamoto, but he does claim he set him up for me. He didn't. My feeling is that he's an honest man but is deluding himself in contradicting the combat mission report to which he subscribed at the time. I think he shot the same bomber down twice. He hit the one going toward the ocean, was distracted by the Zekes, and when he

218   FIGHTER JOCKS

got away from them, shot the same Betty down. It was now out over the water. It's sad because we were friends and he was a first-rate fighter pilot. Rex flew fifty or sixty missions on my wing and never left me once, saving my life several times, and vice versa.

My feelings about Yamamoto today are quite different from what they were then. I don't regret killing him, but I now know more of the truth about him and have come to respect him as a human being. He was opposed to Japan's attacking the United States in the first place; not for moral reasons, but because he knew from his years in America and Europe that Japan could not defeat us in the long run. It's ironic to me that both Yamamoto, when he was going to school in this country, and I myself, when I was growing up, were so taken with Billy Mitchell. In one way or another, our parallel experiences and interest in Mitchell led us to that fatal rendezvous in the Solomon Islands in 1943.

Everyone on the mission was shortly sent home and, after taking time off to get married, I was ordered to report to Hap Arnold. I went into his office in Washington wearing my old green jungle outfit. He looked me over and said, "You know, Tom, my two sons don't fly, so I've adopted a fighter pilot in each theater. Dave Schilling in Europe and you in the Pacific. So far neither of you has let me down. If either of you ever does, I'll have your ass."

Then he added, "But look at you, for Christ's sake! I want you to go out and demonstrate the P-38 to the kids who are checking out in that airplane. They're scared of it because they think that, if an engine coughs on takeoff, they're dead. You know it's not true, so go out and show the airplane off. Oh yes, also tell them about the war." He also wanted me to go on a bond tour. I kind of winced when he said that.

"Don't give me that," said Arnold. "It's important that those people in the plants feel that they're part of the effort. That's where the hero bit comes in and you look like a bum, not a hero." Then he told his aide, "I've ordered a uniform for Tom, with the ribbons and insignia. You see that he wears it and looks like a goddamn hero even if he isn't one." Then he laughed and asked me what my theme was going to be when I talked to those people.

"Well, sir," I replied, "I'm going to tell them that we appreciate what they are doing, that we are all part of the war effort, but that we are all also at fault for one thing. As individuals we didn't pay enough attention to the world beyond ourselves, and our nation allowed itself to get weak. We invited attack. That's why we're at war. Secondly, I'm going to tell them I resent their asking me to go out and kill somebody."

Arnold said, "Tommy, I don't know whether you're going to get away with that. Once the country's honor and safety are at stake, you have to kill. I know I'm a little remote from the dying and killing. You were right on the line, but goddamn it, don't think I don't toss and turn every night about the kids I have to send out, possibly to die."

I'm sure he meant every word, and I respected him for it. I said I would do my best, and my wife and I shared our honeymoon with production workers in Buffalo, Philadelphia, Pittsburgh, Cleveland, and Detroit. You should have seen their faces. Arnold was right. They wanted me to be a hero whether I was or not. You had to play the role. At my very first appearance in Buffalo one of my questioners stood up and asked, without apparent rancor:

"Captain, how does it feel to kill those men who made you an ace?"

This is, roughly, what I remember answering: "My friends, your indifference, and mine, to keeping our country strong enough to deter a Pearl Harbor sent me out there to kill. That's bad enough. But asking those of us who go into combat for you at the risk of our lives is asking a hell of a high price for your prewar carelessness. Even worse is asking us to kill on your behalf. I've done it, and accept it as part of the service I must render for my country. But if your question implies that I should feel guilty about the killing, then join me in the cockpit and share my guilt in action—as you sure as hell do in principle." I got rather a big hand for that response.

In order to teach young flyers about the P-38 Lightning, I had told General Arnold I would need a couple of weeks to learn some of the fine points myself. When we got new airplanes in the Pacific, the ferry pilots just left us the technical booklets. All we knew about them we learned in combat, with the throttle wide open. I never considered the P-38 or any other fighter plane more than an implement of combat. The minute I got in the cockpit, it became an extremity. I don't know why, but I related that way to any airplane I flew. I wasn't interested in what made the ship fly. The crew chiefs kept them working; you could trust them. I recently went to a reunion of one of the squadrons I flew with during the war, and thought I was being very magnanimous when I wound up by saying, "I never knew what went on under the hood and you did." At that point, one old crew chief, rather soused, got up and said, "That's right, you dumb son-of-a-bitch. We knew and that's why you're alive today."

I went to Lockheed, in Burbank, and asked Jimmy Mattern, who was one of their best test pilots, to teach me how to fly the Lightning like an expert. He taught me the routine I would use to convince those trainees that the plane wasn't going to kill them as long as they weren't afraid of it. I'd get on the butt end of the runway, run the engines up full tilt with the brakes on, release them, and hold the ship on the runway until I was doing 180, then raise the wheels by the time I was at the end of the runway. When I started to pull up, I would cut the left engine and go on my way. I practiced that on top of the clouds for two weeks before I tried it on the deck.

While I was in Los Angeles, I met Jimmy Stewart, who was on leave from flight training as a bomber pilot. He knew I was working out in the P-38 and asked me if I'd check him out in the plane. We met the next day at the Marine Base at El Toro and I gave him the full cockpit check. Jimmy is a deliberate sort of fellow, so we went through the routine several times. He finally took off on what was supposed to be a half-hour flight. When 45 minutes had gone by and no P-38 was in sight, I began to worry. After an hour had passed I began to see the headlines: "MOVIE STAR DIES ON ILLICIT ARMY FLIGHT," and the subheads: "James Stewart Rites at Forest Lawn Friday, Lanphier Court-Martial Begins Thursday."

About then, from out of the east, appeared my P-38 flying low and slow, wheels and flaps down, with smoke pouring out of both engines as Jimmy poured the coal to them to be sure of maintaining flying speed. He landed smoothly and taxied back to our position. Jimmy opened the hatch, took off his gear and, looking everywhere but at me, told me he'd forgotten where the lever to lower the landing gear was located. It was right where the famous "purloined letter" had been, in plain sight in front of him.

My tour of the training command bases was an apparent success. I called the colonel at the first base I was going to and told him I couldn't demonstrate the plane with all the safety rules he had in effect. He said, "What safety rules?" Given that unspoken waiver, I said, "I understand." Those base commanders were all old cronies of Arnold's. And so I would come in, fly down the main drag at full bore, loop the plane, and land. By that time I had the trainees' attention. I'd give them a 45-minute light-touch talk, and then we'd go to lunch. After that I'd do my routine, but I'd tell them beforehand that I was going to show off. "For Christ's sake, don't you try this. The reason I'm here is that some of you are said to be afraid of this machine. So I'm going to show you how, if you know the aircraft, it's a safe and nimble bird."

Before I left each flying field, I would fly a 15-minute show of aerobatics, and at the tenth base, somewhere in Texas, I almost bought it. It was hot and muggy. One of the things I used to do was to fly inverted down the runway 50 feet above the ground. My gloves were sweaty and the damn wheel slipped in my hand. The nose went down toward the ground and I desperately pushed forward on the yoke, managed to roll over, and got out of there. That frightened the bravado right out of me, and when I landed at the next base I cancelled the next and last stop of the tour.

I was then assigned to the 72nd Fighter Wing. While there I conned the commander, Felix Vidal, into letting me go to England to fly P-51s, P-47s, and P-38s, to observe British combat tactics, so that we could put them into the training of replacement pilots. Once I was over there, I managed to go on an escort mission to Berlin, in the course of which I learned undying respect for our bomber crews. I came back to the States in time for the birth of our first daughter, and went to work training P-47 fighter pilots who were going to cover the invasion of Japan. I was flying over the Grand Canyon in August of 1945 when I heard that the atomic bomb had been dropped on Hiroshima. I slow-rolled that airplane until I was exhausted because our numbers guys had estimated we would lose half the pilots we were training in the first month of action over Japan. I had a feeling of sheer relief and happiness. The war ended on August 15, and I applied the next day for a discharge, which came through in September.

Assessing what's happened to me in the four-and-a-half decades since I went to war, I must say first that the isolationist "know nothing" in me was converted in the mud and blood of Guadalcanal, and second, that the atomic bomb changed my thinking—as it did for most people. Even Pearl Harbor, with its conventional weapons, was a relatively acceptable form of warfare. You can react traditionally to something like that as a people; that is, strike back with everything you have, every weapon, everything at your disposal. But wars like Korea and Vietnam were different matters. We drifted into a policy of not using the frightful weapons we'd been paying for all along as the keystone of our arsenal. We have no chance of winning such wars. Incidentally, I was there, in the White House, on the National Security Council staff, when Truman proposed to the United Nations through Bernard Baruch—when we alone had the nuclear weapon—that we would agree not to build any more if the Soviets would agree not to go forward with theirs. The USSR turned us down. Are we better off now?

I had never been politically active before the war. That changed in 1946 when I became editor of the *Idaho Daily Statesman*. I moved my family to Boise, and spent the next four years writing editorials criticizing Truman for disarming the Air Force—reducing it from several hundred combat groups to a "paper" thirty or forty. Then, despite those editorials, Truman appointed me as a special assistant to the Secretary of the Air Force, Stuart Symington. I got to respect Truman, who used to call me the "smart-ass kid," but his domestic and international policies, I thought, were the work of fine but fallible men, clumsy in their attempts to maintain our defense position.

I left the government in 1950 when Symington went to the RFC. Jacqueline Cochran got me together with her husband, Floyd Odlum, who asked me to work for him at Convair as its long-range planner, where I got involved with the Atlas Missile program. Odlum was the gentlest, smartest, and most all-around humane man I've met in my life. When the Pentagon decided to drop the Atlas ICBM study for lack of funds, he gambled $3,000,000 of Convair's money until the funds were restored at the advent of Sputnik. Convair was conscientiously committed to developing and building systems to protect this country.

Most of the guys in the war went home afterwards to jobs that had little to do with their military experiences, but I was fortunate enough to be able to use mine while working in government, industry, and the media. I could carry forward what I and most citizen soldiers believed in for the defense of our country. Today, at seventy, I'm starting all over again with television. I'm working on a PBS series on the history of manned flight with the National Air and Space Museum of the Smithsonian. We are doing interviews, covering the whole gamut of aviation, with people as various as Jimmy Doolittle, Anne Lindbergh, Barry Goldwater, Stuart Symington, Jimmy Stewart, Chuck Yeager, C. R. Smith, who started American Airlines, and Fred Smith of Federal Express. I confess that we've started with the older folks first.

It was a rewarding experience to work at Convair when we created the Atlas system. Out of that grew the propulsion system for Mercury, Saturn, Apollo, and other space adventures we cannot abandon. You don't quit. The president and everybody else said that after the space shuttle *Challenger* blew up. We lost lives, but the price of progress in human experience has always been the blood of good men and women. You have to go on these adventures. That's the way it was in World War II. That's the way it is now.

IRON DOG

Edwards Park is a slim, young-looking man, whom we first met at the Smithsonian's facility for aircraft restoration at Silver Hill, Maryland. He looked, if given the opportunity, quite ready to jump into a fighter cockpit and head out on a mission.

Park is a descendant of a long line of clergymen, and those ancestors could find much to approve of in his accomplishments. Retired from Smithsonian magazine, he lives in Annapolis, still pursuing a distinguished career as a journalist. In his memoirs, entitled Nanette *(Smithsonian Institution Press, 1977), Park gives readers a fine picture of what is was like to fly an airplane nicknamed* The Iron Dog *into combat. It may well be one of the best accounts ever written of a man's relationship with a machine of war.*

I think the last P-39 Airacobra was kicked petulantly to death by its pilot. I would meet an old Yale classmate in Brisbane and he'd say, "What are you flying?" and I'd say, "P-39s." He'd say, "Oh, Jesus, not that! How come you're still alive?" That airplane had a terrible reputation. I came to feel that all the planes of that old war had distinguishing personalities. The P-40, for example, was a knobby, arrogant tomboy; the P-47, the Thunderbolt, was more of a dull peasant girl. But of all those old fighters, two could really stir your juice. One was the P-51 Mustang, lovely to look at, honest, efficient, hardworking, and dependable. I know men who married their P-51s and are still faithful to them. The other was the P-39. She was slim, with a gently curved tail section, a smoothly faired air intake, and a perfectly rounded nose cone with its protruding cannon. A man couldn't keep

Edwards Park, right, fighter pilot, has the élan of that daredevil trade. He is today a prolific writer and lecturer, and a regular contributor to *Smithsonian* and *Air & Space* magazines.

his hands off the Airacobra, but she was as rotten as she was sexy.

Back when I was a cadet, I saw one sitting on a strip in Greenville, Mississippi. Two or three of us were looking it over when an upperclassman came by and said, "That's a real dog. She looks great but she won't do anything. She's not fast enough, won't climb, has no ceiling and no range." All of which were true. And then, of course, there was the thing about tumbling. Since I wrote my book, *Nanette*, I've had old P-39 test pilots write to me and say, "You know, you're just carrying on the myth. The P-39 would not tumble." Well, I've tumbled in it. Tumbling is somersaulting, nose first, then tail, then nose. You were literally falling out of the sky, and the airplane had ceased to fly. When it happened, you let go of everything because if you touched anything, it would aggravate the situation. Eventually it would remind you of a pendulum. The nose would start to swing back and forth, and all of a sudden it would straighten out. I could feel the air tighten on the airplane and then I pulled out. That happened at Sarasota. I was doing aerobatics and I got upside down ("and there I was on my back with nothing on but the radio"—a flyer's joke back then) and tried to ease the stick back. Well, you should never do that in a P-39; if you just think about doing that, good-bye. I fell about 12,000 feet before I got the plane under control—absolutely terrifying.

One good thing about the 39, at least the missions were short because the airplane didn't have any range, even with a 110-gallon belly tank tacked on. The Airacobra was built as an interceptor and that's what caused all the problems. The Americans looked at the Hurricane and Spitfire, which were the prototypes of the modern fighter, and said, "We've got to have a plane like that." What we thought of was entirely in terms of the British interceptors, and they needed short-range fighters. It wasn't until we'd been in the war a while that the facts of life made us realize that what we really needed at the time were long-range escort planes.

The funny thing was that I got pretty good in 39s. Coming back from a mission, the loss of altitude over the base was one of our more exciting activities. All four planes in the flight would rock into a vertical bank and do a spiral toward the ground. You tightened that spiral as much as you could and the more you tightened it, the faster you dropped. We would come down from 15,000 feet to 5,000 in about two turns. I'd just touch the stick, with my middle finger adding back pressure, until I felt it quiver and then I'd ease it off again. We'd be streaming condensation off the wing tips. There was a point where I thought, "I'm really flying this bastard now." I didn't give a shit any more. Those wings belonged to me! That's a very dangerous way to feel, but I wanted to get down in a hurry and that was the way I did it. The plane could have stalled at any moment and if it stalled, it would flip and go straight into the jungle. "Augering in," we called it.

I was leading the flight one day and I got the spiral tighter than I'd ever gotten it before. They all stayed in that corkscrew, but they said afterwards, "My God, how'd you get it so tight?" I said, "I really don't know." After that I began to ease off. Doing things like that was dumb and I liked living. If I was going to get killed, I might as well get killed in combat instead of just "augering in" for fun.

We were a good squadron. I was closer to those guys than anyone before or after, closer than I was to my brothers. They were a bright bunch and I never felt I was with anything less than my peers. The prewar guys, who got their wings in '38 and '39, were absolutely one-eyed about flying and fighting. That's all they were interested in, military flying. They were tuned in on that one thing. The newer crowd, replacements like me, who came in after Pearl Harbor, were generally speaking civilian-minded, not military-minded. We still looked back on college days with enjoyment. Then we began to get some younger kids who were just out of high school. They didn't have any college at all. I had a tent mate we all were very fond of, but he was only a kid. He was eighteen and the rest of us were old, twenty-three, twenty-four. This guy, Lundburg, was such a jock. He wanted to play baseball all the time while the old college guys wanted to sit around and drink. He'd come back into the tent just dripping with sweat and we'd say, "For God's sake, you little twerp, why do you come in and sweat all over us?" He'd say, "Never mind, you got some water?" We'd throw him a canteen and he'd go glug, glug, glug and then "Yuckkkkk! It's got whiskey in it." We'd say, "Lundburg, if you're going to live in this tent, you've got to get used to our ways."

There was another guy, honest to God, I think he was trying to kill me. He was one of the older pilots and he thought I was no bloody good. Well, he was right. He read me loud and clear and, through some devilment in the squadron, I was constantly flying his wing. On takeoff, he would turn into me. As soon as he got his wheels up, he'd do a right-hand turn into me, which put me in a position of stalling out, and would have had me cartwheeling into the dirt. I finally worked it out. There was just enough room between him and the trees for me to slide under him and tack on to his left wing. When he saw me skidding under him, he raked me out: "Can't you fly formation?" I said, "Yes, I can fly formation, but I'm not flying formation into the dirt, you silly son-of-a-bitch. If you want to kill someone, you can pick on somebody else." He said, "You don't want to live forever, do you?" The old Army line. I said, "You're damn tooting I do."

The amazing thing was that I was flying his wing when we got into a hairy situation. He was so impatient, he couldn't bear to wait for operations to tell him to do something. This time he got bored flying a patrol and took us on an unscheduled strafing run. He led us down, four of us, and we raked over a Nip area and blew it to bits with the cannons. We started back up and just then got a call that bandits were coming over. We looked up and sure enough, there were six Japanese light bombers and above them the sky was black with Zeros. We climbed up as far as we could and dropped our belly tanks. I didn't know what Old Wild Ass was doing, but I pulled back on the stick, hung on the prop, and blasted off some cannon shots at those bombers. There was really nothing to hit, they were well out of range, but I looked through my sight and sent all those tracers flashing up there. Well, you never saw such a reaction. Every one of those Zeros flipped on his back at once. Twenty-four or so of them were coming down with pulsing ripples of fire from all those guns. Most of them seemed to be firing right at me. I fell off into a stall, straightened it out, and headed for the barn as fast as that little thing would go.

From then on this guy liked me. I'd stuck with him and done something kind of wild myself. He hadn't thought of doing that. I was the one who started to fire first. I liked shooting the guns. Some planes had the 20mm cannon and others had the 37mm. The tunnel went right under you between your legs, and you felt it vibrating when you fired the cannon. It gave sort of a pleasant massage. The 37mm went "whump-whump-whump!" and the 20mm would go off a lot faster. "Bababababa." Some men enjoyed the 20. I was a 37mm man myself.

When he found out that I could drink with him, we would sit around in the farmhouse where we had a little officers' club. We ended up one night sitting on the roof and finishing off a bottle. Neither of us had to fly the next day, but if he had had to fly, it wouldn't have stopped him. It would have stopped me; I was too careful. He could never understand why I was so careful. This night he said, "I majored in English and I bet I can outquote you on the nineteenth-century English poets." I said, "You illiterate bastard, you couldn't possibly do that." Well, he did. In fact, he knew a lot more than I did.

He got killed, the jerk. He was sent home to the Pentagon, and he spent his entire time there hammering on doors to get sent back to the squadron. He couldn't stand it back home. He had to get back into action, and they finally sent him back to New Guinea. I'd already gone home when he got back. He was leading a flight (they were flying Mustangs by that time), and they got into a sortie. Lots of planes with guns firing all over the place. He took some hits and landed on a little strip in the Philippines. It was Japanese-held then and the rest of his flight kept coming over the strip firing to keep the Japanese away and they could see he was all slumped over in his cockpit. His wing man figured they would take him out and play with him if he wasn't dead, so he went around and blew him up. That guy doesn't want to talk about it today.

The Japs were funny little guys and it was pretty hard to read them. We weren't supposed to fly with any markings of rank. You were always a lieutenant. No rank. Then we had a Brit commando come around who had been captured at Malaya and broken out. He said, "Now, I'm going to give you the story on how to handle these guys. Tell them everything. Chances are forty to one that you don't know anything of importance, so go ahead and talk. We're going to beat them anyway. You're no good to us dead, so sing like a bird." He also showed us how to knife them if we did get out. He had this long, skinny knife. It was very sharp. He told us we should go up behind, pull the Jap's neck back and drop the knife in the little place inside the collar bone where it's soft. When it goes in, turn it and your hand will get all warm. We fighter pilots looked at that and I have never seen people blanch like that in my life. I don't think I would have been very good at that sort of thing. The information, however, that he gave us about singing was very important to us. Falling into Japanese hands was a big fear.

★

I have always thought that the main reason I joined the Army Air Forces was that I had to take cold showers in prep school. I grew up in Boston and my father was the minister of the First Church for over fifty years. Among his duties was the "prep school circuit" of New England, preaching on Sunday afternoons to pews full of dark-clad youths with varying degrees of acne and stiff white collars. Prep schools, then, became part of our family conversation, not a big part, but enough so that we were all expected to go to one. The tuition came from somewhere; I don't think it was very much in those Depression days. I ended up in Massachusetts at Middlesex, where the Puritan ethic was pounded into me. Dull sloth is the greatest of sins, followed closely by cowardice, masturbation, smoking, dishonesty, and uncleanliness. A bell woke us up at a quarter to seven and we would pad down the corridor to the huge tiled bathroom where three showers were running steadily, ice cold. Off would come our pajamas and into the shower we would go for a few gasping seconds. It was without any question the hardest thing I ever did in my life. Of course it felt grand when it was over. We would dance out of the misery and rub ourselves down vigorously and snap our damp towels at each other's pink little rumps, and then we would dash back to dress in yesterday's underwear and socks, and today's compulsory clean white shirt, and this term's slightly undersized suit.

We attended strenuous classes, and football was compulsory. I floundered as far as Cicero, destroyed the French language, and enjoyed football, but was far too wispy to achieve glory, ending up with a badly broken left arm. I had sneaked a puff of a cigarette, lied when my cowardice made it essential, and I was tormented by fantasies concerning one master's wife who filled a sweater like no one before or since. I was a disaster.

The only thing I did well was take a cold shower. That frightful little ritual took on a certain significance for me, because it was obviously senseless and therefore had to fit the basic cultural ground rule that I was being taught: if you do something hard, everything will come out O.K.

So there I was in a fighter squadron in New Guinea, winging off on a career for which I was ill-trained and ill-equipped and to which I was morally and viscerally opposed. If that wasn't the biggest goddamn cold shower in the world, it was at least the best I could do.

I was brought up in the glamorous air age. I hero-worshipped a lot and pilots were exciting to think about. I had an older brother who graduated from Yale in 1931. It was the middle of the Depression and Dick couldn't get a job anywhere, so he went into the Marines and he learned how to fly. However, his class lost its appropriation; because the Marines didn't have enough money to keep it going, they withdrew the class just before he would have graduated. He was a reserve officer, so when the war came, Dick went into the Navy and became an Acorn. That's like a Seabee, but based entirely on air stuff, going into a little island and building an air strip, things like that. So, to some extent he turned me on to flying.

Also, my sister married a pilot. He had a Waco that he would fly into fields and give people rides for a few bucks. I was the kid brother because I was ten years younger than my sister, and Elliot tried to butter me up when he was courting her. You know how it is; you go out with a girl and you have to do a little extra work on her brothers and sisters. When I was twelve years old, I got into Elliot's little roadster and we drove up to Lake Winnepesaukee in New Hampshire. There was a float plane tied up and the pilot was a guy named Fogg who was a friend of Elliot's. The two of them talked hangar flying for a while, in other words, swapping lies. Finally he winked at Elliot and said, "Well, do you think it's time we went up?" My first flight was in a seaplane and I loved it. Elliot had made a friend for life.

When I was at Middlesex, I didn't do anything about flying, but there was a field across the road where a guy landed his plane one day and the whole school emptied out to go look at it. He was probably tired or needed to take a leak and found himself surrounded by 130 schoolboys. Those were great days for aviation. Just to get close to an airplane was exciting.

After Middlesex, I went to Yale as part of the Class of 1939 and actually took some lessons in a Piper Cub. I enjoyed it and felt I could handle it if I really got into it. Then the war came along and I was drafted into the Corps of Engineers in 1941. I put in for OCS and was twiddling my thumbs in Washington waiting for an assignment, still a private in the Engineers. I went down to Bolling Field to look at airplanes. A flight of P-40s buzzed the field and pulled up and peeled off one after another with the engines popping and the flaps down, screaming with wind resistance and one after another they landed. Those guys got out of the P-40s, and they looked so sharp! Those wonderful leather jackets and helmets. There was a car waiting for them and they went roaring off to the officers' club. I knew that they would down a few and go into town and raise hell. I thought, "Jesus, what am I doing in the Engineers? Life can be beautiful." I put in for flying and went into the Army Air Corps just as Pearl Harbor broke.

I went to Helena, Arkansas, for primary and flew PT-17s. Our instructors were excellent and it was a very good base. The food was wonderful and I liked the people. It was like being in a little red-brick country university. We had nights when the new guys would have to put on shows for the upperclassmen. The spirit of the place was great. I had one upperclassman who looked after me. They would assign a guy to each of us. He would stand in front of me at 4:30 in the morning, after reveille, and say, "Ah, Park, how is your libido this morning?" If I showed the slightest twinkle of a smile, he would jump all over me. "Wipe that smile off. Throw it on the ground! Step on it!" He'd come late at night with some other guys and you'd think, "Oh, God, there's going to be some more hazing." I'd be busy doing navigational work, something like that. We'd all snap to and they'd say something like, "You're a pretty sloppy-looking bunch of cadets." Then they'd say, "At ease. How is it going? How is your flying? Is there any way we can help?" They were great guys, they really were.

I got through that O.K., and then I went to basic training, which was in Greenville, Mississippi, and flew the BT-13, which we called the *Vultee Vomiter*. It was the only plane I ever chucked up in because the air inside the cockpit was so thick with fumes. After basic, I went off to Selma, Alabama, for advanced. They had a bunch of RAF cadets there under the Empire Training School Act and a lot of our instructors were RAF flyers. They were terrific. The Brit cadets were either very, very bad or very, very good. The American kids were never very bad and seldom very good. We hit more of an average level, and we just sort of stumbled along and did what we were supposed to do. The RAF instructors were very demanding. When you were strafing they wanted you to get right down on the deck until you were kicking up dust with the propeller. The British were hair-assed. The Americans, I think, were a little more safety-conscious.

We were flying the AT-6. Now we had an airplane that had retractable landing gear, a fully controllable prop, flaps, and a good radio. It was a very flyable plane, and we started to learn a lot about night flying, instrument flying, and gunnery. We also flew mock combat, which was a matter of going around and around in tight circles trying to figure out if your instructor was getting on your tail or you were getting on his. It didn't really prove anything and, in fact, was bad training because, if you ever tried to do that with a Jap, you would have been dead so fast you wouldn't have known what hit you. We always underrated the Japanese planes. They were always much more maneuverable than ours. The thing that saw us through the war was that we kept whittling down their best pilots.

I graduated in September, Class of 1942H, and was ordered to Sarasota to join a P-39 operational training unit. I really wanted to be an instructor. I would have been a fine instructor, especially with bad students like me. I hadn't been very good and I understood the mentality of the bad pilot. I could help him. But they said, "No, you're such a lousy pilot you might as well go off and get killed flying a fighter."

I bought a secondhand Ford with another guy, both of us blowing our first pay as lieutenants. It was cheap, but it held together fine to get us down to Sarasota. When I shipped out, the other guy sold it. He never sent me my share because he was killed.

Next we went to San Francisco by train and got on a freighter. Nobody knew where we were going. We were issued a lot of Arctic clothing so we figured it was Alaska. It wasn't. We wove around a lot by way of Hawaii and down through the South Pacific, and ended up in Townsville, Australia. It was a small sugar-cane port on the coast of Queensland. We just scuffed around Townsville for about four weeks. The Army typically didn't have room for us. They didn't know what we were doing there. Then they put us on a train and we went to a little mining town in the interior of Queensland called Charters Towers. It was quite a picturesque little place, but the water was brown and everybody in camp had dysentery.

We did some flying in bad airplanes while we were there. They'd been in combat in New Guinea and were battle-weary. They'd been sent south to die. They actually had Band-Aids on them and when you'd pull them off, you'd find bullet holes. We were still in training and learning low altitude stuff. It was sheer terror flying really low, skittering over those rain forests. Then we went back to Townsville and they loaded us into B-17s for the trip to Port Moresby, New Guinea. We got there late in the evening and after dumping our gear into a tent, we were driven to this squadron hut where all these guys were sitting around. We were so used to all the chicken-shit we had been through since we entered the Army, the indoctrination and formality, that these guys looked practically naked. Most of them were stripped to the waist and wearing raggedy khaki shorts that had been hacked off with a hunting knife. Big old Army boots with no socks and no identification on anybody. One of them had on a T-shirt that said "Purdue AA" on it. This was a real combat unit and that was my kind of uniform from then on.

I said, "Where's the commanding officer?" One of them said, "Right over there." I looked and there was this tall guy with a droopy mustache, playing cards. I went up and saluted. "Lieutenant Park reporting, sir." He said, "Forget that shit." That's a direct quote. Then he said, "You're the new guys?" and I said, "Yes, sir." He said, "Never mind the sir, my name is Ed." He called somebody over. "Hey, Chuck, take these guys up and show them the area, O.K.?" We were flying in 10 minutes in airplanes that seemed brand new. The engine sounded different from anything I'd ever flown before. It had some wallop. This was a line squadron, the 35th Fighter Group, and they cared about those airplanes. They all looked perfectly beautiful, those 39s. Their sleek little bodies were waxed, their engines continuously warm, and their guns armed and taped over the muzzles to keep out rust. As soon as you fired off rounds, you blew out the tape and the plane would whistle. You could hear it from the ground and you knew there had been some action. Everybody would come out as soon as they heard that whistling when the planes came in for a landing.

I had a great feeling flying with that crowd, although fear began to assert itself. When you listened to the older pilots talk, you realized that they had lost a lot of friends. Somebody would mention a name and somebody else would look at him and say, "You stupid bastard. He bought it four weeks ago, don't you remember?" Then, "Oh, yes, yes, poor guy." As for food, I have never eaten such absolute shit in all my life. It was Australian army rations. Front-line stuff. Everything was bully beef and canned salmon. Canned salmon was a huge luxury in Australia and I got so I couldn't stand it because we got it all the time. Breakfast, canned salmon. Lunch and supper, the same. Our poor chef used to try and dress the bully beef up. He would say, "Tonight we are having Boeuf de Bully." We asked him what he was going to do after the war and he said he was going to open an Italian restaurant in Providence.

These were desperate times in New Guinea. In 1942, our squadron was always ready to move out if the Japanese ran the whole place over. And in early '43, when I joined, there was still a funny feeling, almost a sense of release. Impending defeat eliminates a lot of crap in your life. We found ourselves being very honest with each other. Nobody told lies. If you asked a person what he'd done in civilian life he told you. "I sold typewriters." Reading back now, both MacArthur and General George Kenney, his Air Corps chief, were pretty sure we were going to win. However, when we looked at the air strengths that our intelligence was giving us, we figured out that the Japanese were able to put up a hell of a lot more planes than we could.

There were always rumors that we were going to get new planes. That we were going to get real force in there, and we'd get out of New Guinea. We didn't like the place very much. It was very spectacular. Everybody agreed that the mountains were the most beautiful they'd ever seen. But the heat was like being hit with a rubber mallet. We all got jungle-rot and bugs would crawl into our beds. We lived in tents and had to use mosquito nets all the time. Everything turned to mud when it rained and the nearest town was 2,000 miles away.

The local natives were Melanesians, but we called them boongs. We had to learn Pidgin English in case we had to bail out. A planter came to Charters Towers to brief us. You would go up to a native and say, "Balus belong mefellah 'e bugger up finish." ("My plane has crashed.") Then you'd say, "More better you take 'em feller longside man belong Sidney." ("Get me to an Australian.") Finally, "You gaminem mefellah, plenty trouble 'e come behind." ("If you lie to me you're in big trouble.") And I'll never forget the word for piano. "Beg fellah bockis 'e got teeth, you bang 'im 'e sing." We had a laundry boy who grew up in a Christian mission on the island. My first day with the squadron I took my laundry over to him and asked, "You wash 'm lap-lap belong mefellah?" He said, "Yes, lieutenant, just stick it by the tree."

Early in 1944 we were operating out of a steel-matting airstrip and cluster of tents called Nadzab, on New Guinea, when we got our first P-47s. We called them Thundermugs or Thunderjugs, or just "jugs." If you took a milk bottle and put wings on it, you'd have a P-47. It was kind of fun to fly a tail dragger again because you really try to kiss it on when you're landing. The P-39s had tricycle landing gear. It was also a big, comfortable plane with lots of room in the cockpit. I was used to being scrunched into the cockpit. The typical P-39 pilot had a hunched look and a continual tick from looking over his shoulder. If you saw one walking down the street, you knew what he flew.

The old days were gone. When I first joined the squadron, guys were flying in football helmets, anything they felt like wearing. We'd gotten more civilized and now we had brand-new flight suits. Very lightweight and fire resistant. You had to fly all buttoned up. I was now operations officer, and a couple of us went down to Melbourne in March of '44 to pick up the new P-47s with the bubble canopies. We had a thirty-day leave and I met my wife Jeanie about the tenth day. She was a nurse, and we ended up getting engaged. Three months later we were married. A lot of guys in our squadron married Australians and all of the marriages worked out.

We loved the bubble P-47s. They were really great planes. All of the olive drab paint was gone and everything was shiny aluminum. And they were fast! We were waiting for the landings at Balikpapan, Borneo, learning how to fly eight-hour missions. Charles Lindbergh came down and gave us the dope on how to fly long range without using a lot of fuel. I never got to Balikpapan and I thank God for that. I wasn't afraid of flying the missions, but I dreaded sitting on my butt for eight hours. I've never liked to sit down too long since the war.

I became the acting C.O. of the squadron late in 1944 and by this time we had moved to Noemfoor on New Guinea. And then I finally managed to shoot down a Tony, which was a nasty airplane. We were coming back from a strike and my wing man called in and said he had an oil leak. I called our squadron leader and told him my number two had an oil leak and I'd better take him back. He said, "We're going to weave with the bombers. You go straight and we'll see you back home." The two of us broke off and I called in to operations. "Mary, this is Beaver Blue one. I'm bringing back Beaver Blue two and we need a straight-in approach." Mary called back. Mary was the code name for the base. "Beaver Blue one, there are bandits in the area. The field is closed." I said, "Oh, shit." Then they called back and said, "Our area is clear, but the bandits are headed back toward you on the deck." Just as he said that, I looked down and here come a couple of Tonys under me. Nice big fat red meatballs on them and going like hell.

I called my wing man and told him to just stooge around, flipped over, and came out of the sun. One of the Nips was straight ahead of me, right in my sights. He was still a long way off, but I thought I'd better clear the guns, make sure they weren't frozen. I was just going to fire a little "brrrrp." All eight guns went off and it was a wonderful sound so I just crammed on that trigger. The Tony got bigger and bigger and it seemed forever until I hit it, but when I did he actually went sideways in the air. Pieces were all over the place. He rolled on his back and I turned around to look and there was a parachute. I went right by him and he was hanging on his shrouds watching me. He had short cut black hair and sideburns. A flying suit like ours, but he'd lost his helmet and goggles. He looked like a nice little fellow. I was supposed to shoot him, but I couldn't get my sights on him. I was glad because I didn't want to do it anyway. If there was disputed land under you, the rule was to shoot him. If the Aussies were underneath you, you didn't bother because they would capture him and probably kill him. That's how I got my "kill." When my boys had reached the stage where they thought it was glamorous to have a father who had been a fighter pilot, they'd say, "Dad, did you get any?" I'd say, "Yes, Dick Bong* and I got forty-one between us." It took a long time before they figured that one out.

Not long after that I was sent home and ended up at Yuma, Arizona, in time for Christmas of 1944. I had flown 199 missions. I didn't count them until afterwards and had I known, I would have flown one more to make it an even 200. I was glad to be home because I felt that I'd used up my luck. Yuma was the very last choice of a base where I wanted to go. However, they made me officer in charge of ground gunnery and I had a little rank. By now I was a captain and I had a good life at Yuma.

The guy I replaced at Yuma had gotten orders to go overseas, and we'd talk a lot. He was briefing me on what my job would be and also asking question after question about combat. I said, "Look, combat flying is hard to describe. There are tricks to learn." He said, "I got to know the tricks, Park, tell me the tricks." I said, "Let's take a couple of planes out tomorrow and see what we can do." We took off and met each other and I called him on the radio. "Get on my tail and let me show you what I'd do." He dropped behind and as soon as he was on my tail, I banged the stick forward. Hit it as hard as I could. That plane went straight down toward the ground and I heard this little voice, "Park, Park, where'd you go?" Nothing goes down faster than an airplane when you do that. It just vanishes from the sky. You get blood in your eyes and the nickels in your pockets go flying up to the canopy roof. I taught him that and as far as I know he lived through the war. I hope he used it.

I finally had enough points to get out and I was back in New Hampshire when the big bomb dropped. I spent the summer after the war ended in New Hampshire and then I went back to the little school where I taught before the war, Proctor Academy. I taught

*Ed. note: Major Richard I. Bong, USAAF, the top U.S. ace of World War II, shot down forty enemy aircraft.

English, a little science, and a lot of skiing. My wife was still in Australia, so I quit and went back across the Pacific and got a job in an Australian ad agency doing radio work. I was supposed to do 122 10-second ads a week for some kind of cereal. I wrote the words *delicious* and *nutritious* on the wall with all the synonyms that I could think of and I'd use the same copy, just changing the words. I'd finish in no time and in my spare time I wrote a short story about flying in New Guinea during the war. My parents had sent some of my letters to Ted Weeks at the *Atlantic* and he'd published them, so I sent the story to him and he wrote back that it was a marvelous story, check on the way. My boss at the agency found out what I was doing and we had a parting of the ways. Then I went to work on the *Herald Sun* in Melbourne. I worked on a lot of different things for the next five years.

In 1951 we flew back to the States and it took me a long time to get a job. I finally got one at the *Boston Globe* and I worked at the paper for four years. Then I went to the *National Geographic* and spent fourteen years there. Ed Thompson [a former managing editor of *Life*] called me up one day and said, "I'm starting *Smithsonian* magazine, come over and join me." That was a wonderful job and I was there until I retired in 1983. After I got on *Smithsonian*, I began to get paid better, and Jeanie's family started to get itchy to see us and the grandchildren. We managed to get to Australia in the 1970s. My sister-in-law was married to the deputy head of Trans-Australian Airlines. John asked me if I'd like to have a look at New Guinea. I said, "Boy, would I ever." I went up to Moresby and got on a little TAA commuter plane. I went through a lot of emotional thoughts on the way up there. We landed at Nadzab where I had been stationed so long ago. I was met by a TAA ground representative who put me in a jeep and took me to an airstrip that was surfaced and even had an actual airliner sitting at one end. I said, "This isn't my strip." He said, "This is the only one we've got." I said, "You see those little ruts going through the Kunai grass?" "Yeah." "Can we follow them, please? Will the jeep do it?" He said we could make it if I didn't mind going through the nine-foot grass. We came out in a little clearing and I looked around at the hills and it felt so good, so familiar. He scuffed under his feet at a bare spot. Steel matting. We were on my old strip, completely smothered by the grass except for that one little spot.

THE EDGE OF DIGNITY

There's real presence when Roscoe Brown walks into a room. He's slim, lively, and electric in his movements. President of Bronx Community College since 1977, he was one of the best-kept secrets of World War II (as were all of the black fighter pilots of that era). He has always been quite amused by a book, written in the 1930s, which purports to "prove" that a black man simply cannot learn to fly a fighter plane. A member of the famous Tuskegee Airmen, an all-black fighter group, Brown was among the first pilots to shoot down a German jet, which at the time was a much dreaded "super weapon."

When I was a kid, growing up in Washington, I made models from kits and had my own little air force. I'd read all those magazines, *Air Trails, Flying Aces,* and followed the careers of people like Wiley Post and Howard Hughes. At that time, Washington was a segregated town, but the museums were not segregated. One of my big thrills was to go down to the Smithsonian Institution and look at the Fokkers, Spads, the *Spirit of St. Louis,* and all the old flying equipment they had there. I'd really get into it.

My first flight in an airplane was under rather interesting circumstances. My father would take us to see the planes at this airport in Virginia, and I'd always bug him for a ride. You won't believe this, but because of segregation, blacks weren't allowed to fly in the sightseeing aircraft at that time. My dad told me what the realities were and we couldn't do it. I didn't want to know about it and kept bugging him and finally he came up with an idea. He's a light-skinned man so he told them we were the children of a French diplomat and

Roscoe Brown, a fighter pilot of the noted "Tuskegee Airmen," being buck-
led into his P-51 Mustang fighter by crew chief Sergeant Smith. Today Dr.
Brown is the president of the Bronx Community College in New York City.

he was bringing us out for a ride. We kept our mouths shut until we were up in the air. That's how I got my plane ride.

When they began to tool up for the war, I was going to Springfield College in Springfield, Massachusetts. It was an integrated college, and I was quite active in sports. Many of us went to integrated institutions where you might be the only black playing a particular sport. I played in New England most of the time, and the guys didn't give me much trouble. However, we played Army in lacrosse and one well-known All-American football player set out after me. He called me a "nigger" and chased me all around the place with his stick. He finally cracked me on the head. My white teammates were so incensed that they practically caused a riot right there at West Point. There were football teams we'd play and players would be talking to me, "Sunshine, come on over here," and crap like that which you learned to ignore. You just can't let yourself get into something like that. You'd just play a good game and when you came off the field, your head was held high. It was surprising, too, that some of those same people who were calling names would later come over to me and say, "Nice game."

At that time, many of my white classmates were being recruited for Naval Aviation, the Army Air Force, and a couple for the Marines. Between that motivation and my own interest in flying, I decided that I would try to enlist in the Army Air Force. The local recruiter gave me a lot of doubletalk and I got the message. I didn't even think about the Navy at that time. The only thing a black could do in the Navy was wait tables. I finally wrote to Washington to find out if they were going to train any black pilots. When I found out about the 332nd Fighter Group, I wanted in. A. Philip Randolph and the NAACP had gone to President Roosevelt at one point and had threatened to march on Washington if blacks were not allowed to be in combat groups, particularly flying. Roosevelt gave in, and the 99th Pursuit Squadron was formed—completely segregated. After they had proved themselves in the air, the 332nd Fighter Group was formed. I graduated from college on March 13, 1943, and I was called to active duty on March 16.

We went to Keesler Field in the heart of Mississippi and marched in the mud for a couple of months and took a lot of tests. Those tests were very interesting. After the war, I coached at Western Union State College for two years while I was trying to decide what to do. I decided to stay in education, and my basic research was in exercise psychology. Today it's called sports medicine. Part of that research was looking at what made a good combat pilot. I got into reading personality profiles, and I guess I was reading about myself and not realizing it. First, they looked for intelligence, that's basic, and good physical condition in terms of eyes and so on. Then they looked for things like endurance and reflexes. One of the things we found was that you couldn't really predict who was going to be a good pilot from these requirements but we could actually give a paper and pencil test where you have situations and you respond to them. It was called the "critical incidence technique," and it's still used in business today. It gives you critical decision points in management to see how you react. The best selection technique, of course, is actual experience. You get a bunch of people and put them through the process, and the ones who survive, make it; and the ones who don't, don't. However, that's a costly way to do things, especially with pilots flying expensive airplanes, so you try to narrow down the randomness by looking at some of these other variables.

We did very well on the tests, much better than I think they expected blacks to do. At this time the drill instructors were black and the supervising officers were white. The drill instructors were tough regular Army men, and they were there to break in the recruits, especially "smart niggers" from the North who'd been to college. They were right about one thing. We were smart, and we weren't taking shit from anybody, white or black. We took everything they dished out and gave them a little back. It was a very interesting time.

Next we went to Tuskegee Institute in Alabama for preflight orientation. This consisted of some more marching and flying a Piper Cub for 10 hours. Then we moved into the Stearman. After a while we went into the BT-13 and then the AT-6 and worked on cross-country and night flying. The instructors were civilian pilots at Tuskegee, and most of them were black. In fact, Alfred ("Chief") Anderson, who was one of the first blacks to get a pilot's license back in the thirties, was in charge of the instructors. The officer who was in charge of the whole operation at Tuskegee was Col. Noel Parrish. He had a southern background, but he was not a racist. In fact, Parrish fought hard to see that the group was able to stay intact and to make sure we were treated fairly. This was very important because as the officer in charge, if he had been hostile and racist, he could have really made it rough for us. They called it the Tuskegee Experiment because they expected it to fail, but Parrish helped it succeed. After the war, he got his Ph.D. in history and taught at one of the southern universities.

We graduated, got our wings, and went to Waldenborough, South Carolina, which is near Charleston. The first group had taken their advanced training at Tuskegee, but they realized that there wasn't enough room in the sky so they moved north to Selfridge Field, just outside of Detroit. I only spent two weeks up there because Detroit had a race riot, and I think that was one of the big reasons they moved us back down south. I can't describe conditions at Self-ridge Field, but I can talk about what we found in South Carolina.

One of the mechanisms we adopted for dealing with racism and segregation was whenever possible to avoid trouble unless it really dealt with our basic dignity. For example, we could not go into town, go into a theater, and expect to sit downstairs. You're going to sit upstairs! So, if you didn't want to embarrass yourself, you didn't go to the theater in town. Some of the military bases had worked this out after a fashion by building three or four theaters. One would be close to where the black troops were, and they'd naturally go there. However, Waldenborough only had one theater, and so we went and sat where you normally did, in the middle. Some officer came over and asked us to move to the "colored" section. We said, "We're officers and we're not moving." He said "The colonel won't like this." We told him to go get the colonel. He did, and when the colonel showed up, we told him we weren't moving. After a lot of talking, he finally said, "You'll hear about this." Before we got there, blacks in the Air Corps were service troops. They cleaned up, worked in the kitchen, and so on. We were a new group, and we were creating a new environment and attitude. Of course, the theater became a cause, and the next day five or six of us decided to see a movie.

The MPs were waiting for us. "The colonel says you can't sit where you want." We said, "Excuse me," or whatever, and went in. They called the colonel and he said, "You know, you're violating the rules of the base. Colored troops sit in their own area." We explained that we were officers and were going to sit where any other officer sits in the theater. Now he was mad. "You *boys* will be court-martialed if you continue this." To this we said, "If we are court-martialed, we can't fly these airplanes and Uncle Sam spent all those zillions of dollars training us. If we are going to fight for our country like everybody else, we're going to have privileges like everybody else." We probably weren't quite as articulate as that, but he got the idea. You have to realize that a colonel is way down in the bureaucracy. His job was to keep his little part of the plantation quiet. When that didn't work, he must have called somebody and they must have said, "Let's not make a big deal out of this." The next day the ribbons separating the sections were gone, and the theater was integrated.

Just before we left for overseas we went to Fort Patrick Henry in Virginia. They had the whole place segregated. Black mess hall, everything. Somehow we wandered over to the white PX and were told that we couldn't go in. Again I think they threatened to court-martial us. We talked among ourselves—should we go in there, create an incident, and get court-martialed? Or should we step back on this one because we were so close to the larger fight? We felt we could get whatever it was we wanted somewhere else, so we stepped back. We wanted to show them what we could do when we got over there. There was always that feeling of living on the edge of danger—the edge of dignity. Were you willing to give up some of your dignity in order to achieve the larger result?

Remember black folks had been doing this for at least 150 years—our grandparents, parents, all of us, whether we lived in the South or North. People talk about the South, but take New York in those days. You couldn't go to a downtown club; they just wouldn't have you. The type of thing today where you go into a good restaurant and see blacks sitting randomly around like anybody else—that just didn't exist. We had a reality, and our reality was segregation. We knew it was wrong and what it did to us, but we learned to play the game and we were always inching forward at the same time.

The pilots that were training us for combat were white. We didn't know it at the time, but a lot of these people had been returned to the States because they had problems and some of them weren't particularly competent. When they started dealing with us a couple said, "You *boys* do this and that." We let them know very quickly we were officers just like they were and that we wanted to learn, but we were not going to go for that "boy" crap. It turned out that we were better pilots than some of them, and the majority learned to respect us. There was one guy who did show some blatant racism and made a few comments about our race. We decided to teach him a lesson. When we were flying one day, we locked on his wings. Four planes flew in a flight, and we just kept squeezing tighter and tighter on him. He would try to maneuver away from us, and we'd move right with him and it was really getting hairy. Finally he said, "O.K., smooth it out." It was like saying, you got me. From that point on, we didn't have any trouble with him, and we never had to say a word. We beat his racism by showing him that we weren't going to take any shit, and we were as good as he was. In fact, after a while, he got to respect us, and we were the best flight in our particular squadron.

By the time we got into fighter transition, we were flying P-47s. The first group that had gone overseas flew P-40s. They flew with the British in North Africa doing ground support, finally ending up in Sicily. They didn't do particularly well initially because they hadn't been adequately trained and had no experience. The southern congressmen wanted to stop the whole program, and they called the commanding officer, Col. Benjamin Davis, Jr., back to Washington to testify. Just by coincidence, while he was back there, the group mixed it up with some Germans and shot down several planes. He could say, "Hey, we're really a success," and they got off his back. By that time they were flying the P-47, and we got them, too. We used to go up and do a lot of mock dogfighting, which helped us sharpen our skills. You learned to hang the big P-47 right on the prop as you were making a turn. It was a heavy airplane, but it was a good plane to fly.

When we finished transition, we shipped to Naples and were assigned to Ranitelli Air Field. The entire 15th Bomber Command was spaced out along Italy, and when they took off for a mission, they would make up a big circle and we would go up and join them. When we got over there the first thing we did was go through transition to the P-51. You look at that airplane today; it's still beautiful. In my mind I can still hear the sound of that engine as you went down the runway. You'd get your speed up, pull those wheels up, just feel that plane accelerate. We were pretty hot, and I could fly that airplane as low as the damn dust.

One of the things that made the Mustang great was that they were "the ones that went all the way." We could go all the way with the bombers on the missions, out and back. We would fly with two big 110-gallon drop tanks. Most of the time we wouldn't drop them because they cost money and you better have a good reason not to come back with them. If there was air combat or you were on a strafing mission, then you dropped them. We loved to drop them because that's when you really got to be a fighter pilot. You'd yell, "O.K., drop tanks, let's go!" On fighter sweeps we would go after anything that moved—trucks, oil tankers, trains, anything. I was the number one locomotive buster in our group. You'd be sitting with your sight on that locomotive, put those shells in there and "whoooom"—up she'd go. I was doing that one day and almost went in. There was an explosion as I went over the train, and I lost part of my wing. I managed to get it up by using both hands, and flew it back. When we looked at the wing, there were timbers from a railroad car lodged in there, complete with numbers. I liked to fly low, but that was too low.

Most of our flying was bomber escort work. We had a cause and a strong commander, and we provided good cover for those bombers. Good training in anything starts with discipline, whether you coach a football team, manage an institution, or work on creative projects, and we had it! All that crap you hear about somebody leaving the group to go out and shoot the sky up, that's just that, bullshit. If you left, the chances are you wouldn't get back. I think our group had magnificent discipline. In fact, some of us felt that the discipline was a little too tight. Colonel Davis felt that our task was to protect the bombers, period. If the German fighters attacked, O.K., let's get them; but if something's going on someplace else, stay put.

I'd flown about sixty missions and was flying in the back of the group. I was breaking in a new flight leader because it seemed like it was going to be a routine mission. We'd flown up from Naples, over the Alps, Austria, and on into Germany. We were over Berlin and somebody said, "Bogeys," or what have you. The flight leader didn't see them. I don't know if he froze or what, but I told him I was taking over. I told everybody to follow me. It turned out that they were jets. We had seen them on photo recon missions because they'd make passes at us. I think they were trying to scare us and maybe to test themselves out. There was a lot of mystique surrounding them. The jets, however, had to slow down to shoot at the bombers because they were so fast. That's when we'd get them. I pulled down and came up underneath this one jet just as he was slowing down. I climbed right up his behind and got him. In fact, my squadron got three jets that day, and we received a Presidential Unit Citation.

Even on tough missions, I had no feeling of doom. There's a certain kind of immortality that everybody feels when they're twenty. Life goes in seconds anyway. You're driving down the street and a car comes through an intersection. You hit the brakes and you make it. You continue to live. I guess the thing about the air war was that you confronted these challenges to life every day. Every time you completed a mission, you did two things—helped the war and helped yourself by living another day.

We'd gone to Athens twice and lost people each time. On the third mission, I wasn't flying because I was the operations officer. We were getting the planes off and one of the guys, a big talker, all of a sudden got chicken and decided he couldn't fly. That meant they had to go with fifteen airplanes. I ran into the shack and got my parachute and hopped in his plane and flew the mission. No escape packet, map, gun. It was crazy, but fewer planes meant less protection for each plane; and I didn't feel that was fair. I was really angry with that guy. People like that were the exceptions. They would come back early because of engine "problems," get "sick" when the mission would come up. You knew who they were and you didn't fall for it. You'd just wish the flight surgeon would come up and say, "Look, you're out of it."

Most of them, however, were great guys and real characters. John Whitehead was one. He had very high cheekbones and was very thin. When he put his helmet on, he looked like a skull and his nickname was "Mr. Death." Supposedly he ran out of ammunition one day so he flew up next to a train, dropped his flaps and gear to slow down, and pulled out his .45 and shot at the train. Now that's baloney, but it's a super story. Plus the fact that he stayed in the service and became one of the best pilots in the Air Force.

Most of us were tough, and people were always volunteering. I volunteered myself. Why? I guess because it had to be done, and I was a leader by that time. Part of being a leader was to tell somebody else what to do. That's difficult in today's society because now we want to persuade people that something is the right thing to do. You don't want to order people around. But, you know, I find that I'm sitting in a meeting and people are saying so and so and it's dragging on and on and finally I get up, "O.K., we are going to make a decision." When I say we, I actually mean I'm going to make a decision. People are looking for that, from me at least, because that's my personality. When people say leadership roles are complicated, I have to disagree. In the service, I would decide who would fly. Was it a short mission or a long mission? Bad weather or good? Obviously, the longer the mission and the worse the weather, the more I want the leader of the squadron to be an experienced pilot. If you had some new pilots, who would be the best person to take them in? How's so and so feeling? I'd write it out just like I would a batting order for a ball team. Today, when I prepare for a meeting, it's the same. How important is the meeting? Who is going to be there? Things like that. It's the same thing all over again. Always know what's going on around you.

When I'm at a meeting, I'm always watching everybody to see how they're reacting to things. What should I do next? Your own emotions are important. What are you feeling yourself? That helps a person deal with fear. If you're involved with something, really involved, you mobilize your energies. One of the things I do before a speech is to make a little outline. Two or three key words or ideas so if I wander a little, I can look down and pick up a key word and go on. Same thing when I'm running. I have a mental outline instead of a written one. Keep your arms up, Roscoe, breathe regular, things like that. It all came from flying. When I was leading a squadron through an overcast, I'd be doing the same thing. What's the rate of climb? Watch the power, the instruments. Keep the artificial horizon steady. Concentrate; focus on the job at hand. That helps you deal with the tension. I think the flying experience helped me in so many ways. You internalize those things. People say I drive a car the way I flew. Always looking around. If there's an opening, I move for it. These skills become instinct and they help you survive. There were a lot of fine pilots who operated on pure instinct. They were not the best leaders. You didn't become a squadron leader because you were just a great pilot—it was because you displayed good judgment. When I think back I can still feel most of those same emotions and feelings today.

I did what I wanted to do in World War II. I wanted to fly. Every person in that unit wanted to fly. But we also wanted to improve the quality of life for our people. We knew we were different, and everyone was watching us. We were human beings with all the anxieties, jealousies, fears, and all the rest. But we were also black. If you talk today with these men, get below the surface, below the war stories, women stories and so on, you find that's basically the reason we were there. It was more than a bunch of young black pilots flying fighter planes in a war and trying to be heroes. It helped to make us the men we needed to be, to come back and do the many, many things that had to be done.

"KEEP THEM FLYING"

Except for a few odd cases, no one has ever flown an aircraft in war time without an enormous backup in men, materials, and organization. Behind every mission is a vast conglomeration of draftsmen, engineers, manufacturers, suppliers, technicians, instructors, administrators, and mechanics, to name just a few. A mighty army in this age of technology.

Close to the front and sometimes under fire were those who worked directly with the flyers. Some of these men repaired and maintained the airplanes. Test pilots had to check out and fly all the planes that rolled off the production lines. Others looked after the aviators' mental and physical well-being, or helped to plan and evaluate the missions, all with only one purpose: keep them flying.

For the most part far from the fighting, but making a significant contribution, were American women. They, too, kept the airmen flying by building the machines that would bring the war home to our foes. A few lucky ones got to fly. Looking back at World War II, it may have been the most important single liberating influence in the recent history of women.

This airplane inspector was one of many women, civilian and enlisted, who supported the air war. She is checking a BT-15. National Air and Space Museum, Smithsonian Institution.

FIREBALL

One of his friends said it best: "Herb looks more like a company executive than a test pilot." Fisher is a heavy-set man, with eyes that tell a story of dangerous work well done. They're the eyes you'd expect on a man who made his living testing airplanes at the "edge of the envelope." As senior test pilot for the Curtiss-Wright Company in Buffalo, Fisher and his crew made sure the airplanes rolling off the production lines were ready to go to war.

Our conversations took place at his home in suburban New Jersey and at the Wings Club in Manhattan. This prestigious aviators' club is one of his favorite haunts. On the way to our table Herb had to stop and talk to half a dozen people. In the flying fraternity, Herb Fisher has a reputation as a "can-do guy." His many honors include being the first civilian to receive the Army Air Forces' Air Medal, induction into the New Jersey Aviation Hall of Fame and OX-5 Pioneers, and receiving a Doctor of Aeronautical Science degree from the Embry-Riddle Aeronautical University.

There were a lot of times in test programs when I was concerned, but I was never afraid. I really don't feel that I've ever been afraid in an airplane, and I don't think a pilot who says that is bragging. He's also not saying he's better than anybody else, just different. There were pilots during the war, even some of the test pilots who worked for me, the last thing they wanted to do was get in an airplane. They just happened to do it because there was a war and it was a job. Others bring something special to an airplane. They can handle that piece of

The "Fireball Squadron": Herbert Fisher, center, with Ran Reid, left, and Dick Griffin. They are standing in front of a Curtiss P-40. These were the pilots who did the actual flying in the wartime motion picture *Flying Tigers;* you saw John Wayne get in the cockpit but it was Herb in the air. Fisher first flew in 1928 and has been in the aviation business for over sixty years.

machinery and make it perform with confidence and precision. If somebody took all the things I've done in airplanes, there wasn't anything I did that another test pilot couldn't have done. I just happened to be in the right place at the right time. Maybe I brought something to those test programs. Maybe that's the "right stuff," like the book says.

On August 6, 1942, Mr. Burdette Wright, vice-president and general manager of Curtiss Wright Corporation in Buffalo, called me on the phone and said, "Herb, do you have a C-46 going up? I have Killer Caldwell in my office, and he's never been up in an airplane that size." Wing Commander Clive Caldwell was, and still is, Australia's number one ace. I think he shot down twenty-eight Germans in North Africa, and he'd been sent on a mission to the United States to go to each of the aircraft companies to talk to the employees. Stir up production, and as he said, "To help end the bloody war!" I said, "We have one going up at eleven o'clock and I'm flying it." We took off and spent two hours doing all the normal production testing. When I was through, I turned it over to him and pretty soon he was flying like a fighter pilot, diving through the beautiful cumulus clouds we had that day. After he'd finished flying, we started our approach to the field and I told him, "Gear down." He hit the landing gear handle and the main hydraulic line separated. That was the sixth C-46 off our production line and we had no mechanical way of locking the gear in the down position. I had already written it up and sent a memo to the project engineer: "If we have a hydraulic failure, it's inevitable that there's going to be a belly landing." Production at this moment was installing the manual emergency landing-gear system on all C-46s. We were up there for seven-and-a-half hours and you just wouldn't believe the things we tried. When I think back on it now, some of them were rather stupid, but in a situation like that, with seven lives on board and the company's reputation at stake, you try anything.

Curtiss had a Stinson that was used by the executives and they decided to try and get a five-gallon can of hydraulic fluid up to us. If we could put that in the reservoir, they thought we might get momentary pressure and lock the gear down. They put 350 feet of rope on that goddamn can and the plan was that I would fly the C-46 up to the floating can and pull it in the cockpit window. Pretty soon it's floating in the air out in front of me. I got my hand out the window, but due to the flow of air off the nose, the can didn't get close enough. Then they tried to lower a canvas bag with the can and some tools into the large cargo door in the rear of the plane. That came loose and ended up wrapped around the rudder.

At one point the ground magicians decided to try another can.

We had a man laying flat on his belly at the open cargo door. He had two men sitting on him to keep him from falling out. He was holding a rope and they brought an AT-6 under our belly and they tried to hook that rope with the can. The pilot came on the radio, "Herb, hold that thing steady because my propeller is only a foot or two from your belly." One of our Curtiss personnel was in the back seat and just as he was trying to hook the rope, the lid came off the can and the turbulence sucked out the fluid and dumped it all over him. Talk about a comedy of errors. After seven-and-a-half hours, there was no alternative except to bring the plane in on her belly. By that time 125,000 people were at the airport waiting to see if I could get down in one piece.

On final approach, I cut the mixture controls so that both engines would use up the residual fuel in the lines. We skidded along for about 750 feet and stopped without any problems. In fact, you could have jacked that airplane up, put two new propellers on it and flown her out of there. I like to think it wasn't how tough the plane was, but how nicely I slid it in. Clive and I became very close friends during that seven-and-a-half hours and I'm sure he wondered how he got involved in such an operation. While we were up there he asked Mr. Wright to send him up a cup of tea.

★

My parents, Harold and Rose Fisher, came from England, settled in Canada, and then moved to Buffalo. I was born in Buffalo and we moved to Indianapolis when I was three. Early in 1927, my first job was as an office boy at the Chamber of Commerce. I had been there three months when two pilots came in looking for some land to start an airport. They were barnstormers from West Virginia who wanted to settle down and open a flying business. Col. John Reynolds, the secretary of the Chamber of Commerce, called me in and asked me if I would like to take them around in his car to find a suitable spot for an airport. I had a Model-T Ford with no top and he had a brand-new Willys Knight. Here I was, a high-school kid, driving two pilots around in a Willys Knight. I was on cloud nine.

We drove out of town when they saw a nice field, and we got out and walked around. They were talking about the terrain and how the hangar would be laid out. It was quite an experience for me. They made arrangements to meet the owner at the field, and the lease was signed on the hood of the Willys Knight. Things were simpler in those days. There was no hangar, just an open field, and I found a guy who built a little booth where they could sell tickets. A dollar a ride and I was their first passenger. That's where I got the bug for airplanes: at Hoosier Airport.

Following this, my boss, Col. Reynolds, directed me to locate and recommend, in writing, a possible site for a municipal airport. This was accomplished in my memo to him of June 6, 1927. During those years I was doing just about everything involved with aviation in Indiana. When Transcontinental Air Transport, now TWA, started transcontinental passenger service, I handled their press and public relations. I was instrumental in the selection and improvement of thirty-five Indiana airports by the Works Progress Administration and supervised the air-marking program, which painted 300 rooftops of buildings throughout the state to help pilots navigate.

My actual flying began in 1928. I joined the 309th Observation Squadron, which was an Army Air Corps reserve outfit flying out of Schoen Field, and gained a lot of flight experience as a member of that squadron. I resigned in 1937. By that time I was looking for a change, and one day I ran into Ed Berlin, who was an engineer at Curtiss Wright in Buffalo. His brother, Don, was director of engineering in the aircraft division. Don designed, among others, the Hawk 75, the P-36, and the P-40. When Ed got back to Buffalo he called me and said there was a job for me.

My first job at Curtiss didn't have anything to do with flying. I was assigned to the mold loft section where the patterns are cut for the skin of an airplane. Shortly after that I became the assistant to the engineering manager, Alex Noble. I assisted the coordination of his office with manufacturing, inspection, sales and the military, and I also helped him hire new engineers. After eight months I was promoted to assistant service manager and that was what I had been waiting for because this might give me a chance to fly. I had been on the new job for only a week and Lloyd Childs, the chief test pilot, called me. In those days it was imperative that every single airplane that could fly be test-flown by the last day of the month. Those airplanes then got into the books and became money in the bank for Curtiss. Lloyd said one of his pilots was in China, one was in France, and the other one was in Brazil. In those days a test pilot did everything. Production test, high-performance test, sales, and of course, demonstrations. Lloyd said, "I'm the only one here and I'm going to need some help today." That was music to my ears. I left a note for my boss, "Dear Norm, have gone flying," and drove across town to the airport like a dose of salts.

Lloyd put me in a Navy Helldiver, which was a two-seater biplane. He said, "Do you know the cockpit?" I had been hoping that something like this would happen and had been taking the operation manuals home. Of course you can read something, but you also have to practice the real thing. Every time I had the chance, I would go down to production and sit in the airplanes and familiarize myself with the cockpit. Also, I had flown military aircraft in the reserves, but not with all this power. Lloyd got in and said, "Fire it up." I was real fortunate because it started up right away. You know, you really want to try and do everything right with the chief pilot sitting behind you. We taxied out, got clearance and took off. I made a couple of turns, did a complete stall, followed by three turns of a spin, a dive where we pulled around five Gs, then a slow roll, and landed.

He got out and handed me the knee pad and said, "Get up there and check these items out." I took off and went to work and when I called the tower for clearance to land, the first damn airplane that I flew for Curtiss Wright had a major hydraulic failure and the gear wouldn't go down. I called on the radio and the fellow in the flight office said, "Do you need any help, Herb?" I said, "No, I know what to do." There was an auxiliary hand pump and by using that I got the gear down and locked. I landed and made nine more flights that day including some with P-36 fighters. Later that day I flew P-40s, and when I saw that big old Allison engine sticking out in front of me I said to myself, "Well, this is it. This is real flying." I was hooked. Lloyd had personnel transfer me into flight test on the next Monday and I was on my way.

I got married in 1939 and the personnel director at Curtiss needed a secretary. Emily had been working in Indianapolis and they hired her right away. She had all the radio frequencies we had in the airplanes at home and could listen to everything I was doing in the air. When I had the belly landing in the C-46 she listened to the whole thing. I only lived a minute and a half from the plant, in a P-40 that is, and I used to come across the house at 500 feet and say, "Put the soup on in thirty minutes."

I became chief production test pilot in 1939. One of my pilots was having a little party and Emily and I were at his house when we heard about Pearl Harbor. From then on we were flying day and night. The military was breathing down our necks all the time. Get them out! Get them out! Curtiss built about 15,000 P-40s and each one of them had to be flown for one hour. The C-46s had to be flown for two hours and we ended up building approximately 3,100 of those monsters. Curtiss was also building P-47 Thunderbolts under contract from Republic and they had to be flown for an hour. There were five assembly lines of P-40s, two lines of C-46s, and one line of Thunderbolts. Since the Army Air Forces was taking all the pilots they could get, a few of us were doing a hell of a lot of flying. We were also taking on pilots who didn't have a lot of time because we had so many airplanes coming out the back door. My production pilot flight board occasionally indicated a pilot would fly from ten to eighteen hours in any one day.

Bill Schmitz was in the engineering department. He only had 400 hours, but he wanted to be a test pilot. He'd been flying something like a Mooney, nothing too big. I really stretched the point with him because, one, I needed him, and two, whatever he didn't have in flying experience, I figured he could make up with his engineering degree. I put him in a P-40 and told him, "All I ask you to do is bring this thing back down in one piece or neither of us is going to be here tomorrow. Don't just shove the throttle forward, get her up slowly, lift the tail up, and gradually go to full throttle. You won't have any problems with it." I was trying to make it simple for him. However, I also told him he would be moving a lot faster than he'd ever been moving in an airplane before. Not only did he fly that airplane, he made a decent landing.

Old Bill was elated, but he had sweaty palms, and he was glad that first P-40 flight was over. He said, "I'm not going to have any trouble now," which I was glad to hear. Then he said, "I hate to say this, Herb, but don't you think we ought to go to the bar?" We headed for our favorite watering hole and in those days I think he was drinking Old Grand Dad. He flew a lot of P-40s and C-46s after that and never had an incident. Later on Bill followed me over to China and flew the Himalayas in C-46s. After the war he worked for North American and is now with Hughes Aviation in Mesa.

We had a checklist with approximately thirty items for the P-40. Run the gear up and down so many times, flaps up and down, take it up to altitude and run the airplane up to 450, 500 miles an hour in a dive. Due to the production rate and having so many people in final assembly, somebody might be installing instruments and lay one on the floor and forget it. Then it would roll under the seat. There were also all kinds of shavings and nuts and bolts in the cockpit. One of our pilots rolled a plane over on its back and an instrument rolled out from under the seat and hit him in the chin. That can hurt so we came up with a procedure. You'd open the canopy, roll the plane over on its back, and all that junk would fall out. You just had to make sure you were wearing your seat belt.

You name any emergency and we had it. Fortunately, most of us lived to tell about it. At one point we were having problems with the hydraulic valves in the brakes. When you pressed the pedals, they'd end up going all the way to the floor. We'd been crabbing that on the flight cards, a crab was when you put down something that was wrong, and one day both pedals went to the floor. I had to ground loop at the end of the runway and that was the crowning blow. I walked into my flight office and wrote across the big flight schedule board, "ALL P-40s GROUNDED."

That started a sensation. I'll never forget old Oscar Kent, he was in charge of final assembly. He came in and said, "Fisher, you can't ground those airplanes." I said, "I can and I did. I have complained about this to Engineering, Production, and Inspection for the last few months and nothing's been done. I just damn near put one into Genesee Street." I knew I was right. All I could think of was, suppose we kept throwing those airplanes out and some young pilot is coming in and he's not going to have any brakes. To me, that's why we were there.

I got word that there was going to be a meeting in Col. Clyde Mitchell's office in ten minutes. Clyde was the resident representative for the military. All of the big wheels were there. Mr. Wright, Manufacturing, Production, Inspection, Quality Control, plus a couple of the military acceptance pilots, who had also been complaining about the brakes. There was a chair for me right next to Colonel Mitchell and he said, "Well, Herb, looks like you're the black sheep of this group." I thought to myself, "That's a great start." He asked me to tell him precisely what was wrong. I did, and then he asked for comments from everybody else. After everybody was finished, he said to the group, "If these P-40s aren't good enough for your pilots, they're not good enough for ours. Good day."

Curtiss found a DC-3 and loaded every brake system valve they had in stock and even had some men taking out the ones that were already in the airplanes in final assembly. Then they flew them to Cleveland or Detroit, I forget which. I suppose Curtiss called up the subcontractor and said, "Look, we don't care if you work all night, do whatever has to be done. These valves are holding up the production line of Curtiss Wright." That DC-3 was back at our plant the next day at 7:30 in the morning and we had an army of men reinstalling them in the P-40s. We were flying again before noon.

My nickname was "Fireball," and we had a Fireball Squadron in Buffalo. Whenever we had a VIP at the plant and Mr. Wright wanted to show off his P-40s, we'd fly demonstrations. It all started one day when three of us had finished our testing and we were sitting at 15,000 feet about 10 miles south of the factory. I called the tower and told them we were going to make a pass over the plant. I headed right for the main building and we came across at low level, and high speed, then nosed up into a blossom and landed. It just so happened that Mr. Wright was at his office window. Well, Jesus, 15 minutes later I get a call from Esther Grogan, Mr. Wright's secretary. She said, "Mr. Wright would like to see you in his office right away." I figured that this was Fisher's last day at Curtiss. I went up there and he said, "Boy, that formation was great, Herb. Can you do a demonstration like that tomorrow for some visiting military officials from South America?" These flights continued for the next two years.

The Flying Tiger story was hot in 1942 and the Fireball Squadron got to participate in the making of the Republic film about the Flying Tigers. They brought the entire movie troupe to Buffalo and we were assigned three P-40s. The director said, "You're now John Wayne." You don't see us in the movie, but all of the landings, takeoffs, and aerial work were done by Dick Griffin, Ran Reid, and myself. If you happen to see the film on the late show, look close. The P-40s on the ground are made out of wood.

I went overseas in 1943 to do experimental flying over the "Hump," the air supply route from India to the part of interior China not under Jap control. I was to serve as a research test pilot working with engineering and maintenance on the C-46 and the P-40, primarily the C-46, lecturing to pilots on flying technique and actually flying missions. The C-46 had a lot of problems and there were many things the pilots didn't like about the airplane. However, they didn't realize what was going on in Buffalo, where they were just trying to get those airplanes built. There wasn't time for months and months of flight testing and we were doing all we could under those conditions. The C-46 program was very important at that time because China needed the materials that were being carried over the Hump. We didn't have the six or seven years' experience that Douglas had with the C-47 before the war.

I made ninety-six trips over the Hump in some of the worst weather in the world. In fact, I was flying when it was officially closed, so we could definitely encounter severe icing and other weather phenomena as it might affect the C-46. Up until the latter part of 1943 they would have an experienced pilot leave India and he would radio back and tell operations if they should keep the planes on the ground. That was fine, but the demand for the things they were flying to China was more important and I guess there's a feeling that people are sometimes expendable in a war.

One day I happened to be following General Tom Hardin, commanding officer of the Air Transport Command. He was flying ahead of me in a B-25 and the Hump was officially closed. I was in some weather for awhile, but then I popped right out into CAVU sunshine. When I landed I ran into him in the operations office and he said, "Where the hell did you come from?" I said, "I just came across the Hump." He blew up. "That's the damndest thing. Here's a civilian pilot flying and our people are grounded." He didn't mince any words. "From this day on, the Hump is never closed," and in later years he would kid me about that. "Goddamn way to run an Air Force. Nobody flying except you and me."

I was only supposed to be over there for three months. After a year they sent me for two more months to North and Central Africa to work with C-46 crews based there. When that assignment was

260   "KEEP THEM FLYING"

finished I returned to Buffalo and who was there to meet me but Mr. Wright. He and his wife were also there when I left for India and that personal interest and friendship was worth everything to me. My first priority, however, was to see my pretty blonde Emily again.

The war ended and I transferred from the airplane division to the Curtiss propeller division, which was located in Caldwell, New Jersey. I was now chief test pilot and sales representative, and we had some test programs that were pretty fantastic. I made over one hundred high-velocity dives with a Thunderbolt. We were testing very thin experimental propellers to see if they were more efficient than conventional props. We had some scimitar blades that were really wild looking. Curtiss was trying these props because they knew the jets were on the horizon. Now, forty years later, this theory of scimitar propellers is being developed for multi-engine aircraft using turbine-fan propulsion by NASA and Douglas.

Some of those blades were so thin they would flutter at various times on takeoff and in flight. If I accelerated the engine too rapidly during the takeoff roll, the blades would not absorb the excess horsepower and they would bend like a saw blade. My dives started at 38,000 feet. We had thirty instruments on three panels in the cockpit to help obtain all the necessary data during the flight. The engine had 2,400 horsepower, but we used water injection so I was pulling about 2,800 to 2,900. We needed to hurtle those propeller blades through the air as fast as I could physically fly the airplane and still bring back some data on the instruments. There was also a camera behind me that recorded everything during the dive. It might sound kind of simple, but it would sometimes take a week to get ready for one dive. After every flight the airplane was inspected and everything was taken off that could be unscrewed. I used to tell my hangar crew that they were going to wear out those Dzus fasteners. You wouldn't want to start a dive unless everything was functioning, and I would spend 10–15 minutes checking out some thirty items prior to starting my descent. During the first 8,000 feet I would recheck the operation of all my systems, and at 30,000 feet I would be going between 450 and 500 miles an hour. During the next 10,000 feet I would reach my maximum Mach number between 550 to 600 miles an hour. On one dive I hit Mach .83; that's over 600 miles an hour, but that was unusual.

There's one thing I want to get in for the record. There are many World War II pilots who swear they went Mach One in a propeller-driven fighter plane. I get letters from people who say they did this in a P-38, P-51, what have you, but there's no way. At some point the propeller becomes inefficient; at extremely high Mach numbers the propeller becomes a drag rather than a thrust factor. Not only that, the airfoil, tail, in fact the whole configuration of those World War II piston-driven airplanes was not designed to go that fast. Two or three of our very first jet fighters weren't even Mach One aircraft. Scott Crossfield, the North American test pilot, said, "Anyone who claims he pushed a P-47 over Mach One is sucking on a jug of pretty potent stuff." I'm sure those pilots who think they went that fast had two or three minutes that were very exciting, but Mach One? Never.

Once I hit 20,000 feet in the dive, I was required to maintain plus or minus five feet during the entire 100-mile level flight path. There was a thrust meter located behind the propeller and if I didn't hold this precise altitude, the recordings would be extremely erratic. We didn't have then the miracle black boxes that can hold an absolute altitude today. It took a lot of concentration and practice. My flight path would go from Allentown, Pennsylvania, to Montauk Point, Long Island. Airway traffic control would give me clearance because I would have to keep my eyes glued to the altimeters. During that period of level flight I couldn't look out of the cockpit for even one second.

We had our share of problems during this flight test program. An oil line that was under 75 pounds of pressure to a thrust meter directly between the engine and propeller fractured when I was passing through 29,000 feet at 590 MPH. I damn near lost the airplane because that hot oil completely engulfed the engine, penetrated the entire cockpit, and also covered the cowling, windshield, canopy, and fuselage. I was saturated with oil and my instruments were covered with it. At the same time I was becoming nauseated because my oxygen was being mixed with thick smoke and oil. It's a wonder it didn't catch on fire, but it did start to smoke. I was trying to locate the field when I heard a voice on my earphones, "P-47-219, Herb! You're on fire! *You're on fire!*" I didn't see any flames and didn't want to lose that airplane with all its valuable instrumentation, so I thought I would stay with her a while longer.

Since my windshield was all covered with oil, I came around the field trying to look out the back of the canopy. When you are flying out of a field all the time, you know the place. The houses, trees, and everything else on the approach. I knew I was heading directly for the runway. Originally, I was going to belly land her, that was the best way to get in with a problem like this, but again, as a test pilot, I knew the engine would have to come out, the propeller would be busted up and God knows what else, so at the last minute I dropped the gear. I probably made the best landing I ever made because I couldn't see what I was doing. I jumped out and ran blindly from the plane as the fire engines raced across the field toward me. The next day I was up at 38,000 feet again to rerun the aborted flight of the day before.

I took my son, Herb, Junior, up to 30,000 feet and made a dive with him. I think he was two or three years old at the time. My own fuselage was a little thinner in those days and he sat right next to me. I had an oxygen mask for him and he was declared "the fastest baby in the world." He learned to fly, graduated from college with an aviation management degree and was senior operations supervisor for the Dallas-Fort Worth Airport for 10 years, so I guess it didn't sour him on airplanes. Now he's general manager of all ground services of AMR, American Airlines' parent company, at Dallas-Fort Worth.

We also had a testing program with a C-54 and reversing propellers equipped with electronic governors. I could reverse all four propellers in flight, and when you do that you remove 75 percent of the lift over the wing. Some of the airline pilots who were flying the Boeing Strato-cruisers were taking them up to 35,000 feet to get over bad weather. The airlines were afraid that there might be a decompression and the pilot would have to get down to 10,000 feet in a hurry. In those days they had only a pressurized cabin with no individual oxygen masks. We were showing the airlines just how quick you could get down. When I reversed all four simultaneously, and was doing 150 to 200 knots, four seconds after reversal I would have a sink rate of 15,000 feet a minute with complete control of the aircraft.

I put on a demonstration at Caldwell for the New York press. We had hired an American Airlines C-54 and Captain Harry "Red" Clark, their chief pilot, was flying alongside me, in another C-54, on the approach. We told Red to get his plane down any way he could. We were both sitting at 15,000 feet, two-and-a-half miles off the end of the runway, when I reversed the props. My wheels touched the runway one minute and fifty seconds later and I stopped in 700 feet. Clark touched down about five minutes later.

Guy Vaughan was delighted when I'd back up our C-46 and C-54 while he was on board. I was in Ft. Lauderdale and the tower had me park it with the nose right up against a wall. They thought I would be towed out in the morning. The next day I called the tower and asked them if I could have permission to back up. I can't tell you how many tower people said, in almost the same words, "If you can back that big monster up, you have our permission." I wish I had that airplane for demonstrations at airshows today. The real and significant value of reversing propellers was their use when landing on wet and icy runways. I have never heard of the statistics of the number of aircraft saved from overshoots, but I think it would be staggering.

In 1952 I was asked to go to work for Fred Glass, director of aviation for the Port Authority of New York/New Jersey. The Authority had taken over the responsibilities of operating Idlewild, LaGuardia, and Newark airports. They also had the heliports and owned Teterboro Airport. I had contact with the entire aviation industry, with anybody who had anything to do with our airports at that time, because the Authority was always interested in acquiring more traffic. I had a good-sized department and we prepared reports, publications, and exhibits that documented the Port Authority's aviation activities. We had meetings until they came out my ears.

I was also on the first technical committee on noise abatement in the United States. The first day I reported to work, Fred said, "We've got problems with the Lockheed Constellations." That airplane had short exhaust stacks and they really barked. The people around Newark were raising holy hell. I also had to take a ride out to Teterboro Airport. Bendix had a B-25 that they were using to do test work on communications. The boys flying that airplane were going over Hackensack like they were on a bombing run. My first day on the job and I had to go out and explain to a vice-president that we were having a problem with our citizens calling in noise complaints. I mentioned the fact that I had been a test pilot with Curtiss Wright and not some guy who didn't know anything about flying. As it turned out, I knew both of the pilots and we established better flight patterns for their program. Then over the next few months the airlines dumped three airplanes, one into Elizabeth and two into Newark. Three catastrophes and that was just like throwing gasoline onto the fire because the people really got up in arms. Now it wasn't just the noise, they were also afraid. There was a meeting of the presidents of all the airlines and the directors of the Port Authority at Newark Airport, and we had to get the police to protect them. Those people were irate, and the governor closed Newark Airport for a couple of months.

About that time the 707 and 727 came along and the noise was really becoming serious. You couldn't blame the people because there were times at LaGuardia when you had an airplane over those houses every two minutes. We had to work with those people because, after all, we were a public body, so we came up with new traffic patterns. We had thousands of pilots we were trying to indoctrinate into doing something which they hadn't been doing. We installed big signs on both sides of the runways describing the takeoff procedures. Right turns, left turns, immediate climb to altitude, power reduction, etc. This had to be coordinated with the Airline Pilots Organization because the pilots thought it was terrible. We weren't doing anything that would cause safety problems. It was just a change in procedure, as simple as that. I was flying a 727 myself just to make sure that we weren't asking the airlines to do something that reduced takeoff safety. At that time my vehicle had all the radios and rotating lights so I could go right out on the airports. We also installed loudspeakers inside the hood. We spoke to every community around the airports. For instance, we went up to Ft. Lee, New Jersey. Airplanes were coming out of LaGuardia and going right over their houses. The mayor wanted the people to know that he was trying to do something about it. He had the council meet, and I turned on the radio so they could hear the tower operators giving instructions to the pilots. I'd even take some of them right out on the airport to let them see what was going on. I saw in the paper the other day that they are putting insulation in the schools near LaGuardia. There was one school on final approach where the airplanes were coming over the roof at one hundred feet. The school board was raising hell with us 33 years ago and now they are just installing sound-proof insulation.

During my twenty-four years with the Authority I checked out every type of business and commercial jet prior to its permission to land at the New York airports. In fact, I went to England in 1953 and flew their Comet, which was the first commercial jet transport. All the Boeings, the Douglas, Convair, Lockheeds, French Caravelle, Comet, Citation, Sabreliner, Falcon—you name it, I had the opportunity to fly it. This was an edict by Austin Tobin, former executive director of the Authority. One airplane that I really loved to fly was the 747. That's such a wonderful piece of equipment. The only thing I regret is that I retired in 1974 and just missed flying the Concorde.

I had to be lucky during my career, there's no other way. I have 19,351 hours and I never had an accident or violation. Luck is a very important part of any pilot's life, especially a test pilot's.

THE FIRES OF EL AL MILLYA AL HARLAL

Stephen Howell lived in Farmingdale, Long Island, not far from the Republic Aviation plant where he worked for 23 years. He has since moved to Harrisburg, Pennsylvania. At one point during our conversation Howell brought out his squadron scrapbook chronicling his World War II experiences as a crew chief in North Africa. As we looked at the pictures, he pointed out the different men he had known. "I didn't realize it at the time, but these were some of the finest people I would ever know."

He had recently attended a reunion of his 347th Fighter Squadron. "I'm the one who keeps in touch. Two of the fellows hadn't seen each other in forty years. We didn't bring any wives, because they just think it's boring. Besides, when it's just the men, we can give it the flavor of the war. Language-wise, if you know what I mean."

On my twenty-sixth birthday I was flown to the front in Tunisia. The 347th was an advance fighter squadron and we were the guys they sent in first. How the pilot of that C-47 knew where to take me I don't know, because he landed in an area that was simply a dustbowl on the edge of the Sahara Desert. The nearest water hole was over 200 miles away and the only vegetation were some little bushes that didn't look like they were alive. The pilot was screaming at me, "Hurry up! Hurry up! Get your stuff out of here. I've gotta get the hell out of here." He had flown in there without any fighter cover and we were eight miles from the front. I looked at him and said, "What the hell are you crabbing about? I've got to stay in this godforsaken place." I had no idea how I would ever get out of there, who would come to get me, and what I was expected to do while I was there. I

One of the crew chief's unstated duties was to listen intently while "his" pilots described their exploits in "his" airplane. Here Sergeant Stephen Howell, left, assumes the properly intent air while Captain Frank Heckenkamp, a Thunderbolt fighter pilot, shows just how he shot down three Germans in three minutes. The boys seem to be mugging it up a bit for the hometown newspapers.

had no orders, I was just shipped there. You start to think, "I wonder if 'they' know where I am."

Then, a couple of hours later, here comes another airplane and out come some more men and a lot of junk. Pretty soon, up drives a pack of trucks with drums of gasoline, oil, parts, all sorts of things. Then suddenly our airplanes land and we've got to park them somewhere. You don't know where the flight line is going to be so you make a line on the ground with a stick. This is where we're going to park the airplanes, right here. Then I picked a spot and I had a guy put up a flag and then so many feet away we put another flag. That was the runway. It sounds impossible today.

Suddenly, more trucks show up with the bombs, ammo, the pilots, and a board is put up in a little tent. You go in there and look at the board and find that your ship is on duty for four o'clock the next morning. It's supposed to be loaded with gas, ammo, bombs, everything so that pilot can fly a mission. We got it done on time. Where did it all come from? It's too many years for me to remember everything, but it all came together and we became operational.

I consider the roughest part of the entire war to be the living conditions. The amenities of life, whatever you call it. You couldn't put your tent up because the ground was baked so hard you couldn't drive a stake into it. We would dig holes that were nothing more than a little pothole and put our shelter half over that. We lived like that for months. In some places the ground was so hard that we couldn't even dig holes so we'd have to scrape together enough dirt to build up a little wall to protect us from the elements. Somebody finally went to the quartermaster and came back with twenty-penny nails and we drove them into the cracks in the hardpan to hold our tents up. At some point we got wall tents which were larger but there was virtually no way we could keep them up. We'd get these "whirling dervishes," little cyclonic twisters, that would tear through your tent and blow everything all over the place.

We set up a mess hall which was really just a bunch of K-ration boxes. Everything was packed in boxes that were the size of Crackerjack. There was a little toilet paper, candy, soup, soda, chocolate, and some kind of cheese-food and crackers that would swell up and make you feel full. Anything that required water was out of the question because you didn't have any water to make it with. In fact, you had nothing to drink with your food unless you saved your ration for the day. We had half-a-helmet's worth of water to wash with and barely half a cup of water to drink, per day.

In the midst of all this we were ordered to take atabrin for malaria and this affected most of the men. It made us sick, throw up, have the runs, and turn yellow. I remember one night when the atabrin first took hold. God Almighty, you'd see a flashlight come ripping out of a tent door, zigging and zagging, trying to find the latrine. Pretty quick here'd come another desperate case from another tent. Some fellows didn't make it. You can picture what a terrible mess we lived in for a while.

We were still required to do the job seven days a week, around the clock. Our squadron never missed a mission and we were never short an airplane. In fact, we loaned airplanes out to other squadrons. We became known as one of the best operational fighter squadrons in the entire Mediterranean Theater. Every time they had a forward field that had to be operated under the adverse conditions, we were it. The 350th Fighter Group, the 347th Fighter Squadron. We made a name for ourselves and maybe, unfortunately for us, we made the wrong kind of name.

The planes whipped up a lot of dirt with their props. The runway was simply hardpan, cracked clay, and there were sometimes sixty or seventy planes taking off in the morning. The dirt would rise in the air in a large cloud over this dustbowl and it would hang there all day because of the heat. Then, at night, it would cool down and that dirt would drop right down on us. We were so dirty that you couldn't run your hand through your hair. Everybody in the outfit cut his hair off as short as he could get it, because washing it was out of the question. The little water we did have we tried to rinse our mouths with or clean our faces. You didn't bother with your hands because they were going to be right back in grease. Just wipe them off, do the best you could. But just imagine, you're out in the desert, 200 miles from nowhere, and where are you even going to get a rag to wipe them off with? You had to use the end of your shirt-tail or something like that.

One of the reasons that things were so difficult was the fact that we were constantly on the move. We would just get ourselves set up nicely, try to get a little order in our lives and we'd move to a new field. We'd erect a movie screen and set up a little theater, make a squadron bar, and buy local wine. There'd be a place for the fellows to play cards. We'd set up volleyball courts, clear fields for baseball diamonds. You were allowed to play ball if you could find anything to play with. At our squadron reunions, we show pictures of the boys playing volleyball and baseball, that kind of stuff. The women say, "What the hell? Is that all you guys ever did?" They only see what amounts to two seconds out of that entire war. We did have our own baseball, football, and soccer teams, and we played other squadrons. We also played the British. I played in the band so the Air Force supplied me with a set of drums, but this shouldn't be construed to sound as if all we did was play games. We were at war and you do the best you can during a war.

You always had to keep up the flight line. We always had aircraft going and missions flying, but in between or whenever some man got an idea, they'd try things. We were always trying to make the latrines a little better. Instead of just a hole in the ground, we'd build a box and put a tent over it. We had some men who got together and built a terrific hot-water shower. It had a big tank up on a platform with a firehose connected to it with pumps and heaters. We could run twelve showerheads at one time. I found the showerheads and twelve mother-of-pearl toilet seats in a Crane Plumbing Supply in Rome. We built wooden floors and had a big dedication ceremony when we finished it. I mean, we had a super deluxe shithouse. We carried that thing all over Africa with us, up into Corsica and over to Italy. We wouldn't go without it. It almost filled a truck but we didn't care, we wanted that latrine with us. The Army and the Air Force and the whole Mediterranean Theater of Operations didn't give us that stuff. We made it ourselves. Then we put too much napalm in it one time—we used napalm to burn up the waste once a month—and burned the whole goddamn thing down. Sometimes we'd get very discouraged.

★

When I was a kid I used to ride my bicycle from Hollis, which is on Long Island, to Roosevelt Field. There were wooden hangars at the corner of Merrick Avenue and Old Country Road where the Franklin National Bank is today. We'd go out there and hang around and get to know the guys who were flying those early airplanes. They'd give us little odd jobs like picking up oily rags or straightening up the work bin. Then we'd rake the dirt floors so it looked halfway decent, because on weekends they would be giving rides to people. Those old aircraft were very light and the grass field was not well kept up. The airplanes would bounce like the devil, and if the wind caught them they could tip over. They would get a couple of kids and have us keep the wings steady until the pilot got to where he was going to take off. It was around 1925 or 1926, I was ten years old, when I got my first ride in an airplane. I think it got in my blood.

While I was going to school, I would go out to the airport every weekend and ended up getting my pilot's license and my A and E. That's airplane and engine, which meant I was also a licensed mechanic. When I graduated from high school I started working for a pharmaceutical company in New York City. At that time I was also playing the drums nights and weekends so I didn't go out to the airport at all, to speak of, during that time. I worked in New York for a couple of years and then I went on the road selling drugs for the same company. My territory was out in Ohio, and I'd stay a week here and a week there. I would go to see the doctors who still dispensed drugs right in their offices. Most of them were out in the country or smaller towns. I met this guy in a hotel lobby one Saturday morning and we had breakfast together. It turned out that he was an engineer with Goodyear and worked with blimps. He said, "We have trouble getting men to work on the weekend. Would you be interested in a part-time job? I said, "What do I have to do?" He told me that I'd be on the landing party, tie the blimps down, and would also be working on them. That sounded like fun and blimps are sort of like airplanes so I said I'd take the job.

They had just built a huge hangar in Akron and there were a lot of blimps in those days. I was there for about a year, working on weekends. Later, in the war, I think we were the only squadron that had a blimp attached to it. It was helping with the de-mining of the Italian coastline. We had to assign thirty-two men to land and tie it down every night. Bill Kaiser was the commander of that blimp and he worked with me at Republic Aviation. He became the curator of the Cradle of Aviation Museum at Mitchel Field.

The drug company decided to go mail order so they didn't need me on the road anymore. They offered me a job back in New York but I had my ticket for aircraft mechanic and heard that they were hiring at the Watertown Arsenal in Watertown, New York. I got the job and we were installing overseas gas tanks in the lend-lease aircraft that were being flown to Britain: Lockheed Hudsons, Lodestars, and B-25s. They put up a notice on their bulletin board that men were needed to train the British to maintain the aircraft we were sending them. Anybody who was draft-bait could go up to Canada and receive a permanent rank depending on his ability and the job he had at the time. The war was getting closer and it looked to me like we were going to get involved. Because I was a foreman, I became a master sergeant. We trained in Canada with the Royal Canadian Air Force and then they put us on a ship to England. My stay was short because we just walked across the dock and got on another ship going to Alexandria, Egypt. When we got to Alexandria they trucked us out to different airfields and we went to work for the British, who were chasing Rommel around the desert. I think there were about ninety of us and we were teaching them how to fix and take care of the B-25s.

We were considered "advisors" until the day after Pearl Harbor. I listened to the British account of the attack on the radio and that was pretty scary. Then we got orders that we were now combatants and we became gunners for the British on B-25s. We did that for three or four weeks and then got orders that we were being recalled to the United States for retraining. I didn't understand that at all. What would they have to retrain me for? But, of course, there was no way you could argue with the Army and they sent me back. I ended up at a special advanced engine school in Philadelphia. The captain called me in and said, "Why are you here?" I told him that I had tried to fight it. "I'm a trained aircraft mechanic with all kinds of experience on almost anything that can fly. I don't need retraining. In fact, without bragging, I can probably show your instructors a few things." He said, "I've been looking at your record and I feel the same way. I want you to run the engine test stands." They had engines set up on stands with big cages around them so nobody would walk into the props while they were running. The idea was for the fellows to figure out why an engine wouldn't start or what was wrong with it. My job was putting the bugs into the engine. I might take the rotor out of the distributor and put in a cracked one, or maybe put in a cracked spark plug. Sometimes we'd simulate an oil line that was ready to blow. That one was a mess because the kids had to clean up the whole shed after that black oil blew all over the place. We only did that if they gave us a hard time.

I worked there until my time came to ship out. The whole class was leaving and we had a little shindig at Howard Johnson's. The head of the school gave a little talk; we had a couple of drinks and dinner and went on our way. They took us down to the North Philadelphia station and we sat between the northbound and southbound tracks. We didn't know which way we were going until the train stopped. During the whole war I never knew where I was going, ever, until I got there.

We went out and bought one of those cheap, fiberboard suitcases and went over to a liquor store and filled that damn thing with booze. We figured we were going to the Pacific and were all set for a long trip. The train finally rumbled in and it was going north. The guy with the orders gave them to the conductor and he ripped them open. We were going to Trenton! One stop. Here we have all this booze and we never got to open it.

When we got to Fort Dix, this was October of 1942, they weren't expecting us and they didn't know what to do with us. Some of our guys became prison guards and a few were even doing yard work. Because I was a civilian pilot they sent me out to what is now McGuire Air Force Base. At that time it was a grass field with one hangar and a couple of old O-46s. They were big, high-winged monoplanes that looked like they belonged in the First World War. The pilot sat out in the open, no cabin, and the back cockpit was round with a track that had a .30-caliber machine gun mounted on it. You wore goggles and a helmet and my title was gunner-observer. We'd fly in a certain sector off the coast and watch for submarines. I don't know what we would have done if we'd seen a submarine, but I think the people on the ground found it more of a morale booster than anything else. Just seeing those airplanes flying overhead. I flew that every day, two hours on, two hours off for eight hours. They ended up replacing those airplanes with blimps because they could stay on the station much longer without having to go back for fuel.

One morning at three o'clock they woke us up. "Everybody up! Everybody up! This is it, everybody out!" My friend Charlie and I were the last two to walk up the gangplank of the ship that we went over on. It was a South American liner that the Navy had taken over and called the *Hermitage*.

Again, we had no idea where we were going—north, south, east, west—or if we were going to be sunk in the middle of the ocean. The ship held around ten thousand men and I had a bunk approximately 18 inches by 6 feet. That was my little spot for what turned out to be an eighteen-day trip. We had formed a large convoy and any direction you looked, all you saw were ships. We were going very slowly because the freighters and tankers couldn't keep up. On the tenth day we were told to sharpen our weapons. Now, all I had was a gun and I didn't know how you sharpen a gun. Not only that, I had gotten lost from my group. I was a replacement and had only known them for a couple of days and I couldn't recognize their faces on the crowded ship. I just fell in with any outfit that came along. When they announced, "We're going to Casablanca," we all thought we were going to a place with lions and tigers and gorillas. Nobody had any idea that it was a fairly modern city controlled by the French. Guys from Brooklyn were the worst. They thought there was a wall around Brooklyn and that there was no civilized world beyond that.

I went over the side into an LST and we were told to shoot anything that came in sight when we got ashore. At this point I'd like to inject something. I attribute part of my returning successfully from the war to the fact that I was able to joke about things, laugh it off, no matter how bad things got. Can you picture me standing on the deck of that ship with my full fieldpack, my iron hat, and my damn rifle? I even had bandoleers of bullets wrapped around me. I might not have been a real fighting man, but I sure looked like one.

Having worked with the British, I found that the Americans didn't know what the hell was going on over there. They didn't know what combat was all about because they'd never been in it. The people who actually knew anything were still in England. Here we were on an LST, nobody knew anybody, nobody knew anything about combat, nobody knew anything about an invasion, yet we were *in* the North African Invasion.

On the way in to the beach there were still some bodies in the water. We had clips on the harness that held our field packs. They were virtually impossible to open. We had three days' rations, a shelter half, blankets, extra ammo, grenades, and I don't know what all in that pack. When you added our clothes and rifle, we weighed a lot, and nobody knew the undersea terrain where we were getting out of those LSTs. In some spots there were deep holes and we lost a lot of men simply because they couldn't get their packs off. On later invasions they modified the clips, but before that some guys used shoelaces tied in a bow so that they could just pull and it would release. We lost many good men during the war because of some simple little dumb thing like that. Those were the kinds of things that you found out as you went through the war and you had to cope with them. If we had the crybabies of today, the news media and everybody out in the street running around having some kind of a *cause célèbre*, they would have had a field day in World War II with the things that went on. We didn't complain about them because we couldn't. You were caught up in a war, and people were concerned with more important problems than us.

There were things that happened we had never thought of, never heard of, and it never entered anyone's mind that we might have to cope with these situations under battle conditions. We had to perform our work without the support of anyone behind us. Fend for ourselves and still do our job. The enlisted personnel of the Air Force are very low on the totem pole when it comes to singing praises, but without these men there would have been no Air Force. We had some ingenious and talented people and you didn't have to be an Air Force pilot to be a strong contributor to the effort during the war. There were many, many times when I felt the enlisted men went far beyond what was expected of them in order to get the job done. I have found in talking with other guys, after I got back, that almost all of us had the same problems and almost all of us took care of them in the same way, by ourselves.

We got close to the beach in the LST and then waded through the water to the beach. I started sliding on my belly like they taught me and by the time I got to where I could stand up I was in a hell of a mess because the sand was filthy. I stood up, took deadly aim at a tree and let loose with that rifle. I don't even remember if I hit it, but I'll tell you, that really felt good. All that work so I could shoot that damn gun at a tree. There I was, a soldier on a beach in Africa. That was my first thought when I hit the beach, "By God, I'm really a soldier."

There was actually very little opposition. I heard a couple of pops and bangs, but it was pretty much over when we landed. During the next two days I was able to find my own squadron and we went out to the airfield. A couple of days later the guy who was in charge of the group and I took a jeep and drove around Casablanca. Part of my job was to act as a liaison to find local suppliers. We saw a sign, "Atelier de Machine Industriale," meaning machine tool shop. We found it had been turned into a place for making women's items. They had machinery and equipment but no materials—the Germans had taken that—and the people were happy as hell to do any kind of job we wanted. It was the first work they'd had for a long time. We got the allied military government, which could use what was available in a place like Casablanca, to put them on the payroll and see that they got food. If we hadn't had those guys we wouldn't have been able to operate because we didn't have any tools. We waited a couple of months for our toolboxes. When they arrived we were excited. Oh, boy, now we've got American tools. We opened them and found out that some contractor had shafted the government. There was a pair of slip-joint pliers, a black-handled ordinary screwdriver, and a pair of water-pump pliers. That was it and we hadn't gotten any airplanes either.

Then we discovered some Curtiss P-36s that were still in crates. They had been sent to the French but the Germans got there before they could put them together. We didn't have any orders, but we also didn't have any airplanes, so we hired a bunch of French people and assembled them. They were better than nothing.

Then we got our real airplanes, P-39s. They flew them from England to Africa, which was a hell of a trip. Sixty-two started out and forty-nine made it. Eleven were interned in Portugal or Spain and two were lost. The P-39 was an outdated airplane the day it hit the field. It wasn't a bad airplane, in fact, it was a well-built, advanced-design airplane. It did have a lot of innovations. There was a cannon firing through the propeller hub and it was one of the first tricycle-landing-gear-equipped aircraft. You could almost drive it like a car. I taxied many of them and I know what I'm talking about. It also had electric landing gear which did away with heavy hydraulics. It was just unfortunate that it was built at the time it was. High-altitude combat was just coming in and they weren't supercharged.

At this time I was a crew chief and the size of my crew depended on the type of aircraft and the kind of combat we were involved with. I usually had an assistant crew chief, a mechanic, an assistant mechanic, an armorer, and the radio department would supply a radioman. A crew chief had one airplane, that was his responsibility. Later on I was a flight chief and I had seven planes. Of course, there was a crew chief on each of those planes. Then I became a line chief and I'd have anywhere from twenty-four to thirty-six planes under me.

We were in Casablanca for a couple of months and got orders to go to a place called Oujda which is also in Morocco. Of course, we didn't know where we were going. They arranged for us to be moved by train in what the French call "forty and eights." They were boxcars that were used in the First World War and the "forty and eight" meant they could hold forty men or eight horses. They were smaller than American boxcars and only had four wheels, which made them very rough riding. You could barely get forty men standing shoulder to shoulder in there and the ones we happened to be in had been used to transport camels. There is nothing like camel dung. You can't believe it unless you've smelled it.

We were in those cars for three days and two nights. There were thirty-eight guys in my car and we found out that one-third of the men could lie down while the other two-thirds stood. They would get some rest and then after two hours, we'd shift. You had to lie on your side, up against the next guy, and try to get a short cat-nap. Nobody told us how long the trip was going to take, where we were going and when we were going to stop along the way. The officer with us had orders, but I mean, if somebody said to you, "You're going to Oujda," big deal. Where was that? Africa is one hell of a big continent.

We came to stations, but we didn't know if the train was going to stop, and if it did stop, for how long. You might see a bread store, but you couldn't get off the train and run over there because you might miss the train. It was very hot during the day and at night it got cold so you had to keep your overcoat available. It was just miserable. After we were on there for awhile we did figure out one thing. The conductor, a Frenchman, who was up in a little cupola on the last car, would blow a whistle when the train was going to stop. He would go "tweeeeeeet." When he went "Tweet, tweet, tweet, tweeeeeeeeet," that meant, all aboard, let's go. By listening to that whistle we managed to at least get a little something to eat or take a leak along the way.

We tried to heat coffee one morning at a railroad siding. We broke wood pieces off the C-ration crates and had just started some little fires when the whistle went off and the train pulled out. There stood the fires of El Al Millya al Harlal, or whatever the name of the place was.

We finally reached our destination and we didn't even know we'd arrived. They had to tell us. Pretty soon here come some G.I. trucks and they picked us up. They took us out to this muddy field that was almost covered with water. "This is your new air base, fellows." They dumped us off, with all our stuff, in the mud, and there we sat. We put up our tents and here come the airplanes, the gas trucks, all kinds of stuff. Next thing we know, we're operational again. That was living in the Army Air Forces.

While this sort of thing was going on you were, of course, required to maintain the aircraft given to you. That required a knowledge of P-36s, P-40s, P-38s, P-39s, P-47s, and A-36s. We were also working on British Spitfires, Hurricanes, Beaufighters and Mosquito bombers. Each of these aircraft required special tools and equipment. Different-sized jacks. I mean, just take the propellers. Electric, hydraulic, four-blader, three-blader, all of these things entered into the maintenance of those aircraft. We started getting P-38s for high-altitude convoy cover and we had no access to P-38 parts. Some of the P-39 parts fit on one engine of the P-38, but the other engine had opposite rotation and it required all different parts. We had to think of ways to make them.

In a foreign airfield, it's very difficult to get anything, much less parts. You had to try to trade with other squadrons. Go to the British and try to get parts, whatever you had to do, you did. A lot of things had to be made. We had to make nose-gear jacks to keep the aircraft off the ground when we were working on the landing gear. We also had to make yokes for the tail. Each airplane had to have its own equipment. I made tools just to take sparkplugs out because each engine had the plugs in a different place. As far as I can remember, we never had stands to work off. We'd pile 50-gallon drums on top of each other so we could put the battery in a P-47. That was about 12 feet off the ground. The battery was quite heavy and the drums didn't fit together properly. They'd be rocking and weaving around and you'd be trying to work up there. Ingenuity was an important part of the picture. Our engineering chief, George Wixen, was very helpful in making parts for us. He had men under him like Herman Yellin, who was in the clothing industry before the war. He became an excellent mechanic. Guys like Cowles and Mulligan. They were both electricians and did excellent work. We also had a propeller specialist from Boston by the name of Meyerowitz who was extremely good. There were times we worked all night. We didn't have any lights and I remember six or eight of us changing an engine with one flashlight among us. We had to keep switching it back and forth because you could only have the light for a minute. We had that engine running in time for an early morning preflight and that plane went on a mission that day.

The pilots were good, very good. Their situation was different from ours because they were on a rotation basis and after they had completed a certain amount of missions, they would go home. Depending on how many missions we were flying a day, we would hardly get to know the pilot before he was gone. It was tough when a pilot wouldn't come back. You'd be standing there waiting and no airplane. You may have just broken your ass fixing it, too. We never lost an airplane because of mechanical failure. I lost a couple of P-39s.

I had X, that was my letter, and she flew off on a mission one day and never came back. We never knew what happened to it. Then I got double X. That plane flew for quite awhile and then crashed. It was lost in combat, but that pilot was saved.

I never really got attached to one airplane but I had one P-47 that was pretty special. It seemed to have a little more power. The pilots used to say that they liked to get her. Each airplane was different in little ways that you'd learn after working with it for awhile. I'd try to tell the new pilots what they could expect from an airplane. I don't know how many pilots I cockpit trained. My C.O. told me, "You know that cockpit better than anybody. Give them the whole treatment." That morning that pilot would go out on a mission. Now, you know yourself, if you change cars, you don't have all the information. Just think of getting in a strange airplane and going into combat. Those pilots had a dedication that you don't hear about today.

There were thousands of men doing what we were doing and they all did their jobs and did them well. Each outfit thought that theirs was the best. When I look at the pictures in the history book of the 347th Fighter Squadron, I see the tilt of a fellow's hat, the way he looked at you, the way he stood. The entire war effort was something that the American people can be extremely proud of. There are a lot of people who are nearly forgotten, but they did their best. Fine men. We were strangers, brought together by that war.

Today people are talking about World War II and coming up with all sorts of new opinions. There is the big hassle about fire-bombing Dresden. What were the Germans doing to Britain during the Blitz? How many English people were killed? They're still digging bombs out of London today. Why shouldn't we get into a place like Dresden and knock the hell out of it when we got the chance? That was war. Forty years later to be worried about the poor Germans is utterly ridiculous. The same with the Japanese. Two of their top diplomats were in Washington wearing morning coats and top hats. They were acting very diplomatically the day that their country attacked us. Then they gave us a hard time for over three years all over the Pacific. Today you hear people say, "Oh, you shouldn't have done that to those poor people." Poor people, my ass. You had to be scared of those guys during the war. I don't see where it is necessary to have everything from forty years ago dug up by do-gooders who cry about everything they look at.

We chased all over Africa and Italy and every time we thought we'd found a home they'd tell us to pick everything up and away we'd go. Back to riding like sardines in trucks. We went down the coast of Sardinia over roads which were alkali and the entire convoy was covered with white powder. We looked like we'd been dipped in barrels of flour. We went to Corsica on a ship and I don't know how the old thing stayed together. We were in rough weather and I went up on the poop deck. A French corvette came with us and that ship would disappear and the next thing I knew it would be up on a hill of water next to us. We slept on the steel plates of the deck and ate our rations cold. We were nine days on that boat.

At one point I was moved to Parmigliano, which was close to Mt. Vesuvius, and while I was there it erupted. It wasn't bad enough that I had to fight a war, but I was in a volcano eruption. Believe me, that burned up a lot of our airplanes and really put a dent in us because we were trying to work the Anzio beachhead at the time. The Lord didn't do us any good when he blew the top off that thing. We were on Anzio three times and each time we got beat up pretty bad. One time we lost eighty-eight men on our chow line when the Germans hit us with guns and mortars. We did, however, accomplish the missions we were sent in to do.

Whenever we could, we tried to help the local people. In the wintertime, the children used to wait at our chow line. We would try to save a slice of bread, anything we could. We were ordered not to do it but it was common practice to save some of your food for the kids on that line. We didn't want to dump it into the garbage cans and make them take it out of there. We also gave a Christmas party in Pisa, Italy, for orphaned children. We decorated a tent and made things for the children out of candy and stuff we could find.

When the war ended in Europe I had the most points in my squadron, but they had a little deal where they could declare you essential to the war effort and your points didn't mean anything. The idea was that I would go back to the States, have 30 days furlough, and report back to Fort Dix. Then I would catch up with my squadron in the Pacific. I was on a subway train in New York City when I saw the *Daily News* headline, "Atom Bomb Dropped." I didn't know what the hell an atom bomb was. I never heard of atom anything.

I went back to Fort Dix and they gave me another furlough. Thirty days later I went back again and they gave me another one. The next time I went back I told them, "You can't give me another furlough because I have no more money left for car fare. I can't even get back home." At that point I had no job and no money. I was playing in a band a few nights a week to make a few bucks.

I finally got a job at the YWCA in New York making $35 a week. That wasn't too bad a deal, me and six hundred women, but I had just gotten married so it was sort of a lost cause. We moved to Albany where there was more work. I was twenty-nine years old and we had decided it was time to start a family. I got a job with Montgomery Ward and I would go out to Albany Airport two days a week, picking up extra money by doing aircraft maintenance for American Airlines. In 1949 I went to Los Angeles for Northwest Orient Airlines. They sent me to Alaska for two years. Then I came back to New York and went with Pan Am at Idlewild.

Then I hired on as a mechanic at Republic Aircraft in Farmingdale, Long Island. That was 1951 and they were building the F-84s, the D models. I always worked on special projects, experimental or flight test and was a mechanic, foreman, and general foreman at different times. I think I'm a guy who's been pretty lucky because I went from Roosevelt Field, from the days of fabric aircraft, Lindbergh and Admiral Byrd, to the time of the space shuttle.

I've often said the war set me straight, and I've heard other people say the same thing about themselves. I was kind of a silly jerk, drinking, raising hell, playing in bands. Nothing bothered me. I was living it up. The war settled me down, and when I came back I was ready to make something of myself. The war also made me a better mechanic because it gave me hands-on experience. It taught me how to make do and improvise.

At one point they were having trouble with a unit on the F-84 and the whole tail section of the airplane would have to be pulled to replace it. I looked at the job and said, "I don't have to pull that tail. I can reach right up into that hole and take it out." By doing that you don't have to get permission from the Air Force to take the tail off which involved a lot of paperwork and time. All I need is permission to take the unit out. I got up in there and I could feel the bolts but I couldn't turn them because there was a cable in the way. I tied the tools to my wrists so they wouldn't drop down into the fuselage. If they did, you couldn't fly the airplane until you found them. I got a box about eight inches high, and when I stepped on that box I could get my hands up in there and when I stepped off the box I could turn the bolts. I'd repeat the process to put the new unit in. What used to take 12 hours took me 15 minutes.

My friend, Gus Stathis, told me, "Don't tell Lenny." Gus was superintendent of inspection at that time and Lenny was the general foreman. Gus used to get Lenny into things and then take his money away from him. He bet Lenny that I couldn't get that unit out of there without taking the tail off. He said, "Okay, Steve, show Lenny how you do it." Lenny said, "Are you kidding? He'll never be able to do that." I got up there and put my hands in, with the tools on, used my little box and took it out in nothing flat. Lenny said, "He'll never get the new one in." Gus said, "Watch." I went in there again and put the new one in with no trouble at all. Gus said, "Look at that, 10 minutes. Lenny, you watch this old buzzard, if he isn't a good mechanic, then I don't know what a good mechanic is."

THEODORE KARL HIMELSTEIN

BICYCLES, BLACKOUTS, AND BRITISH BEER

His New York apartment overlooks Central Park, which Dr. Theodore Karl Himelstein enjoys calling his "front yard." He is thin, with a controlled professional manner, and his voice became soft as we talked, occasionally trailing off to an almost inaudible tone. As we looked through his medical records from the war years, he seemed amazed at the amount of surgery he and his associates had performed.

The television program "M.A.S.H." made the world of combat medicine a part of many lives and underscored the irony faced by all wartime physicians. Himelstein finds no fault with the medical aspects of the program but, he says, "We didn't have anywhere near the kind of fun or the time off that those TV people had."

I think I was "born" a doctor. My mother would tell the incident of a doctor coming to the house when I was three years old. When he was leaving, the doctor patted me on the head and asked, "Would you like a ride in my buggy?" I answered, "No thank you, when I grow up I'm going to be a doctor and have a buggy of my own."

I was born in Brooklyn, July 4, 1906. It was still what you might call country in those days and there was lots of open space with goats roaming around. When I was eleven, we moved to Highland Park, New Jersey, which is across the Raritan River from New Brunswick. I loved the outdoors and I learned how to swim, fish, ice skate, and paddle a canoe on that river.

I graduated from New Brunswick High School and then went to Rutgers College in the premedical program and received my B.S. in 1928. I worked for a year at Squibbs Pharmaceutical Company in New Brunswick as a biochemist and saved my money because I planned to go abroad to medical school. I took part of my studies at the Rotunda Hospital in Dublin, Ireland, and then studied in London with Sir Reginald Watson Jones, who wrote the now-classic textbook on fractures and dislocations. I received my medical degree in 1933 from St. Andrews University in Scotland.

My decision to become an orthopedic surgeon took place during my third year in medical school. The professor presented to the class a baby born with a club foot. In a club foot deformity, the foot is twisted so that the sole faces upward and is clenched, resembling an ugly knob at the end of a clublike leg. If untreated, the adult limps along with pain and breakdown of skin, in a grotesque shoe. In those days, such unfortunates were seen limping along on the street.

After pointing out the features of the deformity, the professor took that little foot, and with a single deft turn of his hand, made it look normal. "Now we will put on a plaster cast and hold this corrected position, and in three weeks, when he has outgrown the cast, you change it. You make sure the foot is in the right position and repeat that procedure until the child is ready to walk at age one, and he'll have a normal foot." I thought to myself, orthopedics! That's for me, to be a mender of the maimed. Orthopedic surgery is a concrete, "hands on" specialty. You can see the results of straightening a crooked spine, a club foot, or healing a broken bone. To see your patient standing straight and walking again, that was for me.

After graduating from medical college, I spent four years as intern and resident for my specialty training in orthopedic surgery at Metropolitan Hospital in New York City. In 1933, interns, not paramedics, rode the ambulances answering emergency calls. Just out of school, with our heads crammed with theory, we now faced the real test, applying that theory; and a few incidents remain with you forever. Setting a dislocated elbow with a loud "pop" in Grand Central Station during the height of the commuter rush hour. No doctor ever performed to a larger audience. And the sad old lady, living alone, who tried to end it all by turning on the gas. Artificial respiration and oxygen gradually brought her back. She slowly opened her eyes, not sure if it was this or the afterworld, looked around crestfallen, and with resignation said, "Same damn wallpaper."

Orthopedic surgery deals with the bony framework and the locomotor system of the body; bones and joints, and the muscles, tend-

Dr. Theodore Karl Himelstein, a flight surgeon with the "Mighty" Eighth Air Force in England during World War II. Retired from his practice in New York City, Dr. Himelstein was one of the pioneers involved with artificial joint replacement.

ons, and nerves that move them. Treating the deformities, diseases, and injuries which afflict them. We are the carpenters of the human body and adapt a lot of their tools to our practice. Chisels, hammers, drills, saws, that sort of thing. The big difference is that we wear rubber gloves.

To have entered the field of orthopedic surgery in the 1930s was a fantastic opportunity. It was like emerging from the dark ages into a sophisticated, modern age. During that time the basic, seminal discoveries were made which opened the doors to undreamed of possibilities and achievements. In the thirties, Vitallium was produced, a metal alloy that was tolerated by the body tissue and was harder than steel. Before that we had no metal compatible with human tissue to use as bone plates, rods, or screws. Now we could create artificial joints, use metal rods to eliminate three months of bed confinement and traction in the case of broken bones. We also had boneplates to hold together complex fractures, implant metal jacks to straighten severe spinal curvatures—the list is endless.

The blood bank made possible long and complex operative procedures that wouldn't have been possible before its creation. Also, we had the bone bank. To combat infections, which are especially disastrous in bone and joint cases, sulfa drugs came in during the 1930s and antibiotics in the forties. I could appreciate each advance because I had one foot in the past while I stood on the threshold of the future.

One other important advancement should be mentioned. Modern anesthesia, administered by a doctor, a specialist in anesthesia, can best be appreciated when one recalls the open drip ether being given by an intern or nurse. The patient, during induction, would go through a state of excitement thrashing about in a semiconscious state and had to be restrained by two strong orderlies. Induction took 20–30 minutes while the surgeon, with a busy schedule, sat and twiddled his thumbs, waiting to begin. During the operation, in addition to concentrating on the surgery, the surgeon was responsible for events at the anesthesia end and the general condition of the patient. The discovery of pentothal ended all that and we went into World War II with all of these healing weapons at our disposal.

When I volunteered for the service in '42, I was assigned for a year in Louisville, Kentucky, at the Nichols General Hospital. We were taking care of the complicated cases that were coming in from the Pacific Theater, mainly the Solomon Islands campaign.

In 1943 I was sent to England and my assignment was chief of orthopedic surgery section of the 231st Station Hospital serving the Eighth Air Force. Orthopedic surgeons have to carry the major workload in any war. Statistics show that in war, 70 percent of the wounded were orthopedic cases! Now, orthopedic surgeons are not

70 percent of the medical "family." We are only about 5 or 6 percent. You had thoracic surgery which deals with the wounds of the lungs, general surgery which takes care of belly wounds, that sort of thing. A neurosurgeon handled brain and nerve injuries. We also had ear, nose, throat, and eye surgeons and urologists for kidney and V.D. cases, plus the rest of the vast field of medicine. All of those fields together equaled the number of orthopedic cases I handled. We had about thirty doctors for all of the other fields and one orthopedic surgeon, me. There was never any time off and I learned to do without sleep because there were emergencies every night.

I was given obstetricians and gynecologists for assistants. Being surgeons, they knew how to scrub up, sterility, and how to sew up an incision. They couldn't make the major decisions about what tissues could be saved and what couldn't, but they proved to be proficient assistants and got better and better as time went by. We'd have four operating tables going at once. My assistants would open up, I'd do the operation and they'd close up. It was work, work, work, like an assembly line, but a precise assembly line.

In addition, I had noncommissioned corpsmen, sergeants and corporals, whom I trained. One of those young men, Frank Cassese, from Far Rockaway, New York, was a steam fitter in civilian life. I taught him how to put up every kind of traction and he became very proficient. Another one, Richard ("Pinky") Pingstock, from Cleveland, Ohio, had just graduated from podiatry school. He became my chief sergeant and my dependable right-hand man. I taught him, along with the others, Al and Whitey, how to put on plaster casts. A body cast would run from the upper part of the chest down to the toes. Every joint must be in a specific position. The knees bent a little bit, hips straight, spine and feet, just right. It would take forty-eight rolls of plaster to put on one of those casts. Today bandages come with plaster of paris already impregnated in them, rolled up for you, in several sizes. In those days they hadn't appeared yet and you had to roll your own. You would take big sheets of crinoline, cut them into the desired sizes, and rub plaster powder into them and roll them up. We used three hundred bandages a day, day in and day out. I went over my requisition slips at one point and found that in the twenty-odd months I was in England, we had put on ten-and-a-half tons of plaster casts.

After the casts were put on I'd inspect them, and if the cast was just a little bit off, it was unacceptable and I'd have them take it off and do it again. Oh, they grumbled at first, but in the end they were happier being perfect and took great pride in their work. These men were well trained and a big, big help to me. I think they were the unsung heroes of the outfit.

Everyone was inspired. The nurses were very devoted. There were no goldbrick goof-offs, and it was one great devoted family. As for me, I counted myself fortunate in that I had the training to contribute to this great cause at this crucial moment in history. When I went into the Army, Hitler held Europe and was almost to Cairo, encircling the Mediterranean. The Japanese were in the Aleutians, and we were really in a closing vise. The days were black and it looked like it might be the end of the world, the free world as we knew it. But there was always an air about the men. Especially the flyers and the British people. If we gave it "our all," we felt we could win. I felt that way and that's why I didn't spare myself. At one period I went nineteen months without an uninterrupted night's sleep and without a day off. The colonel had to order me out of the hospital for a weekend in London. If you've ever watched "M.A.S.H.," the television show, it gives you a realistic idea about the patient-doctor relationships and the problems you had in medicine during a war. But, I want to tell you, we didn't have anywhere near the kind of fun, or the time off that those TV people had. None of that. It was as I said before, work, work, work.

We were called a station hospital. That was an old First World War term. There were general hospitals, station hospitals, and field hospitals. The general, or base, hospital takes care of everything; long-term recuperation, major elective operations, making the dispositions to send men home or back to duty, that sort of thing. A field hospital takes care of medical emergencies, close to the fighting. Now, anywhere you have an Army installation, you need a hospital to take care of the people stationed there, the station hospital. You're not supposed to have combat casualties; you just take care of the people on the base. You're also limited to 750 beds. Now, it's true, we were in England, at an air base, and not in the combat zone, but the war was brought to us. The bombers would leave in the morning and would fly home to us in the afternoon with their casualties. We were a field, general, and station hospital all wrapped up in one operation. It turned out that 750 beds were not enough. That was fine when we were just taking care of the Air Force, but after the Normandy invasion, when they started sending in trainloads of three hundred ground casualties at a time, we had to have more beds. Instead of 750 beds, we now had 1,500. Some of these casualties had had emergency care before they got to us, but their open wounds and shattered bones now required definitive treatment. We'd take the temporary casts off, set their bones, sew up their wounds and put on proper casts or apply traction when indicated.

We were located in the county of Norfolk, about 10 miles south of the city of Norwich. Our outfit covered quite a lot of acreage. The laboratory, headquarters building, mess hall, and officers' barracks were temporary square wooden buildings. The patient wards were Quonset huts, each with a fifty-bed capacity.

We had a saying, "The field of orthopedics is best fertilized by the blood of warriors." You see so much so fast during a war. Mass injuries. Not one or two, but hundreds. With every war we've gained, at great cost, significant surgical advancement. During the First World War they had no antibiotics so they tried to sterilize the wound against infection. If a man got a compound fracture of the limbs, he would be placed in traction and a tube put in the wound with Carrel-Dakins solution constantly running through it. This solution generated nascent chlorine which they thought would kill the bacteria and control infection. It didn't.

Toward the end of the First World War, a new concept was introduced. Instead of trying to sterilize the wound with caustic chemicals, they would remove all dead and devitalized tissue from the wound, no matter how extensive, in the hope that the remaining healthy tissue could fend for itself against infection. It is dead and devitalized tissue on which germs thrive.

This procedure was called debridement, which means, literally, housecleaning a wound. Snipping away everything that's dirty, devitalized, and foreign. The wound would then be left open and immobilized in a cast. Just let it smolder in there. The cast would become stained because of the discharge from the open wound and it might even ferment the juices and cause a nauseating odor. But, when you took the cast off, there was a nice healthy bed of tissue with the skin gradually growing in from the edges. However, it would take months to heal a large, deep wound and when healed, it would leave an adherent, deep scar.

It was late in the First World War when they first tried it but it wasn't until the Spanish Civil War (1936–39), the next European affair with mass casualties, that it got a real mass trial. A surgeon by the name of Trueta, a Spanish loyalist, was the first to do the procedure on a large scale. His results were so impressive that Dr. Trueta was awarded the orthopedic professorship at Oxford, breaking tradition by giving this prestigious post to a foreigner.

In World War II, we went a step further. We would do the debridement, but if five days later we found no infection, we'd sew up the wound. If there wasn't enough skin left, or the wound too large, we'd apply a skin graft. By doing this the wound would heal more rapidly and leave a much more acceptable scar.

Before the Normandy invasion, we'd get twelve to twenty casualties a day from the bombing missions and we could afford to spend an hour and a half on a debridement. Also, consider this: These were clean men in those airplanes; they had a shower that morning, clean clothes, and a warm breakfast; their wounds reached us within the "golden period" of six to eight hours. The infantrymen were a different story. Living in a foxhole, dirty, cold, and hungry. They might be in some fertilized field covered with a lot of manure loaded with bacteria. When we started getting three hundred a trainload from Normandy, and from the Battle of the Bulge, things were different. We didn't have that hour and a half to spend on a debridement. Now we had wounds that were four or five days old. When the invasion came we had penicillin, but antibiotics can't take the place of a good debridement. We would end up with about 1 percent infection on those soldiers, even with penicillin. We had no infections with the Air Force cases who had meticulous debridement and no penicillin. Methods may change, but basic principles are forever.

One Christmas came and went. Another Christmas came and went. You suddenly realize you have forgotten your own home telephone number. You forget exactly what your wife looks like. Her image has become fuzzy. You're in an entirely different world and you haven't got time for anything else. It was so consuming, so absorbing. I don't care how exciting your life was afterwards, after the war, you could never experience the sustained intensity again. You had ten or more lifetimes of professional experience. When I got back into civilian practice, I found that I couldn't talk to my civilian colleagues about the numbers and experiences that surgery entailed. Let me give you an example.

We used to have a saying, "Hitler's secret weapon is composed of three Bs: bicycles, blackouts, and British beer." The men from the air base would ride their bikes down to the local pubs and have a few beers, try to ride back in the blackout, and take a fall. A falling person instinctively puts his hand out to stop himself, landing on the outstretched arm. The type of fracture sustained depends on his or her age. The child breaks the weakest part, which is the growing bone at the bottom of the forearm. A young adult breaks the scaphoid, one of the key ballbearing bones in the wrist; an older adult sustains a Colles' fracture, a break in the spongy part of the bone. In an army you've got thousands of young adults who are all basically the same age group. Almost anybody who falls off a bicycle, or slips off the wing of a plane while he's loading bombs, is going to sustain a fracture of the scaphoid. A civilian orthopedist might see a dozen or two in a lifetime. In England, I had 310. I was once rushing through the x-ray department and something caught my eye. An x-ray film was hanging up to dry and it showed a fracture that had to be somebody at least forty years old. I said, "Who's the patient?" It turned out to be a middle-aged WAC. When I got back home and reported that I had

310 scaphoid fractures, I could see my nonveteran orthopedic colleagues smiling at each other as if I was inventing the numbers. I resolved, no more war stories. They must have sounded like fish stories to those men and women.

There were other things you had to get used to. The constant noise of planes in mass formations coming from and going to bomb Europe. We were located in East Anglia, which is that rounded southeastern bulge on the map of England. It was one huge, flat airfield and home for the Eighth Air Force and the RAF. We were flying daylight missions and the British were flying at night. They would start up the motors before dawn and leave in formation by eight, be over the target at noon and back at the base, if they were lucky, by four or five in the afternoon. By that time the RAF were forming for their night missions. You had the steady roar of planes overhead and it permeated your life. You'd have a stethoscope over a patient's heart and you heard those airplane engines in your ears. When you talked on the telephone you had to talk louder. You made a gradual adjustment to those things and when the war was over, the silence was so striking because you suddenly realized there was such a thing as quiet.

There were other things. You had no privacy. You could never shut a door and be alone. We lived six officers in one hut. You showered and ate with a hundred guys. There were no chairs so you sat on footlockers, benches, or a cot. Seeing a child was a shock. You hadn't seen a child or an old person in such a long time. All of those things would become important. My wife saved all my letters I sent home. I dug them out and read three or four of them before you came. You can sense somebody under an awful lot of tension. I frequently wrote, "I don't think I can take any more of this young torn flesh."

Those flyers used to say, "The flak was so thick you could walk on it." They saw some terrible things. One plane was hit and the men bailed out. Some of the parachutes were on fire and one fellow was screaming and tearing at his chest. They talked more to the psychiatrist, but some of them talked to me. There was one officer, he had been a college professor. A very intelligent man who went into the war on an intellectual basis. He wanted to fight the forces of evil. After a couple of those terrible experiences up there he said, "I can't fly anymore." He explained his emotional reaction to those horrors in a very articulate way. He had become a tormented man.

We had periodic air raids by the Luftwaffe and during one of those, a bomb hit our power plant. The whole place was suddenly dark. We had emergency lights in the operating room and I was in the middle of an operation. I put a dressing on the wound, a protective cast over that, and got an ambulance to take him to Oxford. I believe that there was a silent agreement between Germany and England that they wouldn't bomb Oxford or Heidelberg since they were both university towns and have very little strategic value. We knew we could send a patient to Oxford and be almost sure of his well-being.

Just when you thought you had reached your limit, something would happen to bring you back to the other side of life. Something happy, positive, and constructive. Among the casualties brought in was a young tank officer. He had had a brief romance with one of our nurses before they went overseas. After he was wounded in Normandy, he managed to have himself sent to our hospital because he knew she was there and they decided to get married. The Army was equal to that mission, too. They had a bridal gown, matron of honor, and maid of honor gowns sent up from London. Everything was white, even the post chapel was decked out in white flowers. There was music and happiness and it was wonderful after such a long period of destruction and depression. The first pleasant thing that had happened to us in so long. Such a contrast to the suffering around us.

I took care of so many of those youths that it's hard to remember too many specifics about each one, but two cases do come to mind. This young tail gunner on a B-17 was brought in. He had been shot through the thigh and the main artery had been severed and the limb was turning black. They flew those bombers at five-mile altitudes where the temperature was about 40 degrees below zero. These men were not only subject to wounds, but frostbite as well.

Almost all of the compound fractures were caused by either 20mm cannon shells or by flak. Chunks of metal of varying size from one-half to six inches. The missile not only shattered bone, it cut everything in its path. They would go through skin, muscle, tendons, nerves, veins, arteries; the entire cross section of a limb. That's what had happened to that gunner's leg, and I had to do an above-knee amputation, which is far more disabling than below the knee. He would have to wear a harness and there'd be a definite limp. I often think of the artificial arteries that can be transplanted today and often restore circulation. In our time, if the major artery was gone that leg couldn't survive and it would have to come off to save a life. If some of those fellows had been born one war later, we would have saved their legs with today's technology.

I found that amputees have to go through a severe emotional adjustment to the loss of part of their body. Everyone has his own way to get through it. Some fellows were brazen. One was going to take his pension money and open a bar on Third Avenue in New York City. It, he said, was the best thing that had happened to him. Very macho. This young gunner, however, wasn't taking it well at all. I don't think he'd ever been away from his mother's apron strings before the war. He looked so young he must have faked his age so he could get in the Air Force for the so-called glamour. Every time I came around to see him he was crying. I asked him, "What are you crying about, soldier?" He said, "My ambition in life was to go to college after this was over, become an accountant for the big mining company in town, and get married and have a family. What girl will have me now?" He needed a little build-up. We had a WAC working around the operating room who had a pretty good rapport with the boys. Cheerful kind of person with an open manner. I said to her, "Do you see that soldier over there crying? I want you to shave him every day." She came back and told me that he didn't shave yet. I said, "Never mind, shave him anyway. Keep talking to him." And do you know, within a few days that kid was smiling when I made my rounds. His stump healed well and we shipped him home.

Years later, I was back practicing in New York, when I got a call at the office. "Dr. Himelstein?" I told him I was. "Were you a doctor with the Air Force in England?" "Yes." "You wouldn't remember me, but you were my doctor. My name is Jim Baxter." I said, "Jim Baxter, I had over six thousand of you fellows." But then I remembered, "Hey, aren't you the kid from the mining town in Appalachia?" He told me that I had it right and that he was now in Atlantic City on his honeymoon. He wanted to come up and see me. I told him I'd be delighted and up he came, with his new bride, and my wife and I took them out to dinner. We had a nice time and ended up at the Astor Hotel. We had a number of drinks and when we were about ready to part, I said, "Now Jim, you have to tell me something. Frankly, what would prompt a man to interrupt his honeymoon and come up to see the doctor who chopped off his leg?" He looked at me and said, "Doctor, I never figured you chopped off my leg. I figured you saved my life." Secretly, I think he came back to thank me for that WAC. He'd gone to college, became an accountant, and was getting on quite well. He had made it.

The other fellow was a flyer who had gotten a piece of flak in the center of his knee. So much damage could have been done by that piece of rough metal, but this one had done hardly any. It was as if a trained surgeon had picked the safest route to get inside that knee. I told him, "You're the luckiest man I've operated on. That Nazi gunner must have gone to medical school to get that piece of flak in your knee so carefully from five miles away. You're going to make a full recovery and what's more, this is going to be your ticket home." Somewhere along the line I asked him where he lived. He named a town in New Jersey where my wife's brother lived and I said, "When you get back, will you call my family? Tell them you saw me in England and everything is all right." He said he'd be glad to.

Seventeen years later I was in that town and my brother-in-law had a party at the local country club. People were chatting, standing around in groups, and this fellow was looking at me. Pretty soon he came over and said, "Don't I know you from somewhere?" I told him that I was having the same feeling. After a few minutes it suddenly dawned on me that this was that town in New Jersey and this must be that fellow who had the flak in his knee. "Pull up your trouser leg; I think I've got my trademark on you." He pulled it up and there it was, the scar. I said, "How's your knee?" With that, he did a deep knee bend and walked around me. Said he never had any trouble with it, and that made me feel pretty good.

When the European war ended, the unit breakup came. It was rather sad because we'd become a very close family of over two hundred people. Some of us were sent here and some were sent there. I was ordered to the army of occupation in Bavaria. We went from having an incredible amount of work to idleness. From twenty-two operations a day to an occasional sprained ankle from a baseball game or a jeep accident. I now had time to travel, which was exciting. It is a beautiful country and we were in the foothills of the Alps. I was also able to visit the concentration camp near Munich, Dachau. I got in there quite early after the liberation and it was a sight that made you a different man when you came out. I used to say that when you are a young doctor, there are a couple of experiences that you go through that make you a different person. Assisting a birth for the first time. It is one of the most amazing experiences to see a new life launched. It gives you a whole new perspective. The other is your first autopsy. When somebody you saw a day or two before alive on the wards is now cold meat on a slab. You see all the giblets that remain. You knew all of this from your textbooks and dissection classes, but this was different. That visit to Dachau was another one of those experiences for me. One of the cadaverous survivors acted as our guide and took us through the place. We saw the ovens with the human ashes and bones still in them, the killing grounds with blood still on the earth, and we also stepped into the vast gas chambers with the fake shower heads still present on the walls. You could see dirty footprints on the walls almost to the top of the 12-foot ceilings in the rooms where they stacked up the corpses waiting to be cremated. There was a room of victims' clothing. It was a shattering experience. You had heard about it, but when you saw it, that was different. The mute evidence that shrieked at you and now, 40 year later, there are those who would deny the fact that this ever occurred.

I also got to Hitler's "Eagle's Nest" in Berchtesgaden. He lived with his cronies above the clouds and it was there he was supposed to have gotten all his inspirations. It was way up on the top of a mountain and I expected to have at least an interesting view. All I saw looking down were clouds, because it was above the cloud line. Martin Borman's house was next door with the nameplate still in place. What impressed me about Hitler's house was the fact that there was a movie projector behind the wall in every room. Evidently he liked movies. It was an experience that I would also remember, but the Dachau visit, nothing will ever equal that.

I spent about six months in Germany and then came home and was demobilized. You felt like a stranger to your family. Four years is a long time to be away and you had to get reacquainted. It took a while getting back into civilian habits and practice. My practice actually came back much quicker than I thought it would after a four-year absence. I resumed my teaching post at New York Medical College, clinical professor of orthopedic surgery and chief of fracture service at Metropolitan Hospital.

When I think of all the great advances that took place during my professional life span, I realize and appreciate the good fortune to have lived and worked on the threshold of the future. The amazing things being done today with total joint replacement. The actual replacement of worn-out parts in the body. New concepts in healing fractures that we couldn't even imagine. And I think it's only the beginning. New miracles we haven't dreamed of will come from research. As far as my career goes now, I retired from surgery at age seventy-five, but kept up my consulting practice in the office. I hope to be able to continue as long as my health permits.

I made a sentimental journey back to England a few years ago. I wanted to take my wife and show her where all that intense hospital activity took place. We got a driver in London and drove up 100 miles to Norwich. A little dirt road seemed familiar near the little town of Wymondham, but we couldn't find any trace of the hospital. We tried a couple of other side roads, but no luck. There was a minister walking along the road so we stopped and I asked him if he remembered an American army hospital that was located in that vicinity during the war. He said, "I've heard of it. I think it's over where that college is now." We had been criss-crossing that college campus for awhile and I think by that time the driver thought I was some crazy Yank looking for something that never existed. We decided to try one more time and drove onto the campus again. After going for another tour of the school we were just about to give up and then, there it was!

They had saved one building. It was just a weather-beaten wooden shack with a faded caduceus, the medical insignia, and the words, "U.S. Army Laboratory" on it, but I don't think any archaeologist was more jubilant over a historic find as I was that afternoon. Our laboratory building preserved in the midst of that college campus.

You should have seen that driver. He was more excited than I was.

It was a warm, sunlit day and the students were strolling about the campus, others sitting on the grass in small groups. The scene radiated a mood of peace and serenity. These young men and women building their futures were not yet born when those turbulent events took place on that site. World War II is something in a history book to them. I wondered if they ever gave any thought to that unobtrusive, weatherbeaten relic in their midst.

What if, like the Ancient Mariner, I gathered them around me and told them of those teeming events; the bleeding and suffering of people of their own age; the frenzied activity; the supercharged atmosphere with the constant drone of war planes overhead? All of which might have been necessary to make possible their present peace and security.

I left England after that visit, feeling that my own mission was now completed.

BEATRICE HAYDU

YANKEE DOODLE GALS

*When we visited Bee at her home, a pleasant Cape Cod in rural New
Jersey, there was a "for sale" sign in the front yard. She has since moved
to Florida, where she and her husband Joe flew an immaculately restored
World War II Stearman trainer until recently. Now they are in the process
of restoring a BT-13.*

*There is something very youthful and vivacious about her. She still
displays the same qualities that helped her win the Silver Wings of a
WASP over forty years ago. In those days a WASP was not a "White
Anglo-Saxon Protestant" of current usage but a "Women's Army Service
Pilot," in the abbreviated style of WACS and WAVES. They served at
army pay as training, ferry, and utility pilots, saving men for combat
duty, but timid government did not award them status as veterans until
1977, after a long political battle.*

Our war ended December 20, 1944. We had heard the rumors, starting in September or October, that they were going to discontinue the
WASPs [Women's Army Service Pilots]. We were told, initially, not to
do anything. Everything was under control and we shouldn't worry.
General Arnold and Jacqueline Cochran were going before the Congress, and we would be militarized. We would be part of the Army
Air Force. Sometime in November we got an official notification that
we were going to be disbanded. They started calling us the "million-
dollar glamour girls." The CPT pilots said we were taking away their
jobs. They were the civilian instructors who were working for the
Civilian Pilots Training Program. The government was winding
down the flight training programs because they didn't have the des-

perate need for pilots anymore. What they needed was men in the infantry. The CPT pilots didn't care about us until they saw themselves in the walking army. General Arnold tried to explain that we weren't taking jobs away from anybody, that we were doing an important job, but by then it had become a very hot political issue and he was fighting a losing battle.

All of the commanding officers were told to take photographs of the women stationed at their base. They took our picture in front of a B-25 and that was that. When I got the notice that we were being disbanded, I sent letters to aircraft manufacturers, airports, airlines; anyone I could think of to try and get a job in aviation. I never saw "no" written in so many different ways.

I left Pecos and went out to California because I decided that the movie studios might be interested in doing a movie about the WASPs. I rang some bells and tried to convince people that it would make a good story. They all thought it was a great idea if I would sit down and write it. I told them, "I'm no writer." They said, "Oh, yes you are. You just sit down and try." I started a story, but just as I told them I found out I wasn't a writer. My funds started to run low and I realized that the only job in aviation open to women was going to be flight instruction. I flew back to New Jersey and started to work on my flight instructor's rating.

★

We were Depression kids. I grew up in Montclair, New Jersey. My father owned a couple of taxicabs and there wasn't enough money to send two kids to college, so my brother went to school and I ended up as a private secretary at a zipper company in Newark. I enjoyed the work, but I also spent a lot of time feeling unhappy because I couldn't go to college. Then I said, "Stop feeling sorry for yourself and do something about it." I decided I would go to night school at Newark Academy and take aviation courses. Aviation looked like it was an up-and-coming thing. I was working at the zipper company during the day and took ground-school courses at night. Navigation, meteorology, theory of flight, power plant, all of that. There were a few other women in the class and we decided to take flying lessons together.

Our instructor at Newark Academy, Charlie Groeder, had a flight school that was located at Martins Creek, Pennsylvania. He used to have an airport in Paterson, but in World War II the defense line was drawn through New Jersey, and no private flying was allowed in the entire state. Martins Creek was just across the Delaware River. He had rented a farmer's field, that's what the airport really was. We would find someone with a car and all chip in for gas. One of

Beatrice "Bee" Haydu, shown during training as a WASP pilot, was one of the women aviators who delivered fighters and bombers during the war. Among those responsible for the WASPs receiving veterans' status, Bee (a friend said she flew like a bumble bee) donated her wartime uniform to the National Air and Space Museum in Washington, D.C.

the fellows who used to drive us up there was stopped for speeding. The state trooper came up to the car and kind of smirked. "Let me see your pilot's license." So he pulled out his pilot's license and got away with a warning instead of a ticket.

The field was full of stones. Charlie had rigged a platform with wheels and would attach it to the back of his car. He would drive the car and we would follow it around picking up the stones and putting them on the platform. We were his airport slaves. He had four Taylorcraft airplanes and there were always more people who wanted to fly than planes. If the weather was bad and we couldn't fly, he'd always find something for us to do. He was building a hangar, and I can still remember carrying the cement blocks up the ladder. That hangar is still there, but today it's a skating rink.

Going out there for a weekend was like a camping trip. Charlie rented a house and we would go out Friday night and stay over for the whole weekend. We all put in money for food and one of the instructors' wives would do the cooking. We'd go swimming in the Delaware River or take a ride into town on Saturday night. It was lots of fun. Most of the students were women because the men had all been drafted. There were some older men flying and the young man that we used to ride out with was 4-F. We, the women, all wanted to get into the WASPs because we had heard that they were thinking of using women pilots in some kind of military capacity. Women were being used as ferry pilots in England, and Jacqueline Cochran had taken some American women to fly with their British counterparts. She was pushing for the same thing in this country. We all wrote to her in Washington and found out that they were going to be interviewing in our area for the WASPs. You had to be an American citizen, a high-school graduate, and have a personal interview with Jacqueline Cochran or one of her staff. At one time the requirement was 200 hours, but they found that the fewer hours you had the better, because you hadn't developed a lot of bad habits. They started you out from scratch anyway, as if you didn't know anything.

I set up an appointment, and after having a personal interview and showing my log book, I was sent for a physical. It was the same physical that the men who were going into the Air Force had to pass. Twenty-five thousand women applied and twenty-five hundred were accepted for training. About 50 percent of the women who were accepted actually graduated. Out of our little group of six girls who flew together at the airport, who all went into the WASPs at the same time, three made it and three didn't.

There was no opposition from my parents. My mother was the type of person who would say, "I wish I could have done something like that. You are so lucky to have the opportunity." She always encouraged me in anything I wanted to do and my father was the same way. The only time my mother got a little upset was when she came down for my graduation. My sister and mother got there three days before the ceremony and I still had to finish up my night flying. I was out on the flight-line, getting into an AT-6, and my mother was watching with some of my friends. It suddenly dawned on her that her daughter was going solo into that very black sky. The next day she said to me, "Why didn't you call when you got back? I was worried all night about you." She didn't know what had been going on for the last seven months.

The six of us took the train down to Sweetwater, Texas, to begin our seven months of training. We had to pay our own way down. We also had to pay our own way home. The name of the airport was Avenger Field. It was originally a municipal field that had been converted to military use. The town of Sweetwater named it that because the pilots trained there would "avenge" Pearl Harbor. They gave us a salary and we paid room and board out of that. The whole program was set up as an experiment. We weren't military, but the government told us that if it worked out, we would be militarized. In fact, we all had to sign a paper that we were willing to go into the military if it worked. A few of the women didn't want it, but the vast majority did. It was very rigid. We were taught military discipline. You lined up to go to mess and classes. When your instructor came into the classroom, you stood at attention. We were in a very awkward situation; we couldn't get military insurance because we weren't part of the Army. Yet nobody else would give us insurance because we were flying military airplanes. We ended up flying without insurance, and thirty-eight WASPs were killed during the two years we were in existence.

When we got to Sweetwater, the weather had been very bad and the previous class had to make up its flying time. We were supposed to go to ground school half a day and fly half a day. Since we couldn't fly—the other class was using the planes—we had half a day on our hands for awhile. I got together with some of the girls and said, "Let's put on a show for the base about our first impressions of what Army life is all about." One girl could write, another could sing; we came from all walks of life. There were debutantes, doctors, athletes, aviators. You name it, we had it. Julie Jenner was an actress who was in another class and she helped us put the show on. We called it the "Eager Beaver Show" and I was the MC. It was such a success at our base that they had us do it at a nearby men's field. I hope I never have to walk into a room again where the audience is all men and already sitting down. We had to walk down the aisle because there was no way to get through from the back of the stage. You should have heard the hollering and whistling. They said the show was so good that they wanted us to take it on the road. We had the choice of taking the show around the country or going through the WASP program. We came there to fly, not to be showgirls. That was the end of the "Eager Beavers."

We started flying Stearmans and the instructors were, for the most part, good. I have the feeling that they were almost hand-picked. None of the men whom I knew had a bad attitude toward us and I think if they had, they would have been fired. If you felt that you had a personality clash with your instructor, you could ask for another. We were told when we started that it wouldn't be held against us. A lot of the girls wouldn't do that. They were afraid, proud, or something like that, and ended up washing out. You were not allowed to fraternize with the instructors because they didn't want anybody passing his girlfriend. If you were caught going out with an instructor, you were washed out. The only instructor we spent any time with was married. We had Sundays off and there was no place to go in Sweetwater. Our primary instructor and his wife would say, "Come on over to our house." All you wanted to do was sit in someone's living room and visit. The training was rigid and the pressure was incredible because you knew that at least 50 percent of your class was going to wash out. Let's face it, we weren't all lily white, but you weren't going to throw away this chance on a romantic fling.

The problem wasn't that all of the women couldn't learn how to fly. Well, anybody can learn to fly, but the WASP program didn't want the ones who would take a little bit longer to get the hang of it. If you didn't solo in a certain number of hours, you were washed out. If you couldn't do your spot landings, same thing. We took a civilian flight check and an Army flight check at the end of every phase of our training. We had to pass both of them.

We did all of our flight training at Sweetwater. We didn't move from base to base for primary, basic, and advanced like the men did. We had four auxiliary fields to keep the traffic from getting too heavy at Avenger Field. With all those people practicing takeoffs and landings, you couldn't possibly use one airport. We used to drive out to those auxiliary fields in the "cattle car." They put wooden benches in the back of this old truck and we'd go bumping out to the flight line in that contraption.

After the Stearman we went directly to the AT-6. Normally, the cadets would go from Stearmans to BT-13s and then the AT-6. The military wanted to see if they could eliminate that middle step and they tested it out on us. I don't know if we were the first class that worked that way, but we were among the first. That was a big jump because the AT-6 was a lot more airplane.

Washing out was crushing and you were always aware of it. I was on a solo cross-country flight, and as I was coming in to land I noticed fire coming out of the right exhaust stack. It's funny the things that go through your mind at a time like that. "Should I jump? Should I try to land this thing? What should I do? If I jump, I'll have to fill out all sorts of forms and I'll have to go through a check ride. Maybe they'll wash me out. I think I'll stick with it a little bit longer." I wanted to graduate no matter what. I called ahead and told the tower that I was going to make an emergency landing and got down without a problem.

When somebody washed out, she would be gone the next day. They didn't want it to affect the morale of the girls who remained. You would have a bay, our room, of eight girls, now suddenly, there's six left. Then there would be four. They used to start moving us into rooms together so we wouldn't be looking at those empty beds. Training was rough and you really got tired. Reveille was at six o'clock in the morning and after five hours of ground school and four hours on the flight line, you just wanted to get into bed.

Jacqueline Cochran was the director of women pilots and her headquarters were located in Washington. She was a very aggressive woman and I admire her for it. If it hadn't been for her, I wouldn't have had that great experience. Leoti Deaton actually ran the base. Dedie had worked with the Red Cross before she joined the WASPs. She was a strict but very fair woman. Every once in awhile Jacqueline would fly in for an inspection. One time she was walking down the flight line and stopped in front of me. You were supposed to have short hair, but if you had pigtails it was okay. She called Dedie over and said, "She's got long hair." Mrs. Deaton smiled and said, "Yes, but she has it in pigtails." That was that.

Jacqueline Cochran came from very meager beginnings. She used to tell us that she didn't have to say how old she was because she really didn't know. I think Jacqueline got a job in a beauty shop when she was a teenager and by the time she was in her twenties was working at Saks Fifth Avenue. She used to do Floyd Odlum's wife's hair and that's how they got to know each other. She later married him. Jacqueline was very attractive. It was Floyd who suggested that she take flying lessons.

We had a WASP meeting in Cleveland in the 1960s and Jacqueline asked if anyone wanted a ride to New York in her Lockheed Lodestar. Two of us went with her. After we'd been in the air for awhile she turned to me and asked, "Do you still fly?" I said, "Yes."

She looked at the copilot, who was a man, "You, out!" She was always very forthright in whatever she did. I got in the copilot's seat and she gave me the controls. I guess she liked what I was doing because I stayed in the seat for quite awhile. At one point Jacqueline turned to the other girl. "Are you flying?" She said, "No," and started apologizing. Jacqueline just looked at her and said, "Then you don't fly now." Oh, she used to bawl us out. "You women aren't doing things. You should be out there setting all kinds of flying records. Look at me, I've flown jets." She'd go on about this and that. Well, she had a husband that could pay for all of that. A lot of us couldn't afford to fly a jet. But she was definitely pushing women to make names for themselves. I think Jacqueline thought that everybody could accomplish what she did if they pushed themselves.

I graduated in September of 1944 and was sent to Pecos Air Force Base, Pecos, Texas. I was doing, among other things, engineering flight testing. If a student wrote up an airplane, said that it was flying with a wing low or the engine was running rough, I'd take it up and see if it was the airplane or the student. After an engine had been overhauled, the plane had to be flown at a prescribed speed, slow time, for several hours to break in the engine and I'd do that. I also flew as a utility pilot. If somebody had to go someplace, I would take them. One time I was gone for three weeks flying a ground school instructor to different states so he could inspect their operation. If you mention today that you were a WASP, the first thing people say is "Oh, you ferried airplanes to Europe." A couple of newspapers did articles about me and I'd pick up the paper the next day and it would say, "She ferried aircraft over to England." We were not allowed out of this country. Nancy Love and Betty Gillies got as far as Goose Bay, Labrador, in a B-17, but General Arnold found out about it and ordered them to come back. They didn't want us in combat areas. They only wanted us in the States to relieve male pilots for active duty.

Women were also towing targets for training gunners and that was dangerous duty. Col. Bruce Arnold, General Arnold's son, was stationed at Camp Davis, North Carolina, which was one of the largest antiaircraft artillery training bases. He said the two target planes would fly along the beach. First the small guns would fire at the target, then the larger ones, and finally the really big ones. There was a fellow who sat in the back seat of the plane who would reel the target sleeve out and bring it back in when they were finished. One of the girls said that this one fellow bent down to do something and a bullet went through the airplane, right where he would have been sitting. Another WASP was killed because a bullet lodged in her engine and, as she was coming in for a landing, the engine quit. Another girl told me that she dated the captain who was in charge of all those gunners. She wanted to make sure she wasn't going to get shot up because he would say, "Hey, guys, take it easy with my girlfriend."

After the WASPs were disbanded I started freelance instructing. I was living in East Orange with my parents and working at airports that were close to my home. This was 1945 and it was getting pretty close to the end of the war. The government had started the G.I. Bill and one of the things veterans could do was take flight training. A lot of men who hadn't flown during the war were coming out and taking lessons. Quite a few of the men who did fly in the war didn't want to ever see another airplane.

The flying schools had been unable to buy airplanes during the war because everything was going to the military. Now private planes were being manufactured again and the factories wanted professional pilots to deliver them. It looked like more fun than instructing so I decided to start a ferrying service. I had a long list of pilots who had come back from the service and wanted to do flying to build up time. This was not a long-term operation because I figured it would only last about a year. By that time the manufacturers would make other arrangements. I figured out my costs and how much I had to charge, checked out the pilots to make sure they could fly, and I was in business. We'd pick up Cessnas in Kansas City and Aeroncas in Ohio. I used to get bored always flying the same routes so I'd trim the plane and knit socks. They weren't too big and I could grab the stick if I had to. I think Jacqueline Cochran told me she used to do the same thing, knit or do embroidery when she was flying long trips.

While I was ferrying the Cessnas, I met the distributor, who was located on Long Island. He said to me, "Why don't you take a Cessna dealership?" I was going into all of those airports anyway, and if you could sell twenty airplanes in one fiscal year, you would come out with a pretty good chunk of money. I'd fly in and demonstrate the airplane, just like you'd sell a car. Show them all the features. While I was flying from airport to airport trying to sell airplanes I found out that the operation at Woodbridge Airport in New Jersey was for sale. A group was getting together to buy it and they asked me if I would like to get in on it. There were eight men who were veterans and myself. My financial contribution to the group would be the airplane so I didn't actually have to lay out the money. It was a Cessna 140. What a wing span that thing had! You'd be landing and just float and float and float.

I started instructing again and really enjoyed it. You met all kinds when you were instructing. If somebody came out and didn't want to fly with a woman, we'd just give him a male instructor. I'd just say, "That's up to you." I remember my first student. He was the easiest guy to teach because he was a bulldozer operator. They have great coordination. The women who were taking lessons kind of identified with me. I had done it.

We were successful and having a lot of fun until the Garden State Parkway came along. We looked out one day and saw a bulldozer at the end of the runway. We went out and asked him, "What are you doing?" He said, "We're putting in the Garden State Parkway." Back in those days they didn't have to give you any notice. They took part of our runway and the CAA said, "You're closed." The runway wasn't long enough for safe operations so we moved to Hadley Airport.

I decided that I didn't want to spend the rest of my life working at an airport. All of my friends were out having fun, doing things on Saturdays and Sundays. I was getting up at six o'clock on Saturday mornings because I had an early student, flying until it was dark and then pushing planes into the hangar. I found a job with the Indamer Company in New York. They used to sell airplanes and aircraft parts to India. They were also a Beechcraft dealer. The job was still in aviation and my boss had a Beechcraft that he let me fly whenever I wanted to. I think he was very happy to find somebody who knew something about aviation. I left Indamer in December 1950 to get married and have a family.

In about 1964 my husband Joe and I were taking the children to Washington, and I couldn't wait to get them into the Air and Space Museum and show them what their old mother used to do in those years. The museum was in a Quonset hut at that time. I went in there expecting walls of photographs and there wasn't one word about the WASPs. I was mad and Joe said, "Well, quit being mad and do something about it." I wrote to Paul Garber, the curator of the museum. I told him I'd been down to Washington and there wasn't anything about the WASPs. He wrote back and said, "You're right." He asked me if I had anything that I would like to donate to the museum. I wrote back and asked him if he'd like my uniform. They set up a little ceremony and I donated my uniform and they put it into mothballs. In fact, they managed to lose the hat. It was six or seven years later when they finally put it on display.

The WASPs were a close-knit group for about six years after the war. Then, somewhere along the line, people lost touch with each other. They were busy with families, careers, what have you. One or two of the women tried to get us declared official World War II veterans, but it never worked out. We had our thirtieth reunion at Sweetwater in 1972. There wasn't too much left at the field. Some of the buildings had been torn down and the plaque that General Arnold had presented to us had been stolen. It was originally at the bottom of the wishing well. We'd throw a coin in there when we had to take a check ride. When we passed, our classmates would throw us in.

Bruce Arnold came to that reunion, and he likes to say, "I had two martinis too many and promised to help." He is a retired Air Force colonel and works as an aircraft manufacturer's representative in Washington, D.C. Bruce more than lived up to his word. I became the president of the Order of Fifinella* (the name of the WASP organization) and held that for three-and-a-half years. What really irritated us was when the Air Force started saying that the women who were graduating from flight school at that time were the first women to fly military aircraft. What about us? What happened to the WASPs? We really sizzled. While I was president, I wrote to the graduate Air Force girls and sent them each a decal of Fifinella. A few of them wrote back and said they had kind of heard of us at some point.

Bruce Arnold thought he would put an amendment on a bill to make us veterans and that would be that. Well, it turned out that it wasn't quite that simple. The government said, "You are asking us to open a Pandora's box." If the WASPs are classified as veterans, groups like the Civil Air Patrol, Merchant Marines, Red Cross, correspondents, and the Auxiliary Military Police, to name just a few, will want it too. They had a whole list of groups and some of them were ridiculous. The WASPs had been started with the "intent and expectation to militarize," and our operations were under military circumstances. Let's face it, the Merchant Marines did face danger. However, they were well paid. They were not on a serviceman's salary, like we were. They didn't have to live on military bases like we did. We felt we were military.

There was some dissension in our organization because a few of the women wanted to hire a "smart lawyer." Others wanted to get the feminist movement involved. We felt anything like that would have made it difficult for us. It also went against my personal way of doing things. We decided to do it politically and stuck to it. Bruce Arnold was calling the shots. He had the knowledge of Washington ways, and he also knew the people, some of whom were Representatives Margaret Heckler and Lindy Boggs and Senator Goldwater. Barry Goldwater flew as a ferry pilot during the war and made a couple of trips with our women. He often tells of the time he flew formation on a trip with a WASP in a P-51.

I'd be back and forth between New Jersey and Washington. I kept after everybody through the newsletters and I convinced a large

*Ed. note: Fifinella was a cartoon character, a lady gremlin, designed for the WASPs by Walt Disney.

aircraft company to give me the use of their Watts line two evenings a week. I would telephone all over the country, tracking down the girls and trying to get their enthusiasm whipped up or documentary information we needed. Everybody in my family, very fortunately, was very busy doing their own things at that time so they didn't know half the time I spent on the WASPs. It became almost a full-time voluntary job.

Everything had to always be done immediately. Bruce would call and say, "You've got to get in touch with this senator, that congressman. Send night letters. Get everybody to write." I had it set up so that—theoretically—I would just make three phone calls and then each of those people would have a list of ten names they would call. They, in turn, would have ten names, and so forth. When the women would come to Washington, we'd ask them to come and see us at headquarters and we'd try to get them appointments with their congressmen or senators. If they didn't come to Washington, we'd have them write. It was that personal contact that did us a lot of good. That, plus the fact that we got out and got publicity. I have a box full of news clippings. I would also attend as many functions as I could. Groups like the P-47 Thunderbolt pilots. I went to their reunion and asked them to get on the bandwagon. They were fantastic. We got thousands and thousands of signatures from all over the country. Everybody was running around getting signatures and mailing them back to headquarters. We put them together and made this huge roll which we presented to Lindy Boggs on the Capitol steps the day of the House hearing, September 20, 1977.

Antonia Clayes, who was the assistant secretary with the Air Force, was also very helpful. She was concerned with the effect the defeat of our bill would have on the women who were already training with the Air Force. The Veterans Administration was against us, if you can believe that. All we needed were a few kind words and instead they were dead set against us. Again, "Pandora's box." We were fortunate that our friends outnumbered those who were against us, and the bill was passed by the Senate on November 4, 1977. President Carter signed the bill on November 23, 1977, and we had our honorable discharge and we are now considered veterans. We had won.

After this was all over, Joe got a letter in the mail. It was from a guy out west who was asking him to join an organization that was going to try and get the same benefits for the CPT instructors. They wanted him to send money and were going to get the same benefits those women got. It was just the way it was worded, *those* women. I asked Joe very sweetly, "Can I answer this letter for you?" I just wrote a couple of paragraphs and told him that "I happen to be married to one of 'those' women and everything they got was justified."

After the fight in Washington was over it was a bit of a letdown. When you've been working so hard for something and finally get it, you wonder what you're going to do with your time. One of the things that I've been doing is building up hours in our Stearman. It's fantastic flying, like we did in 1942. Open cockpit and goggles. Joe, being the born instructor he is, said, "I'll check you out." We flew around a few days and he finally said, "Okay, take it around the pattern." I took off and when I got on my downwind leg, the engine started running rough. I climbed up and came in high so I'd be sure and make the field, brought the power back and slipped it in. After I landed I turned off the runway and cut the engine. Joe came tramping up the field. It was a hot day and he was very annoyed. "Why the hell did you let it stall?" I said, "I didn't let it stall. It was running rough so I turned it off." He gets in and gets it going. It purred like a kitten. Now he's telling everybody, "Oh, after all these years she's got soloitis. Bee got scared and imagined the engine was running rough."

About three days later we were flying together to another airport and all of a sudden the engine started running rough. I said, "See, I told you so." It turned out that the engine is made for 80 octane fuel and we have 100 at our airport. It was running a little too rich and the plugs were fouling up. When we fly we lean the mixture out a little bit and it runs just fine. I was so happy when the engine started to act up. Men!

JOSIE THE RIVETER

Her kitchen is her pride and joy and Josie Rachiele immediately tries to feed anybody who stops by her Long Island home. The meatballs are delicious.

Then, there are the airplanes. A model P-47 Thunderbolt sits in the living room, two miniature F-84 Thunderjets adorn a dining room shelf, even the ceramic teapot is a fat little airplane. "I'd love to have a real P-47 in my backyard." Her scrapbooks contain newspaper articles, photographs, and newsletters about the airplanes Josie helped build for over forty-five years. Since our conversation she has retired.

I was scared to death when I first went to work for Republic Aviation. There were so many people and the buildings were so big. I used to get lost going to the ladies' room. Somebody would ask me what shop I was working in and I would be so confused that I would forget. I was so miserable that I would call up my father and say, "Pop, would you please pick me up? I don't feel good." He'd come and get me and my family couldn't understand why I was coming home during the day. But then I stopped doing that because I had to get used to working there. I was patriotic and wanted to do my duty for my country.

Working in the plant has made me a lot more worldly than when I went in there. I'm not worldly in today's sense, but I know I've changed. I'm happy that I'm able to do a lot of things that other women can't do. It's been interesting working in an airplane factory

Josie (Josephine) Rachiele put both heart and hand into her job as a riveter building P-47 Thunderbolt fighters at Republic Aviation on Long Island. Josie, center, is shown with her "Home Front Sisters," Sarah, left, who was a drill grinder, and Theresa, an executive secretary.

and I'm glad I stayed even though there have been problems every once in awhile.

My parents were born in Italy. They got married over there and then come to this country in 1921 and became naturalized citizens. My parents bought this piece of land in 1934 when there was nothing out here. Just a dirt road, no homes, nothing. It was pretty desolate.

My father was a carpenter and he built our house from the ground up. I went to West Babylon grammar school until the ninth grade and then my mother decided I should go to work because we were kind of poor. She worked at a coat factory in Lindenhurst and I went to work with her. I sewed buttons, trimmed threads, and hung a size tag on the button. We made summer coats in winter and winter coats in summer. When the war broke out, all garment factories had to make something to help the war effort. We were making Navy nurses' uniforms.

I was in the first war-bond drive we had at the coat factory. My boss asked me to go around with these cards for everybody to fill out. People could sign up for fifty cents or a dollar a week. We had all these older ladies sewing and they were complaining that the money was going in my pocket. Sadie was hollering; they were all hollering that they couldn't afford it. I said, "The money is not for me, you're helping your country." I signed up a lot of people.

Then my two sisters and I heard about them hiring at Republic Aviation. My older sister, Theresa, went to Republic training school in Bay Shore, New York, for sheet metal work. Terry didn't like that kind of work so she went into secretarial work and ended up on mahogany row working for Col. Tom Murphy, who was a vice-president. The girls who worked upstairs in the offices looked down their noses at the girls who worked in the shop. Occasionally, Terry would come down and eat lunch with me. Everybody would say, "Your sister from upstairs comes down and eats lunch with you?" I said, "She's my sister, what's the big deal?" Sarah, my younger sister, was seventeen years old when she was hired. She was a drill grinder, which meant she sharpened drills. Kids like Sarah, we called them kids, went home after eight hours. Everybody else worked ten hours a day, and three Saturdays in a row. We worked eight hours on Saturday and it was a big joke that we only worked half a day. Sarah didn't like shop work either and she eventually went to production control and did paperwork. They called us the "Home Front Sisters." Sarah stayed until 1954 and Theresa quit a few years later.

I applied for a mail-girl job but they didn't have any openings so I became a riveter. I've been there ever since. I stayed at Republic because I picked up a talent working on all of those different airplanes and the money was good. I have been self-supporting most of my life.

"KEEP THEM FLYING"

My two sisters and I met our husbands at Republic, but I was only married for five years.

When I was working at the coat factory, I was getting paid $10 a week. I started at Republic making sixty cents an hour. With all the overtime it came out to about $31 a week. We also got an incentive bonus. I had my own lunch box and a tool box. They gave us a list of ten different tools we would need. A hammer, screw driver, chisel, I forget what else. We had to buy them ourselves and I still have my original tool box, someplace, that cost $1.98 in 1943.

It was a drastic change to go from the feminine atmosphere in the coat factory to the masculine conditions in the shop. I didn't have to go to school because when they hired me they needed people so bad they wanted us to start working immediately. The first day I started, they took me right out on the floor. The foreman showed me what had to be done and then he took me to meet the girl who was going to teach me how to do the work. Her name was Annie Sweetman and she had been working there for awhile. I found it kind of difficult at first holding on to a drill motor. Somebody would tell me to take a rivet out. The head of the rivet is round and it's got a hole in the middle where you put the drill. I would be skidding all over the place because I just couldn't drill straight. I would come home and tell my mother that I drilled my finger or somebody caught their hair in a drill motor and she'd say, "Oh, please, quit that job. You're giving me heart trouble." It took a while, but I caught on to that type of work.

I also had a terrible time learning how to buck rivets. You started out holding the bucking bar, which is a piece of metal, against the skin of the airplane and your partner is shooting the rivets from the other side. Annie would shoot the gun and my bar would go all over the place. She was a very nice girl and very patient with me. There were times when I had a job all by myself. I would put the rivets in the holes; we called it loading up the job, and then I would take the piece to another woman who was operating the riveting machine. That's a big C-shaped machine that you put the piece in and then you use a foot pedal to squash the rivet. At that time we were using rubber cement to hold the rivets in position. Today we use masking tape. It's a lot different today in a lot of ways than it was during wartime. I'm now classified as a structural assembler. That's a lot different from when I first started as "Josie the Riveter."

Eventually I graduated to speed riveting. There were a lot of silent competitions between the girls. We would see how fast we could go down a line of rivets on those big skins. That way you could also make production. It was fun shooting all those rivets as fast as you could, but you should have heard all the noise! My ears ring all the time and I lost some of my hearing from it. I think we all got deaf.

They didn't have ear protectors then. Now if you work in an area where there's noise and you don't have ear protectors on, your department gets a demerit. It's too late for me, though.

I'm going to be retiring soon and the boys are all saying, "Josie, when are you leaving? I want your badge number." I've got a low badge number because I've been there so long and I guess they think that's some kind of status. I didn't like the first badge they gave me in 1943 because the photograph was terrible. I said, "Oh, my God, is that me?" One of the girls told me to lose it and get a new one. If you lost your badge, you had to pay for a new one, fifty cents. It was worth it, and after the war, when we had to turn in our badges, I gave them the lousy one and kept the good one. That picture was kind of cute because I sometimes used to wear pigtails in those days.

We all used to have long hair and eventually they made all the women wear turbans or the caps with a snood in the back where you put your hair. They did that to keep your hair from getting caught in the machinery. A lot of the girls wore overalls, but even if you didn't, you had to wear slacks. After the war we eventually could change to pretty things but you still had to wear pants. We'd start wearing blouses with frills and bows. When we could take off the caps the women started to worry about their hair. We were able to doll up a little, bows in our hair, things like that.

We had to buy our own overalls and we could get them in the company store, which was in the tunnel under the plant. The tunnel was also used as an air raid shelter because there was always the fear we would be bombed. They had sighted a submarine off Long Island and we were scared that somebody would attack the plant. The building where I worked, Building Seventeen, was huge; overhead we had a tremendous amount of glass windows. The company had painted all of the windows black so there wouldn't be any light showing at night. I heard later, although I never saw it, that the top of the building was painted to look like a golf course. I would have liked to see that if it actually was up there.

We made P-47 Thunderbolts during the war. That's all we made, and we built over fifteen thousand of them. It was so crowded in the plant because there were over twenty-five thousand people working there then. I think I got along better with people who worked there during the war because we were all fighting for the same thing. A lot of the women had relatives and husbands in the war. The shop was well organized and I liked the factory better then. We had a big sign at the end of final assembly, "Keep the Line Rolling," and the assembly lines were on each side of a wide aisle we called Broadway. It's still called that to this day. We were making fifteen airplanes a day. Of course, they weren't as complicated as the ones we make now. They used to have all those long lines working, all those P-47s, all lined up nice and neat. God, it was beautiful. We were so proud when those airplanes rolled out the door. We'd see them going out to the runway and flying off to the war.

Security was good during the war. We had all kinds of posters around the plant. "A Slip of the Lip Will Sink a Ship," "Button Up Your Lip," and, of course, you had to open up your lunch box when you left. They would check it carefully. They would tell us that production was important, but we didn't need to be told. We would push ourselves. We knew there was going to be an extra check at the end of the month, the bonus, but we were more into the war effort than the money. People were really dedicated then. The plant is a whole lot different place to work at today. The kids like the pay a lot more than they like working. There's hardly anyone left who can remember anything about the war years. I think I'm one of the few. My friend, John Roedel, put a little sign on my tool box one day. It said, "Grandmother of Aviation." Once in a while one of the kids will ask me how it was during the war. They wonder if I miss the place like it was a long, long time ago. It doesn't seem that long to me and I would rather work in those conditions than what we have today. Of course we were young and gay, and I didn't get tired as easily then.

Tommy Dorsey made an appearance during wartime and the girls were all excited. They took a picture, and I was able to climb up on the wing of a Thunderbolt with my sister Suzie. He was down below with his arms around two girls and one was my sister Terry. The company would bring in Joe Varvaro's band and have them play some music during lunch hour. That was for morale. The main buildings were separated by a set of railroad tracks. There was a small drawbridge which connected the buildings. Somebody would bring in a victrola and records and we would dance between the buildings. All of the forties music. "Don't sit under the apple tree with anyone else but me" was one song I remember.

There were occasions when the girls would decide to go to New York City and we would bring our clothes to work in a suitcase with the dress hanging in a bag. We'd get dressed, take the train to New York and have dinner at the Brass Rail or maybe Jack Dempsey's, then do something like go see a show at the Paramount. It was really nice and we did that quite often. We'd tour the city and I've got pictures of my two sisters and myself on top of the Empire State Building and at Coney Island. I often wonder what happened to all those young women I worked with during the war.

We had a foreman at one time who would say, "You can take ten of my men and give me four women." I think the women were, and still are, dedicated to doing a good job. A lot of the men want to fool around. You see these guys today, hollering and yelling around the shop. That's all you hear some days, a bunch of commotion. The jobs don't get done when that's going on. I even take part in it once in awhile. You hear somebody yelling and I bend over my bench and start yelling, too. I like to have a little fun with the kids and they're nicer to you when you join them and act crazy once in a while.

I was working a few years back on some longerons, which are very long parts of the airplane's fuselage. It is a major assembly and the drilled holes have to be very straight. Before I went on vacation, I explained the job to this man who was going to work on it while I was gone. I told him that there were holes underneath these three clips and they were the only ones to be drilled. I even marked the job up for him. When I came back from vacation, he had a big hole in the wrong place and he wanted me to plug it up. No way I am going to plug a big hole. He wanted me to do it without the boss knowing, and I can't hang myself for him. You have to get an inspector to check something like that and then the engineers will figure out if you can do it. They did plug it up eventually, but I wanted to be sure. You read all about these plane crashes, especially the ones with cracks, and rivets missing, and I don't want to fool around with stuff like that. People's lives are at stake in those airplanes. I'm very conscientious about what I do. I try not to make mistakes, but you can't always be perfect, and when I do make a mistake, I break out in a sweat. My boss says to me, "What's the matter, Jo?" I tell him, "I made a boo boo." I guess I'm a worrywart and I want that airplane part, when it goes away from me, to be perfect and that's that.

My sisters and I used to write to our G.I. friends when they went overseas. Almost every night we wrote to our buddies. Some were from the neighborhood and they would give our names to other soldier friends and we'd write to them too. We used to send them things we baked, like cookies, and cheese and crackers, all kinds of candy, and writing paper and pens. Anything that we thought they might like. Two of our friends never came back. One of them, Frankie Columbo, was killed in one of the invasions in Europe and I still have my letter that was returned to me marked "deceased."

Another friend went out to Yaphank, out east on the Island, on maneuvers and he brought me back a piece of a P-47. He said, "Here's one of your Thunderbolts." The pilot had nose dived into the ground and was killed. The rivets were broken and the piece was all bent. It still had mud on it and I saved that piece of airplane for years in a shoebox and then somebody in my family threw it out. They probably thought it was just a piece of junk. I don't know what I was going to do with it, but it was a memento from those years. My sisters can't understand why I have airplanes all over the house. I've got two photographs signed by the designer of the P-47, Alexander Kartveli. I saw him once in the plant, but I never met him personally. I wanted to buy a model of the T-46. That's the trainer plane they're working on now. Seeing that we work in the plant, you'd think they would sell it to us for a little discount. No, they want $60 for a little model plane.

We had a lot of layoffs, years back, usually at Christmas time. I was laid off in 1964 and went back in 1965. When I was laid off the last time in 1972, I went to work for Grumman, and they were excellent employers. I was only there about three months and they called me into the office. They had this big yellow paper with these things written down about me. "You're cooperative, you pay attention, you're courteous, and the work you do is excellent." I was thrilled. I went back to Republic when I was recalled in 1974 because I had my seniority and pension plan there. Before I left Grumman, I was there two months, they called all of us Republic women into the office and tried to get us to stay. They said that production went up and the quality of the work was better. That was good news and made us feel good, but I couldn't lose that seniority.

Then we got back to Republic and they were telling us we're doing everything wrong. I'm not back two months and they're telling us we start too late, quit too early, and we're not doing enough work. Every morning they are giving us a sermon on how bad we were. At Grumman they were just the opposite and I didn't do as much work as I did at Republic. I can't believe this place. It's Fairchild, not Republic. We old-timers agree that it was a different place to work in when it was run by Republic Aviation.

Oh, we had so many nice things. The bowling league, the chorus. We had a personnel recreation director, Oscar Frowein, and he was always coming up with all sorts of things. We had Christmas shows that were just like Broadway shows. I was in three of them and they were wonderful. At one time they had the Turkey Caravan come around the shops. It was a truck fixed up to look like a turkey and they'd stop in every department. If they picked your badge number, you won a turkey. There was also a Miss Republic contest for two or three years. I wasn't in them, I was in the audience. The girls looked so lovely in their gowns.

When the war ended in Japan, one of the executives came down to the shop. He stood on a bench and announced, "The war is over." Just like that and it was over. We were all yelling and crying and what a ruckus there was. I was crying.

I've worked on the P-47, the F-84, the F-105, the A-10, and I did some work on the C-5, the big cargo planes. I've made hundreds and hundreds of parts and I can't remember all their names. I made the dorsal fin on the F-84. Right now I work on the SF-340, which is the Saab Fairchild commercial plane. I've made all sorts of parts for that airplane and what I sometimes do now takes a lot of time and a little knack. They call the parts "fuel tank access doors," and they have to be covered with aluminum foil. They're made out of fiberglass and the aluminum has adhesive on the back. You lay it on the part and then I use a nylon piece to take out all the bubbles and wrinkles. It has to be perfectly smooth. Then I trim it with an exacto knife, make it nice and neat. Then the surface has to be abraded. That takes the shine off. I'm making hundreds of them because they use twenty per ship. It's an interesting job because you have to have a special touch and it's nicer than drilling holes.

We use a lot of different fixtures. They hold the job secure while you're working on it. There have been jobs over the years where I had to sit on the floor, lay down on the floor or go right underneath and stick my head up in the job. That's where you really lost your hearing, riveting inside the job. Once in a while I would put the cardboard down on the floor and lay down and everybody used to say, "Josie, are you taking a nap?"

We had midgets working at Republic during wartime. Maybe half a dozen of them. They used to work in a fuselage or any area where people my size couldn't get in. They were very handy and it was so funny to see them walking down the aisle in the plant, these little guys trying to keep up with everybody when thousands of people were walking along with them.

I heard about the P-47 Alumni Association from my friend Danny Pflug, who used to work at Republic. He has been involved with restoring the airplanes that they have at the Cradle of Aviation Museum in Farmingdale. They have quite a few planes there, including the ones that Republic and Grumman built on Long Island. When they first started the association, it was only for people who were associated in some manner with the P-47. Pilots, mechanics, crew chiefs, and whatever. Now, I think if you're really interested in the Thunderbolt you can become a member. They put out a very nice newsletter with all sorts of information about the airplane and the people who care about it.

I said to Danny, "Gee, I'd like to belong. Do you have any women members?" He said, "No, the only women who come to the meetings are some of the wives and they make the refreshments." I joined in 1982 and I really enjoyed being with the people I worked with and other members. Sometimes they have speakers at the meetings and they're very interesting. I heard Herb Fisher [see beginning of this chapter], who was a famous test pilot, and he was wonderful. When I retire, I would like to help them restore some of those airplanes. I know how to drill a hole and I know how to rivet. They have people who stand up at the meetings and tell how they were involved with the P-47. I could never get up because I don't know what I would say except I made small parts, put holes in them, and riveted them. Eventually, I'll speak up, I guess. I did my job to the best of my ability and am proud to have been one of the thousands of "Rosie the Riveters" during World War II.

"TRUCK DRIVERS"

However destructive its object, war was also creative, especially in technology. Global war constantly required newer and faster means of getting men and materials to the places where they were needed, and before it was over cargo planes vastly augmented the traditional ships and ground transport. The Army and Navy between them had created an airline system that reached every continent and every front. Thousands upon thousands of young men who had once fancied themselves flashing through the skies in fighter planes and bombers found they were instead delivering supplies, ferrying men, evacuating casualties, toting the heavy impediments of war, dropping paratroopers, and towing combat gliders. Out of this work, often conducted at great hazard and with heavy losses, came many of the skilled pilots for the airline industry that blossomed after peace returned.

A C-47 Skytrain, military version of the DC-3. Many of these versatile aircraft are still flying today. National Air and Space Museum, Smithsonian Institution.

ALBERT GEORGE LEONARD MORGAN

WHERE'S PEARL HARBOR?

Len Morgan has the kind of confident manner that Tom Wolfe described in
The Right Stuff: *"A particular folksiness, a particular down-home
calmness." The assured voice of the airline pilot you hear over the
intercom. Morgan retired from Braniff Airlines after 33 years and lives on
St. Simons Island, Georgia.*

*He is also a respected author and has written extensively about
airplanes and men who fought in World War II.*

I was born in Terre Haute, Indiana, but raised in Georgia. My father
was a Presbyterian minister, and we moved to Monticello when I was
six weeks old. When I was fourteen we moved again, to Louisville,
Kentucky, and I graduated from high school there in June of 1940. I
started going to the University of Louisville and had this crazy idea
that I wanted to be an aeronautical engineer. Ridiculous when I think
back on it. I had no flair for mathematics, chemistry, or physics. In
fact, I hated all of that stuff. I lasted one quarter. I didn't flunk out,
but I knew there was no way in the world I was going to be an
engineer. I transferred to the liberal arts department, and that was
just as bad. Of course, you know what was going on in 1940. Things
were getting hot over in England. One day I looked in the paper and
read an article about this boy, Merlin Kehrer, who had been a student
at the U. of L. He had joined the Royal Canadian Air Force and was
back in town. I went around to his house and talked to him about it. I
asked him if you needed a college education and he told me all you
had to have was a high school diploma. It sounded good so I thought
I'd go up and give it a try.

Albert George Leonard ("Len") Morgan joined the Royal Canadian Air Force in 1940, and wound up in Africa as a sergeant-pilot before transferring to the American Air Force flying transport planes. After the war he had a long career as a pilot with Braniff Airlines.

I can only imagine now what my parents' reaction to all this was. Remember, the United States was still at peace and a lot of people thought we were going to stay that way. "No way are we going to go over there and do what we did twenty years ago." My parents were British, and that made a difference for us. My father listened to the radio, and we would hear Edward R. Murrow saying, "This is London." My dad had one brother, two sisters, and numerous cousins still in England. My mother's sister and mother were also over there, and my parents were very sympathetic to what was going on in England. Now one of their kids wants to go over and get into it. Of course, they knew a lot more about what was involved in a war than I did, having gone through the First World War. They knew that this could very easily be a one-way ticket. No point in getting that return ticket until you find out if you're going to come back. My parents weren't any help at all while I was trying to make up my mind. It was my decision. I finally told them, "I'm going to do it." Dad bought me a bus ticket and gave me a ten-dollar bill.

When you came out of the tunnel between Detroit and Windsor, Ontario, there was the RCAF recruiting office with a big sign. A good-looking guy with a flying helmet on and it said, "Adventure in the Skies!" I always thought that was sort of done on purpose. I went in to see them and the recruiting officer said, "Yes, you can get in." It seemed too good to be true. You have to remember that the United States Army Air Corps and the Navy in those days required a minimum of two years of college if you wanted to fly, and they were highly selective. Even if you had two years of college you might not get in if you hadn't been nominated as an All-American. At least, that was the impression given in all those movies about military flying, things like *West Point of the Air.*

I was flying back from Vietnam on a 707 in 1968 when as a Braniff pilot I was in the Pacific/Military Airlift Command, contracted to move personnel and materials to the Far East. The hostess came up to the cockpit and said that we had a VIP on board. I said, "Who is it?" She said, "Some old guy named Pat O'Brien." I told her to go back and bring him up front. We could get away with stuff like that out there. When he got up to the cockpit he looked exactly like he did in the movies. He stayed up there with us for three or four hours. I said, "I want you to know something, Mr. O'Brien. You and James Cagney and John Wayne and the rest of them are the reason I'm sitting here right now." He laughed. "I've heard that a thousand times. I should have gotten an award for recruiting."

Enlisting with the Canadians was very simple. It wasn't slap-dash, but it was quick. You had to show them your high-school diploma and two letters of recommendation. If you showed up without them the squadron leader would send you downstairs to see the sergeant and he would tell you about a little print shop down the street. They could make you up anything from a letter of recommendation to a Harvard degree. This kid from Cleveland didn't have his and when he got back from the shop the officer said, "Oh, I see you found your papers." They were still wet. That squadron leader was a fine old boy and he got the ten or fifteen of us Americans who had enlisted that day in a room, and I remember the little speech he gave us. "Now, men, this is not a game. This nation is at war and you will be trained to be pilots and in all likelihood you will be sent overseas. More than likely you are going to be in combat. This means that some of you, maybe all of you, are not going to come back. You can walk out this door right now if you want to and there won't be any hard feelings. You are Americans and we don't ask you to swear allegiance to the Crown. We only ask you to serve with our forces for the duration, plus six months."

That speech was food for thought. But, by gosh, when you're eighteen years old you're immortal. I also think there was something different about that bunch of Americans who went up there. I think we had the flying bug a little worse than most kids. I went over to Detroit and walked out on the waterfront that looks over the Detroit River and toward Windsor. I stood there for a while thinking that I could take those papers and throw them in the river and go home. That would be that. But instead I hopped on the train for Trenton, Ontario. They put us in this enormous exhibition hall which was on the Ontario fairgrounds. There were hundreds of double bunks. We were the raw material that was coming into the Air Force. They began to pump us full of shots and I was sick as a dog for about three days. We were air crew recruits and to be trained as pilots, navigators, bomb aimers, as they were called in the RCAF, and gunners. Which one you'd end up as would be decided later. I met three Americans there and we stuck together, more or less, through a great deal of the war. Don Vogel was from New Jersey and he was shot down and captured, and finally liberated by the advancing American army. I just got a letter from him the other day. Charlie Woods was burned very badly in a crash. They said he was the worst burn case in the Air Force to survive. It didn't keep him from making $60,000,000 since the war. He owns a big piece of downtown San Diego. Bill Baldwin never made it back. He was on the south coast of Arabia and they took off at night. The airplane went right back into the ground. It was supposed to be his last trip and when he finished that one he was going to come home with Charlie and me. He was a good fellow. There were about eight thousand Americans in the RCAF by the end of the war, and 20 percent of them were killed while they served with the British, and more after transferring to the U.S. Army. I tried to trace down the twelve Americans in my class, and as far as I can tell, six survived. Just two years ago, I happened to be going through a list of Americans who had served with the RAF and I came upon a fellow from Hibbing, Minnesota, named Wendt. That name jumped right out at me. "Wee Willy Wendt." Big, tall, gawky farm boy, and there was his name. He was tall, all arms and legs, but a hell of a nice guy, and he went to Berlin and never came back. I noticed that he had the DFC and bar and the British didn't hand out the DFC to just anybody. Me, I got off scot-free. I led a charmed life all through the war.

From the fairgrounds they sent us across town to the Eglington Hunt Club, which was a swanky gentlemen's fox hunt club. We were put in the stables. They had been painted, but you could still tell who the original tenants were. They called this initial training school, and we went through six weeks of basic math and physics. The idea was to see if you knew enough math to cope with the ground schooling that was coming up. In July 1941 we went to St. Catharine's, which was down near Buffalo, to No. 9 Elementary Flying Training School. It was a nice grass field with, I'm guessing, seventy-five or eighty students. There was a small cadre of RCAF people, and all the rest were civilians. There was the C.O., the M.O. [medical officer], a couple of tough sergeants, and a few flunkies to make sure it was being done the military way. We were flying fleet trainers, biplanes. I was assigned to an instructor named Al Bennett. I went back up to St. Catharine's a few years ago and walked around the airport looking at the hangars. I ran into the guy who managed the field and he asked me who my instructor was. I said, "An old fellow, probably long gone, Al Bennett." He said, "Hell, no, he's right downtown running a big insurance agency." I went down and walked in to his office and there he was. I told him that he had taught me how to fly about thirty years ago. He said, "I had three American students who had last names which started with M and you're one of them." I said, "Morgan." He said, "Yeah, what are you doing now?" I told him that I was flying the Pacific in 707s. He said, "I must have taught you well."

We eliminated quite a few more at St. Catharine's. In most cases it wasn't those crying scenes you see in the movies when a guy washes out. Most of them realized that they weren't suited for flying and one or two of them actually walked in to see the C.O. and said, "I don't think I'm cut out for this and I'm wasting government money. Give me a shot at navigation school." It was very concentrated ground school and not a great deal of flying. It's a shame that somebody didn't have a movie camera at some of those old primary fields. We didn't lose a boy, but they were really tearing up the airplanes. There were Canadians, Englishmen, New Zealanders, Australians, and the Americans. We called it the Royal California Air Force because there were a lot of guys from California. The Canadians operated in a peculiar way considering that they were hard pressed to get people overseas. We had a five-day week. Come five o'clock on Friday, everything stopped and if you had behaved yourself, you got a 48-hour pass. I think it made a lot more sense than the 24-hour-a-day, seven-days-a-week thing because you got a chance to catch your breath. We would hitchhike to Buffalo or Detroit on the weekends, and I really enjoyed that.

From there we were sent to No. 14 Service Flying Training School at Aylmer, Ontario. Now it was strictly military and all business. All the instructors were RCAF, and we had lots of parades, marching around and firing rifles, machine guns, and pistols, all of that. We flew the *Harvard*, which is what the British called the AT-6. Years later, I did a story for *Flying* magazine about the AT-6, and it was wonderful to fly that airplane again. It was such a handful of airplane for an eighteen-year-old boy, and today it seems so tame. You still have to stay on top of it, any airplane can get you into trouble, but it wasn't near the big thing that I had built up in my mind. I graduated from Aylmer on November 21, 1941, and my folks drove up with my two brothers to see me get my wings. The man who gave them to us was Jerry Nash, a famous First World War fighter pilot, and we were tickled to death to get them. By the time we finished we had lost about 50 percent of the people we started out with due to washouts and I had about 160 hours logged.

The American system had primary, basic, and advanced schools. A student would end up with 200 to 250 hours. The British had elementary and service schools and then they would send you to an operational training unit in England. I wanted to be a fighter pilot and shoot down Germans. That was the image we got from the movies. My instructor wanted me to go into twin-engines. When you left elementary, your instructor would recommend you for either twin- or single-engine training based on his assessment of your personality. All my friends were going to single-engine and I didn't want to fly a bomber or flying boat, something like that. I went to see the C.O. and it turned out that they were one man short on the quota. In retrospect, my instructor knew what he was doing. There's a fighter pilot temperament and I don't have it. He's a wild man because he has to be a wild man. I've talked to many fighter pilots, and they had to be highly aggressive to have a prayer. I can see now that I was much better in a more plodding type of flying. Flying big airplanes is more procedure than anything else and that's not to belittle anybody. It took a rare brand of guts to sit in a B-17 or a Lancaster and head out knowing before you started that the chances of 15 or 20 percent of those airplanes not coming back were excellent. I have enormous respect for those people as well as the fighter pilots. In the final analysis, however, the fighter pilot was an individualist. Once the formation broke up and they got into battle, he depended on his own wits and luck to keep himself alive.

I flew the *Harvard* well enough to get through school, but there's no point in kidding anybody. I was just an average pilot. I wasn't above average and I certainly wasn't below average. I think that's what I've been all my life, an average pilot. We went home for about 10 days and then we went to a camp near Halifax where the ships were that would take us overseas. We're sitting there one Sunday and a guy walked in and said, "The Japanese have attacked Pearl Harbor." We all said the same thing, "Where's Pearl Harbor?" We'd heard of it, but it's like Mozambique, where's Mozambique? There were a lot of rumors, and two Americans took off to head back to the States. I don't know what happened to them but they just picked up and left. The majority of us stayed right there and we were like the people I've read about in the First World War. We were terrified that we were going to get there when it was all over. It wasn't going to last long enough for us to get over there. Little did we know that there would be four more miserable years of this horrible affair.

We went across and it took us 13 days. I drew bridge duty and got a chance to ask the master of the ship how the trip compared in his experience. He said, "Son, I have never in all my life on the North Atlantic seen it this rough." The ship was designed for 400 people and I think we had about 3,700. Very few of the pilots got seasick, but the soldiers were the most miserable bunch of bastards that I have ever seen. Maybe flying helped us with that kind of motion sickness. We never had our clothes off during the whole voyage and we wore our life vests at all times. That old captain also told me another thing. "Don't complain about this weather, Sonny, because there are subs out there and they can't hurt us as long as this is going on. You pray this goes on until you see the Irish coast." We quit our bitching.

We came into Liverpool on Christmas Eve, 1941. They put us on troop trains and of course, they were unheated. I don't think there was any heat in England at all during the war. We got in an awful lot of trouble at one of the camps by tearing up the floor in the barracks and burning it in the stove. Another bunch of guys raided the officers' club one night and took all the furniture and burned it up. As they say in the RAF, headquarters took a dim view of that.

They sent us down to Bournemouth, which is a seaside town on the south coast of England. On a clear day you could see the coast of France, and that was the first time I really realized what I had gotten into. That's where "they" were. The Germans were not in the paper anymore, not in the Movietone News, they were right over there. We were there for about two weeks, and Bill Baldwin and I were bitching about the weather one day when a sergeant came into the barracks. He stopped over by us and asked, "Do you fellows know so and so?" whoever they were. We said we didn't know them, but what did he want with them? "Well, they're being posted to the Middle East and I've got to find them and get them on a troop train." Bill said, "Middle East, where's that?" This guy was a professional British sergeant, and he told us that he had done a tour of duty in the Middle East and "it's hotter than hell out there." Bill looked at me and I looked at him and he said, "You looking for two men?" We were on a train that afternoon for Edinburgh and this was during the big blizzard they had in England during the winter of 1941. It took 21 hours to go from Edinburgh to Glasgow and I think it's normally an hour's run.

We got on the *Viceroy of India*, which was one of the old P&O liners and thought, "So long, Charlie Woods, Don Vogel, and all of you other guys. We're going to where it's warm." We were on the ship for 44 days. The first stop was Freetown, West Africa, and then Durban, South Africa, where we got off the ship for four days. It was wonderfully warm down there and we were wearing shorts and pith helmets, really playing the part. Bill and I were walking down the street and he said, "Hey, look!" Here came Charlie Woods and Don Vogel. They were on another ship in the same convoy and we didn't know it. We all ended up in Egypt at Suez. The story was—I never knew if it was true, but the timing was right—that we were on our way to Singapore. When Singapore fell we got orders to reroute to Egypt. There were something like eight hundred pilots in this convoy, and there was nothing for us to do there. They didn't have a school and the desert air force was stretched to the limit. They were almost out of equipment and not about to turn any of those fighters over to us for training. We sat there for 14 months in a tent city. This, with the war raging all over Europe and the western desert. If you flew 30 minutes west from where we were, you were right in the middle of the Afrika Korps. We could see the bombers taking off and coming back and it was a very frustrating experience for a young pilot who was itching to get into it. How are you going to explain this when you get home? "What did you do in the war?" "Oh, I sat on the edge of the desert on the Suez Canal drinking beer for 14 months." It looked like Rommel was going to succeed in invading Egypt and could take over Alexandria. You could sit in the nightclub on top of the hotel in Alexandria and see the artillery fire out on the desert, it was that close. They put us on ships and sent us down the Nile. We were then put on a train to Khartoum in the Sudan and we stayed down there for a month. Montgomery succeeded in pushing the Germans back and we came back to Cairo. In Khartoum we were living in barracks made out of camel dung bricks and they were fine until it rained and they got damp. Then their true nature was revealed.

Every once in awhile we'd see an American airplane go through. A B-25 painted in "desert pink," some C-47s and B-24s. It was the Ninth Air Force, and we found out that they were headquartered in a hotel in Cairo. We went down there and hung around in the lobby until we saw this master sergeant, three up and three down, walk through the lobby, go up some stairs and through an unmarked door. We followed him in and there's a bird colonel sitting there, a couple of enlisted men, and the sergeant. The officer asked us what we wanted. "We're looking for the headquarters of the Ninth Air Force." He said, "This is the headquarters of the Ninth Air Force. What the hell do you know about the Ninth, this is supposed to be quiet." We told him that we were Americans and the RAF didn't have anything for us to do and we wanted to join the U.S. Army and get in on the war. His name was Sory Smith, later on he became a general, and he said, "As if I didn't have enough trouble and you guys show up. I will get a telex off to Washington and we'll see what happens. You guys keep in touch but don't be noising it around about the Ninth Air Force."

In due time the Ninth showed up *en masse*. I mean, when the American Army shows up, boy, they show up. Shiploads. Up went the barracks, up went the quartermaster's corps, here come the airplanes, and all of a sudden, the Americans were there. We were sergeants in the RAF so they made us sergeants in the Army Air Corps and the Canadians were delighted. They said, "Good show, we're just sorry we couldn't put you to work." There was no hesitancy to let us go over to the Americans and they were completely fair about it. Oh, we had some arguments when we were with the Brits. "You Americans couldn't build a good airplane if you tried," and that kind of stuff. For the most part, it was good-natured. The British and Canadians were great people in all respects.

At that time Pan American World Airways was contracted by the Army to establish a trans-African airline to haul freight and personnel, and they sent us to do that. All of the pleading we did about getting into P-40s didn't do any good at all, and that's where I spent the rest of my time overseas. We were based in Accra, Gold Coast, and flew through Kano, Maiduguri, Ft. Lamy, El Fasher, and Khartoum to Cairo—or east to Ethiopia. Or up the west African coast through Dakar and Marrakech to Oran. Those were the main routes and we operated them on schedules.

All we had were C-47s (militarized DC-3s), but we had an operation that was almost airline quality because it was operated by Pan

Am and lots of other pilots from other airlines were there. They were civilians working under contract, and the pilots wore a pseudo-Army uniform. They were suntans but with peculiar insignia on them, and we used to call it the "lion tamer's suit." That was not appreciated. There were old guys from TWA, American, and Braniff, and we flew copilot for them. They were old airline hands and good pilots. We weren't losing anywhere near the number of airplanes that we were allowed to lose. We did have a few go down but it was, for the most part, safe flying, even though we were usually flying overloaded airplanes. I'm not going to try and put any heroics on it. Compared to what the people on the Hump were doing, ours was an easy life. We were called the African Middle East Wing and we had a huge terminal at Accra. It was much larger than anything back in the States. You name it, we'd haul it. Everything from personnel, aircraft engines, food, mail, to medical supplies. A lot of it was going to fight the war in the desert and some of it went straight over to Ethiopia and across the southern part of Asia and then on over the Hump into China. By that stage of the war the German planes pretty much left us alone. There were occurrences of C-47s being shot down, but the Germans were too busy trying to protect themselves to give us any real trouble. We were bombed a few times in Egypt but they were more nuisance bombings than anything else.

In the public's mind, training command, I suppose, was at the bottom of the heap. We in Air Transport Command (ATC) were next. We were "Allergic to Combat" or the "Army of Terrified Copilots." But they had to have those people in training command and they had to have air transport. The thing that didn't dawn on me until after the war was the fact that air transport was the only air activity in World War II that was entirely new. The First World War had fighters, reconnaissance, and at the end of the war, the RAF was massed in France to start heavy raids against the Germans with big four-engine bombers. Transporting large loads of cargo and people that could turn the tide of battle was something completely novel. By the end of the war the Naval Air Transport Service in the Pacific and our ATC planes were running a global airline, and there wasn't an ocean or continent we weren't going to. I'm not trying to build up the Air Transport Command compared with combat situations, but it was an unusual opportunity, and for anybody interested in going into the airlines it was ideal training. I think the airlines preferred us because it made sense to the average airline vice-president. If you had been flying transports, you had the right attitude.

In August of 1943 they began a rotation policy, and if you can believe it, they brought out a new rule that our British time didn't count. Well, one of the elders in my father's church, Gaylord Gilbert, was a reserve officer in the Kentucky National Guard before the war. When the war started, he quickly rose to lieutenant colonel and was in the inspector general's department. That's the outfit that keeps the rest of the Army straight. I'm walking through the mess hall one day in Accra and I hear, "Hey, Len." It's Colonel Gilbert. He said, "What's with the sergeant's stripes?" I told him and he said, "We can't have that. All our pilots are going to be second lieutenants." I told him, "Wait a second, there's sixteen of us." In two days we were all lieutenants. When this thing came up about our time not counting, I dropped around at Colonel Gilbert's office and he said, "You're going home." And that was the end of that.

When I got home there were two places open. Ferrying bases at Dallas and Memphis. I chose Memphis because it was closer to home. You talk about a chicken outfit, that was it! I got crossways to my C.O. right off. I don't think he liked the fact that I wore my RAF wings on one side and my Air Force wings on the other, and he assigned me to some miserable duty. I flew a PT-23, which is an open seat trainer, from Chicago to Alabama, in the winter. I hadn't been there three months when orders came through for me to go back overseas. In the meantime I had married Margaret and I thought, "We've got six hundred pilots on this base all chomping at the bit to go overseas, how come I have to go back?" I got on the phone to Colonel Gilbert, who was now in the Pentagon, and said, "Look, I'm the last one to complain. If defeating the Axis powers depends on my going back over there, I'll go, but I just got married and I want to stay here a little longer." Two days later I went to see the C.O. and he said, "Who do you know?" I said, "I don't know anybody." Margaret and I piled everything in our 1940 Dodge and drove to Reno, Nevada, where I went to C-46 school. I was there for a year and a half and that's where Terry was born. The C-46 was a good old airplane in a lot of ways, but you still hear it bad-mouthed everywhere you go. If they crashed a C-47, it was pilot error. If they crashed a C-46, it was the "Curtiss Calamity."

I was then sent down to Florida and went through C-54 (militarized DC-4) school, and that was a beautiful airplane. I was really beginning to like this multi-engine flying. At the end of the summer of 1945 I was sent out to what is now Travis Air Force Base, took my check ride in a C-54, and qualified as a first pilot. The next day the war ended. It was amazing how one day there could be all of this feverish activity, flying, students, all of the goings on of a big air base, and the next day it all ended. They said some kind of new bomb had been dropped and it was all very mysterious. They called us in and offered us a chance to sign up for one additional year. There wasn't going to be much flying so I chose to get out and started sending off

332

applications to all the airlines. They all said I needed two years of college so I went to the University of Louisville on the G.I. Bill. I sent out a second round of applications and ended up putting in 33 years with Braniff.

Braniff's failure is a long story. John Nance's book, *Splash of Color*, tells only part of it. It was a sad thing, like a death in the family. We saw what was happening but we really didn't think it would ever come to total collapse. Under the old system it was almost impossible for an airline to go broke. The CAB would have forced a shotgun marriage with another airline because they wouldn't want it to go under. Under deregulation things changed. The one thing that each airline had that was worth anything, its route system, was gone. Also Harding Lawrence was, I don't know how to describe the man, part genius and part gambler. He thought those graphs were going to go up forever. But things started falling apart all at once. Deregulation, gross mismanagement, the recession, the fuel crisis, and the PATCO strike. We signed too many long-term agreements, and they'd pay anything for a gate at an airport. On the other hand, Lawrence did things like painting those airplanes bright colors. I flew the Calder 727* quite a few times. People would hang around the airport and that was the one airplane they would talk about. Our name wasn't on it anywhere and they'd ask whose plane it was. That was real promotion. Somebody said it looked like a seagull that had flown through a plate glass window.

When it all ended, they just padlocked the terminals. Every time you would turn on the TV for the evening news the Braniff logo would be up in the corner. Oh, no, here comes another story about the bankrupt Braniff. The paper began falling off the billboards around town. Here we're advertising London and Hawaii and the billboards are starting to fall down. Those multicolored airplanes were parked in rows and started to look grubby. We liked Texas, Margaret thinks of herself as a Texan even though she's from Kentucky, but it was depressing when the parking lot at the hangar was starting to grow up in weeds, and I was glad to move to North Carolina.

An airline is not like any other kind of company. It's almost a family, and it was very depressing to see that family break up. I used to go out in the back yard and when I'd hear a jet turning onto final approach for Dallas–Fort Worth I would look up to see if it was one of ours. Looking up at a plane is a habit a pilot never outgrows. It took me a little while to realize that it wouldn't ever again be one of ours.

Ed. note: Braniff commissioned Alexander Calder, noted painter and sculptor, to paint a 727.

WILLIAM TAYLOR

MILITARY BEARING

William Taylor's life proceeds from Kansas City to Harvard—then to hazardous days as navigator of an Air Corps C-47, a DC-3 with all of the amenities removed. Taylor and his crew spent the war dropping paratroopers, towing gliders, and transporting the lading of war. When the war ended he returned to Harvard and teaching. For the past twenty years he has been a professor of history at the State University of New York at Stony Brook. He tells his stories in a charming, deadpan fashion.

I had this feeling after the war that I didn't want to have my life overwhelmed by this experience that took place when I was twenty years old. It was rather like having a famous father or something like that, and you had to live it down, or live up to it. I think a lot of people kept it at a distance, at least I did. It was close to a conscious effort to keep the whole experience in its proper place. After all, although it was very exciting, it was only three years of my life. What I always wanted to do, but have never succeeded in doing, was to see the war as a kind of interim period. A period of time taken off from real life when things were on hold. An interruption in my life rather than the high point. That doesn't mean I'm always successful in assigning the war to that place, but I try.

In the courses that I teach I almost never talk about wars. I don't really have to in the kind of things that I do, but wars have had a profound influence on all of the material I'm talking about. My first book, *Cavalier and Yankee: The Old South and American National Character*, was about the antebellum South. It explained the myths created about the North and South in the first half of the nineteenth century,

The *Harvard Freshman Redbook* of 1939 displays a serious William Taylor. In the war he was a navigator in an Air Corps C-47, serving in supply, airborne, and glider operations. Afterward he returned to Harvard for his Ph.D., and is now a professor of history at the State University of New York at Stony Brook.

based on newspapers, novels and correspondence of the time. The book came out at the time of the Civil War Bicentennial and it was often listed as a Civil War book. The result of this was that a couple of times I ended up going off to talk to Civil War roundtables. I did a lot of traveling in the South while I was writing the book. Going to plantations and going through letter collections, things like that, but the people at those roundtables were not interested in that. I think they felt there should have been more hardware or at least more about the war itself in my book.

I could never understand that kind of mentality. Not completely. It's a kind of time-stop mentality. Going back and getting into "it," whatever the "it" may be. I'm always amazed that people actually feel that way about World War II. I suppose for veterans who were lifted out of humdrum lives for two or three years and then went back into them, after the war, it must have been hard not to have that kind of outlook. Give a guy like that a P-38, nothing will ever be as great again.

There was enormous optimism during the war that I took for granted and that my whole generation has never fully abandoned. All of us must have believed that the United States was essentially doing the right thing and it all was going to come out in our favor. We thought the "American Century" was just beginning. I must have assumed I was never going to go anywhere I would be ashamed to be an American. I've been many places since, where it was clearly an embarrassment to be an American, and I think our reputation in the world has altered since the war for the worse.

I don't think the grim termination of the war in Japan, Hiroshima and Nagasaki, gave most people, including me, much pause at the time. I thought it was gruesome, and I suppose in some tentative way I debated if dropping the bomb was necessary, but it was only a qualification on the otherwise unblemished record of national prowess. I wish now I could report that I had been deeply troubled. There have been other changes. There was also a feeling that Americans were natural soldiers. Bring these people in, so the myth went, dust them off, and before you knew it, they'd be out there fighting, indomitable. I think in some ways we all absorbed that sort of belief and perhaps even exemplified it. Retroactively, I have considered a lot of the events leading up to the war and I have a somewhat different view now.

It wasn't the people so much as the politics, including Roosevelt's own provocative behavior. I don't think war at that point could have been avoided, given what was going on in Europe. I don't think the United States could or should have stayed out of it. But, beyond that, I have a lot of doubts about it.

I myself started out as a pacifist. When I was going to Harvard, Rufus Jones, a Quaker pacifist, came through the Boston area and gave some impressive and very convincing lectures about what was going on in Europe. I marched in a couple of antiwar parades and felt for a time that we should stay out of Europe. This was, of course, before Pearl Harbor. For most people, certainly for me, Pearl Harbor meant that America had been attacked and that completely changed our perspective.

I grew up in Kansas City, Missouri. Kansas City had a big airport because Transworld Airlines had their largest operation located there. I guess it was called Transcontinental Air Transport at that time and my father would take me out to watch the Ford Tri-motors take off. When I was nine, I flew in a plane with my grandmother. She paid five dollars, and the two of us went up in an open cockpit plane and flew around Kansas City. Like everybody else, I made model airplanes, but I didn't think of myself as having any particular interest in flying. I was surrounded by kids who were much more interested in aviation than I was. Where this Air Force thing came from, I don't know. It could have been the movies I went to see at that time, films like *Dawn Patrol*. The glamour of flying that was in all of those First World War movies.

I always felt that I was born with a silver spoon in my mouth. Having been adopted, I was raised by some good people. My father was a dry goods merchant. He owned a department store, John Taylor and Sons, which was in downtown Kansas City. It was a big store, six stories. It's now R. H. Macy's downtown store. When I was a child, the whole first floor was yard goods. Women came in with dress patterns and bought the material to make their own clothes. By the time I left for school, it was a pretty complete and modern department store. There was a men's department and a beauty parlor, things like that.

As a child I had a lot of fun in that store. There was an elaborate arrangement of package chutes between the floors. You could slide down four floors in them. My friends and I were always swooping down those chutes and landing on top of some person's recent purchase. Because I was the owner's son, nobody ever made much of a fuss about it. I really had a privileged childhood except for a troubling time when I was sent to a military school in Minnesota.

It was one of those midwestern gothic campuses, Episcopalian in addition to being military. The school was beautiful, but it was bitterly cold up there. I remember playing hockey one day when it was 32 degrees below zero. The school was full of kids from Minneapolis, St. Paul, various towns in Iowa, and a few people, like me, from Missouri. The conception we had was that we had all screwed up in some way. I'd been kicked out of a couple of schools. It seemed to me that everybody, well, not everybody, but a lot of people there had disciplinary problems. I remember my father saying, "You'll have military bearing when you come home." I had an uncle who had gone there, and everybody said he had "military bearing." I had no idea at that time what military bearing was. I thought it was some kind of mechanical device. I have to admit that I've always had good posture as a result of that school.

There were some good teachers there, but you had to dig them out. I had one excellent English teacher who taught me a lot and was interested in helping me learn how to write. I think that's what you need if you're going to earn your living with words. Somebody to get you excited about it. The military side of the school was interesting to me. I was scared to death of it beforehand and loathed it afterwards, but somehow the drilling and all that stuff wasn't as bad as it probably sounds. It certainly made the Air Force seem a lot more normal. Shattuck Military Academy graduates, if they were the right age when they graduated, became lieutenants in the Army reserve. I was younger than most of the boys in my class so I didn't get a commission. My class, almost to a man, turned up in those early battles in North Africa and almost two-thirds were killed. In this sense, I was saved by being younger, though it was painful for me at the time.

Shattuck also gave me some self-discipline. By the time I went to Harvard, I had acquired some of the academic skills necessary to get along. The man who was in charge of advising students about college said, "You can't get to Harvard from here." Most of the students went to the University of Minnesota. Midwestern colleges were the most popular. A few graduates who were rich enough went to eastern colleges, but at that point there wasn't much interest in the Middle West in going to Ivy League schools. I applied to Harvard, somewhat to my father's disappointment since he had gone to Princeton. I was accepted and started school in September of 1939.

I volunteered for the Army Air Corps and entered flight training in early January of 1943. We were sent to Atlantic City for basic. The weather was extreme, and I had a difficult time. Our drill sergeants used to condition us by putting us in overcoats and full packs and running us up and down the sand in 15- or 20-degree weather. You'd sweat and your uniform and overcoat would be soaked through. Then they'd stand you at attention and you'd have to wait for another activity. I really learned the meaning of hyperventilation.

Even after Shattuck, basic training was a brutal experience. We lived in the President Hotel. One incident stands out in my memory. They caught some poor bastard stealing from our footlockers and instead of arresting him, turned him over to the other trainees in the hotel. They kicked him down six flights of stairs. I'd never seen anybody beaten up as badly as that, even after years of military school and hazing. The moral was, doubtless, that you don't steal from your buddies, but I was stunned by the extraordinary brutality.

At this time, the Air Force wasn't able to keep people on their training schedules, because the flight schools were all filled. Cadets were sent to various colleges to wait for things to get caught up. When we finished basic, in March, we got on a train, and much to my amazement, as I squinted through the blinds, we started north. I saw all these familiar signs, Hartford, Springfield, and before I knew it, we were in Northhampton, Massachusetts. Then, they put us on a bus and took us to Amherst. I had a girlfriend, whom I subsequently married, in Smith College. I was able to see her all the time, and we would tryst in the library at night. We were at Amherst for about eight weeks. They tried their best to fill our time with academic busy-work. I took a course in world history while I was there, and an English course where I wrote themes on subjects like "why I want to be an air cadet" and "why we're in the war." No one took this part of our training seriously, including the instructors.

Then, I think it was early April, we were sent to Nashville to the Air Force classification center. We went through aptitude tests, and that sort of thing. I was classified a navigator, which had been my preference. In the test you could tell what the pilot questions were. They were all about fixing your car, mechanical things. Navigator questions all had to do with geography and directional sense. Bombardier questions were hard to identify. I think most bombardiers were usually failed pilots. I had no particular desire to be a pilot. I think I liked the idea of somebody else's driving the bus.

While I was in Nashville, I got married. I remembered that my mother thought it was foolish of me. I asked her if it was because I was going to get shot and leave her with a widow to take care of. She said, "No, it's just foolish in general, freestanding foolish." My wife and I walked under the crossed sabres of all my fellow air cadets, and we had a 36-hour honeymoon at the Andrew Jackson Hotel. I was always glad I was married because it seemed to give my life a little more focus during that crazy period while I was out of the country.

By the middle of June, I was in basic flight training in Monroe, Louisiana, learning how to identify Japanese naval vessels in a thousandth of a second. Being shown the difference between the smokestacks of an American and Japanese destroyer. We were sitting in tar-paper barracks where the temperature rose to 200 degrees, watching training films, and learning how to behave if we escaped from a prisoner-of-war camp. Fliers who had escaped came and talked to us about their experiences. It seemed at the time that a sense of humor was something that had to be generated because it wasn't part of the plan. It was August when I left Monroe and went to advanced training.

I ended up in a school run by Pan American Airways in Miami Beach. We were put up in a gorgeous old hotel, and all of our flight training was in ancient Pan Am Clippers. We were taught by Pan Am navigators, and by the time we left we were extremely well trained. I got so airsick in training, I almost washed out. It was real agony. I got over the worst of it by the end of the war, but I have never really enjoyed flying. I mean, despite the thrill of it, there's the feeling that you get in your stomach when you're in turbulence. It's still a painful experience for me to take the shuttle to Boston. If I fly to California, I'll have a couple of drinks, and we'll be up there above the clouds, and I'll start to think, "Well, this is wonderful." Then, two hours later, the seatbelt light will go on and the pilot will say, "We're heading into a little light turbulence." All those memories will come back to me. Those Clippers were always full of bilge water and the combination of puke and bilge was frequently too much. I still remember sitting there at our navigation desks with a couple of other cadets riding through those turbulent Caribbean nights, trying to learn how to do astral navigation.

We were in Miami through November and then I said good-bye to my wife and went to Fort Bragg in North Carolina. We were trained there in paratroop operations and in pulling gliders. The decision to put us in C-47s had been made before we went to Florida. I assumed for a while that I would be put in the Air Transport Command, which I thought would be good because I would get to come home occasionally. I guess I would have rather been in a bomber, but I got over that preference quickly. What I was doing seemed more interesting because there was more actual navigating to do. Except for the big invasions, we weren't involved in the huge operations that the bombers were. The navigator in a bomber was there, for the most part, in case you had to get home alone.

We flew all over North Carolina and I got a real sense of what paratroop operations were really like. We also pulled gliders, which turned out to be all right, but it was a very slow business, and you always felt that anyone with a slingshot could have shot you down. We were flying at 3,500 feet at 90 miles an hour. It seemed awfully slow, even then.

While we were there, we crashed. Our plane was involved in a 36-hour maneuver that was training for endurance. We'd flown all night and had just unloaded a jeep. Jeeps were secured in C-47s on two big steel ramps like the ones they used in service stations for oil changes. We got rid of the jeep before dawn and took off. We were flying in close formation with nine planes. I was standing up between the pilot and copilot and we were talking and laughing. Once it gets light outside, you feel things are better in the air, even if they aren't. Next thing I knew, the plane heaved and there was the sound of crunching metal. Then, the plane started going down. The pilot said, "What the fuck?" There was no way for us in the cockpit to tell what had happened. The crew chief, who had been back in the cabin, rushed forward, told us that our elevator was gone, and rushed back into the cabin. The pilot moved the wheel back and forth and nothing happened. He said, "Well, we're in trouble, guys." We continued down. The only way we could control the descent was by using the throttles. It turned out that the plane that was flying on our right had crushed the elevator and we had no up or down. By using the throttles and flaps, Peterson, the pilot, was able to slow the plane down and get the nose up.

We had been flying over woods for an incredible amount of time and we were now below the level of the trees and we could hear branches scraping the bottom of the plane. Suddenly, we came upon a tobacco field and as we started to settle down, I whipped out of the cockpit and went back into the cabin. I remembered this class we had in basic about securing yourself if you were crashing. When I got back there, I said to Eberle, the crew chief, "We're going down." He said, "You think I don't know?" We braced our backs against the bulkhead and the plane came down. I couldn't see much except things that were flying past the door. We settled down and slid along for an incredible amount of time, hit a ditch, which turned the plane around 180 degrees, and we started skidding backwards. The ramps came forward between us at what must have been 70 miles an hour, and went right into the cockpit between the pilot and copilot. As soon as the plane slowed down to a sort of scraping crawl, we went out the door and the guys in the front went out the hatch over the cockpit. We ran like hell and got pretty far away, but we could still feel the warmth on our faces when the plane went pufffft and caught on fire.

We looked around and then looked at each other and started laughing. About 20 or 30 minutes later a plane flew over and then after a while a truck turned up and took us back to the base. We were debriefed and immediately put back in another airplane and sent up that afternoon. They didn't want us getting spooked by that experience.

It never occured to me, until after the war, that I could have been killed. I realized that people were being killed all the time, but they say when you are that age you feel sort of immortal, despite the scary things that are happening around you. I remember crossing Harvard Square as an undergraduate and having a truck almost peel the buttons off my overcoat, and I didn't think of it as a close call. I mean, that truck almost got me. It took me a while before I really began to sweat. I think that was true of the war. When these missions were going on, both training and operational, I don't think any of us faced the fact that the odds were what they were. They were high, and not in our favor. On a mission we flew to Holland, I think we lost half our squadron. I don't mean that everybody was killed, but that's how many planes went down. A lot of them, however, did go up in fireballs.

I remember feeling, when we were flying over Europe and under fire, how little stood between me and the bullets. It wasn't as if you were in some sort of solid metal container. I felt that aluminum was very thin protection. We caught a lot of ground fire, but the German gunners never learned to "lead" C-47s enough. It may have been the fact that we seemed to be flying more slowly than we actually were. The result of this was that 90 percent of the ground fire that we caught went into the toilet at the back of the plane. It was always called the "death chamber" and anybody who wanted an orthodox evacuation had to take incredible risks. We also flew with the plane door off, which meant that you could get sucked out of the plane if you didn't watch yourself in moving to the rear of the plane. I wouldn't have been anything but, literally, "caught dead" in that part of the plane.

From North Carolina we went to Ft. Wayne, Indiana, and picked up the plane that we took overseas. There was this big thing about naming our plane. We suddenly realized this was the plane we were going to be flying to war. The proprietary feeling that we had about the airplane is difficult to explain. It was brand new and had that smell that cars have when they're new. We flew in it for a long time. We cooked in it, slept in it, and spent God knows how many hours just sitting on the ground waiting to take off. It was really like a second home. I felt much more at home in that airplane than I ever did in any barracks we lived in. We sat around for a whole day figuring out a good name and having it painted on the plane. We ended up calling it "Snoopy." There weren't any what you might call nasty or warlike names on C-47s. They were thought of more as "angels of mercy."

As a matter of fact, I would say that 80 percent of the time I was airborne we were flying evacuation and supply missions. They used us like delivery boys. Right after Paris fell to the Allies, we flew electric heaters into SHAEF headquarters. Load after load of those heaters to warm up those hotel rooms. I thought to myself at the time, "Here I am, risking my life to keep those damn staff officers warm." Another time we flew up to Edinburgh to pick up cases of

Scotch and flew them to SHAEF headquarters in London. It was one of the most dangerous flights I was ever on because our pilot got so drunk that he tried to land the plane on automatic pilot. We had to coax him into releasing it and going on manual control.

We did, however, have a wonderful time in Edinburgh. We arrived with our transportation, since we had a jeep in the plane, so we had some wheels to move around with. I spent the day driving around looking at eighteenth-century buildings and trying to interest my crew chief in what we were seeing. We had a five-man crew: pilot, copilot, navigator, crew chief, and radio-operator. We had a real good pilot. Peterson, a big talker, knew how to fly. He was some kind of graphic artist who had worked for *Time* before the war. I flew with him a long time and I always respected him. We got along well. Eberle, the crew chief, was a general's son and another guy I really respected. While I was sitting reading books, he was out there sweating the fuel lines. When he said the plane would fly, I always believed it would. I forget the copilot's name, but he was a consummate anti-Semite. There's someone like him in every movie about World War II, the one who makes the smart crack during briefing. He was very crude but at the same time he was very funny. Our radio operator also could have jumped out of any number of movies. His name was Flanagan and he had a Brooklyn accent. He sat right behind me and didn't seem to know anything whatsoever about radios.

There was that element of death and danger which sort of heightened people's sense of craziness. We never bombed any English bases as they did in *Catch-22*, but I think for the right amount of money you could have gotten this one pilot who lived with us to do almost anything. He thought up incredible schemes for making money. At one point he flew into Paris with a whole suitcase full of wristwatches that he'd bought on rest leave and sold them to pilots who in turn sold them to the Russians in Berlin. He was selling twenty-five-dollar watches for five hundred dollars. Occasionally, our crew would steal things from the RAF bases. We'd get back in the plane and the pilot's jacket would be all swollen out. I'd say, "What have you got in there?" He'd say, "I've got the mirror out of the men's room." This after we'd been treated to a free meal and beer. Even so, that side of the war is really much more attractive, in a way, to remember. The thing that Heller captured in *Catch-22* is the kind of madcap, frenzied, crazy, scheming stuff that went on. That includes all of the crazy sex.

I was the intellectual of our little group. I had a place right behind the pilot. There was a navigational desk and a bookshelf built right into the plane. Once we started flying in Europe, I realized that I wasn't going to have to use a logarithm to get anywhere. I took all of my navigation books, put them in my footlocker, and filled the book-shelf with books I wanted to read during those incredibly long times we'd be sitting around waiting for this or that, or just circling around once we got in the air.

I never was a reader as a child, not even in college. I read what I had to and that was that. The war made me a recreational reader. I read things I wouldn't have dreamed of before or after. All of those little blue Oxford books. I read two volumes of Milton's poetry. At one point I had laryngitis and I did the first reading I had ever done about American history. Sitting in an Army hospital reading Charles and Mary Beards' *Rise of American Civilization.* It was also better to read than to brood on the things that could happen to you. I guess I used books the way other people used the bottle.

Our unit was the 438th Troop Carrier Group. When we first got to England, we were based near Nottingham and then we were moved down near Newbury. All of our operational missions from England were flown out of that base. That was just prior to the inva-sion. The gliders went in on D-day and the 438th was the first group to go in. We had people from all the news services in our planes and a reporter from the New York *Herald-Tribune* in our plane. I don't re-member his name, but I don't think he was any more scared than I was. He filed a story that my mother actually read. He mentioned the name of our plane and it was a great moment for her.

Normandy was not what we had been led to expect. We didn't lose anybody from our group. Not a plane. We went in very early, and as we flew across Normandy we could see the lights coming on. There was flak by the time we flew out again, but we didn't catch any. The people who came in later took the brunt of it. We were lucky, we just went in and out. We flew back the next day first with more gliders and then, a day later, with a load of the *Stars and Stripes!* Within two or three days we were doing evacuation missions. That June we must have piled up hundreds of hours in the air.

At the end of June our unit was given orders to fly to Civitavec-chia, which is north of Rome. We were there for the invasion of southern France, which was in July. That was a very uncontested landing. We were dropping paratroops, condoms, *Stars and Stripes,* what have you. Only the first two operations were military. The rest were supply missions so this was almost like a vacation for us. The base was really grungy and we were absolutely driven crazy by fleas. We were living in tents and I was dusting my sleeping bag all the time. It was like trying to get cockroaches out of a New York apart-ment. One of us would fly into Rome every day and pick up mail. I would always try to get on that flight and I made it about six or seven times, enough to get some feeling for Rome as a city. That was a pleasant break.

Then we went back to Newbury and flew the mission to Holland. That was in September, and it was the first time we made a drop in broad daylight. We had the hell shot out of us. I can remember that day as well as anything in the war. We were flying at 3,500 feet, and at that altitude you can see a cat move on the ground. They were throwing up all that flak and our nightmare was that we'd get hit by tracer bullets with our tanks half-full of gas. You've got all those fumes and the plane just goes pouufff. I corrected our course at one point on that mission because I felt if we went in and followed the other squadrons, we would go right over the same flak barrages and we'd get the same thing they were getting. We went in north of the assigned flight pattern and even so, we still lost a lot. I mean, there we were, flying that low in broad daylight over some very angry Germans.

That was my last mission. I had met the head of the Information and Education Branch while I was still flying. He had been a professor at Columbia. They were looking for officers to do information and education briefing for staff-grade officers who would then go back to their groups and brief the troops. "I and E" was really, in a sense, a propaganda detachment. An informed soldier is a good soldier. A whole series of curriculum units were developed on such subjects as *Our Ally: Russia* and *Our Enemy: Japan*. I and E was based in London when I was offered a job with them. By the time I joined them, they had moved to Paris. Most of the time I was simply preparing and dispensing materials about what was happening in the various theaters of war. It was an easy job and I felt as though I'd betrayed all my friends when I took it. My war, in terms of flying, was all over by September of 1944.

That was an exciting time for me. There I was in a big European city without any responsibilities after two o'clock in the afternoon. I had told them I spoke fluent French when I got to Paris. I thought there was bound to be some advantage to that. I'd studied French in school, but the way the Americans do, so I told them it would help my accent if I had a tutor. The guy who taught me French was an Estonian who later became professor of romance languages at the University of Iowa. He was a superb teacher, and he taught me how to move my tongue around and make the proper sounds. When he finished, I was having dreams in French.

Through him, I was inducted into this world of international refugees then living in Paris. There was a Yugoslavian who later became an official in the Tito government, and a Chinese guy who became a kind of eminence in the Chinese government before the Cultural Revolution. I haven't heard from him since. They were both graduate students at the École de Science Politique studying political economy with a group of Estonians and a few French people. All of them had intellectual ambitions of some kind. I was brought into the group because they wanted someone to read Whitman to them. We would have these sessions where I would read Thomas Wolfe or Whitman and they would sit around and clap. Our little group would go to concerts and the theater and talk through the night. The I and E office would get tickets from the French government for the officers who were there for training. They would always post a list on the bulletin board saying what was available. Tickets to the Follies were gone by nine in the morning, but anything in French would just sit there. Some wonderful concerts and plays would go begging, so I would get the tickets and take all my new friends. We could go to the officers' club for dinner, and I could take my guests for about a buck apiece. Those were wonderful times.

When the war ended in Europe, the staff school moved to Oberammergau in southern Bavaria. Then they dropped the bombs on Japan and I can remember going to the little church in town on V-J Day to hear Mozart's *Requiem.* I can remember seeing Nazi coins in the collection plate. There was an enormous feeling of relief that the war was finally over.

We got our orders to terminate the staff school. After a complicated trip across Germany and France by truck and train, they put us on a boat and I ended up at Fort Devens, Massachusetts. They released me and I haven't done anything remotely military since.

I think the war may have awakened my historical interests. I had majored in comparative literature before the war, but when I came back, I entered the doctoral program in history, again at Harvard. I later taught for three years at Amherst. When I finished with my Ph.D., I taught at Harvard for five years and then went to the University of Wisconsin. Then I was offered a job when Stony Brook expanded in 1968, and I've been here ever since, teaching history.

I've never attended college reunions, school reunions, that sort of thing. However, the first time I went back to England after the war, I rented a car and drove to the air base near Newbury where we were billeted for all that time around the invasion. It turned out that it was in the process of being reshaped into a jet base. I managed somehow, despite the bulldozers and construction equipment, to find the Nissen hut where I'd lived. Just as I found it, a bulldozer pulled up to one end of the hut and I watched the place where I lived during the war torn down before my eyes. It was an incredible moment.

I then drove up the road to where the pub had been. I went up to the door and walked right in and this very startled couple were in there, sitting in their living room. I said, "I'm sorry, this used to be a pub." The man said, "Do you know how long ago that was?" He told me that they'd bought the pub 10 years before and made it into a house.

I was drawn back there one more time when I spent a year in England in 1975. This time there was security like you wouldn't believe because it was now a big American jet base. All I could do was drive around the peripheral road and even that alerted a patrol car that followed me around for a little while.

ABLE, BAKER, AND CHARLIE

J. Dawson Ransome has been flying since he was sixteen years old. Today, though he is past sixty, airplanes are still very much a part of his life. Founder of Ransome Airlines, a Philadelphia-based regional, he recently sold the highly successful firm to Pan American Airways. However, he has not retired. A board member of several major corporations, Ransome keeps his hand in with his favorite pastime—flying aerobatics in his vintage Luftwaffe trainer. Throughout 1944–45, Ransome was flying transport planes over the perilous "Hump," between India and China. It was during those turbulent years that he developed the outstanding flying skills that would later be needed to compete in the modern aviation market.

There was a fellow who lived in my home town named Sonny Wright, and I'll never forget him. He was a bachelor and just loved kids. Every weekend Sonny would come over in his big Packard touring car, and we couldn't wait for him to show up. Everybody would pour into that Packard, and he'd take us out to get ice cream. Sonny knew how much I liked airplanes so he made arrangements for me to get a ride. It was a biplane flying boat with a big Liberty engine. I grew up in Riverton, New Jersey, which is on the Delaware River, right across from Philadelphia. I was nine years old and can still remember putting my arm out and feeling the wind blowing it back: that started all this airplane business. I soloed when I was sixteen years old on a little grass strip, and I've been at it ever since.

I went through the public school system in Riverton and then attended the Episcopal Academy, a private school on the so-called Main Line here in Philadelphia. I didn't go to college. In fact, I didn't

J. Dawson Ransome began his wartime experiences as a civilian instructor. Not wanting to "miss out on the war," he went out to fly cargo planes over the "Hump," the treacherous route between India and China across the Himalayas. After the war he started his own airline, and for a hobby flew aerobatics at air shows all over the country.

even finish high school because I just plain quit and went up to Canada in the fall of 1941. I think I was prompted by a combination of patriotism and adventure. One of the things that inspired me was a bunch of British sailors my dad had invited to our house in Riverton. After dinner I took them up for a ride in a Waco F biplane. They were telling me horror stories about getting torpedoed crossing the Atlantic. From them I got a firsthand indication of how rough the war was, and that helped make up my mind to get into it. To be truthful, however, adventure was probably more of a factor.

I went up to Ottawa with a grand total of 300 hours. They were going to use me as a civilian instructor, but I had a very short tenure. The United States got into the war, and I came right back and became an instructor, still as a civilian, with the Army Air Corps at Decatur, Alabama. Instructing was tough because you were dealing with young men who, in most cases, wanted to fly so badly. I remember one man who was a football player with the New York Giants. He was a huge fellow and just about the roughest bastard on the controls I ever flew with, but such a likable guy that you wanted him to make it. I worked with him and worked with him and finally got him soloed after 18 or 20 hours. Most of my kids would solo after eight or ten hours. We were out at an auxiliary field where he was practicing takeoffs and landings. When you were teaching a student in primary, everything he did was mechanical. Takeoff, climb to 300 feet, level off, level turn, climb to 500 feet, that sort of thing. On the downwind leg, you had what was called the key position and at that point you cut the throttle and glided in for a landing. He took off, leveled off, and everything looked good, but instead of turning toward the runway, he kept going, going, going. He got about two or three miles from the field, finally turned around and started to head back in. I was standing next to another instructor, Jack Heggie, who incidentally just retired from Delta Airlines, and I said to him, "Goddamn, that son of a bitch is going to hit that tree." Sure enough, he hit the tree, WHAM!, wiped out the complete left side set of wings and crashed upside down.

There was a huge cloud of dust and Jack and I started running like hell toward the wreck because we thought we were going to find a corpse. Out of the dust stumped that hulk of a guy and he was bawling like a baby. I said, "Jesus, are you hurt?" He said, "No, but that's the end of my flying." He did manage to get into the war as a bombardier, but never got to fly as a pilot. That was not his, or my, best day. I guess I shouldn't have taken him as far as I did but you became so involved with those guys you hated to quit on them.

After putting over twelve hundred students through primary training at Decatur I started to get itchy. I wanted to fly better equipment than Stearman trainers and didn't want to miss out on the war. There was a group of us who wanted out of instructing, and after making a lot of noise some of us made it into the ferry command. I was working out of Memphis, Tennessee, and ferrying airplanes all over the place. For instance, I took four DC-3s to Ceylon, just off the tip of India. Those trips were very long hauls, especially for a young crew, and the first one I made was quite an experience. There were four of us, copilot, radio operator, mechanic, and me. We flew from Kansas City to Newfoundland and then sat on the ground because the visibility was zero-zero for almost two weeks. Finally a big cold front came through, the weather cleared, and we launched. The whole 12 hours from Newfoundland to the Azores was nothing but thunderstorms. The radio operator's name was Chuck Suzza, and he had the ability to mimic personalities. Al Jolson, Jimmy Durante, he could do them all, and he managed to keep us entertained all the way across the Atlantic.

I was pooped when we got to the Azores, but we decided to fly directly to Africa. When we finally got to Casablanca, I had been up for something like 50 hours, but it was my first trip to that part of the world and I had to go downtown. I wanted to see if Humphrey Bogart or Ingrid Bergman was still there. The first thing we did was go into a corner cafe and I ordered French wine and snails. You have never seen a sicker guy in all your life.

We went from Casablanca across North Africa, and this DC-3 I was flying had the first radar altimeter that I had ever seen. I was anxious to play with the thing and so I was soon flying right down on the deck and watching the altimeter when all of a sudden there was a loud sound, "Braaaaaap!" Braaaaaaap! Braaaaaap!" I thought, "Oh, my God, I've hit the sand with the props," and yanked the airplane up. Everything was running all right, nothing was shaking, and then I heard it again. This time I saw dust kicking up in front of the airplane and felt a breeze on the back of my neck so I opened the door behind me. There was Suzza, sitting in the open cargo door with the .45 submachine gun that we carried on the plane, shooting at everything he saw on the ground. Rommel had just been driven out of Africa and there were tanks, trucks, and all sorts of equipment all over the desert. There were also a lot of natives cannibalizing that stuff, and Suzza must have scared the hell out of them. It was a wonder that he didn't shoot the wing off our plane.

When we got to Cairo I said, "Chuck, I'm going downtown to the officers' club. Want to come with me?" He said, "I'm a sergeant, I can't go down there with you." I gave him a set of bars and wings, dressed him up like an officer, and we went down to the club and had a ball. I probably could have gone to jail for life, but things were different over there. We never wore a tie or cap and it was all very loosey-goosey.

My job with the ferry command lasted for about a year and then I was assigned to go over and fly the Hump. I deadheaded over in a C-54, that was December of 1944, and was assigned to Mohanberi, India, which is up in the Assam Valley, bordering Tibet and Burma. Primarily, we were flying between Mohanberi and Kunming, China. I wasn't over there too long when I got my commission as a second and then a first lieutenant. Up to that time my rank was that of a flight officer service pilot, a civilian pilot who went directly into the service. We were carrying a lot of fuel into China and Burma for the fighter squadrons that were based there—Chennault's group.

Conditions—and people—were rather primitive. There were women building the runways. They didn't have stone crushers and they'd just beat rocks all day long and throw them into baskets. Take big rocks, crush them with a hammer, and make them into little rocks. Once in a while we would carry troops and I can tell you a horrible story about that. A C-46 was carrying a bunch of Chinese troops, and when it was on its takeoff run, they all got up and ran to the tail of the airplane. The weight and balance were thrown out of kilter, the airplane spun in and killed everybody on board. As a result of that, on all future flights, the radio operator would sit in the back of any airplane that was carrying Chinese troops with a .45 so everybody would stay put.

The biggest problems flying the Hump were getting the altitude we needed and the wear and tear that inflicted, particularly on the engines. We were flying the C-46, which for some reason to this day has a terrible reputation. It was a big airplane for those days, and we used to call it *The Flying Cigar*. As far as I am concerned, it was a hell of a good machine for the mission we had to do. First of all, the C-47 couldn't get up to the altitude we needed to clear the mountains when we flew the northern route. There were three routes, Abel, Baker, and Charlie. Abel was the most northern, and we needed a minimum of 18,000 to 20,000 feet. Baker was down around 16,000 and Charlie was the lowest. You could clear that one at about 12,000 to 13,000. I actually flew over Mount Everest in a C-46. When I became operations officer for our base I could fly check rides and one day I took a 46, empty, and just managed to struggle over that mountain. The airplane was just barely holding altitude because I was flying at about 30,000 feet and she didn't have much left. (Everest is 29,028 feet high.)

Another big headache was navigation. We had ADFs, low-frequency automatic direction finders, and high-frequency short wave. The short wave was just for reporting our position. We'd send back coded messages to show our position as we passed these various radio stations going over the Hump. The ADFs were subject to all kinds of atmospheric problems, and if you got into thunderstorms, and we got into a tremendous amount of them, there was a lot of static. The ADF will automatically seek the station you have it tuned to, but when you have a lot of static in the air the needle just flips all over the place and you can't really tie onto the track you're trying to hold. At that point you could take it off automatic and rotate the antenna manually. You heard a tone in your earphone and when the tone faded, the null, you would know that was the station's direction. When we would get a combination of thunderstorms and turbulence, we'd be trying to listen and copy code, attempting to dig it out of all that racket, and it took a lot of interpretation, luck, and experience to get through.

I have been a ham radio operator since I was sixteen years old, I am still active today, and that radio experience helped me a great deal. Sometimes I would trade off with the radio operator and let him go up and sit with the copilot. I built a radio station at our base scrounging anything I could get my hands on, and we would work with the base information officer to give the local news, play music, things like that. We didn't have a lot of power, and what we were doing was rather illegal, but as I said, things were different in those days because we were a long way from home. Our call letters were MON, for Mohanberi, and sometimes when I was coming back from a mission I could hear our station 100 miles out.

The winds in that part of the world are usually the same as they are here, west to east. You could almost depend on them being somewhere out of either the southwest, west, or northwest, depending on the weather. I'm talking, of course, at about 18,000 or 20,000 feet. They would generally be in the neighborhood of 50 or 60 miles an hour and that was a real problem for the kind of airplane we were flying. To show you how things have changed since those days, today I sometimes run into winds of 130 knots when I'm flying my Citation, and it's no problem at all. I often think what it would have been like flying the Hump if we had the stuff we've got to work with today. In that jet I can punch in Miami on the flight management system and the computer will give me the direct route and fly the airplane there for me. All I have to do is sit back and watch the route on the CRT.

At any rate, you usually ended up with a tailwind going over, which was good because you were loaded, and a headwind coming back when you were light. This one particular night, however, a front came in and the wind was out of the south at about 90 miles an hour. The whole area was a solid mass of embedded thunderstorms, and of course, we didn't have any radar. The only thing we had were those pilot reports which the weather people would use to draw a cross section of the Hump on a piece of glass. They would try to keep that thing updated as much as they could and we would look at it just before taking off. That particular night, with all those thunderstorms and all that static, a hell of a lot of airplanes were blown into the Himalayas and crashed. It was pathetic to listen to what was happening on the radio. There I was, a twenty-three-year-old kid, and I was lucky enough to have a copilot who in civilian life was a captain for Pan Am. I think between his previous experience flying the Pacific and my experience with the radio, we were able to hold the track and get through. There were a lot of men who didn't make it through that night. We lost thirty-six airplanes.

Some people who bailed out over the Hump managed to be rescued. We were one of the few bases that had a search and rescue group. They had a B-25 and a couple of C-47s that were used to parachute guys into the field to rescue crews that had gone down. At one point they ran some tests with a rig that was similar to the old "All-American" airmail pickup system that was used in the 1930s. A kit would be dropped and the guy on the ground would set up two poles which had a cord strung between them. Then he would get into a sling, facing toward a DC-3 which was flying at 120 miles an hour toward him. The airplane was rigged with a winch that would play out a rope with a hook on it, snatch the pilot off the ground, and then the pilot would pull the airplane almost up into a stall. Obviously you'd want to yank him off the ground instead of dragging him along the ground or through the trees. The winch would play out with a friction clutch. Also, the rope was nylon and designed to stretch a lot and help get rid of the shock. If all that didn't work, you were history because your guts would be ripped out. I've never bailed out of an airplane in my life, but I did try that rig. They were running some tests and I volunteered so I ended up going up instead of down. Don't ask me why I did it. I was young.

We experienced some Japanese fighter attacks, but not in the air. The weather over the Hump was bad enough for us, almost impossible for fighters. Most of the attacks we had were Zeros strafing our fields in China and Burma. We came in and landed at Kunming one night and were just pulling off the runway when a Jap came in with his lights on, just as if he was one of our group. There he was, in the pattern, and that guy laid a whole string of bombs right down the runway. He got out in one piece because it was such a surprise.

I had a roommate in India who ultimately couldn't take the gaff. He started to crack and told me, "I don't want the responsibility of command anymore." Command of an airplane. He asked if he could be my permanent copilot, which I agreed to. He was a nervous type, but a hell of a nice guy. We were taking off out of Mohanberi and it was about 100 degrees. Aircraft performance is affected by the temperature and the hotter it gets, the worse it gets. I'm rolling down the runway and the cylinder temperature gauge started going up and the engine started to detonate. I knew exactly what was coming, the engine would just quit. The blower seal on the R 2800 had failed and raw oil was getting into the fuel induction system. I was too far committed to quit and I hollered out to him, "The right engine is going." He never said a word to me and I never said a word to him. He sucked the gear, feathered the right engine, closed the cowl flaps, did everything perfectly in sequence. I had to make a big wide-ass turn, 360-degree turn, to come into the runway because I was only 50 feet above the trees, and just before we hit, thump, he put the gear down and we rolled to the end of the runway and the other engine, the left one, seized up. Tighter than a bull's ass. It just proves the point that a lot of the hotshot bastards in this world, when they are under pressure, become unglued. This guy showed all the opposite tendencies, and then when he had to, he did everything just right. Del Cassada was his name and when the chips were down, he came through.

Once in a while the Chinese would fly P-51s into our base and they'd follow us over to China. We'd have to wait until the weather was good because they didn't have navigation worth talking about in those fighters. The Chinese were some of the craziest pilots I've ever seen in my life. When they came into Kunming, they'd be ground looping all over the place. Just tearing up the airplanes. I think a lot of it might have been that they just didn't have the exposure that American kids had gotten to machines. Most of us had been fooling with cars or airplanes since we were kids and that made a hell of a difference.

Near the end of the war I flew a black Cadillac automobile over the Hump for Madame Chiang Kai-shek. It seemed to me that it was a hell of a waste of our resources hauling something like that, but I suppose that it had been promised to her. Even during the war politics had to be taken care of. After the Japanese surrendered, we had to stay and keep the supply lines open to China, just as General Tunner promised we would. I was there for two months, and when we finally got the word that I could come home I decided that it wasn't going to be in a war-weary airplane. I got on a boat in December of 1945 and three or four days later wished I had taken any airplane, no matter what shape it was in. It took us 45 days, but coming in to New York harbor was almost worth the trip. There were fireboats pumping water, the whole works. I had tears coming down my face when I saw the Statue of Liberty.

Prior to the war I went to work as a mechanic for my father's company. Just before I was born, he had started, along with another fellow, a construction equipment business, Giles and Ransome. They sold wheelbarrows, concrete mixers, and that sort of thing. After the war I moved into the sales end of the business and a few years later became vice president of marketing. We were also a Caterpillar tractor distributor, and I'm still on the board of directors.

I maintained my interest in flying and bought an AT-6 for, if you can believe it, $600. I got rid of that for an Aero Commander 520, flew that for a while and then sold it and bought a P-51 Mustang. I put in a seat where the radios used to be so my wife, Maryann, could ride with me. We would put our suitcases in the areas that used to hold ammunition and our golf clubs on the gun racks. It was a hell of an airplane, but I decided to get rid of it because my wife didn't particularly like it. She'd be sitting in the back of the thing with that 12-cylinder engine barking and all those fumes coming in, which wasn't her idea of a good time. One weekend we were going to play golf at Pinehurst and before we left she asked me if the bag she was packing could fit in the airplane. I said, "Oh, sure," without really thinking about it. We got out to the airport and sure enough, it didn't fit, so she proceeded to take all of her clothes out of the bag and stuff them in the ammo area. Off we went and just about the time I was lifting off the runway, the damn latch came loose and her clothes were being sucked out, one at a time. Blouses, bras, and everything else were all over the countryside and when we got down to Pinehurst I had to buy her a whole new set of clothes. Right after that incident, we decided to sell the Mustang and buy a twin Beechcraft.

It was at that point I decided it was time we got into the aviation business. One of my brothers had gotten interested in flying and we convinced my father and other brother that it was a good idea. They were originally very much against it. "Those things don't look like tractors to us." We concluded that the then-emerging regional airline business was the best deal and started flying our first scheduled flights on March 2, 1967, between North Philadelphia Airport and Washington, D.C. Allegheny Airlines was flying out of Philadelphia International, but we concluded that we were closer to the center of the economic center of gravity up here in north Philadelphia. We had eight flights a day when we started and we were using the Beechcraft and a Turboliner, a turbine-powered Beechcraft.

We started in a construction trailer and a T hangar. Our present head of maintenance loves to say, "When you went to the can at

Ransome Airlines, you really went to the can." What he was alluding to was the fact that we didn't even have a toilet in the hangar when we started, just literally, a can.

At one point I went up to New York City to see American Airlines. I was trying to develop some joint fares with them that would be competitive with United Airlines. I was going up in the elevator with the district sales manager, Spence Rice, when the door opened and this great big hulk of a guy got on. Rice said to him, "Mr. Smith, I'd like to introduce you to Dawson Ransome." C. R. Smith was one of the real pioneers in aviation and he started American Airlines. C. R. looked at me and said, "Ransome, how's that little pipsqueak airline of yours doing?" I said, "O.K." "Are you making any money?" I said, "Hell, no, I'm losing my ass." He told me to stick with it, and then he said, "On second thought, come upstairs, I want to talk to you. Rice, you go downstairs and wait for him." I told C. R. that we were at the point of quitting the business because we were having a hell of a time. He spent more than an hour with me going through the early days of American and really gave me the fortitude to carry on. He was a big tough old pussycat and it was one of the highlights of my life to have a guy like that sit down with me and show me how it was done.

Another tremendous influence on me was Les Barnes, who at that time was the president of Allegheny Airlines. He recently retired as chairman of Ryder Trucks. When we were having all that trouble I just decided to call him up. Never met him in my life, but I got hold of him on the phone and said, "Les, you don't know me, but. . . ." He said, "Oh, yes I do. You're the guy who put the big outdoor billboard on the expressway advertising cheap seats to Washington." I told him that I'd like to come to see him and just philosophize a bit about the airline business. He said, "When do you want to come?" I owe a lot to both of these men; they really helped me make our operation successful.

We hung on and today we fly out of fifteen airports, but it was a tough haul. We bought twelve French Nord aircraft which Lake Central had been operating. They were pressurized, had a flight attendant, and carried twenty-seven passengers. The airplane had developed a terrible reputation because Lake Central had very little experience with turbine aircraft. We did our homework, put them into service, and that airplane has been phenomenal. We still use some of them today, but the airplane that really made us is the Dash-7, a fifty-passenger, four-engine STOL (short takeoff and landing) airplane. We pioneered the concept of flying our own low-level routes which are designed to keep us away from the other jet traffic, and landing on a 2,000-foot runway that converged with the major runways the major carriers are using. It has been very successful because it takes our airplanes out of the daisy chain, so to speak. When you move an airplane out of the conventional pattern, you allow one more airplane to land, and that increases the airport's acceptance rate. We also save about 40 miles of flying by using these routes, which means we save a hell of a lot of fuel. The whole flight profile is preprogrammed into the on-board computer, and it's almost autoflight because the computer virtually flies the whole trip. I can see the day when the whole commercial airline system will be designed this way, but it is very difficult to get this kind of advanced technology accepted by the FAA. I don't mean to sound critical in any way, but the FAA is a typical, cumbersome government agency. Now that our operation has been sold to Pan Am, I head up a lot of special committees that will be involved with just that sort of long-range planning.

The opportunity with Pan Am presented itself almost by accident. They called me and wanted to know if we could work with them, as well as with Delta, whom we've been associated with for three years. I told them that I didn't think it would work because it isn't possible to serve two masters. Then I said, rather casually, "Why don't you buy us out?" A couple of weeks later they called back and said that's exactly what they would like to do. The only thing I'm interested in is maintaining my office and having an interest in whatever the entity is.

If you want to look at an airline, generally speaking, I think you should look at the top management. Look at their philosophy, the way they run their outfit. I think people, for the most part, want to do a good job. Particularly people who have responsibility for other people's lives. It's a matter of making the people who work for you as happy as you can in their work environment. Make them feel as if what they are doing is important to the success or failure of the company. I also think somebody has to be the boss, but one of the things that a lot of the original pioneers had to go through was making the transition from being the sole driving force to being able to delegate responsibility and create a management team with a diverse group of personalities.

What worries me today is that we are losing our basic industries. The kind of industrial and technological advantage that we used to have. World War II wasn't just won by the guys who were fighting it, but also by the tens of thousands of people who worked in the factories and the little machine shops who had the capabilities to make the materials we needed. The small operation run by the guy with an idea made this country strong. Everything today is merger, merger, bigger, bigger, and I'm not sure if that's the way to go. The whole management structure is set up for short-term rewards, not long-term goals. How much money did the company make this year? When the annual reports come out the most important item is profits, not future plans. We can't go from a highly productive, creative entrepreneurial society to a service society without losing our position in the world marketplace. I guarantee you that we're going to go down the tubes if we keep it up.

ODD MAN OUT

C-47s tow Waco CG-4A gliders in a training mission. Collection of John Lowden.

We conclude this book with two men who fought unique and different wars. John Lowden flew gliders, carrying men and equipment on a one-way trip into battle. Once a glider pilot was on the ground, he became an infantryman until he could get back to friendly lines. The "best of both worlds."

Hughes Rudd went into combat in a military version of a Piper Cub. That is, he carried a pistol. His job was that of artillery spotter and scout, a job formerly entrusted to horse cavalry and balloons in earlier wars. Rudd sums up the experiences of World War II aviators as well as anybody. "I don't think a day goes by that I don't think about the war. I'm sure that is true of everybody who went through a combat experience."

"NEVER, EVER VOLUNTEER"

Tall and polished, a retired communications executive who now lives in Florida, John Lowden speaks about his hair-raising war experiences with an observer's detachment. "You were either bored to death or scared to death. In gliders, there was no in-between." In fact, flying combat gliders was extremely dangerous duty. Records show that a 40 to 50 percent combat casualty rate was anticipated for some missions. A product of the unique conditions of World War II, the combat glider has faded into history. John Lowden thinks that's just fine.

The Waco CG-4A glider was designed and built with seat configurations that required parachutes for the pilot and copilot to sit on so that they could reach the controls. One day an airborne lieutenant said to me, "If you leave this glider using that 'chute, you're going to look like a bunch of grapes because all my troops and me are going to be hanging on to you."

We substituted for the 'chutes with two small tubular sandbags placed side by side on each seat. These sandbags, which did the job perfectly, were nothing more than wheel chocks for the gliders. Then as a safety measure we scrounged up armorplate to go under the sandbags, which were made more comfortable by putting a cushion of some sort on top of them. Sometimes this was something as simple as a bed pillow folded in half. We all felt much safer with the armorplate. We didn't by any means like the idea of taking a bullet from the ground in the foot or leg. But we were even more antsy about taking a random bullet or piece of shrapnel in the butt or in the family jewels.

At boot camp in Tacoma, Washington, in January 1941, John Lowden, right, poses with a friend, Russ Mulvaney. Washing out in pilot training, he "volunteered" to become a glider pilot and flew missions during the invasion of Germany. After the war he had a long career in advertising. Today he is writing a book describing his perilous career in the legions of silent wings.

Some of the glider pilots from my squadron trained with the British before Normandy. I was one of them. We considered ourselves pretty good in the CG-4A. But we considered ourselves exceptional after learning to fly the British Horsa, which had a tricycle landing gear, could carry thirty-two fully equipped airborne troopers (or the equivalent weight in combat vehicles and gear), was towed with a Y-shaped hemp rope which attached to slots on either side of the Horsa's "flight deck," and had flaps which worked off two compressed air cylinders. That is, each flap worked off a separate cylinder. If the pressures in the cylinders were not equal one flap would come down sooner than the other, which gave the Horsa glider an annoying—not to mention horrifying—tendency to attempt a slow roll on the final approach. You can be sure that the pilot and copilot kept an eye on both flaps while landing. (By contrast, the CG-4A had spoilers on top of the wings. When opened fully by the pilot the glider sank at a rapid rate because wing lift had been "spoiled.")

The flaps ranked right up there with the Horsa's nose gear, which had a way of collapsing if the Horsa were landed too hard in a plowed field or on rough terrain. And let us not forget the hemp tow rope. Problems arose when the main rope broke—or when one of the ropes which formed one arm of the Y gave way, which caused the glider to fly sideways just long enough to scare hell out of the tow pilot and make gibbering idiots out of the glider pilots. In both cases, an unscheduled landing was in order.

I much preferred the American CG-4A. It was more maneuverable and easier to land. Also, the CG-4A tow rope was made of nylon, about one inch in diameter and 350 feet long. It could and did stretch about one-third of its length so it was always relatively taut, unlike hemp, which had little elasticity. And, the nylon tow rope attached to a single spot on the CG-4A's nose. When the American glider program was started, the pilot was supposed to drop the CG-4A wheels once he had taken off, and land on skids. But they found the glider was almost uncontrollable after it hit the ground. Wheels gave the pilot some braking control (the CG-4A was equipped with hydraulic brakes), but not much because at that time "blitz" landings at speeds up to 100 MPH were still standard procedure.

The Army Air Corps finally decided to leave the wheels on and decided that a low-spead landing around 50 or 60 MPH was much more practical. With the wheels on, the pilot could make a nose-high, three-point landing and have braking control. Also, a low-speed landing made it a damned sight easier to put down a fully loaded glider in some farmer's potato patch without taking out his fencing as well as the fencing of his neighbor. But there was one thing that had to be carefully watched. Two skids curved up from under the nose like a pair of skis. If the glider, even with wheels, were rocked forward onto the skids to help slow it down in a short-field landing, the tips of the skids could dig in and the glider then usually flipped over on its back, which created a hell of a mess inside if the glider happened to be loaded with men and equipment. I learned this the hard way—which cost me some front teeth, the copilot a broken back, and eight troopers assorted broken bones, cuts, and bruises.

Those of us who had trained in the British Horsa glider were scheduled to go into Normandy on D-day +2 with British airborne troops to fight a 48-hour diversionary action some miles behind the German lines. We were 15 minutes from takeoff when the mission was scrubbed. Two reasons were later given to us: an American general officer had seen the battle plan and said, "You can use your own pilots for this mission but you'll not use Americans," or that the invasion troops had not punched inland from the Normandy beachhead as far as they thought they would in two days, so the mission was scrubbed because its objective was too heavily armed. This would probably have prevented a link up with troops fighting inland from Normandy. I'd like to think the real reason was the former, but I am inclined to put more stock in the latter.

Then there was the invasion of southern France, called Operation Dragoon. My squadron leader came into the barracks calling for volunteers. There was a big silence. Eventually, a few hands went up. The squadron leader turned to me. "What about you, Lowden?" I asked, "Where are we going?" He said, "I can't tell you, it's top secret." I said, "So keep your secret. I'm not going." He said, "You're not setting a very good example for the men in your flight—after all, you are a flight leader." I said, "Let me tell you a little story—something my father passed on to me just before I caught the bus to boot camp. My father was a First World War infantryman. He once volunteered to crawl out at night before a major attack to cut barbed wire and then crawl back to his lines. He made it but a couple of his buddies didn't. So at the bus depot he didn't tell me about loose women or the evils of booze or venereal diseases or being true to my Catholic faith or anything like that. He gave me a single piece of advice: 'Keep your eyes open, your mouth shut, your bowels free, and never, ever volunteer.'"

I said, "Now if I'm ordered to go, I'll go. But you give me a choice, and I'm not going." I didn't want to be hanging up there as God's yo-yo at 300 feet, under heavy ground fire and barely in control and have to say to myself, "If it hadn't been for your stupid volunteering, Lowden, you'd be sitting on your ass in a bar someplace." The squadron leader got his volunteers and away they went to help liberate southern France. They were gone about 30 days. I heard later that if something could go wrong it did, especially where my squadron was involved. There was one volunteer from our squadron who was a tough steel-mill type from Toledo. For some reason we never seemed to get along. Nothing overt, we just avoided each other. When he got back from the mission, he walked up to me and put out his hand. He said, "Lowden, I want to shake your hand. We may never have gotten to be buddies but I just want you to know that I've come to the conclusion that you're the only son-of-a-bitch in this squadron who has any goddamned common sense."

I wasn't a coward. Just cautious. I was a Depression kid. I was leery as hell of people with authority. During the Depression the guy with the clout made some people in the world jump or dance a little jig, at the very least. I was in the U.S. Army Air Corps almost a year before Pearl Harbor. (Hell, in those days Pearl Harbor could have been one of our local hookers in Walla Walla, Washington! That's how much I knew about world geography.)

Anyway, I had a scholarship of sorts to Whitman College in Walla Walla, but I needed some kind of work to fill in the blank spots—even though I could live at home. I went to the president of the college and asked for a three-year raincheck. The draft was in effect and anybody who read the newspapers in 1940 would have had to be stupid to believe that the U.S. was not going to get involved in the war in Europe. So one Saturday night I said to my favorite drinking buddy, "All we do is sit around and drink nine-cent bottles of beer and bitch about the fact that the world is passing us by. Let's enlist!" We shopped the services. The Marines wanted four years. That was too long. The Army was out of the question. We didn't like the Navy uniforms so we ended up deciding on the Army Air Corps.

On January 18, 1941, we were both sworn in and in a few days started our basic training at McChord Field near Tacoma, Washington. The pre–World War II Army was tough, but it wasn't as bad as we expected. Living quarters were decent and the food was edible. The pay wasn't much: $21 a month for openers, which in a few weeks went to $30 a month where it stayed until a promotion. I was nineteen years old at the time and by the time I got out of the military in December of 1945, I did a lot of growing up. I had a pretty short temper as a kid. I wasn't a troublemaker, but I didn't accept discipline very easily. All this changed quickly in the Army. You do it their way or forget it. Their way or the stockade. There was no option.

After basic training I was assigned to a B-25 group as a photographer-gunner. To the 89th Reconnaissance Squadron, to be exact, and our home base was Pendleton, Oregon. Late in 1941 we went on maneuvers—from Pendleton to Houston to Augusta, Georgia—and we enlisted men did all our traveling by truck. It was the pits. Then one day in late November we got orders to return to Pendleton. We made Pendleton in early December and after all the mickey-mouse stuff got sorted out, we were given two weeks for furlough. I left Pendleton on December 6 for my home town, Walla Walla, just 47 miles away. The next day—you know what happened December 7, 1941—I turned right around and hustled my ass back to Pendleton and spent that evening and most of the night helping to drape and tie down bed sheets over the wings and tail surfaces of the B-25s. The brass was afraid, and rightly so, that a heavy frost might interfere with the planes getting off the ground in a hurry.

Some of the guys also spent a good deal of time painting out red and blue crosses on the sides and wings of the planes. While on maneuvers, these designated the Red Army and the Blue Army. Since these crosses hadn't been painted out before the planes returned to Pendleton some of the locals thought the Germans had landed! Then there was a report that a Japanese carrier was off the coast of San Francisco in a fog bank. Every B-25 and crew went on standby, but no carrier developed. There were also tales of Jap submarines cruising all up and down the West Coast. But these turned out to be true. I recall that a B-25 from our squadron was the first to destroy one.

Once things quieted down a bit, I applied for flying school and was accepted. I was in Class 42-H and was shipped to Santa Maria, California, to the John Hancock College of Aeronautics for primary flight training. Out of a class of about 120 only about 30 of us graduated and went on to basic training at Lemoore, California, in the San Joaquin Valley, where the summer temperatures were almost unbearable.

It was while in basic training in Lemoore that I learned that my friends in the B-25 Group had flown off the aircraft carrier *Hornet*, and bombed Tokyo. One of the gunners from my old 89th Reconnaissance Squadron is reported to have shot down seven Jap intercepters.

But, anyway, something went wrong in basic training. I don't know whether I got too cocky, lost interest, was too slow on the uptake, or just wasn't as good as I thought, but eventually I washed out. My main problem was learning blind or instrument flying. I felt bad about this because it was the first time in my young life that I had failed at something of consequence. I was assigned to a quartermaster company and figured my flying days were over. Little did I know! The company executive officer called me into his office one day and told me all about a new program involving combat gliders, which he thought I might be interested in. I thanked him for his concern about my future but turned down his suggestion that I volunteer for this new glider corps. So to make sure I didn't have time to sit around feeling sorry for myself for having washed out of pilot training, he assigned me to do an inventory of G.I. blankets which were stacked in a warehouse where the temperature must have been over 90 degrees during the coolest part of the day. I spent two days on the inventory. The morning of the third day I was standing in front of the adjutant's desk and said, "Sir, I have given careful reconsideration to your suggestion that I volunteer for the glider corps and I have decided to do so." He said, "I thought you might see it my way."

I was immediately given staff sergeant stripes and sent off to Plainview, Texas. There we flew Piper Cubs and Aeroncas up to 5,000 feet, day and night, cut the switch, and glided in deadstick. The daytime stuff didn't bother me much. But the first night I reported to the flight line and asked for my instructor I was told, "He's up with another instructor. He's never had any night flight training." I don't know how we survived the required thirty hours of training, but we did. We lost a few planes but we didn't lose a student or an instructor.

Most of us were then sent to Fort Sumner, New Mexico, for sailplane training. We would be towed up to about 2,000 feet and the idea was to get the feel of free flight. I could ride thermals [rising air currents] for as long as my rump could hold out—usually around four hours. Training in free flight and a long final approach to a landing did us little good when we saddled up for a combat mission in a CG-4A which could carry its own weight—about 3,800 pounds of cargo, or fifteen combat-equipped men. Usually the cargo was a mix of men, munitions, high-octane fuel, maybe a jeep or baby bulldozer, or a burial detail with white stakes and gray canvas bags. A long, final approach to a combat landing was also just asking for concentrated ground fire.

From Fort Sumner we were shipped off to Albuquerque, New Mexico, where about 800 of us stooged around for weeks because the CG-4A, which was to be the advanced trainer, hadn't been built in quantity yet. I finally got my wings in Lubbock, Texas, and was eventually transferred to Bowman Field in Louisville, Kentucky. There a cadre of infantry officers made our lives hell for eight weeks. We were all hacking around the officers' club or taking frequent 48-hour passes into Louisville, when a notice was posted that all glider pilots would be assembled the next day in Class "A" uniform on the parade grounds.

The next morning we were all standing at attention in that miserable Louisville summer heat facing the reviewing stand on which a bunch of infantry officers seemed to be sharing some sort of private joke—and all the glider pilots seemed to know what the joke was all about. There we stood—pale, fat, and totally out of condition. One of the infantry brass walked over to the microphone, and as he looked us over said, "They tell us you men are pilots. I can't comment on that. However, you are not soldiers. I can see that even from here. We're going to change that during the next eight weeks."

Those infantry guys put us through a training program that had us qualifying in everything from the bayonet to the use of antitank weapons. I came out of that program ten pounds lighter and a damned sight more confident than when I went into it. After all, before the program started I doubt that most of the glider pilots had done much more than fire a rifle.

The training continued in a remote area of North Carolina. Night maneuvers could be especially hair-raising. I was part of a double tow one night. That is, one C-47, the standard American tow plane, would pull two gliders. The nylon tow ropes made a V-shape and were attached to a D-ring coupler which in turn attached to the tow plane's tail. One glider flew the left-hand position about 350 feet behind the tow plane and the other glider about 425 feet back in the right-hand position, which was my position this night, with a full load of troops.

For some reason both arms of the tow rope were about the same length, and we were no sooner airborne than the glider on my left started drifting into me. I don't know if the pilot had a bad case of night blindness or the shakes but his right wing tip kept trying to punch a hole in the side of the nose of my glider. I was finally forced to cut my glider loose at about 1,000 feet. I didn't know where the hell I was at that point. I did know there was nothing below me except acres and acres of scrub pine trees. Fortunately, there was some moonlight and I spotted a little tobacco patch that some farmer had cleared, so in we went. It was tight, believe me. I flew a close down-wind leg, started using the spoilers on the base leg, and on my final approach used the spoilers and had the glider in a sideslip. I came out of the slip a few feet off the ground and put the spoilers full on and pulled the nose up a bit more than usual, so we touched down very gently at about 55 MPH. Since the field was plowed we didn't roll more than 100 feet. We walked out on roads that were not much more than cow paths and got a ride back to the base in a truck that had been sent to look for us. I don't think the glider was ever recovered. It was so far back in the boondocks.

Later, while I was flying a daytime maneuver, the tow rope pulled out of the tail of the tow plane at about 200 feet. Since the rope was nylon and under tension it snapped back toward the nose of my glider and from where I sat I could see that the heavy metal coupling device, which attached to the tow plane's tail, just might come through the front of the glider, taking out me and the troops aboard. I pulled the nose of my glider up sharply and as the coupler went under us, I released the tow rope from the nose of the glider. Instead of the rope falling free, the end that had been attached to the glider wrapped around the right wheel. Since the rope was 350 feet long and we were 200 feet up, I could feel it snagging on trees. I knew if I tried to make a forced landing at normal speed, the rope would almost surely hook on a tree and we would do a partial nose-down outside loop into the ground. Again, a small clearing in the trees appeared and I dove the glider into it. The glide angle was shallow enough to give us some chance of survival, and the speed was such that I hoped that the rope would not have the time to get seriously involved with a tree or fence. We survived with a few broken bones and bruises.

Sometime in March of 1944, I shipped out for Europe. Those of our group that didn't fly to Europe by way of northern Africa headed for Liverpool, England, on a converted French cruise ship called the *Louis Pasteur*. It had been transformed into a troop ship by the British and it was cramped. We crossed alone from New York to Liverpool in four days and twenty-two hours, without any sort of escort. The ship cruised at about 27 knots so an escort could not have kept up with it. The weather was terrible and nearly everyone was seasick.

From Liverpool we traveled south to our base near Exeter in the southwest part of England. Training continued, but sporadically. Then we moved to Fulbeck, which became an enormous staging area for airborne of all types. It was from Fulbeck in September of 1944 that we took off for the invasion of Holland—called Operation Market-Garden. The names of Dutch cities and villages like Arnhem, Nijmegen, Oosterbeek, and Groesbeek are today mentioned prominently in military history books. This was the first mission of the newly formed First Allied Airborne Army, which included, among others, the U.S. 82nd, 101st, and 17th Airborne Divisions, the British 1st and 6th Airborne Divisions, and the U.S. 9th Troop Carrier Command. Two thousand American gliders and seven hundred British gliders made up the largest single glider operation of World War II. This combined airborne and tank operation was designed to open a clear road to Berlin and end hostilities. The mission has been called a limited success. Actually, the Nazis kicked our Allied asses good. This is not to say that the Allies did not give a good account of themselves, especially the British at Arnhem and the Nijmegen bridge. But the fact is the Nazis held their ground, and the war did not wind down that September as the Allies had hoped.

My part in the Market-Garden was interesting, but not so much because I flew a CG-4A into a small field near Groesbeek—and almost put down in a minefield while I was at it. Once on the ground, we were to rendezvous at a certain point, but darkness came too quickly and I got lost. I ended up with a bunch of others who had lost their way—mostly Americans and a few British. We dug in finally, for to be moving around, lost and in the dark, was an invitation to get shot. Dawn finally arrived and we hadn't gone a hundred yards down the road when we ran into a British truck convoy that was going into Brussels to pick up medical supplies, ammunition, food, and so forth. Or so they told us. I've often wondered why this stuff couldn't have been dropped by parachute. Anyway, the sergeant major in charge of the convoy said, "Hey, Yanks, how'd you like to finally do something to earn all that money you've been getting all these years?"

He explained that even though we were surrounded, the convoy had to get out and it needed protective firepower. They had none of their own, but he could see we eight American glider pilots were loaded for bear (our British friends had gone off in another direction), with a bazooka, automatic weapons of all sorts, hand grenades, and the like. He told us, too, that the road was going to be opened long enough for the convoy to get out. And just about then we heard the start of a heavy firefight not too far away. We jumped in to the trucks—one glider pilot with each driver in the cab and the rest of us split up and riding in the rear, crouched down behind the tailgates.

A signal was given and off we went. Considering how close the fighting was around us, I didn't think we had a prayer of getting through. But we did, and we were roaring down this two-lane highway when the convoy comes to a sudden stop. We, the Americans, thought we'd been ambushed, so we bailed out of the trucks and took cover. But the British had stopped for "high tea" [or "elevenses"] with their gasoline soaked cans of sand serving as hot plates and other makeshift paraphernalia. Once tea was finished, we were off again for Brussels at full speed.

They dropped us on the outskirts of Brussels. We Americans split then to go our separate ways. A buddy of mine and I headed immediately for downtown Brussels and checked into the Metropole Hotel wearing full combat gear. The man in the striped pants and cutaway coat behind the registration desk never turned a hair when he looked up and saw us. You would have thought that every day he had people who looked like us—helmet, battle fatigues, submachine gun, knife in boot, all that nonsense—checking into his hotel.

Brussels had been liberated by the British for only a couple of weeks, and there was a lot of celebrating still going on. Since we were some of the first American soldiers in Brussels following the liberation, we did some "sightseeing and partying" for a few days. But the British had other ideas. And since they were running the city at that point, they ran all American glider pilots out of the city. I'm not sure, but I think now that the Brussels military airport was our rendezvous point with our own C-47s for transport back to our bases in England.

I discovered later that a test case charging desertion in the face of the enemy had been brought against one of our group who had visited Brussels, but the case was dismissed—which saved a lot of hassle for a lot of us—on a technicality. The defense attorney proved that in the Market-Garden briefing, one of the glider pilots had gotten to his feet and asked, "After we hit the ground, what do we do then?" and the briefing officer's response was, "Don't worry about it, you'll find plenty to do!" It was this ambiguous statement that was the key to our man's acquittal and which certainly saved a lot of us from going to trial. As nearly as I could find out, every American glider pilot in Brussels had arrived there because he had served the British military forces in some way. We made the mistake of not getting some sort of written statement to that effect, whether it was from the convoy's sergeant major or from British headquarters in Brussels.

Then along came Operation Varsity in March of 1945. This was the crossing of the Rhine River at Wesel and landing on German soil. I'd been scared before but never as much as I was on that one. I was leading my flight in at about 500 feet and we were about a quarter of a mile from our landing zone, when a Nazi gun emplacement opened up. Our line of flight was taking us directly over it, and the gunner was doing real damage to the flights in front of us. Then, out of nowhere, a British Typhoon fighter with a full load of rockets came boring in at about 200 feet and blew the gun emplacement into oblivion. Some of the dust and smoke was still rising when we flew over the spot. To make it even more interesting, the British had laid down a smokescreen to protect troops crossing the Rhine and it had drifted over our landing zone. We went in blind but broke out at 300 feet.

I was now on my final approach. I'd learned that what's behind you can sometimes be as dangerous as what's in front of you. So I leaned well forward and looked out over my right shoulder through one of the ports. I saw that a glider on my right had been hit, and it looked as though it was going to collide with mine. I put my glider into a dive to get out of his way. I was then going to pull up and put the spoilers on and get on the ground as quickly as possible. My copilot, another glider pilot, panicked, so he grabbed the controls. When this happened, I thought we'd had our tail shot off. But instead of being frightened, I felt relieved. Here was the moment of truth—the moment I'd been fearing since I first got in a glider. I'm 150 feet in the air and it will all be over in a few seconds. Then, I noticed that the goddamned glider was flying along quite nicely. I looked over at the copilot and he stared back at me as all kinds of shit from the ground was pinging through the glider's tail. I took over the controls and in a few seconds we were on the ground. We spent two days on prisoner guard duty and the Hitler Youth, even that late in the war, were real hard noses. Young kids, sixteen or seventeen years old, who would as soon spit on you as look at you. But the sixty-year-olds who had just been drafted into the front lines weren't about to give anyone a hard time. For them the war was over. We marched thousands of prisoners to the Rhine, where British amphibian vehicles took us across the river to a British fighter base where our own C-47s picked us up.

After every mission we were entitled to a week someplace in Europe. Someone said, "Where are we going to go?" Somebody else said, "Jesus, there isn't a city in Europe that isn't crawling with soldiers." We had a Cajun in our outfit who spoke French and we told him, "Go down and talk to the trainmaster and find out where the hell we can go to find some peace and quiet." He came back all excited because the day before they had finished putting down the railway tracks linking Orleans and Biarritz. The next day seven of us were on the train to Biarritz, which is on the French coast near the Spanish border. While we were there, the war in Europe ended. Biarritz had been isolated since the Nazis pulled out, and we were the first Allied soldiers they had seen. It was refreshing to walk into a town and be welcome. After four years of war it didn't matter what uniform you wore. You were still a soldier and there were hundreds of thousands of others just like you creating problems with traffic, in bars, in whorehouses, in police stations, and everywhere else. When the lights went on in Biarritz the seven of us were invited to cocktail receptions, celebrations, dances—we were the conquering heroes.

We got back from Biarritz—I think we were back two weeks— and the squadron executive officer walked into the barracks one day and said, "Who wants to go home?" We were told to be packed and out in front of the barracks in two hours. The C-47 was "rarin'" to go! We landed in Stone, England, which was a reverse replacement depot. From there guys were going home by ship or plane. Many of the Air Force officers that had been shot down and survived prison camp were there. Some were guys who had only made one mission and had been drawing all their pay during the war. They had gambling tables set up with armed troops guarding them. There would be as much as twenty to thirty thousand dollars on the table some of the time. A lot of guys lost everything and others won enough to go back home and start a nice business.

I flew home by way of Greenland, landed at Miles Standish Air Force Base in Massachusetts, got 30 days at home during which the atomic bombs were dropped on Japan, went to Santa Ana, California, and officially got out of the service on December 23, 1945. After five years in the service, I was told that I was going to miss it severely. I didn't think I would and I didn't. In a week you'd have never known I'd been in the Army Air Corps.

I promised myself a month on the beach for every year in the Army. I went to Hollywood and found myself a room in a boarding house. Then I bought myself a used Chevrolet convertible and went to the Santa Monica beach everyday and made the clubs every night. When I ran out of money I packed it in and enrolled at Whitman College in September of 1946. I later matriculated at the University of Nevada, in Reno, from which I graduated with a degree in English. After that I went to the University of Oklahoma for advanced writing courses. By the time I got through college and started my first steady job I was twenty-nine years old.

At that point I wanted to be a writer, but I thought I'd better find work to pay the rent and buy food, so I went to San Francisco and signed on with an insurance company as a claims adjuster. In my travels I ran across a broker who said, "I've been listening to you and watching you. You don't belong in this business; you really belong in advertising." I said, "I tried to get an ad job for months, but nobody would take me." He picked up the phone and within two weeks I was working as a writer in a small agency in San Francisco for fifty dollars a week. After that I went to Campbell Ewald in San Francisco and Washington, D.C., and worked on the Chevrolet account. Next I joined Erwin Wasey, Ruthrauff & Ryan in New York City. I was the account supervisor on the British Rootes Motors account, which was almost as harassing and horrendous as completing a glider mission. We couldn't do advertising that was different, daring, or unusual, and bad advertising leads to bad sales.

After that I spent a few years at General Dynamics in New York and thought I'd found a corporate home. But when losses of $450 million were reported in the development of the Convair 880 and 990 commercial jets, wholesale firings took place almost immediately. I was one of those unfortunates. However, one good thing did come of my sojourn at General Dynamics: it was there I met my wife, Janet. So my family and I moved to Los Angeles—I had a daughter, Susan, by this time. I signed on with Foote, Cone & Belding, an advertising agency, and went to work on the Hughes Aircraft account. Fourteen months later I was recruited by ITT in New York as advertising manager, and in November of 1963 I had relocated at 320 Park Avenue, where I spent the next 21 years. I retired as vice-president for advertising and sales promotion in December of 1984.

Like most glider pilots I think we've been neglected by the military history books. And by the film industry, for that matter. But at least there are some museums around that help tell the story. One that was underwritten or sponsored by the World War II Glider Pilots Association is located near Terrell, Texas, about thirty miles east of Dallas. Also, in the U.S., there's a permanent exhibit in the National Soaring Museum in Elmira, New York. In Holland, of course, there's the famous British Airborne Museum in Arnhem, and another not too far away in Groesbeek. The museum opened originally in Nijmegen but later was relocated to larger space in Groesbeek. This Groesbeek museum is a pet project of a Catholic priest, Father Gerard Thuring, pastor of a little church in Groesbeek. He was six or seven years old when the invasion took place. He was on the roof of his house with his sister and she said, "Look at those funny airplanes. There are strings between them!"

My elder son, Jonathan, visited the museums in Arnhem and Groesbeek and came away impressed—impressed with the fact that we gray panthers really fought and won a war with equipment and armament that he called "right out of the Stone Age."

HUGHES RUDD

MAYTAG MESSERSCHMITT

*Retired, Hughes Rudd now lives in France, but before he moved abroad,
we met in the elegant old bar at the Mayflower Hotel in Washington,
D.C. His face is a bit older than you remember from Rudd's years with
CBS News, but the voice is unmistakable. It sounds as if it were being
filtered through layers of gravel. Listening to him, it's obvious that his
famous sense of humor, a necessity if you were flying around Europe
during World War II in a Piper Cub, is still very much in tune.*

I've often thought of the view that I had of the war. A rifleman was
usually in the woods hiding behind something. The bomber pilots
were flying too high to see anything, and the fighter pilots were
flying too fast. There I was at 3,000 feet and going all of 75 miles an
hour. It would have been a perfect place for a National Geographic
photographer.

When they bombed Monte Cassino, my assignment was to fly
around looking for German flak batteries. We had been assaulting the
mountain for months with infantry and not getting anyplace, so they
decided to bomb their way through. The Army used guys like me
because the Germans were on the high ground and the Americans
were on the ground, period. We were the best method of observation
they had. When the front finally broke loose and they'd send everybody full bore down the highway, I would be flying point out in
front. If I saw a roadblock or enemy troops, I'd get on the radio and
warn them. A colonel told me once, "You men are my cavalry." I've
thought about what he said and that colonel was right. During the

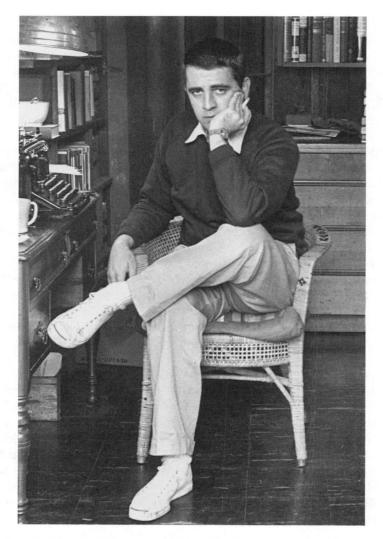

Hughes Rudd took this portrait of himself with a self-timer while he was a student at Stanford, ten years after his days as an artillery spotter fighting Germans in a Piper Cub. How much younger could he have looked then? Starting out after the war as a newspaperman, Rudd first brought his distinctive style to the television screen in 1969. Retired, he lives today in France.

American Civil War the cavalry wasn't used in head-on charges. They were really scouting troops who rode sturdy horses.

The first attack on Monte Cassino was made by P-40s. They dropped 500-pound bombs, and as they zoomed all around me, their slipstreams rocked and jolted my L-4. That was awesome enough, but when they came back with the medium and heavy bombers a month later, I never saw anything to equal that. The sky was full of bombers, and when they dropped their bombs, the smoke and debris were flying up almost as high as I was. The air was actually shaking, and I could see ripples running across the ground as though an earthquake were in progress.

They were also very inaccurate. I was flying long figure-eights back and forth, and I could see bombs bursting 10 miles behind the American lines. They were dropping them all over the fucking landscape. Maybe it was true that they could hit a pickle barrel with that Norden bombsight, but there were no pickle barrels in the Liri Valley that day. Enough bombs hit Cassino town to turn it into rubble, making it impassable for American tanks, which were ready to attack. The abbey was also destroyed and 1,400 years of history was blown away that morning. After it was all over, the British infantry put up a sign next to a bombed-out British tank which said, "American precision bombing."

I grew up in Waco, Texas, and I can't remember when I wasn't fascinated by airplanes. The cadets who were training at Kelly Field in San Antonio would have to fly a triangular course at night as part of their graduation exercise. San Antonio to Waco to Temple, and back. About once a year one of them would run into a water tower on the edge of Waco. You'd hear that "bong" all over the city and you knew, there went another cadet.

After high school I went to the University of Missouri and at one point I quit school and tried to join the North American Field Service. I wanted to go to North Africa and drive an ambulance with the British Army. It was a burst of misguided romanticism and my parents wouldn't let me go. I ended up at Fort Hayes, Kansas, in early 1942, hoping to become a fighter pilot. One eye tested 20/40 so the Army Air Forces gave me to the regular Army to become what was called a "liaison pilot," meaning artillery spotter.

The Army put us through primary and basic at Fort Hayes, where we were taught by civilian instructors. Our airplanes were Aeroncas, tandem two-seat monoplanes with 65 horsepower. They terrified us, but aroused only contempt from our instructors, who were accustomed to heavier stuff. An Aeronca or Piper Cub can kill you as dead as an F-14, but my instructor acted as if it wasn't an airplane, but merely sort of a tricycle which occasionally found itself in the air.

After about 25 hours of solo flying at Fort Hayes, we were shipped to Fort Sill, Oklahoma, where we took what they called "the Short Field Course." You got about 200 hours learning how to take off and land over obstacles, land on roads and plowed fields, and how to adjust artillery fire. We were now flying the L-4, which was the Army's version of a Piper Cub. It was made of aluminum tubing with doped linen stretched over it, and one man could pick one up by the tail and pull it along behind him. This lightness meant we could take off and land from places unthinkable for real airplanes and everybody knew, once we were in combat, that we were going to be in a lot of unthinkable places.

Not everybody could get it right, and a lot of guys washed out. Others went the hard way. The Army didn't make it a point to tell us about fatal crashes, but young men died often enough in those harmless-looking little airplanes, without ever seeing a German or a Japanese. I was sitting in the waiting room of the base hospital one day, waiting to be treated for some minor medical problem, when I noticed a terrible odor. I asked the orderly what it was, and he said the lab was boiling the brain of a student who'd been killed that morning, to see if there was any alcohol in his system. Rumor had it that if you were killed with a hangover, your insurance was cancelled. Since we were restricted to the post all during the week, this was rarely a problem.

On the weekends a lot of us did overdo it in the fleshpots of Lawton, Oklahoma, which has been catering to soldiers since before Custer and the 7th Cavalry were stationed at Fort Sill. We even sang songs, just like soldiers in the movies. There was a song about us, to the tune of the "Artillery Song," the one where those caissons go rolling along. Our song went something like this. "Over trees, under wires, to hell with landing gear and tires, we're the eyes of the artillereeeeeee. We don't mind the mud and sand, we don't need much room to land, we're the eyes of . . ." etc.

Those of us who survived the short field course graduated, and we all got our wings, which had an "L" for liaison on them. I was then assigned to the 93rd Armored Field Artillery Battalion, and I found out the Army didn't know why they had these airplanes and pilots. Since we were pilots, we were issued a leather flying jacket and aviator's sunglasses, and the 93rd didn't like that at all. However, there wasn't a damn thing they could do about it because they were Government Issue, G.I. They also used to insist that we wear those lace-up leggins (and the word was leggins, not leggings). The Cub had exposed rudder cables and they would catch in the little brass eyelets. Get those caught in the cables and you were all through. I'd get in the airplane, taxi out, and take my leggins off. Then I'd stick them under my butt and sit on them. They also wanted you to fly with a steel helmet on. The aileron cables would rub across the top of the helmet, so you took that off, too. You had to outfox the Army all the time.

Another thing, the officers of the 93rd thought that L-4s were "vehicles," with the accent on the first syllable, and while we remained at Fort Sill they were forever after us to grease our véhicles. You don't really grease an airplane, you don't even wash it very often. Still, the 93rd believed in washing all véhicles, including Sherman tanks, so we washed the L-4s. All of that nonsense ended when we got overseas. The 93rd realized what we could do and nobody cared what we wore and we didn't have to grease our véhicles.

In the latter part of 1942 we went to North Africa on a converted banana boat. Our airplanes went with us and were packed inside huge crates. There was a manifest on each box which said, "Aircraft, L-4, cost to U.S. Govt., $800; Crate, 1942 M-2, cost to U.S. Govt., $1,200." I had my first real intimation that the Army might not be taking us too seriously if the crate cost more than the airplane.

I was commissioned while we were in Africa. A lot of Cub pilots didn't get commissioned until much later, when we got to Italy, because their battalions were slower to appreciate their worth. The idea to use light aircraft as spotters was started by some civilian pilots who approached the Army before Pearl Harbor. The Army didn't think it would work, but during the Louisiana Maneuvers, which were the last big peacetime war games, they tried it and it worked like gangbusters. The top brass and generals got the idea immediately, but down at the battalion and regimental level, they didn't. If the observer was on the ground, they would have to use a very complicated system of geometry to adjust fire. Put that same observer up in a Cub at 3,000 feet and he's looking right down on the target and doesn't need all that math. The Army, being the Army, found it very hard to accept that. They had spent years learning their system and some nineteen-year-old guy comes along in an airplane that cost $800 and shows them how it could be done better.

I was with a self-propelled artillery battalion in North Africa. The guns looked like Sherman tanks, but instead of a turret, they had a 105mm howitzer. Our "air section" consisted of our planes, two pilots, a mechanic, an armored half-track and driver and sometimes, a two-and-a-half ton truck. The half-track was used to beat down the grass in the fields we used for landing fields and the truck would pick up gas or anything else we needed.

When we first got there, we would land as close to the front as possible, but we found out that the Germans took us more seriously, in the beginning, than the American Army did. The minute the Germans saw us land, they'd start shelling the field. From then on, we'd keep the airplanes behind a hill so they couldn't see where we were landing.

I don't think there's any way to teach a young soldier what it's like to be shot at. They had us crawl under live machine gun fire and all that business, but there wasn't any way to prepare people for what it was like in an airplane. They couldn't put you up in a plane and fire flak at you and try to just miss. So when it first happened it was quite a shock. If a machine gun was pointed at you, you'd hear the muzzle blast over the sound of the engine. The first time I heard that "pop, pop, pop, pop," I thought there was something wrong with the engine, a broken piston ring or something. Then I saw the tracers going by and they looked like snowballs. It was a terrible realization. God, this is really serious. It certainly wasn't like the movies. You never saw John Wayne in a Piper Cub.

We went over with ten pilots whom I knew and two came back. They were killed by a dumb move or just plain bad luck. There was a lot of luck involved in that kind of flying, but some of them who were killed were just plain dumb. Doing something like flying down a valley without looking at a map to see if there were high tension lines.

One guy was killed at Anzio. He was hit by one of his own battalion's shells, which was always our worst nightmare. The parabola that the artillery shells described was very high. I think a 105mm shell reached 50,000 feet at its zenith, but you were frequently very close to that parabola on its way up or down. With all eighteen guns going, sometimes the shells would come so close that the plane would shake as if it were in a violent thermal. I don't know whether they were 500 or 100 feet under me, but they would really shake me up. The other pilot in our section, Miller, was up one day and all of a sudden the engine started to go to pieces. He managed to get the plane back and the propeller and crankshaft were both bent. We looked at the prop and there was a gray smear on it. That was paint off a white phosphorous shell and we figured out that shell had just kissed that prop. That's what I mean about luck.

I got a stove lid from a farmhouse and put that under my seat pack when I flew. I figured that would guard against getting shot in the butt. Later on, I got a piece of armor plate off a half-track that had been shot up. We didn't think of wearing flak vests, but they would have weighed too much anyway, and you wouldn't have gotten out of those short fields. Most of the time you couldn't even carry an observer because you were lucky to get over the trees that always seemed to be at the end of the field. We didn't have luxuries like flaps or a variable speed prop, just 65 horsepower.

I'd go on leave to the Riviera or Naples, and we'd be in a bar and one of those bomber guys would see my liaison wings and say, "My God, are you flying those little Piper Cubs?" Well, I couldn't believe that those guys could go up there and fly in those B-17s for eight or ten hours over Germany. I was at Naples Airport at one point, and there was a B-17 that had made a forced landing. I had never been aboard one so I asked one of the gunners if I could go inside. I walked in and couldn't believe how small they were and how uncomfortable it was to move around. The thing stank of vomit, urine, feces. It was like an outdoor toilet. The vomit smell in the oxygen masks was just awful. Hollywood would show you the glamour of flying in those bombers, but that's just crap. Those people had it bad.

One of the marvelous things about our Cubs was the fact that they were easy to maintain, about the same as a motorcycle. You could pull the cylinders off and grind the valves right out in a plowed field. When I was at Fort Sill they sent the pilots to a modified mechanics school. That was in case the mechanic was killed or got sick so that we could maintain the aircraft ourselves. I remember squatting down in a field for a whole day using compound to grind those valves. One of the problems the Army has with helicopters today, they do the same job we did, is that every 50 hours they have to be completely overhauled. Those little Cubs just went and went.

We flew every day unless the weather was right on the deck. I had 368 missions, all during the day because the L-4 didn't have the instruments and we didn't have the training to fly at night. Besides, you couldn't see the ground references, such as road intersections, bridges, or farmhouses which corresponded to the references on your map. Without those, you couldn't tell the guys where to shoot. You didn't say, "Jesus! There's a Panther tank over by the woods!" You said, "Baker One Able, this is Baker Three Able. I have a target for you, coordinates one niner niner three, six niner two, enemy tank, one round smoke when ready."

The Germans used a plane called the *Storch* (for stork) to do what we did in the Cubs, and one would appear occasionally at Monte Cassino. I saw him one day and flew straight at him. He turned and flew away because they could cruise at 90 miles an hour. We could only go 60. The Germans also had a captured Cub that they would occasionally put up. However, it had the wrong markings. We had big block letters on the side of the fuselage indicating our battalion, and the Germans never quite figured that out. Every time we saw him we'd fly at him and he'd always go away.

All we carried for protection was a pistol in a shoulder holster.

One pilot wired up bazookas on the struts and had the mechanics rig up a battery that sat on his lap. When he touched the wire to the battery, the bazookas would fire, but there was no aiming device. He fired at a light tank near Monte Cassino and missed him by at least 100 yards. Once in a while we would throw out five-gallon cans of gasoline which burst like napalm, but again, I don't think we ever hit anything. It was hard work and not worth the effort. Our artillery did the damage and it was literally suicide for the Germans to move anything during the day within the eyesight of anyone in an L-4. My battalion consisted of eighteen howitzers, and at my command they could pump a dreadful rain of high explosives on the target and do it incredibly fast. By the time the first shell reached the target from any given gun, the sixth shell was leaving the muzzle. In fact, the gun crews worked so fast that the ejected shell had to be knocked out of the way by one of the gunners to make room for the fresh shell going into the breech.

After the war, when I was working for CBS News in Russia, a Canadian came over to my apartment one night and he brought a German with him. They were both in the timber business and we got to talking about the war and the German said he was at Monte Cassino. I said, "My gosh, so was I." He drew a map and I said, "No, that's all wrong. Here you had this rocket position." He said, "No, no, you have it all wrong." Finally it occurred to somebody to turn the map around. We were both looking at it from the "wrong" side. He remembered the Piper Cubs very well because every time we came over it would get very uncomfortable for him. He was in intelligence, and they referred to my battalion as the one that had the automatic 105mm cannons. There was, of course, no such thing. Even now there isn't. Our guns were so good that the Germans thought we had some kind of wonder weapons.

A couple of years ago, my son gave me a model of a Tiger tank for Christmas because I destroyed one with artillery fire. You weren't supposed to be able to do that because that was the biggest tank that ever saw combat. He was going down the road in broad daylight and that tank was so big he actually hung over the sides of a two-lane road. He couldn't have been doing more than five miles an hour. It was one of those rare times when I had an observer with me, a guy named John Buchfelder, and we started calling fire down on the tank. The 105mm shells just popped like firecrackers against the heavy armor, so we "went upstairs," as the argot had it, and asked for 155mm Long Toms. They had more effect, and a dead crew member appeared in the road behind the tank. He had apparently been killed by concussion and was dropped through the escape hatch. Even those high-explosive shells weren't penetrating his armor but there was a gazogene unit on the back of the Tiger. It was a device that burned charcoal, and when they weren't in combat, the Germans would burn methane to save gasoline. A 155mm shell burst squarely on that unit and it started a small fire. The tank ended up going down a cliff where it burst into flames. I got a Tiger tank with my $800 airplane!

With that marvelous peripheral vision granted the young and healthy, while those shells were bursting around the tank, I saw a horse bolt out of the woods with a German soldier holding on to the bridle. By that time we were down to 300 feet and I could see that soldier as though he was on the other side of a street in New York City. He dragged the horse back into the woods, and I knew exactly what that meant—horse-drawn artillery. When the tank started to slide down the cliff I switched the fire on to those woods and what must have been a regiment, horse-drawn artillery pieces, caissons, field kitchens, and wagons came plunging out of there and headed pell mell down the road. That road ran straight as a string for fifteen miles and just happened to lie on the gun-target line, and every round burst on that road for fifteen or twenty minutes. It was marvelous.

Before the invasion they built plywood decks on LSTs, and we took off from them like baby aircraft carriers. That was the only way we could be there for D-day. We took 15-gallon gas cans out of the Jeeps and put them in the back seat of the Cubs. We had a wobble pump so we could pump the gas from the can into the plane's tank, which only held 12 gallons. With that rig we could stay up for six hours which meant you were dying to pee. That was the worst part of an invasion!

For southern France, they loaded the planes and us on ships in Italy. We all thought it wasn't going to work and we'd all end up in the drink. We were also worried about what would happen if the infantry didn't take the beach and we didn't have any place to land. You couldn't land on the LST, no way, and the Navy had told us not to try to land on any of their carriers. "If you do, we'll push you over the side before you get out of the cockpit." You couldn't blame them because if they were in operation, they would be going so fast that they wouldn't have time for a Cub. All our fears were unfounded since the invasion was successful, and I got down without any trouble in a field about a mile from the beaches.

While I was flying on D-day, I adjusted naval gunfire because none of our guns had come ashore yet. The shells were coming from a battleship off the beaches, and I was twenty miles inland. There was a big bridge over a deep ravine, it must have been 500 feet deep, and the Army wanted it knocked out because the Germans were retreating over the bridge. The Navy can hit anything, but it would take about thirty minutes to get the first round out of them. I couldn't talk directly to the Navy, they were too far away for my primitive radio and on another frequency, but I would talk to my battalion and they would pass it on to the Navy. They finally said, "one on the way," and the first round burst right in the middle of the bridge and at least 50 feet of it fell down in the ravine. God, could they shoot!

The Navy, however, did have one problem. They could never distinguish between a Piper Cub and a Messerschmitt 109. About once a month, I had to fly a sack of confidential shit to Anzio, from Monte Cassino. They would have four or five Spitfires orbiting because this sack was important, and you had to fly way out to sea and then hit a precise spot on the beachhead. That supposedly told the Navy that you were friendly. On one side, you had Germans, who you knew were going to shoot at you. On the other side, the bay was full of Navy ships and, son-of-a-bitch, every time you started to go over, everything in the harbor would start to fire at the Cub. But they were used to shooting at airplanes going 200 or 300 miles an hour and they never came near me. All that stuff would be cracking out there, 200 or 300 yards ahead of me, and I'd be yelling, "Goddamn you bastards." It never failed, I had to make that run seven or eight times and they did it every time. Bill Leonard, who was later vice-president of CBS News, was a gunnery officer on a destroyer during the war, and once when he and I were exchanging war stories, it gradually developed that he had personally shot at me all over the Mediterranean.

As far as German fighters went, most of them were occupied in Russia, but there were some in the West. If you did run into one you turned into them and dived. He would be going too fast and couldn't maneuver fast enough to get you.

There were funny things that happened during the war. To keep your sanity, you had to laugh once in awhile. We had a pilot killed in the group, and I flew the spare airplane up to Rome. Miller flew up in another plane to bring me back. We dropped the plane off and it was close to dusk when we took off. I wasn't paying attention because I was in the back seat and all of a sudden I hear "pop, pop, pop," and I looked up at the gauges to see if the tachometer was fluctuating because it sounded like a broken piston ring. All of a sudden it got louder, "POP, POP, POP," and the snowballs started to come by. This ninny, Miller, had gone down the wrong valley. We were flying at about 500 feet, and there was a Panther tank with a guy squatting on the turret shooting at us with a machine gun. Then Miller, the jackass, turned toward the tank instead of the other way. He missed us, but by now we were right on the deck, totally lost. We were just hedge-hopping, laboring up a hill in that underpowered airplane and just falling down the other side. At one point we flew right over a farmhouse with eight German infantry men sitting out in the yard, and we could see them running like hell to get their weapons. We flew right through a tank battle, damn near hitting an antenna on a tank. I was bawling the shit out of that guy, screaming, "Miller, God Almighty, look at the compass! At least go south!" He finally made a 180 turn and got out of there. When it was over, it was hilarious, but at the time I could have killed him.

I still want to kill Miller, for a number of reasons. He'd gone in the Army in '38 or '39 and learned all the bad habits of the old Army. In order to get out of that hard duty he got himself transferred into the Air Corps. He was a good pilot, physically, but he was also an absolute goldbrick. He thought we were really down in Louisiana on maneuvers and sooner or later this shit was going to stop and everybody was going to stand up and go home. He thought we were the "blue army" and the Germans were the "red army" of the peacetime maneuvers. I thought he was a fool, but realize now that it was his way of preserving his sanity. We all had our methods so we didn't go bananas.

Our mechanic was a really interesting man. Wedel was a lot older than we were, about thirty-five, and he'd been a medical student in Berlin before the war. A German-American from St. Louis who spoke fluent German, and naturally the Army made him an airplane mechanic. Wedel and Miller would team up against me because I was a straight-arrow type of soldier and took it all very seriously. I couldn't get it through their heads that there was a war going on.

The Cub had a tail wheel and when you were landing you couldn't see over the nose. I had just touched down in a cow pasture and there was a terrible crash. I thought, "Oh my God, they're shelling the field." The airplane spun around and the right wing hit the ground. I fought my way out of the wreck and there was an Italian burro on his back with all four legs kicking in the air with this peasant trying to get him on his feet. I went running for my tent because I was so mad I wanted to kill that burro and the peasant. By the time I finally got my .45 out of my barracks bag, both of them were running across the field. I emptied the whole goddamn clip at them, but, of course, I missed. Then I had to go down to the depot to Naples to pick up a new wing and strut assembly. They asked me why I needed it and I told them, "I ran into a burro."

You couldn't help but see odd things when you were flying. I remember seeing Roman roads running through cultivated fields in Italy. I kept seeing Cicero's tomb on this ordnance map we were using. It was on the Gulf of Gaeta and the front line finally moved beyond it and I flew over to have a look. It looks just like a miniature Leaning Tower of Pisa, about 50 feet high, without the lean. The classical symmetry was ruined by a half-track with its nose parked under one of the arches. Two G.I.s were sitting down there cooking their rations over a little stove. I'm sure they were oblivious to what the hell the building was they were using for a kitchen.

We had to take a flight test every six months and at one point I flunked it violently. There was a brass plate with a little bitty hole in it and you had a needle at the end of a wire. You held the needle in the hole and if you were shaky, it touched the edges of the hole and made a noise. I couldn't hold the thing steady because I was plain worn out.

The Army grounded me, and I was sent to an Air Forces Tactical Reconnaissance squadron. They were flying P-51s, and my job was to debrief them when they came back. It was an awful bore, and those guys were pissed off because they weren't fighting. I always thought the AAF was the glamour outfit, but these guys were living like dogs in a bunch of old broken-down French barracks with rain coming through the roof. In the Army we knew how to do things. We'd make a stove out of an oil drum to heat our tent. If we wanted to tear out the seats in our Jeep and put in overstuffed chairs, that's what we'd do. These guys didn't even have transportation. I was used to having my own Jeep and half-track and if I wanted to go someplace, I went.

These pilots were living like rookies, but they did have a squadron bar and the wall was papered with enormous charts of Europe. One of the things they had to do was adjust eight-inch howitzer fire and they didn't know how to do it. That was the sort of thing I did all the time and they wanted me to teach them how to do it. I'd explain this and that and none of them would get it. One night we were all drunk in the bar drinking highballs and I grabbed an ice cube and said, "Now look. If you're trying to hit Frankfurt," and threw the ice cube at the map. It hit, pflatt!, and I said, "That's 200 over." Another guy said, "Oh yeah? Let me try that." The first thing you know, we were all throwing ice cubes and then the glasses at the charts yelling, "That's 400 over! That's 400 right!" This colonel came in and wanted to put everybody in jail.

When the war ended, we didn't know it because they didn't tell us at our level. We were in Austria, and when I took off one morning I couldn't believe my eyes. The roads were just choked with German equipment from horizon to horizon. Bumper to bumper, truck-drawn artillery, tanks, everything. I was just hysterical on the radio calling in coordinates and battalion called back. "Roger, wait." I waited and five minutes later I got on the radio again. "Come on, I gave you coordinates, why wait?" They finally said, "Cease all forward action," which was the same as saying return to base. As usual, the higher-ups had screwed up. It was the cease-fire and the Germans were all going to these huge fields to park their equipment. I was really going to have a last hurrah.

I landed and discovered that the war was over. I always thought the war was never going to end and I never thought I was going to live through it. You'd think I would have been deliriously happy. A rifleman probably was, but it was a terrible letdown for me and it took me years to get over it. Maybe I never have. All I could think of was, what now?

My in-laws had a cabin in northern Minnesota, and when I got back, I went up there with my first wife and stayed for a year. I was mad at everybody, and civilians in general annoyed the hell out of me. I remember the first night I got up there, drinking a whole bottle of Scotch and not even getting tight. Recently I've been reading a biography of F. Scott Fitzgerald. All about the kind of drinking that was done in the thirties, and it seemed that after the war everybody was celebrating the same way, being back and alive. There was an awful lot of booze, and you didn't go out and have a few drinks, everybody just got wacky. For most people it began to taper off after two or three years, but my wife turned out to be an alcoholic and by the time I realized it, I was too young and dumb to know what to do about it. It got worse and worse until we finally divorced in 1954.

It was hard on the people who stayed behind. The woman I'm married to now worked in a defense plant in Los Angeles and her first husband was killed in the war. She then spent a year with the WACs. When she and I talk about the war, which we do all the time, we know what we're talking about. For couples where one of them doesn't have that experience, it could be very tough.

My first job was with a little weekly newspaper in Hampton, Iowa. One of the things I had to write was the wedding announcements, and one came out, "Smith/Brown nuptials. Groom just discharged." They fired my ass because they thought I did it on purpose. Next I went to Sabetha, Kansas, another weekly, and then to the *Kansas City Star*. I left the *Star* in 1950, spent a year or so at the *Minneapolis Tribune*, and then quit and went back to school. I'd never graduated from college and the G.I. bill was about to run out so I went to the University of Minnesota for two years. Then I got a writing fellowship at Stanford, went out there and fell in love and had to start making money again. I ended up editing a paper in Rock Springs, Wyoming. The Rock Springs *Daily Rocket and Sunday Miner*. I had two kids helping me who were semiliterate, and since I was working seven days a week, I tried to train them to put the paper out on Sunday so I could get one day off. I told the kids to just take the copy off the UPI wire and measure off what they needed to fill up the paper between the ads. I didn't care what it was, hog futures, or whatever. Also, I told them, no headlines bigger than two columns.

The first Sunday, I got up and went outside in my bathrobe and there was the paper. That was the weekend that Eisenhower had the diverticulitis attack in Denver. He could have been dying, for all anybody knew, but they still had only a two-column head on it, just like I told them. Well, that was all right, but when I flipped the paper over, and I'll never forget this, there was a little one-column, eighteen-point Caslon headline. "Search continues for two-headed boy. Albany, New York, UPI: Authorities say they are still unable to locate John Schwartzkopf, four-year-old missing two-headed son of Mr. William Schwartzkopf. . . " Of course, it was *tow-headed*. I had forgotten to tell them about transpositions on the wire. I jumped in the car and went down to the paper and they were sitting there, so pleased with themselves. I said, "Jesus, if you really believed it was a two-headed kid, why didn't you put it above the fold?"

After Rock Springs I went into the industrial movie business in Kansas City and we used Walter Cronkite as a narrator before he was famous. In 1959 I was fed up with films about things like the Caterpillar Tractor Company and by that time Walter *was* famous so I called him up and asked about a job at CBS. He told me they were looking for an ex-newspaperman to come back to New York and they'd probably hire me. He was right.

I started out as a writer for the *World News Tonight* on the radio and did that for almost a year. Then they put me on the assignment desk for a while and that was where you really learned how to be a correspondent. From there I went out and started to do local stuff. I had worked for CBS for two years and my wife said, "I don't understand what you do." She couldn't figure out what I was doing because we didn't have a television set. I was afraid it would get our child screwed up. I told her that I talk into this mike and then say, "Back to you, Walter." I think she really thought I was running girls on Times Square. We finally had to buy an old black and white set.

After New York I went to Atlanta and started the southern bureau and from there I went to Chicago. Television people were more interesting 25 years ago than they are now. I think today they are rather bland young people who are mainly interested in office politics, not what the politicians are up to. I heard an ABC correspondent who was in Tripoli say, "Those decorations you see on the screen are leftovers from the Moslem Christmas." Of course he meant Ramadan because Moslems have no Christmas. Twenty people must have heard that in the network offices, looked at the copy, and it still got on the air. There are exceptions, guys like Roger Mudd and Sam Donaldson. Both of them understand what's going on. But most of these young reporters nowadays are very dull and they often get some of their facts just flat wrong.

I think that all started in Vietnam. In the beginning the normal correspondents would go, but they didn't want them to stay out there forever. It was too dangerous, so they started rotating. So, to get more people, they hired reporters from local stations who never should have been with the networks. Their thinking was that when the war was over, they'd fire these people, but they didn't. Now they're embedded in the field because they needed these marginal people to hold a microphone up near a fire fight in Vietnam.

I was out there for the first time in 1961. I went back in 1968 but by that time, I was too old to hop around the boonies. In '61 it was a very small-scale war and we wandered around the delta looking for fire fights. We finally found one, and when it was over, the South Vietnamese major in charge of the infantry took a dozen North Vietnamese prisoners and shot them with this machine gun while we were rolling film. When the producer saw it in New York, he got up and ran out of the room saying, "We can't put that on the air." Four years later, it got so that if you didn't have something like that, you couldn't *get* on the air.

There's no comparison between World War II and Vietnam. In some ways Vietnam was worse, in other ways it was no war at all. The infantry only had to spend a year, and that's not any way to run the infantry. The best way to get infantry to fight bitterly and well is when they're absolutely without hope unless they win. Those guys would put in ten months in Vietnam and then a lot of them were really backing off. They always say they fired more rounds in Vietnam. Well, hell, it was the first time everybody had automatic rifles. Everybody was carrying an M-16, and they got into this reconnaissance by fire. They'd see a tree line up ahead, 400 yards away, and instead of walking up to it or trying to go around, they'd just fire everything they had at it. They had beer airlifted out to them, things like that. It was, as I said, a terrible war in many respects but also often a comfortable one for the Army. The Marines didn't do as well with creature comforts.

I don't know how the infantry did it during the Second World War. I saw them in Italy in the middle of the winter when it was fifteen below zero and they'd be lying in a hole half filled with snow with nothing but a blanket. Everybody had trench foot, trench mouth, even I got that. I don't know how those guys did it and they still got up and fought.

I went to Russia for CBS in 1965 and spent two years working there. We were just stunned how wrong everything was that we had been told about the Soviet Union. Stories of these shuffling, sullen people walking along the streets of Moscow. Well, go out and stand at the corner of 79th Street and Broadway in New York and see what people look like in the winter time. If they aren't shuffling, I don't know what they're doing. The wire services got away with that for years because there wasn't anybody there to tell it differently.

In 1973 I became the anchor man on the *CBS Morning News* and after that I did features for CBS in New York. I left CBS and went with ABC in 1979 and retired in November 1986.

The kids of today could do what we did. If they felt the United States was threatened, they would. Don't forget the English young men debating at the Oxford Union. They voted in 1936 or 1937: "We will not fight for King and country." Three or four years later a lot of those same men were in Spitfires. Another thing, if you live in New York or maybe even Washington, you tend to think the people in this country have gotten very cynical. If you go to Wichita or Dallas or Denver, that's not the case at all. There's a lot more patriotism. And God knows, the American South, they still believe what people in New York, or at least Manhattan, don't.

Everybody ought to be exposed to absolute, naked terror once in their life. Otherwise, you don't know how marvelous it is just to go down to the corner drugstore and buy a tube of toothpaste. I don't think a day goes by that I don't think about the war. I'm sure that is true of everybody who went through a combat experience.

APPENDIX

WARBIRDS—THE AIRPLANES THAT WON THE WAR

The total output of American military aircraft in 1939 was 921, including trainers. When the Japanese bombed Pearl Harbor, the Army Air Corps had less than 500 combat aircraft and fewer men than were in the field artillery. The standard Navy fighter, the Grumman Wildcat, was no match one-on-one with the Japanese Zero, and the Douglas Devastator torpedo bomber was considered obsolete.

By the time the war ended, American production lines had produced over 300,000 airplanes, a Herculean effort even when looked at from forty-plus years afterward. Some of these airplanes were conventional, others revolutionary. A few became legends and others were just plain dangerous.

Because of this bewildering array of aircraft, the authors felt it would be useful to include a brief description of some of the more important examples. In no way is this to be considered a complete directory of American World War II aircraft. Tomes have been written on the subject, some of them hard to lift off the coffee table. Ours is just an abbreviated look at the airplanes the men and women in this book flew, fixed, or built.

★

The undisputed queens of the sky were the heavy, four-engine bombers. The Boeing B-17 was first delivered to the Air Corps in 1939, and was designed to replace the Martin B-10. Carrying up to thirteen machine guns and a normal bomb load of 6,000 pounds, it lived up to its name, the Flying Fortress. Steadily improved during the war, one version, the B-17F, had over four hundred modifications, and the vast armadas of B-17s battling their way to Germany became the symbol of the Eighth Air Force.

Laboring in the shadow of its more illustrious counterpart, the Consolidated B-24 Liberator served the Allies in more versions, for more purposes, than any other aircraft in history. The twin-tailed bomber flew in every theater of war with fifteen Allied nations. Relative merits of the B-17 and B-24 will never be settled as long as there are men alive who flew them.

Not only was the B-29 Superfortress the largest bomber flown during the war, it was a major advance in aviation technology. Built by Boeing, the B-29 used new and revolutionary structures, materials, systems, power plants, armament and flight environment. It was not without some growing pains, and pilots sometimes wondered whether the battle was with the Japanese or the B-29. However, once the bugs were worked out, the mighty flying dreadnought brought the war home to the Japanese mainland, culminating with the dropping of the atomic bomb.

Smaller than their big brothers, but faster and more maneuverable, the twin-engine medium bombers came in a variety of configurations. The A-20 Havoc was originally produced by Douglas for the French air force. Extremely fast, the A-20 had one very unusual feature, an emergency control column in the rear gunner's cockpit in case the pilot was killed. It seems to us that it would be most difficult to fly an airplane from the "back of the bus."

Named after Gen. William Mitchell, the testy but fearless officer who was court-martialed in 1924 for his outspoken belief in air power, the North American B-25 was considered by many to be the best in its class. The Mitchell was the airplane used by Lt. Col. (later Lt. Gen.) James H. Doolittle's famous raiders on their daring and morale-raising attack on Tokyo, April 18, 1942.

Not as universally praised as the Mitchell, the Martin B-26 Marauder gained an early reputation as a "widow maker." When the design was submitted it looked so good that 1,000 of them were built without the development of a prototype. The airplane had a very high wing-loading which resulted in extremely high landing speeds. This in turn greatly disturbed the crews. After modifications to the wings and tail surfaces the B-26 proved itself to be combat worthy and, in the hands of the right pilot, an incredible weapon.

After seeing the success that the British were having with radar-equipped night fighters, the Air Corps decided that it wanted one of its own. The result was the Northrop P-61 Black Widow, a large, high-winged aircraft that went into service in 1944. Painted an ominous glossy black, and equipped with four 20mm cannons, four machine guns, and 6,400 pounds of bombs, the P-61 more than lived up to its name.

One of the few aircraft to be conceived, designed, developed, produced, and used in large numbers during the war, the Douglas A-26 Invader was an exceptional aircraft. Bristling with machine guns, the Invader went on to serve in Korea and Vietnam, with a few examples still in combat units thirty-three years after they were first delivered, a record no other type of aircraft can equal.

By far the most widely used military transport in history, the Douglas C-47 Skytrain was a military version of the famous DC-3. One of the real workhorses of the war, the C-47 carried just about everything imaginable, including paratroopers. It also served as a glider tug and a couple of specialized versions included one equipped with skis and another on pontoons.

Developed by the Curtiss-Wright Company to compete with the DC-3, the C-46 Commando was totally redesigned as a military transport. Plagued with problems when it first went into service, the C-46, with its excellent high-altitude performance and high load capabilities, became one of the outstanding "flying trucks" of the war.

Another airplane slated for the airlines was the Douglas DC-4. The Army requisitioned the first batch, designated them the C-54 Skymaster, and modified them for their new duties. Wide cargo doors, stronger floors, and larger fuel tanks were among the modifications. One C-54 was even equipped with an electric hoist to accommodate President Roosevelt's wheelchair.

A variety of trainers was used to teach the future bomber, fighter, and transport pilots of World War II. Probably the best known is the Stearman PT-17. Over 20,000 of the open-cockpit biplanes were produced for both the Air Force and Navy. The Navy version, the N2S, was painted all yellow, and naturally acquired the nickname "Yellow Peril." It was in fact one of the safest and strongest airplanes ever built.

Fairchild's primary trainer, the PT-19, was a low-wing monoplane and almost as many of them were produced as were Stearmans. Rather underpowered, and not very popular with pilots, the PT-23 and PT-26 were variations on the same theme.

After the fledgling airmen had mastered the primary trainer, they moved into the North American AT-6 or Beech AT-11 Bobcat. The AT-6, called the SNJ by the Navy, was an excellent single-engine ship with retractable landing gear and enough power to give the pilot the feeling of the fighter he was soon going to fly into combat. If you were going to be a bomber pilot your advanced trainer was the AT-11. Nicknamed the "Bamboo Bomber" by the men who flew it, the AT-11 was also used to train navigators and bombardiers.

Somewhere between the Stearman and the AT-6 was the Vultee Valiant, the BT-13. A low-wing, closed-cockpit airplane, it was known as the "Vibrator" or even worse, the "Vomiter." We haven't talked to a pilot who liked it.

When the Japanese bombed Pearl Harbor, the Army Air Corps had only one fighter, the Curtiss P-40 Warhawk. It wasn't outstanding, but was the only thing around when more sophisticated and soon to be more famous fighters were still months from delivery. The P-40 proved itself to be the most important Air Corps fighter for the first two years of the war, especially in the hands of the legendary Flying Tigers.

Republic Aviation produced over 15,000 P-47 Thunderbolts, the largest single-engine fighter flown during the war. Affectionately called the "Jug," as in juggernaut, the P-47 was a real street fighter and became a much-respected long-range escort and ground-attack bomber. Using its eight wing-mounted machine guns, pilots roamed the European and Pacific theaters in the big fighters, shooting at anything that moved.

Some airplanes are special and one of those was the P-38 Lightning. Built by Lockheed, it was a revolutionary fighter with its turbocharged twin engines and distinctive silhouette. The Lightning's firepower was so murderous that German pilots called it the "Fork-Tailed Devil." Able to sustain a phenomenal amount of damage and still get home, the P-38 fought throughout Europe and the Pacific.

Another radical design, the Bell P-39 Airacobra, isn't remembered with as much admiration as the Lightning. The P-39's engine was mounted behind the pilot and a cannon fired through the propeller hub. The first fighter with tricycle landing gear, it was a good-looking airplane, but because of a serious lack of power at high altitude the P-39 was used sparingly by the Army. The Russians, on the other hand, loved the Airacobra and found all that firepower to be perfect for low-altitude tank busting.

The P-51 Mustang was North American Aviation's first fighter and they got it right the first time. Quite possibly the finest propeller-driven fighter ever built, the P-51 was designed and produced in record time. First delivered with Allison engines, the fighter came into its own when the British suggested North American mate the airframe with a Rolls-Royce Merlin engine. A classic was born. Using the drop tanks, the Mustang was the first fighter that could "go all the way," escorting the B-17s and B-24s over the heart of Germany and the B-29s to the islands of Japan.

★

When war broke out the Grumman Wildcat was the front-line equipment on Navy carriers and with Marine land-based units. Designed in the mid-1930s, the tubby F4F carried the fight during the first half of the war. Extremely agile, it was a tough airplane and could survive a great deal of battle damage.

When the Navy asked Grumman to build them a "better" Wildcat the Hellcat was born. Following the basic Grumman design philosophy to "make it strong, make it work and make it simple," the company produced the F6F, whose job was simple; shoot down Japanese fighters. It had 2,000 horsepower and could do 400 miles per hour in level flight; it was heavily armored to protect the pilots, with leakproof fuel tanks to protect the plane from fire. These were advantages the Japanese designers had sacrificed to make the rival Zero more maneuverable. Generally a hit was fatal to a Zero, and the pilot was often killed. Navy and Marine pilots flying the Hellcat ended up with a kill ratio of 19:1, a mark that has never been equaled.

Grumman's last effort to see combat during the war was a bold design, the twin-engine F7F Tigercat. Arriving late, it saw very limited service, mostly in a two-seater night fighter version used by the Marines. The Tigercat went on to fight in Korea.

The Chance Vought F4U Corsair is another airplane that has become a legend. With its distinctive gull wings, the Corsair was the plane flown by Marine Maj. Gregory "Pappy" Boyington's Black Sheep Squadron in the Pacific. Going into service in 1942, the Corsair quickly helped the United States gain air supremacy over the Japanese. The airstream screaming through the cooler inlets caused the Japanese to call the Corsair, "Whistling Death."

The only thing devastating about the Douglas bomber, the TBD-1 Devastator, was its name. Delivered to the fleet in 1937, the TBD-1 was the first production monoplane to be based on carriers. These planes were withdrawn from service after the Battle of Midway, where their losses were excessive; thirty-five were shot down during one attack.

Douglas redeemed itself with the SBD Dauntless. It was the mainstay of both Navy and Marine dive-bomber operations in the Pacific from 1940 until the end of the war, and it sank more Japanese shipping than any other Allied airplane. Playing a major part in the Battles of Midway, in the Coral Sea and the Solomons, the Dauntless was a very popular airplane with the men who flew it.

Much less popular was the airplane designed to replace the Dauntless, the Curtiss SB2C Helldiver. Despite a fine war record, the Helldiver was never a big hit with Navy pilots because of its poor handling and stability. It became known as "Son of a Bitch, 2nd Class." Again, we didn't talk to a pilot who liked it.

Filling out the Navy's carrier-based arsenal was the Grumman

TBF Avenger. It had a twin, the TBM, produced by General Motors. Large, the TBF had a three-man crew: pilot, gunner and radio operator. It was primarily a torpedo bomber, although later versions were modified for antisubmarine and airborne early warning duty. The TBF's debut in combat wasn't spectacular. At the Battle of Midway, when six were sent against the Japanese fleet, five were shot down and the sixth came back a flying wreck. From then on the Avenger's performance was brilliant and along with the SBD helped destroy Japan's sea power.

Produced in greater numbers than any other flying boat, the Consolidated PBY Catalina performed some mighty exploits in the early years of the war. In 1942 Patrol Squadron 12 used its "Black Cats" to attack the Japanese at night and one PBY even attacked a carrier in broad daylight after radioing "Please inform next of kin."

Produced by Martin, and never given the credit it deserves because of the fame of the PBY, the PBM Mariner was a larger patrol flying boat with many advanced features. The design was tested by constructing and flying a quarter size scale model. Its distinctive gull wings and tipped up rudders were a welcome sight to many a downed aviator as it landed to pick him out of the sea.

The Navy had its own version of the B-24 Liberator, called the PB4Y, modified for the Navy's special needs. The most striking change was the replacement of the Liberator's twin tail with a conventional rudder. Some of these airplanes are still flying today, but instead of dropping bombs, they are "bombing" raging forest fires with retardant.

★

Two other airplanes deserve mention, not because they bombed the enemy into submission or engaged their fighters in aerial dogfights but because they, in their own unique way, helped win the war. They were flown by two men who appear in this book and did their own special job.

First, the Piper L-4 Grasshopper. The first Piper Cubs used by the military were stock civilian models loaned by the manufacturer for the 1941 Army maneuvers in Louisiana. Later, Piper built the L-4 "military version," which basically meant more window area, a two-way radio and an olive drab paint job. The unarmed Cubs served as the eyes of the Army and at $800 a copy they were probably one of the few bargains in the war.

Lastly, the Waco CG-4: this was the only American combat glider to see service during World War II. The pilots who flew the CG-4 seem to have a strange love/hate affair with the airplane. Constructed of welded steel tubing, wood and fabric, the CG-4 was no thing of beauty. One pilot went so far as to describe it as a "ghastly sight." The CG-4's main claim to fame was the fact that it could carry more than its own weight and that inexperienced pilots could fly it. It was not a howling success, and one can only consider how many glider pilots' lives were saved when the atomic bomb ended the war. The Army had large numbers ready for the planned invasion of Japan.